Japanese Financial Markets

Edited by Junichi Ujiie
President and CEO Nomura Holdings, Inc.

Second edition

NOMURA

WOODHEAD PUBLISHING LIMITED
Cambridge England

Published by Woodhead Publishing Limited, Abington Hall, Abington
Cambridge CB1 6AH, England
www.woodhead-publishing.com

First edition 1996, Gresham Books, an imprint of Woodhead Publishing Limited
Reprinted 1996 (twice)
Second edition 2002, Woodhead Publishing Limited
© 2002, Junichi Ujiie
The author has asserted his moral rights.

British Library Cataloguing in Publication Data
A catalogue record for this book is available from the British Library.

ISBN 1 85573 596 2

Typeset by SNP Best-set Typesetter Ltd., Hong Kong
Printed by TJ International, Padstow, Cornwall, England

Contents

Contents

Contents

Preface

The first edition of this book, which was edited by Shigenobu Hayakawa (then the managing director of Nomura Research Institute's Securities Research Division) and published in 1996, focused on the changes in Japan's financial markets in the decade from the mid-1980s to the mid-1990s. The positive response to the book allowed us to follow up with this second edition (the Japanese version, *Nihon no Shihon Shijo*, was published by Toyo Keizai Shinposha earlier in 2002).

In the five or so years since the first edition came out, the markets in Japan have changed by an even greater extent than in the decade covered by the first edition. To give a few examples of the major developments that indicate the far-reaching nature of the changes in the market environment, then Prime Minister Ryutaro Hashimoto announced the Big Bang programme of financial deregulation in November 1996; a number of major financial institutions went bankrupt a year later; the government followed up with policies to stabilize the financial system by recapitalizing banks with public funds; and the authority to supervise the financial sector was shifted away from the Ministry of Finance. In conjunction with these changes, the Nomura Group has reorganized its research operations, and decided not to revise the previous edition but rather to completely rewrite it under the direction of a new team of editors and authors. This book is the result of these efforts.

Most of the book was written by senior specialists from various divisions within Nomura Securities and the Nomura Research Institute. In line with the approach used in the first edition, the book is divided into four parts. Part I provides a general survey of the financial markets in Japan by outlining the historical performance of the various markets and the reforms of the past few years. Part II looks at the market participants and Part III the different financial markets, in terms of the changes in each area up to September 2001, the remaining challenges and issues, and the outlook. As a sort of afterword, Part IV conceptualizes the issues that need to be addressed to expand the functionality of Japan's capital markets. Corporate pension plans, investment trusts and other institutional investors are addressed in separate chapters, and the public sector is analysed not just as an issuer of bonds but also as an investor, in the form of managers of postal savings and life insurance assets. New topics addressed in this edition include mortgage- and asset-backed securities and venture capital. These efforts have resulted in a significant increase in the number of chapters from 13 in the first edition to 20 in the current one, and a book that is not merely a guidebook on Japan's financial markets but a detailed handbook for practitioners who deal with the markets and financial services business in Japan.

The authors have been given the freedom to express their own opinions and writing style. Accordingly, some slight differences of opinion may be evident among the different chapters. The opinions expressed by the various contributors to this book do not necessarily represent the official views of Nomura Securities or Nomura Research Institute.

Money and information flows are crossing national borders with increasingly greater ease, but there is still a shortage of available information in Japan and other countries for understanding Japan's financial and capital markets. This book is an attempt to clarify the rapidly changing market environment in Japan today.

Finally, we would like to thank Pai Hwong, CFA, of OnJapan, Inc. for his professional and consistent translation of the original Japanese version of the book, and the editors and staff of Woodhead Publishing for once again making this English version possible. We dedicate this book to all those with an interest in Japan's financial markets.

Junichi Ujiie
President and CEO Nomura Holdings, Inc.

Contributors

Chapter 1	Yasuyuki Kato, Quantitative Research Department, Financial Research Centre, Nomura Securities Co. Ltd; Visiting Assistant Professor, Kyoto University Institute of Economic Research
Chapter 2	Yukihiko Endo, Nomura School of Advanced Management
Chapter 3	Daisuke Ochiai and Masanobu Iwatani, Capital Market Research Department, Nomura Research Institute
Chapter 4	Shunsuke Kasuga, Quantitative Research Department, Financial Research Centre, Nomura Securities Co. Ltd
Chapter 5	Masahiko Igata, Management Planning Department, Nomura Securities Co. Ltd; Akiko Nomura and Motomi Hashimoto, Capital Market Research Department, Nomura Research Institute
Chapter 6	Junji Kawahara, Quantitative Research Department, Financial Research Centre, Nomura Securities Co. Ltd
Chapter 7	Haruhiko Urushibata, Capital Market Research Department, Nomura Research Institute
Chapter 8	Daisuke Ueno, Economic Research Department, Nomura Research Institute
Chapter 9	Eiji Katayama, Capital Market Research Department, Nomura Research Institute
Chapter 10	Naoki Hirai, Investment Banking Research Department, Financial Research Centre, Nomura Securities Co. Ltd
Chapter 11	Kiichi Murashima, Economic Research Department, Nomura Research Institute

Chapter 12   Sadakazu Osaki, Capital Market Research Department, Nomura Research Institute

Chapter 13   Sadakazu Osaki, Capital Market Research Department, Nomura Research Institute

Chapter 14   Kazunori Tanaka, Trading Compliance Department, Nomura Securities Co. Ltd

Chapter 15   Kazuo Kakuma, Quantitative Research Department, Financial Research Centre, Nomura Securities Co. Ltd; Koichi Okada, Nomura Holding America

Chapter 16   Kunio Yokomizo, Equity Quants Sales Department, Nomura Securities Co. Ltd

Chapter 17   Seiji Ogishima, Quantitative Research Department, Financial Research Centre, Nomura Securities Co. Ltd

Chapter 18   Yoshikazu Okano, Structured Finance Department, Nomura Securities Co. Ltd

Chapter 19   Akihiro Nakashima, Quantitative Research Department, Financial Research Centre, Nomura Securities Co. Ltd

Chapter 20   Yukihiko Endo, Nomura School of Advanced Management

Abbreviations

ABCP	asset-backed commercial paper
ABS	asset-backed security
ADR	American depositary receipt
ATS	alternative trading system
BIS	Bank for International Settlements
BOJ	Bank of Japan
bps	basis points
CBO	collateralized bond obligation
CBPI	Nomura Convertible Bond Performance Index
CD	certificate of deposit
CDO	collateralized debt obligation
CFROI	cash flow return on investment
CLO	collateralized loan obligation
CMBS	commercial mortgage-backed security
CME	Chicago Mercantile Exchange
CP	commercial paper
CPI	consumer price index
CTD	cheapest to deliver
CY	calendar year
DCF	discounted cash flow
DDM	dividend discount model
D/E	debt to equity
DTC	Depository Trust Company
DVP	delivery versus payment
EBO	Edwards–Bell–Ohlson
ECB	European Central Bank
ECN	electronic communications network
EFP	exchange for physical

EPS	earnings per share
ERISA	Employee Retirement Income Security Act
ETF	exchange-traded fund
EVA	economic value added
FB	financing bill
FDICIA	Federal Deposit Insurance Corporation Improvement Act
FILP	Fiscal Investment and Loan Programme
FSA	Financial Services Agency
FTSE	Financial Times–Stock Exchange 100 share index
FY	fiscal year
GDP	gross domestic product
HLC	Housing Loan Corporation
IAS	International Accounting Standards
IPO	initial public offering
IRR	internal rate of return
ISDA	International Swaps and Derivatives Association
ISMA	International Securities Market Association
IT	information technology
JASDAQ	Japan Securities Dealers Association Automated Quotation system
JASDEC	Japan Securities Depository Center
JCR	Japan Credit Rating Agency
JGB	Japanese government bond
JR	Japan Railways
J-REIT	Japanese real estate investment trust
JSDA	Japan Securities Dealers Association
JT	Japan Tobacco
LBO	leveraged buyout
LDP	Liberal Democratic Party
LIBOR	London Inter-Bank Offered Rate
LSE	London Stock Exchange
LT	LIBOR-Treasury
LTCB	Long-Term Credit Bank of Japan
M&A	mergers and acquisitions
MBO	management buyout
MBS	mortgage-backed security
MITI	Ministry of International Trade and Industry
MITI Law	Law Relating to the Regulation of Business Concerning Specified Claims (1993)

MMC	money market certificate
MMF	money market funds
MOF	Ministry of Finance
Moody's	Moody's Investment Service
Mothers	market of the high-growth and emerging stocks
MRF	money reserve fund
MSCI	Morgan Stanley Capital International
munis	municipal bonds
NASD	National Association of Securities Dealers
New SPC Law	(Special Purpose Corporation) Law on the Securitization of Assets (2000)
Non-bank Bond Act	Law Relating to the Issuance of Corporate Bonds for Lending Activities by Commercial Lenders (1998)
NPFA	National Pension Fund Association
NRSRO	nationally recognized statistical rating organization
NTT	Nippon Telegraph & Telephone
NYSE	New York Stock Exchange
ODR	official discount rate
OSE	Osaka Securities Exchange
OSF50	Osaka Stock Futures 50
OTC	over the counter
P/B	price to book
P/E	price to earnings
PBGC	Pension Benefit Guaranty Corporation
Perfection Law	Law Concerning Exceptions to the Requirements for the Perfection of Assignment of Receivables under the Civil Code (1998)
PPP	purchasing power parity
pps	percentage points
PTS	proprietary trading system
R&D	research and development
R&I	Rating & Investment Information
REIT	real estate investment trust
repo	*see* RP
RMBS	residential mortgage-backed security
ROA	return on assets
ROE	return on equity
RP	repurchase agreement

RTGS	real-time gross settlement system
S&L	savings and loan
S&P	Standard & Poor's
S&S Limited Partnership Law	Law Concerning Small and Medium Enterprise Limited Partnership Contracts (1998)
SCAP	Supreme Commander of the Allied Powers
SCLC	Securities Coordinating Liquidation Committee
SEC	Securities and Exchange Commission
SESC	Securities and Exchange Surveillance Commission
SFAS	Statement of Financial Accounting Standards
SIMEX	Singapore International Monetary Exchange
SNA	System of National Accounts
SPC	special purpose corporation
SPC Law	Law Concerning Securitization of Specified Assets by a Special Purpose Corporation (1998)
SPDR	S&P Depositary Receipts ('Spiders')
SQ	special quotation
TB	Treasury bill
TL	Treasury-LIBOR
TOPIX	Tokyo Stock Price Index
tr.	trillion
TSE	Tokyo Stock Exchange
TSR	Tokyo Swap Reference
UIT	unit investment trust
VC	venture capital(ist)
VWAP	volume-weighted average price

PART

I

Overview

1 The historical performance of Japan's financial markets

This chapter provides a review and an analysis of the past performance of Japan's financial markets, specifically the markets for stocks, bonds and short-term assets. Japan's modern-day financial and securities markets are essentially a postwar creation, given that Japan rebuilt itself under a new system after much of its economic wealth and infrastructure were destroyed during World War II.

The stock market

In May 1878, the Tokyo Stock Exchange Company, the forerunner of today's Tokyo Stock Exchange (TSE), was established in accordance with the Stock Exchange Ordinance, and trading began on 1 June. Trading continued until the economic chaos in Japan toward the end of World War II brought disorder to the securities markets. Trading was suspended in August 1945, and the TSE was not reorganized until April 1949. Other exchanges were established in Osaka and Nagoya around the same time and trading started up again in May. Eventually, nine exchanges were opened, but as a result of closings and mergers, by the end of 2000, only five exchanges remained, including those in Tokyo and Osaka.

In addition to the exchanges, an over-the-counter (OTC) market, JASDAQ, was established by the Japan Association of Securities Dealers in 1983 for the stocks of companies that were not as established as those listed on the TSE. And two new markets were launched in 2000 for relatively young but fast-growing companies: NASDAQ

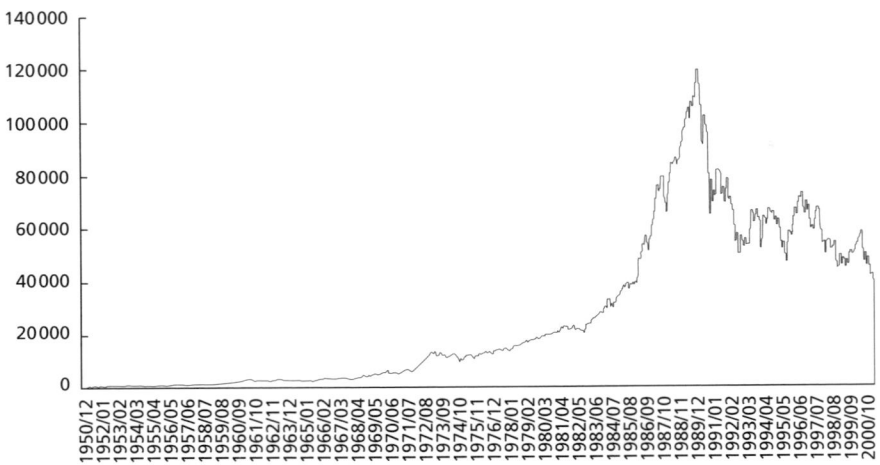

1.1 Historical returns of stocks (total return of the Nikkei Average).
Note: Data are from December 1950 to October 2000, indexed to 100 as of
December 1950.
Source: Nomura.

Japan, a joint venture of Softbank and The National Association of
Securities Dealers (NASD) of the US, and the TSE's Mothers, a market
for high-growth and emerging market stocks.

In terms of trading value, the TSE is still the dominant exchange,
or market, in Japan. As of the end of June 2001, 1447 stocks were listed
on the first section of the TSE, 580 on the second section of the TSE,
1253 on the Osaka Securities Exchange, 579 on the Nagoya Stock
Exchange, 57 on NASDAQ Japan, 35 on Mothers and 880 on JASDAQ.[1]

THE PERFORMANCE OF THE STOCK MARKET

Figure 1.1 shows the annual rates of return of the Nikkei Average
(the Nikkei 225), Japan's oldest stock index, over the past 50 years.
The Nikkei 225, a price-weighted index of the share prices of 225
leading stocks listed on the TSE, is calculated using a frequently
adjusted divisor, in much the same way the Dow Jones Industrial
Average is. The Nikkei 225 can be thought of as the total value of
a portfolio containing 225 individual stocks, and Fig. 1.1 as representing the growth of the leading stocks in Japan over time. The
TOPIX (a market cap-weighted index including all the stocks listed

1 Note, however, that some stocks trade on multiple markets.

on the first section of the TSE) and the RUSSELL/NOMURA Total Market index (a free float-adjusted market cap-weighted index that includes the top 98% of all the stocks, in terms of market capitalization, listed on all the exchanges and the OTC market in Japan) are alternative indexes that represent the Japanese stock market,[2] but here the Nikkei 225 is used as a measure of the performance of Japan's stock market over long periods because of the availability of the historical data and the index's familiarity among ordinary investors.

Figure 1.1 provides an indication of the historical growth patterns of Japan's major stocks.[3] With the starting point indexed to 100, the figure shows the change in value over time of ¥100 invested in Japanese stocks at the end of 1950. The index climbed from a value of 100 at the end of 1950 to almost 120000 at the peak of the market bubble in late 1989 and had an impressive compound annual rate of return of 19.90%. By the end of 2000, however, it had fallen about two-thirds from the peak level. Nevertheless, in the 50 years between the end of 1950 and the end of 2000, Japan's stock market rose at a compound annual rate of 12.67%.

For each 10-year interval, Table 1.1 shows the compound annual rate of return (including dividends) of the Nikkei 225, the average dividend yield on TSE first-section stocks, the average total market value of TSE first-section stocks (the average of year-end totals), the total market value of TSE first-section stocks at the end of each 10-year period and the total number of TSE first-section stocks.

From the end of World War II to the peak of the market bubble in the late 1980s, Japanese stocks steadily increased in value. Despite some hiccups in the 1960s, when stocks slumped on a number of occasions, the market continued to grow strongly in conjunction with the economy's rapid expansion. Stocks increased in value even during the 1970s, when Japan's economic growth rate slid from

---

2 The TOPIX and the RUSSELL/NOMURA Total Market index (one of a series of indexes jointly created by the Frank Russell Company and Nomura Securities Financial Research Center) could be considered better indexes than the Nikkei Average, in light of the problem presented for the continuity of the Nikkei Average as a result of the significant changes to the component stocks in April 2000.

3 The returns include reinvested dividends; for the period from the end of 1950 to the end of 1964, the average dividend yield was used; from the end of January 1965 to the end of 1968, the average dividend yield for the component stocks of the Nikkei Average was used; after January 1969, the average dividend yield for the TSE first-section stocks was used.

Table 1.1 Stock returns over 10-year intervals

	Nikkei Average (total annual compound return, %)	Dividend yield (%)[1]	TSE 1st section avg. market value (¥ bn)[2]	TSE 1st section market value (end of period; ¥ bn)[4]	No. of TSE 1st section stocks (end of period)
Entire period (12/50–12/00)	12.67%				
1950s (12/50–12/60)	35.44%			5411	664
1960s (12/60–12/70)	8.21%	4.07%[3]	10983[3]	15091	801
1970s (12/70–12/80)	15.87%	2.02%	45650	73221	966
1980s (12/80–12/90)	13.86%	0.91%	254664	365155	1197
1990s (12/90–12/00)	–6.08%	0.85%	339098	352785	1447

Notes: **1** Dividend yield figure for December 1950–December 1964 is actually the average dividend yield for the Nikkei 225 Average for January 1965–December 1968; thereafter, the dividend yield figures are the averages for the TOPIX stocks.
2 Averages for the end of each year.
3 Average for January 1965–December 1970.
4 The highest year-end market value was ¥590909bn at the end of 1989.
5 The total returns for the Nikkei Average were calculated by Nomura, based on Nikkei Average figures.

© Nihon Keizai Shimbun, Inc.
Source: Nomura.

Table 1.2 Japan's GDP growth rate

1950s (1953–1960)	8.1%
1960s (1961–1970)	10.2%
1970s (1971–1980)	4.5%
1980s (1981–1990)	4.1%
1990s (1991–1999)	1.3%

Note: GDP growth rate figures are annualized averages for the 10-year periods.
Source: National Accounts Yearbook (Cabinet Office); Kazushi Okawa, *Kokumin Shotoku*, Toyo Keizai Shinposha, 1974.

double digits to roughly 4%, and throughout the 1980s. Then, in 1989, the bubble burst. Marked by economic stagnation and negative returns on stocks that were unusual even by historical standards, the 1990s have come to be known as the 'lost decade'. Table 1.2 depicts Japan's annual average GDP growth rate for each decade.

DIVIDEND YIELDS AND TOTAL MARKET VALUE

Since most Japanese companies paid (and still do) more or less a fixed dividend each year, dividend yields declined steadily in the postwar years at the same time that stock prices rapidly rose. The average dividend yield was more than 4% in the 1960s, but then it fell below 1% by the 1990s. The total market value of Japanese stocks on the TSE rose sharply during the bubble years of the 1980s and eventually exceeded the total market value of stocks on the New York Stock Exchange (NYSE) at one point in 1989. During the 1990s, however, the market value of Japanese stocks tumbled.

PERFORMANCE BY SECTOR

Table 1.3 shows the returns of the NOMURA400 index (an index of 400 major Japanese stocks maintained by the Nomura Securities Financial Research Center) and the excess returns (the return for each sector minus the overall return of the NOMURA400 index) for the 21 sectors that make up the index from the end of 1970 to the end of 2000. The totals are based on compound annual returns, not including dividends. Excess returns of sectors allow the relative performances of each sector to be easily compared.

Table 1.3 Excess returns by sector

	1970s (12/70–12/80)	1980s (12/80–12/90)	1990s (12/90–12/00)	Entire period (12/70–12/00)
NOMURA400 return[1]	13.12%	13.72%	−1.35%	8.27%

(figures below are excess returns relative to the NOMURA400[2])

Construction	−7.37%	4.63%	−11.77%	−5.44%
Housing/real estate	−6.61%	−0.69%	−3.14%	−3.50%
Building materials	−1.81%	−0.09%	−1.55%	−1.18%
Textiles	−2.27%	−1.20%	−2.81%	−2.14%
Pulp/paper	1.02%	0.44%	−2.28%	−0.38%
Chemicals	−0.75%	−2.99%	0.20%	−1.12%
Steel	0.13%	−2.23%	−9.47%	−4.23%
Nonferrous metals-composite	−2.47%	0.68%	1.54%	−0.02%
Machinery	−0.78%	−3.29%	−3.12%	−2.44%
Electrical/electronics	0.51%	−4.46%	6.40%	0.99%
Shipbuilding	−2.41%	−1.68%	−4.79%	−3.07%
Automobiles/auto parts	5.45%	−3.34%	6.97%	3.13%
Drugs	2.42%	−0.82%	8.20%	3.44%
Foods-composite	−0.14%	−1.39%	−1.58%	−1.07%
Trading companies	2.76%	−4.18%	−3.66%	−1.83%
Consumer	−2.92%	−1.86%	0.69%	−1.28%
Oil/coal	12.64%	−9.12%	−6.98%	−1.83%
Communications	1.69%	1.15%	6.41%	3.22%
Transportation	−1.55%	1.22%	−2.34%	−0.98%
Utilities	−5.17%	1.46%	−2.29%	−2.05%
Financials	2.13%	7.66%	−5.69%	0.88%

1 The NOMURA400 index is maintained and published by the Nomura Securities Financial Research Center.
2 Sector returns are excess returns relative to the NOMURA400.
Source: Nomura.

The data in Table 1.3 reflect the changes that have occurred in Japan's industrial structure during the last three decades. From the 1970s to the 1980s, Japan's traditional industry sectors, as well as the financial sector that supported them, outperformed the other sectors. In the 1990s, however, as Japan's economic structure evolved, the service sector, high-tech sector and other growth sectors that were not supported heavily by banks began to establish a leading role in the economy. Because of the bursting of the market bubble that left the vast majority of banks with a large number of non-performing loans, however, excess returns in the financial sector and in the sectors supported by banks worsened. Throughout the entire period from December 1970 to December 2000, less than a handful of sectors outperformed the NOMURA400 index, namely, electrical/electronics, automobiles, pharmaceuticals and communications. The market was thus led by a few sectors composed of large-cap blue-chip companies.

PERFORMANCE BY INVESTMENT STYLE

Investment style – such as value versus growth or large cap versus small cap – also accounts for significant differences in stock returns in Japan's market. Value stocks are those with relatively low price-to-book (P/B) or price-to-earnings (P/E) ratios and are regarded as having relatively low growth potential. Growth stocks, in contrast, have relatively high P/B or P/E ratios. Large caps consist of those stocks with large market capitalizations, and small caps those with small market capitalizations. Table 1.4 shows the returns (including dividends) for various RUSSELL/NOMURA style indexes. Since the early 1980s, when the RUSSELL/NOMURA style indexes were created, value stocks have outperformed growth stocks most of the time. Yet in the late 1990s, when dot-com fever dominated the market, growth stocks outperformed value stocks by a substantial margin. With the collapse of Internet stocks in 2000, however, growth stocks lost their dominance in the market. Over the long term, in both Japan and the US, value stocks have outperformed growth stocks. With regard to market capitalization, small-cap stocks had poor returns in the early 1990s as a result of the weak economy. Style differences have become more marked since 1997, when the financial Big Bang (see the next chapter) and other structural changes began to exacerbate the strains that were already evident in Japan's economic and financial system. Style selection has thus become an increasingly important determinant of investment performance.

The bond market

Following World War II, Japan's bond market did not fully develop until roughly the mid-1960s. Until then, the primary fixed-income

Table 1.4 Stock returns by style (RUSSELL/NOMURA style indexes)

(units: %)

Year	Total market	Value	Growth	Large	Small	Large value	Large growth	Small value	Small growth
1980	9.19	13.14	5.40	8.90	10.73	13.04	4.74	13.72	8.42
1981	17.04	24.23	9.81	20.64	−0.90	28.31	12.67	1.60	−2.99
1982	6.03	5.05	6.96	6.56	2.78	5.51	7.53	2.46	3.13
1983	27.15	22.02	32.28	25.07	40.64	19.64	30.22	34.83	48.85
1984	18.74	24.56	12.59	18.39	20.76	24.75	11.76	23.52	17.62
1985	15.39	22.96	7.85	14.86	18.33	21.66	8.13	30.02	6.24
1986	51.62	55.90	47.63	57.49	21.76	60.33	54.80	31.85	13.30
1987	6.73	18.45	−4.32	3.16	30.54	14.36	−6.86	41.08	16.43
1988	39.58	51.87	26.66	40.85	33.09	54.16	27.32	41.17	22.88
1989	23.75	31.32	16.17	18.05	54.68	25.57	10.72	60.19	48.36
1990	−39.12	−38.68	−39.56	−40.08	−33.76	−39.50	−40.71	−32.40	−34.60
1991	−2.02	−2.03	−2.00	−1.70	−3.43	−2.41	−0.92	0.33	−5.90
1992	−22.74	−22.21	−23.26	−21.93	−26.56	−21.41	−22.47	−26.37	−26.72
1993	10.85	12.01	9.72	11.89	5.60	13.21	10.64	6.38	4.68
1994	9.57	15.64	3.78	8.81	13.74	14.91	3.32	19.00	6.90
1995	1.45	2.09	0.83	2.65	−4.57	3.41	1.93	−4.22	−4.95
1996	−4.32	−2.75	−5.91	−2.84	−12.03	−1.24	−4.40	−9.72	−14.93
1997	−17.71	−25.88	−10.19	−13.19	−42.72	−21.96	−5.42	−44.91	−40.21
1998	−4.71	0.23	−9.07	−5.53	2.48	−0.07	−9.75	1.74	4.65
1999	55.26	30.16	79.01	56.97	40.66	32.28	77.40	19.54	113.74
2000	−21.62	−3.26	−37.09	−22.95	−6.44	−3.97	−37.30	1.39	−31.53

Note: Figures represent total returns.
Source: Nomura.

product was 10-year NTT bonds. The government did not issue any new bonds until 1964 partly to avoid repeating the painful experience of runaway inflation that had developed right after the war, when the government issued a massive number of bonds that were purchased by the Bank of Japan (BOJ). In addition, the government had no need to issue debt; the nation's rapid economic recovery up until then had contributed to a substantial increase in tax revenues. In 1966, however, the government began issuing seven-year bonds each month to finance improvements in the nation's infrastructure.

The performance of Japan's bond market is significantly determined by the performance of Japanese government bonds (JGBs), since the latter account for a far greater proportion of the bond market than corporate bonds and other types of bonds do in terms

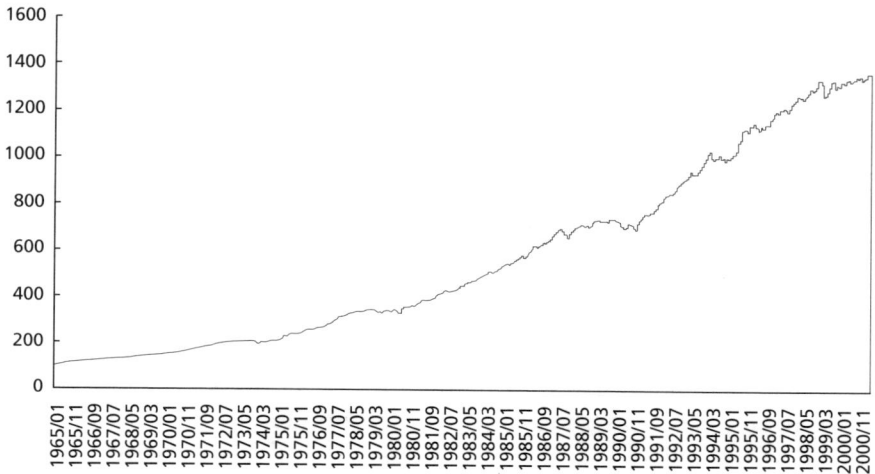

1.2 Bond market returns (NOMURA-BPI index).
Note: Data are from January 1965 to November 2000, indexed to 100 as of January 1965.
Source: Nomura.

Table 1.5 Bond market returns by period

	NOMURA-BPI compound annual return	Annual average amount of bonds issued (¥ bn)	Amount of bonds outstanding at end of each period (¥ bn)
Entire period (1/65–12/00)	7.55%		
1960s (1/65–12/70)	8.79%	4 486	21 077
1970s (12/70–12/80)	8.24%	21 703	154 086
1980s (12/80–12/90)	7.43%	64 716	342 785
1990s (12/90–12/00)	6.28%	127 333[1]	578 316[1]

1 As of the end of December 1999.
Source: Nomura.

of outstanding amount, and an even greater proportion in terms of trading value.

Figure 1.2 illustrates the trend in the NOMURA-BPI (a bond market index created and maintained by the Nomura Securities Financial Research Center) since the end of January 1965. One hundred yen invested in the bond market in January 1965 would have accumulated to ¥1367 by the end of November 2000 – a compound annual rate of return of 7.55%.

For each interval since the mid-1960s (only five years are included for the 1960s), Table 1.5 shows the compound annual returns of the NOMURA-BPI index, the annual average amount of public and corporate bonds issued and the amount of bonds outstanding at the end of each period. Bond market returns remained relatively stable until the 1980s, when total bond returns declined steadily in line with the long-term downturn in interest rates. Although interest rates fell markedly during the 1990s, as the recession set in and the BOJ adopted a zero interest rate policy in 1998, bonds performed relatively well in the 1990s, especially compared with the negative returns of stocks during the same period.

The outstanding amount of bonds rose sharply starting in the latter half of the 1970s, when the government issued a large amount of JGBs. In the hope of pulling the economy out of an ever-worsening recession, the government continued to issue more JGBs in the latter half of the 1990s to finance spending on public works. Moreover, the outstanding balance of government bonds is set to increase even further; public sector corporations currently using *zaito* funds (funds from the government's Fiscal Investment and Loan Program (FILP), or *zaito*) are now required to issue *zaito* agency bonds (more or less equivalent to JGBs) as a result of *zaito* reforms, implemented in April 2001.[4] The amount of *zaito* agency bonds to be issued is expected to match the current outstanding amount of JGBs.

Japan's convertible bond market expanded tremendously during the 1980s, when many companies were keen on using convertibles for financing. Figure 1.3 highlights the trends in the NOMURA-CBPI (a convertible bond index created and maintained by the Nomura Securities Financial Research Center) since the end of June 1970. One hundred yen invested in convertible bonds in June 1970 would have accumulated to ¥2269 by the end of June 2000 – a compound annual return of 10.78%.

For each 10-year period since the 1970s, Table 1.6 shows the compound annual returns of the NOMURA-CBPI index, the annual average amount of convertibles issued and the amount of convertibles outstanding at the end of each period. Because stock prices rose steadily until the end of the 1980s, convertible bonds were in the money nearly the entire time, and their returns were closely tied to stock returns. But when stock returns declined in the 1990s, convertible bond returns held up because of their fixed-income component, which provides downside protection. The convertible bond

---

4 For details, see Chapter 9.

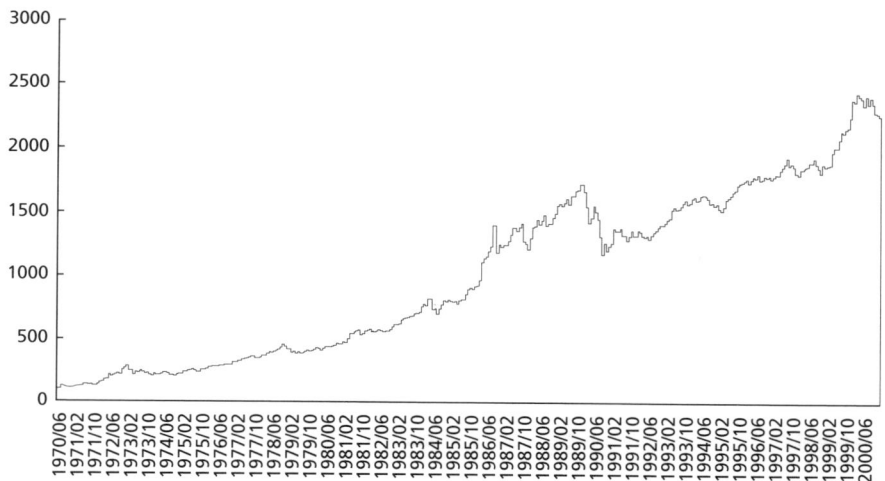

1.3 Convertible bond returns (NOMURA-CBPI index).
Note: Figures are for June 1970 to June 2000, indexed to June 1970 = 100.
Source: Nomura.

Table 1.6 Convertible bond returns over 10-year intervals

	NOMURA-CBPI compound annual return	Annual average amount of bonds issued (¥ bn)	Amount of bonds outstanding at end of each period (¥ bn)
Entire period (6/70–12/00)	10.78%		
1970s (12/70–12/80)	15.61%	222	1 150
1980s (12/80–12/90)	10.41%	2907	16 091
1990s (12/90–12/00)	6.25%	1125	11 741

Source: Nomura.

market grew to more than ¥16 tr. by the peak of the market bubble in the late 1980s, which helped convertibles become recognized as a significant asset class. Since then, however, the market for convertible bonds has steadily shrunk.

Short-term assets

The primary short-term products for Japanese investors are bank savings accounts, short-term bond funds and postal savings accounts. Table 1.7 displays the returns on two-year postal savings

Table 1.7 Returns on two-year postal savings accounts by decade

	Postal savings accounts[1]
Entire period (1/65–12/00)	3.36%
1960s (1/65–12/70)	4.08%
1970s (12/70–12/80)	4.16%
1980s (12/80–12/90)	3.62%
1990s (12/90–12/00)	1.90%

1 Figures represent compounded annual returns, assuming principal
and interest income are rolled over at maturity.
Source: Nomura.

Table 1.8 Risk and return for major asset classes

	Stocks	Bonds	Convertible bonds	Postal savings accounts
Return	12.67%	7.55%	10.78%	3.36%
Risk	19.63%	3.55%	13.38%	–
Time period	(12/50–12/00)	(1/65–12/00)	(6/70–12/00)	(1/65–12/00)

Source: Nomura.

accounts (the only product for which long-term data are available) from the end of January 1965 to the end of December 2000 and for 10-year periods in between. The return calculations are based on the assumption that principal and interest are rolled over at maturity into the same two-year postal savings accounts. The returns on two-year postal savings accounts started to decline markedly in the 1990s, in tandem with the long-term downturn in interest rates. In the second half of the 1990s, short-term rates were below 1%, partly as a result of the BOJ's adoption of a zero interest rate policy in the late 1990s.

Comparison of performance by asset class

Table 1.8 shows the risk and return for stocks, bonds, convertibles and short-term assets over the long term. Risk is measured in terms of annualized standard deviation of monthly returns, and the returns are annually compounded figures. Risk was not calculated for short-term assets. As shown in Table 1.8, the standard deviation of stock returns between January 1955 and December 2000 was almost 20%.

For long-term investors, returns are meaningful only when they are adjusted for inflation, so as to measure the actual growth of purchasing power. Stock returns have more than compensated for inflation over the long term, except during the 1990s, as indicated in Table 1.9, which shows the real returns for the major asset classes (adjusted for changes in the consumer price index). Bonds have consistently generated positive real returns since the 1980s, but their real return was negative in the 1970s because of high inflation. Short-term assets failed to keep pace with inflation between January 1965 and December 2000.

The lost decade

From the end of World War II until the late 1980s, rapid economic growth contributed to strong returns on financial assets in Japan, especially for stocks. The popping of the market bubble at the close of the 1980s, however, changed everything. The lost decade of the 1990s denotes a period when all asset classes in Japan, except bonds, performed dismally. Interest rates decreased and remained at very low levels, and returns on stocks were negative in this decade. Japan's economy and financial markets have continued to stumble because of the slow pace of structural change and the debilitating impact of the massive amounts of bad loans that are a legacy of the bubble years.

The recession in the US that followed the 1929 stock market crash offers a parallel to Japan's lost decade. The 1929 Crash, which was an event of global significance, has been considered as a contributing factor to World War II. At the end of 1929, the Dow Jones Industrial Average stood at 164.58. Only 16 years later did the index recover, reaching 192.91 at the end of 1945. The performance of Japan's stock market since the market bubble burst mirrors the performance of the US market in the wake of the 1929 Crash. Nevertheless, from 1926 to 1997, the compound annual rate of return for US stocks was 10.6%.

Some observers believe that Japan's slump dragged on and turned the 1990s into a lost decade because of the slow response to change that is characteristic of Japanese society. But changes have

Table 1.9 Real returns for major asset classes

	Stocks	Bonds	Convertible bonds	Postal savings accounts	Inflation[1]
1950s (1/55–12/60)	28.70%				1.31%
1960s (12/60–12/70)	2.29%				5.92%
1970s (12/70–12/80)	6.96%	–0.67%	6.70%	–4.75%	8.91%
1980s (12/80–12/90)	11.94%	5.51%	8.49%	1.70%	1.92%
1990s (12/90–12/00)	–6.65%	5.71%	5.68%	1.33%	0.57%
Entire period (1/55–12/00)	6.38%	3.66%	6.89%	–0.53%	3.89%
Time period	(1/55–12/00)	(1/65–12/00)	(6/70–12/00)	(1/65–12/00)	(1/55–12/00)

1 Compound annual rate of change in the CPI.
Source: Nomura.

occurred – progress has been made in economic and financial de-regulation, and the labour market has become increasingly flexible. In the financial and capital markets, the mentality of investors and corporate managers is changing for the better. These changes are explored in the following chapters.

CHAPTER 2
The financial system crisis and the financial Big Bang in Japan

This chapter examines major changes that have occurred within Japan's financial system during the second half of the 1990s. Specifically, the chapter summarizes the implementation of measures intended to stabilize the Japanese financial system, such as the injection of public funds into the nation's banks and Japan's financial Big Bang, which was designed to enhance the global competitiveness of Japan's capital markets and financial services companies. Because these changes relate to the main theme of this book, further details are discussed in each of the following chapters.

Breakdown of the government's gradual-reform policy

Japan's financial system in the postwar years was characterized by the restricted flow of capital between Japan and overseas markets as a result of various regulations, such as the Foreign Exchange and Foreign Trade Control Law and the Foreign Investment Law, and the allocation of capital based on government policy rather than market forces. Under this system, the government kept market interest rates low and favoured companies in industries it deemed important from the perspective of industrial development by providing low-interest loans through government-affiliated financial institutions. Much of the government's postwar industrial policy was implemented through banks, which acted as intermediaries for the implementation of the government's economic policies. The role of the capital markets in Japan following the war was to a large extent limited, both because of the lack of a link between the primary and secondary markets (issuance terms in the primary market did not reflect conditions in the secondary market) and because of various restrictions on market participants.

Once this basic postwar financial system was in place, reforms came about at a relatively gradual pace. When the government implemented systemic adjustments in response to a multitude of environmental changes, it often did so in conjunction with policies designed to minimize the extent of sudden drastic changes to the existing system in order to protect vested interests. The government mitigated price competition as well as other forms of competition among financial institutions, partly in an attempt to maintain the stability of the financial system by preserving the health of individual financial institutions. Because financial institutions did not have to compete, they failed to innovate, and consequently the efficiency of Japan's financial system barely improved.

Foreign countries increasingly pressured Japan to deregulate during the 1980s. Beginning in 1984 in particular, when the US–Japan Yen–Dollar Committee completed its work, systemic reforms were implemented on a predetermined agenda and timetable. Nonetheless, the Japanese government's gradualist approach did not change. Even after the government implemented the Financial System Reform Law in 1992, which permitted banks, securities companies and trust banks to enter into each others' businesses, the actual pace of deregulation remained relatively slow.

During the second half of the 1990s, however, various environmental factors forced the government to increase the pace of deregulation of the Japanese financial system. The first factor was a non-performing loan crisis. Soon after the economic bubble burst in Japan, the amount of Japanese banks' non-performing loans stemming from declines in the value of stocks and real estate rose sharply. The disposal of these non-performing loans was delayed because of expectations among the government and private sector that an economic recovery would resolve the problem within a relatively short period of time; however, underestimation of the seriousness of the bad-loan dilemma resulted in a series of major failures of financial institutions and, consequently, the emergence of systemic risk within Japan's financial system during the second half of 1997.

A second factor was a deterioration in the global competitiveness of Japan's capital markets and its financial institutions, which occurred in part because of the non-performing loan crisis. During

19

the economic bubble years, and helped by the strong yen, Japanese financial institutions built up a presence in New York, London and other major international capital markets that was often viewed as a threat. This trend, however, completely reversed during the 1990s.

Whether Japanese financial services companies have ever been truly competitive by international standards is debatable. Japan's financial and capital markets have been constrained by various regulations and customs, and the costs associated with conducting transactions in these markets have been relatively high. In 1994, pressure began to mount for improving Japan's markets. One of the major arguments for the need to improve Japan's capital and financial markets was based on concerns over a so-called hollowing out of Japan's markets. These worries were triggered mainly by a decline in the number of foreign companies listed on the Tokyo Stock Exchange and a rise in the number of Japanese companies that chose to raise capital in overseas markets. Under the government's gradualist approach to reform, decisions were conducted by 'specialists' (regulatory agencies or ministries and financial institutions, which acted as intermediaries for implementing the government's economic policies). The opinions of market participants had only a limited impact on financial system reforms. Starting around 1994, however, it became more and more widely recognized that the relative inefficiency of Japan's capital markets could be detrimental to the health of the overall economy.

Because the two aforementioned factors became serious issues at about the same time, the government was forced to abandon its gradualist approach to reforming Japan's financial system. Instead, it decided to implement wide-ranging, comprehensive changes. The authorities sought to achieve two goals simultaneously: in order to foster the development of a financial services industry and develop a financial system infrastructure on a par with that in the leading global financial markets, they strived to maintain the stability of the existing financial system while promoting the Big Bang package of reforms.

Japan's policies to resolve the financial system crisis

The problem of non-performing loans existed even before the emergence of the economic bubble. The extent of the problem was limited, however; the regulators typically intervened and persuaded healthy financial institutions to acquire struggling entities before any major problems became public, and details were rarely disclosed even after a resolution was achieved.

THE FINANCIAL SYSTEM'S PROBLEMS IN THE 1990S

In contrast, non-performing loan problems during the 1990s afflicted most Japanese financial institutions. Even financial institutions that had previously rescued struggling companies were not immune to problem loans. As a consequence, the government's conventional method for resolving bad-debt problems was no longer applicable. In March 1992, an unorthodox bailout scheme was adopted for the first time. Toyo Shinkin Bank, which went bankrupt because of a scandal involving forged deposit certificates, was split up and acquired by several banks, including Sanwa Bank, rather than by a single financial institution.

In December 1994, the Ministry of Finance and the Bank of Japan used funding from the central bank and private banks to establish Tokyo Kyodo Bank to take over the operations of the bankrupt Tokyo Kyowa Credit Union and Anzen Credit Union. This move was part of the government's emergency measures to maintain the stability of the financial system.

In December 1995, the finance minister announced various modifications to the rules and regulations regarding Japanese financial institutions. The main changes included a decision by the government to force Japanese financial institutions to take full responsibility for managing their loan portfolios as well as steps to improve the transparency of government regulation over financial institutions. The government made this announcement primarily in response to heightened criticism concerning the authorities and their regulations. Major complaints stemmed from the lack of transparency in the regulatory process and the strong influence of the banks over the regulators, which were supposed to be overseeing the banking sector. Criticisms were also triggered by a series of scandals, such as the massive bond-trading losses incurred at Daiwa Bank's New York City office.

In November 1996, the finance minister issued a 'cease-and-desist' order to Hanwa Bank after the government determined that the bank was unable to effectively restructure its operations independently. This intervention was the first time since the war that this legal provision was applied to a failing Japanese financial institution.

In April 1997, Nissan Mutual Life Insurance was also ordered to cease operations. Following these incidents, this approach became the government's standard procedure for dealing with insolvent financial institutions.

In June 1996, a new law regarding the use of public funds to restructure the housing loan companies, or *jusen*, was enacted. The housing loan companies were not categorized as banks because they were not allowed to accept deposits. As a result of the large amount of loans they extended to real estate companies during the bubble years, the amount of non-performing loans at the housing loan companies rose sharply. The government decided to use public funds to liquidate the housing loan companies in order to minimize any negative impact on the banks and financial institutions for agriculture and forestries, which had extended loans to the housing loan companies. In July 1996, the Jusen Resolution Corporation, which was fully funded by the Deposit Insurance Corporation, was established to take over and collect on the loans of the housing loan companies. Subsequently, the housing loan companies were liquidated.

Shortly thereafter, three key financial laws were enacted to improve Japan's financial system. These laws included various measures for dealing with struggling financial institutions. So-called prompt, corrective action measures forced banks to deal with capital adequacy and other problems at a relatively early stage. Separately, the first formal measures were instituted for liquidating bankrupt financial institutions. One drawback, however, was that these measures applied only to credit cooperatives. In addition, a temporary freeze was placed on the imposition of a ceiling on the amount of deposits insured by the Deposit Insurance Corporation; deposits were to continue to be fully insured to March 2001, but the full coverage was extended for another two years for deposits used for transaction settlements and for another year for other types of deposits.

MAJOR BANKRUPTCIES

Financial institutions continued to fail in Japan. November 1997 marked the beginning of a series of major bankruptcies. Among the first was Sanyo Securities, a leading second-tier securities company that filed for corporate reorganization. The company also defaulted on its call loans, the first such incident in Japan, and sent the money markets into a panic.

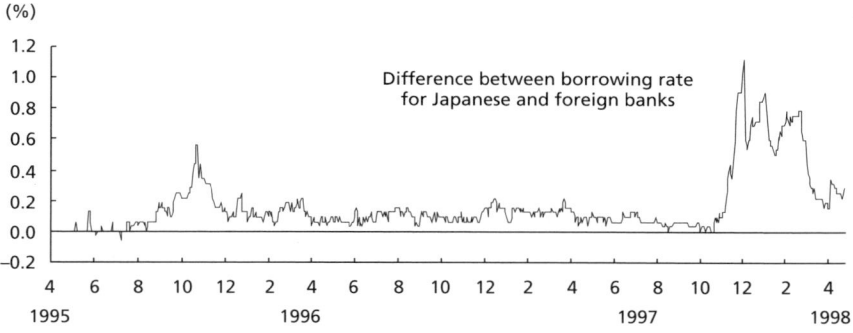

2.1 The Japan premium (for borrowing in dollars).

Hokkaido Takushoku Bank, which was established in 1899 as a national policy-related bank and later recategorized as a city bank, was the second major financial institution to file for bankruptcy. Unable to raise funds, the bank was forced to pull out of the banking business. Hokkaido Takushoku Bank's collapse was significant in that it demonstrated that the Ministry of Finance was unable to hold up its tacit pledge to prevent Japan's major banks from going under.

The third major financial institution to go bankrupt was Yamaichi Securities, which was established over a century ago and was considered to be one of the four major Japanese securities companies. It filed for bankruptcy as a result of a scandal relating to the illegal transfer of non-performing loans to affiliated companies.

This string of major bankruptcies severely damaged the public's confidence in the financial system. The volume of transactions in the capital markets declined, and the withdrawal of deposits from banks that were rumoured to be in trouble accelerated. Furthermore, Japanese banks found it extremely difficult to raise dollar-denominated funds because of an increase in the so-called Japan premium, or the extra amount that Japanese banks were charged to borrow in international markets (Fig. 2.1). These events indicated that problems were spreading from individual financial institutions to the Japanese financial system as a whole.

THE USE OF PUBLIC FUNDS IN THE BANKING SECTOR

In response to the bankruptcies mentioned above, the ruling Liberal Democratic Party (LDP) drafted a package of emergency measures for stabilizing the financial system. The most relevant measure called for the preparation of ¥30 tr. in public funds to fully insure bank

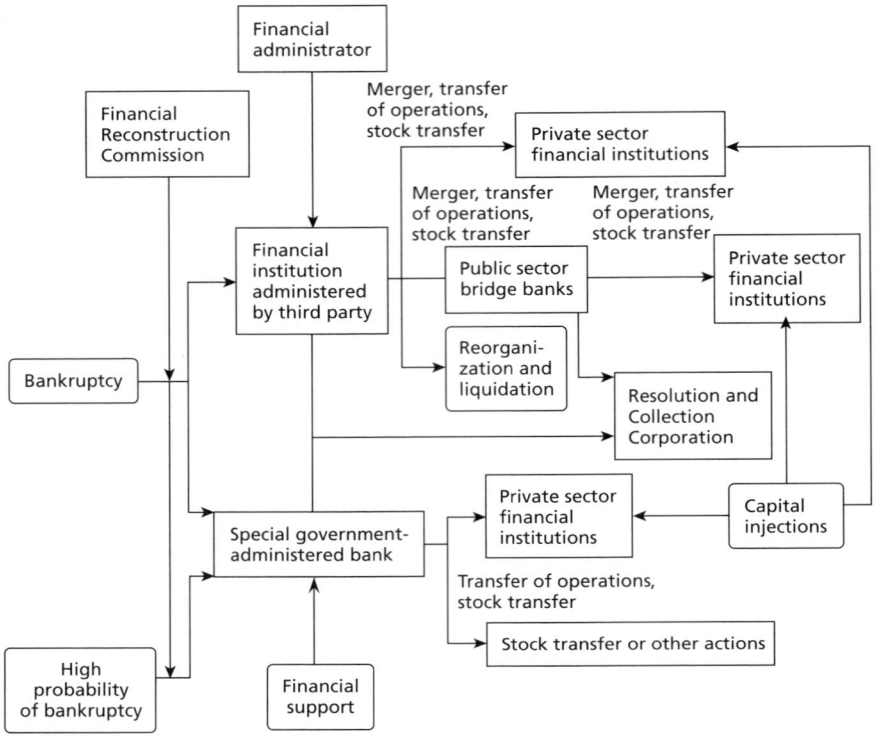

2.2 Liquidation under the Financial Reconstruction Law.
Source: Financial Supervisory Agency, *The First Year of the Financial Supervisory Agency, 1999*, p. 230.

deposits and recapitalize banks. In addition, in February 1998, two provisional financial stabilization laws were passed that were effective only until fiscal 2000. In March 1998, the 21 major Japanese banks received an aggregate ¥1.8 tr. in capital through the sale of preferred stock and subordinated debt to the government.

Furthermore, in October 1998, the Financial Reconstruction Law and the Financial Function Early Strengthening Law were passed to establish arrangements for liquidating insolvent banks and providing capital to healthy banks to ensure the prompt restructuring of the financial system. The total amount of public funds that the government set aside for restructuring the nation's banks was doubled to ¥60 tr. (Fig. 2.2). Both measures were originally scheduled to expire in fiscal 2000 but have been extended indefinitely, and the total amount of public funds made available for the capital injections was further increased to ¥70 tr.

The liquidation arrangement provided for failed banks to be taken over and liquidated by either financial administrators or the government, which temporarily nationalized the banks. The nationalization option was established mainly for emergency purposes for dealing with the failure of a major bank. Under both arrangements, the Resolution and Collection Corporation would purchase the nonperforming loans of a failed bank and sell the performing loans to private entities. The Resolution and Collection Corporation, which was a Japanese version of the Resolution Trust Corporation of the US, was established by combining the Resolution and Collection Bank, which was the former Tokyo Kyodo Bank, and the Jusen Resolution Corporation. If the bankruptcy administrators were unable to find a private company to accept the performing loans of an insolvent bank within a year, the loans could be transferred to a bridge bank funded by the Deposit Insurance Corporation. But if the administrators were unable to find any private entities to take over the loans within two years, insolvent banks were liquidated. A gradual approach for liquidating failed banks was adopted to minimize any negative impact on borrowers.

The Long-Term Credit Bank of Japan was nationalized in October 1998, immediately after the Financial Reconstruction Law was passed, followed by Nippon Credit Bank in December 1998. In 1999, several banks were taken over by financial administrators, including Kokumin Bank in April, Kofuku Bank in May, Tokyo Sowa Bank in June, Namihaya Bank in August and Niigata Chuo Bank in October.

In March 1999, the government provided a total of ¥7459.2 bn in capital to 15 major banks, and in March 2000, it supplied six regional banks with capital totalling ¥575 bn through the purchase of preferred stock and subordinated debt issued by these regional banks.

ARRANGEMENTS FOR LIQUIDATING FINANCIAL SERVICES COMPANIES OTHER THAN BANKS

A safety net for the failure of securities companies is provided by the Deposited Securities Compensation Fund, which was established in 1969 and protects the assets of clients of securities companies that go bankrupt. When Sanyo Securities and Maruso Securities went bankrupt in 1997, however, this fund did not have sufficient funds to cover the entire amount of assets of the customers of both securities companies. The amount of compensation coverage required was made larger by the fact that the brokerages commingled their working capital and customer assets.

25

To ensure adequate funding, the Securities Investor Protection Fund was established in December 1998 as a corporation based on the revised Securities and Exchange Law. Originally, the fund was to be financed by all securities companies in Japan, including non-Japanese securities firms, and securities companies were to be allowed to borrow from the fund. Instead of one fund, however, two separate funds were created, partly because of complications related to the introduction date for a system of managing assets on a segregated basis. The two entities are the Securities Investor Protection Fund, participants of which are mainly non-Japanese securities companies, and the Japan Investor Protection Fund, in which other securities companies participate.

In the insurance industry, two insurance policyholders protection corporations, one for the life insurance companies and one for the casualty insurance companies, were established in December 1998 to strengthen the former insurance policyholder protection fund. All Japanese insurance companies are members of these organizations, the main functions of which are to financially support insurance companies that assume responsibility for policies issued by insolvent insurers and to take over policies of failed insurers if no insurer is willing to accept the policies. Until the end of March 2003, these organizations are eligible to obtain government funding with the approval of the Diet (the Japanese parliament) if their contribution reserves are insufficient for dealing with bankrupt insurers.

Because of the implementation of these various measures, the financial system crisis that hit Japan now appears to be under control.

JAPAN'S FINANCIAL BIG BANG

In November 1996, then Prime Minister Ryutaro Hashimoto announced that the creation of a financial system reform package was one of the most important tasks confronting his administration. The core goal of the package was to transform Japan's financial market into a global financial market on a par with New York and London.

This package was referred to as Japan's financial Big Bang, echoing the 1986 Big Bang deregulation of the London Stock Exchange. As the name suggests, the government hoped to depart from its past ways and achieve its goals quickly and comprehensively. The reform package could be referred to as a 'Bigger Bang' than that of the UK because it targeted not only the securities markets but also all other financial markets.

The reform package was significant for a number of reasons. First, it was crafted by a prime minister who was not a financial market specialist. Second, the package took a fresh approach by including a wide range of specific measures for improving Japan's financial markets that were governed by three guiding principles – 'free' (functioning on the basis of free market forces), 'fair' (transparent and reliable) and 'global' (leading and internationalized).

Under Prime Minister Hashimoto's supervision, the package was reviewed by the Ministry of Finance's relevant councils. With the revision of the Foreign Exchange and Foreign Trade Control Law in April 1998, capital transactions between domestic and overseas entities were liberalized, and a Financial System Reform Law was passed in December 1998. The majority of the measures proposed in the package were implemented by May 2001 (Table 2.1).

Consequences of reform

In addition to the factors mentioned above, other considerations that prompted the reforms of Japan's financial system included pressure from foreign countries, such as the Japan–US insurance negotiations of 1996, and scandals, such as illegal payments to *sokaiya* racketeers. The need for economic stimulus packages also served as a catalyst for the reforms.

The implementation of these extensive reforms has led to various transformations in Japan's financial system. Even just a decade ago, many of the organizational changes among regulatory authorities that have occurred were never expected. Furthermore, several new stock markets have intensified the competition to list and trade shares of emerging-growth companies. These topics will be addressed in more detail in Chapters 12 and 13. In addition, the behaviour of market participants has evolved, as manifested by a rise in the unwinding of cross-shareholdings, a subject that will be treated at length in Chapter 17.

Although financial system reforms have affected many business sectors to date, their impact on the financial services sector has been the most pronounced; specifically, these reforms have resulted in increased consolidation and the entry of new participants.

Table 2.1 Key components of Japan's financial Big Bang and its rollout schedule

	Fiscal 1997	Fiscal 1998	Fiscal 1999	Fiscal 2000	Fiscal 2001
I. New asset management alternatives					
Improved infrastructure for establishment and distribution of investment trusts					
Consolidated investment accounts	Oct				
Corporate-type investment trusts		Dec			
Privately placed investment trusts		Dec			
Retail sales of investment trusts by banks	Dec (Investment trust companies rent space at a bank to sell investment trusts)	Dec (Banks market investment trust products directly)			
Introduction of new derivative instruments					
Options on individual stocks	Jul				
OTC derivatives on marketable securities		Dec			
Policies to improve the appeal of stock market investing					
Measures to promote the use of stock option programmes	Jun				
Measures to promote the use of profits for share buybacks	Jun				
Reductions in the round-lot minimum for stocks	Jul				
Introduction of depositary receipts to facilitate non-Japanese companies listing on Japanese markets		Dec			
II. Increased availability of instruments for raising capital and measures to facilitate companies raising capital directly from the capital markets					
Introduction of new corporate bond products					
Perpetual bonds	Jul				
Equity index-linked bonds		Dec			

Medium-term notes	Jun	
Development of a system for establishment of special-purpose companies		Sep
Introduction of policies for helping companies go public		
Introduction of a book-building system	Sep	
Adoption of a registration system for listing	Dec	
New listing criteria	Dec (Osaka Securities Exchange)	Jan (Tokyo Stock Exchange)
Measures to improve the functionality of the OTC market		
Introduction of a stock lending system	Jul	
Introduction of margin transactions and issuance-day transactions	Oct	
Efforts to improve the non-core market status of the OTC market		Dec
Introduction of a market-maker system		Dec
Changes to the OTC registration system		Dec
Improvements in the market for unlisted companies		
Elimination of restrictions on securities companies' ability to handle shares of unlisted/unregistered companies	Jul	
Lifting of regulations that prevented investment trusts from investing in private companies	Sep	
III. Measures to improve the variety of financial services		
Securities companies allowed to offer new services		Dec
Liberalization of commissions on stock trades	Apr (Commissions for trades in excess of ¥50 m liberalized)	Oct (Complete deregulation)
Liberalization of premium rates for members of non-life insurance rating organizations		Jul
Measures to improve the asset management business		
Introduction of subadvisory system		Dec

Table 2.1 *Continued*

	Fiscal 1997	Fiscal 1998	Fiscal 1999	Fiscal 2000	Fiscal 2001
Revisions of operational restrictions		Dec			
Adoption of a registration system for trust agreements		Dec			
Increase in funding choices available to banks		Oct (Elimination of restrictions on the issuance of straight bonds)			
Increase in funding choices available to non-banks		May (Allowed to use bond issuance proceeds to finance lending activities)			
New entry restrictions eased					
Introduction of registration system for securities companies to replace licence-based system		Dec			
Introduction of registration system for investment trust companies to replace licence-based system		Dec			
Elimination of restrictions on the activities of the subsidiaries of securities companies and trust banks	Oct (Some restrictions relaxed)	Oct (Complete elimination)			
Insurance companies and other financial institutions allowed to enter each others' businesses	Dec (Brokerages and insurance companies allowed to enter each others' business domains)	Oct (Insurance companies allowed to enter the banking business)			

Measure	Timing
Banks allowed to market insurance products over the counter	Apr
Allowed use of the holding company structure	Mar
IV. Measures to improve the efficiency of Japan's capital markets	
Transactional and market infrastructure improvements	
Stock exchange transaction improvements	Nov (Establishment of an off-hours trading system); Jan (OSE J-NET market established)
Regulatory groundwork laid for stock exchange mergers	Dec
Elimination of rules that required trades to take place on exchanges	
Introduction of proprietary trading systems	Dec
Development of an infrastructure for stock lending	Dec
Improvement in the infrastructure for trading and settlement activities	Dec
Expansion of system trading	Dec (Osaka Securities Exchange); Apr (Tokyo Stock Exchange)
Improvement in bond settlement and delivery systems	Dec
Improvement in the flow of shareholder information between the depository institutions and issuers	Dec
Improvement in the infrastructure for netting transactions	Dec
V. Measures to ensure the fairness of transactions	
Improvements in rules and regulations to ensure the fairness of transactions	
Expansion of fair trading rules to encompass new financial products	Dec
New short-selling rules	Oct

Table 2.1 *Continued*

	Fiscal 1997	Fiscal 1998	Fiscal 1999	Fiscal 2000	Fiscal 2001
Tougher insider trading penalties	Dec (More stringent penalties)	Dec (Violators required to disgorge unfair trading profits)			
New measures to prevent conflicts of interest		Dec			
Improved dispute settlement system		Dec			
Clearer definition of marketable securities		Dec			
Improved disclosure					
Transition to consolidated accounting	Jan (Tax-allocation accounting) Apr (R&D expenses)	Apr			
New accounting standards for financial assets		Apr (Pension liabilities, mark-to-market accounting for financial products)			
VI. Measures to improve the health of financial institutions and establish liquidation procedures					
Change in minimum capital-adequacy ratios					
Revisions of minimum capital-adequacy ratios to encompass broader range of business activities		Dec			

Clarification of procedures for requiring institutions with insufficient capital-adequacy ratios to go out of business		Dec
Improved disclosure for financial institutions		Dec
New regulations for the subsidiaries of banks and insurance companies		Dec
Establishment of a framework for protecting the clients of bankrupt financial institutions		
System of segregated account management		Dec
Investor protection fund		Dec
Improved procedures for dealing with bankruptcies and restructurings at securities companies		Dec
Insurance policyholder protection corporations		Dec
VII. Other significant changes		
Changes in the securities transaction tax	Apr (Lowering of the securities transaction tax and the exchange tax)	Apr (Elimination of the securities transaction tax and the exchange tax)
Increased liberalization of capital market transactions between domestic and foreign counterparties		
Comprehensive financial services law		

Source: *Monthly Finance Review*, published by the Ministry of Finance (data taken mainly from March 2000 issue).

Table 2.2 Major consolidations among Japanese banks

	Amount of deposits (March 1997; ¥bn)	At April 2001
1 Bank of Tokyo-Mitsubishi	55 760.8	With Mitsubishi Trust & Banking and Nippon Trust Bank formed Mitsubishi Tokyo Financial Group
2 Sumitomo Bank	39 833.8	Merged with Sakura Bank
3 Sanwa Bank	38 608.9	Merged with Tokai Bank and Toyo Trust & Banking to form UFJ Holdings
4 Fuji Bank	38 279.1	Merged with Dai-Ichi Kangyo Bank and Industrial Bank of Japan to form Mizuho Holdings
5 Sakura Bank	38 270.5	Merged with Sumitomo Bank
6 Dai-Ichi Kangyo Bank	38 243.8	Merged with Fuji Bank and Industrial Bank of Japan to form Mizuho Holdings
7 Industrial Bank of Japan	32 275.9	Merged with Fuji Bank and Dai-Ichi Kangyo Bank to form Mizuho Holdings
8 Long-Term Credit Bank of Japan	23 227.0	Following its nationalization, the remaining entity was sold to Ripplewood Holdings of the US and renamed Shinsei Bank
9 Asahi Bank	22 791.3	
10 Tokai Bank	22 550.1	Merged with Sanwa Bank and Toyo Trust & Banking to form UFJ Holdings
11 Daiwa Bank	12 309.5	
12 Nippon Credit Bank	10 867.3	Following its nationalization, the remaining entity was sold to Softbank and renamed Aozora Bank
13 Bank of Yokohama	9 672.6	
14 Hokkaido Takushoku Bank	7 142.3	Following its bankruptcy, its assets were sold to North Pacific Bank and other banks
15 Chiba Bank	6 713.2	

Note: The above consolidations do not include the transfer of individual operations between banks.
Source: *Nihon Kinyu Nenpo*, summer 1998 edition.

Table 2.3 Major consolidations among Japanese securities companies

	Total assets (March 1997; ¥bn)	At April 2001
1 Nomura	7786.7	
2 Daiwa	6585.1	Spun off wholesale division; established a joint venture with Sumitomo Bank (Daiwa Securities SB Capital Markets)
3 Nikko	4234.3	Spun off wholesale division; established a joint venture with Citigroup (Nikko Salomon Smith Barney)
4 Yamaichi	3151.9	Following its bankruptcy, the retail branch offices were sold to Merrill Lynch
5 New Japan	980.0	Merged with Wako Securities to form Shinko Securities
6 Kokusai	864.0	Nomura Securities sold its shares in Kokusai to Bank of Tokyo-Mitsubishi
7 Kankaku	484.1	Merged with Kokyo Securities to form Mizuho Investors Securities
8 Wako	479.0	Merged with New Japan Securities to form Shinko Securities
9 Sanyo	446.9	Bankrupt
10 Okasan	264.0	
11 Dai-Ichi	209.1	Merged with Universal, Taiheiyo and Towa to form Tsubasa Securities
12 Tokai Maruman	184.6	Merged with Tokyo Securities to form Tokai Tokyo Securities
13 Tachibana	179.6	
14 Cosmo	172.9	
15 Tokyo	165.1	Merged with Tokai Maruman Securities to form Tokai Tokyo Securities

Note: The brokerage subsidiaries of banks are excluded.
Source: *Nihon Kinyu Nenpo*, summer 1998 edition.

Table 2.4 Major consolidations among Japanese non-life insurance companies

	Total assets (March 1997; ¥bn)	At April 2001
1 Tokio Marine & Fire	5144.1	Announced it would merge with Asahi Mutual Life, Kyoei Mutual Fire & Marine and Nichido Fire & Marine (the new entity will be called Millea Insurance Group)
2 Yasuda Fire & Marine	3706.1	Announced it would merge with Nissan Fire & Marine and Taisei Fire & Marine (the new entity will be called Sompo Japan Insurance)
3 Mitsui Marine & Fire	2760.1	Merged with Sumitomo Marine & Fire (the new entity is Mitsui Sumitomo Insurance)
4 Sumitomo Marine & Fire	2713.3	Merged with Mitsui Marine & Fire (the new entity is Mitsui Sumitomo Insurance)
5 Nippon Fire & Marine	1938.0	Merged with Koa Fire & Marine (the new entity is Nipponkoa Insurance)
6 Nichido Fire & Marine	1702.9	Announced it would merge with Asahi Mutual Life, Kyoei Mutual Fire & Marine and Tokio Marine & Fire (the new entity will be called Millea Insurance Group)
7 Dai-Tokyo Fire & Marine	1543.5	Merged with Chiyoda Fire & Marine (the new entity is Aioi Insurance)
8 Daiichi Mutual Fire & Marine	1429.6	Following its bankruptcy, insurance policies were transferred to the Non-Life Insurance Policyholder Protection Corporation
9 Koa Fire & Marine	1384.5	Merged with Nippon Fire & Marine (the new entity is Nipponkoa Insurance)
10 Fuji Fire & Marine	1319.0	
11 Chiyoda Fire & Marine	1294.2	Merged with Dai-Tokyo Fire & Marine (the new entity is Aioi Insurance)
12 Dowa Fire & Marine	1029.1	Merged with Nissay General Insurance (the new entity is Nissay Dowa General Insurance)
13 Nissan Fire & Marine	976.7	Announced it would merge with Yasuda Fire & Marine and Taisei Fire & Marine (the new entity will be called Sompo Japan Insurance)
14 Kyoei Mutual Fire & Marine	806.5	Announced it would merge with Asahi Mutual Life, Tokio Marine & Fire and Nichido Fire & Marine (the new entity will be called Millea Insurance Group)
15 Nisshin Fire & Marine	583.8	

Source: *Hoken Nenkan*, 1996 edition.

Table 2.5 Major consolidations among Japanese life insurance companies

	Total assets (March 1997; ¥bn)	At April 2001
1 Nippon Life	40038.3	
2 Dai-ichi Mutual Life	28032.5	
3 Sumitomo Life	23390.1	
4 Meiji Mutual Life	16709.1	
5 Asahi Mutual Life	12014.0	Announced it would merge with Kyoei Mutual Fire & Marine, Tokio Marine & Fire and Nichido Fire & Marine (the new entity will be called Millea Insurance Group)
6 Mitsui Mutual Life	10208.5	
7 Yasuda Mutual Life	9233.5	
8 Taiyo Mutual Life	6703.5	
9 Chiyoda Mutual Life	5816.3	The bankrupt company was purchased by AIG and renamed AIG Star Life Insurance
10 Kyoei Life	5725.0	The bankrupt company was renamed Gibraltar Life Insurance
11 Daido Life	5059.2	
12 Toho Mutual Life	4509.5	Following its bankruptcy, the company's insurance policies were taken over by GE Edison Life Insurance
13 Nippon Dantai Life	4047.3	Established a tie-up with AXA Life Insurance
14 Daihyaku Mutual Life	3318.6	Following its bankruptcy, the company's insurance policies were taken over by Manulife Century
15 Nissan Life	2061.0	The bankrupt company was renamed Aoba Life Insurance

Source: *Hoken Nenkan*, 1996 edition.

CONSOLIDATION

Since 1998, significant changes have taken place among the major banks, securities companies and insurance companies (see Tables 2.2–2.5). The number of bankruptcies and takeovers has risen sharply, and both inter- and intra-industry consolidations have increased. As a result, the number of large companies in each industry has decreased considerably, while the amount of assets of each of the remaining companies has expanded markedly. Some consolidations were thought to be impossible just a few years ago, such as mergers between companies from different *keiretsu* groups (like Mitsui and Sumitomo) and consolidations involving three or more companies.

NEW ENTRANTS

At the same time, an increasing number of companies backed by non-traditional sources have entered the financial services industry. Some non-Japanese companies stepped in to take over failed Japanese financial institutions, and others boldly went into areas where deregulation lowered the barriers to entry. One such example is the securities business, in which a licensing system was replaced by a registration system. In addition, Japanese non-financial companies have been entering the financial sector in increasing numbers. These companies typically use established brand names to target certain niche markets or use unique business models to differentiate themselves. For example, when Japan Net Bank obtained a licence to operate as an Internet bank in September 2000, it became the first Japanese bank since World War II to be issued a banking licence. Also, the bank received financial backing from traditional investors, such as banks and insurance companies, as well as a number of technology companies. In April 2001, IY Bank and Sony Bank became the next banks to obtain banking licences.

Market participants

3 Individual investors and the investment–savings balance

This chapter outlines the financial asset allocation of households, the primary source of funds for Japan's economy. Examining the investment–savings balance[1] by sector and how individuals have chosen to invest their savings reveals meaningful investment patterns during the postwar years, namely, the entrenched savings habits of Japanese individuals. The reform package initiated in 1996, the equivalent of a financial 'Big Bang', has begun to have an effect on where people choose to invest. We then consider the outlook for private savings in the twenty-first century.

Postwar changes in individual investors' behaviour

THE INVESTMENT–SAVINGS BALANCE

Many changes have occurred in the investment–savings balance since the end of World War II. The government, corporate and household sectors consistently suffered deficits from 1945 through the early 1950s, as Japan struggled to recover from the war. By the mid-1950s, however, individual savings began to rise sharply, reaching a surplus exceeding 10% of nominal GDP in the 1970s. They have since remained at high levels, even by international standards, and individual savings have been more than sufficient to provide

1 The investment–savings balance, which is the difference between savings and investment in each sector of the economy (the household, corporate, government and overseas sectors), indicates the fund surplus or deficit in each sector.

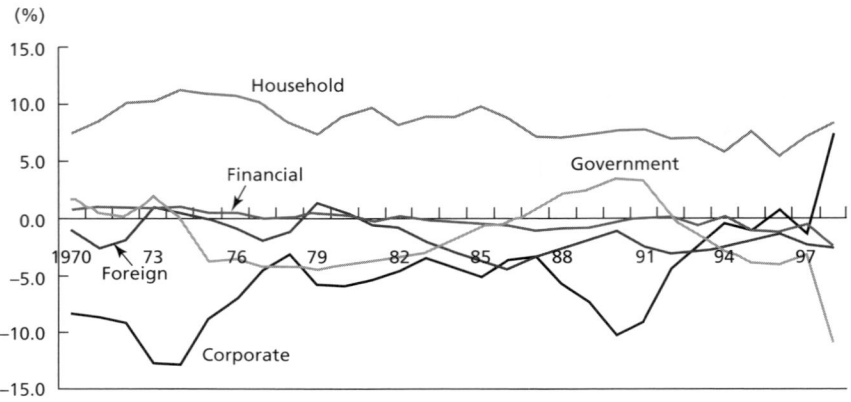

3.1 Investment–savings balance by sector (as a proportion of nominal GDP).
Note: Based on the former SNA (System of National Accounts) 68 methodology.
Source: Economic Planning Agency, *Annual Report on National Accounts*.

for the financing needs of the government and corporate sectors. Thanks to the ample supply of household savings, Japan has maintained a current account surplus ever since the mid-1960s, except during the oil crises of the 1970s.

Figure 3.1 shows the investment–savings balance by sector over the past 30 years. During the 1952–73 period of rapid economic growth, the corporate sector had the greatest deficit because of its substantial capital investment needs. The investment–savings deficit in this sector amounted to roughly 10% of nominal GDP.

After the first oil crisis, however, corporations worked to slim down as the economy slowed, and 1974 marked the first post-war year in which the economy had negative growth. And as the corporate sector's deficit shrank, the government sector's deficit widened. The government increased spending on public works and the social security system to stimulate the economy and expand its investment–savings deficit until, by the mid-1980s, it ran a deficit on a par with that of the corporate sector. With the slowdown in economic growth, tax revenues dwindled, and the government was forced to issue large amounts of bonds.

Following the two oil crises, the government sector reduced its excess investment in order to improve its budget deficit. While the corporate sector's deficit remained unchanged relative to GDP, Japan's current account surplus rose (i.e., the external sector had an investment–savings deficit). This surplus generated trade friction with the US, which had the largest current account deficit at the time and urged Japan to make domestic demand rather than export demand the driver of its economic growth.

In 1986, the Bank of Japan (BOJ) began to loosen monetary policy. By 1987, when Japan's official discount rate dropped to a historical low of 0.25%, an economic boom on a par with the *Izanagi* boom (1965–70), the longest period of expansion since the war, had begun. The corporate sector expanded its investment, and as a result of growing tax revenues from the booming economy the investment–savings balance in the government sector swung from a deficit to a surplus.

The 1990s, however, proved to be a difficult decade in all sectors, and Japan's economy collapsed. In both 1996 and 1998, the corporate sector, which typically ran the largest investment–savings deficit, had a surplus and had to get rid of the excess capacity that had built up during the end of the 1980s. But as tax revenues declined and public spending rose, the government sector saw its investment–savings deficit rise each year in the 1990s. By 1998, the government sector's investment–savings deficit had exceeded 10% of Japan's GDP.

THE SAVINGS RATE OF INDIVIDUALS

One of the most distinctive characteristics of Japan's investment–savings structure is the substantial surplus of savings in the household sector (see Fig. 3.2). The savings rate exceeded 20% in the 1970s. It has since decreased along with investors' disposable income, but it remains high by international standards. At the end of 1992, the balance of personal financial assets in Japan stood at more than ¥1000 trillion.

Individuals' financial asset allocation

SAVINGS ACCOUNTS

Table 3.1 shows the composition of personal financial assets in Japan for five-year intervals from 1955 to 1995. During this time, individual savings and other deposits accounted for an overwhelming

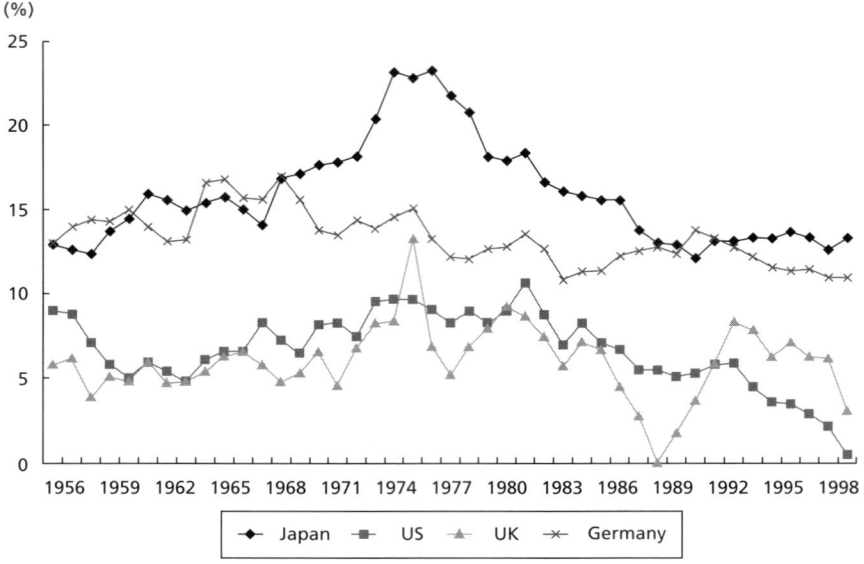

3.2 International comparison of household savings rates.
Source: Bank of Japan, *Comparative Economic and Financial Statistics – Japan and Other Major Countries*.

proportion of personal financial assets in Japan – consistently more than 50% and sometimes more than 60%.

When interest rates were regulated in Japan, deposit rates were linked to the official discount rate. In the 1970s, however, when the government issued a substantial amount of Japanese government bonds, a secondary market for JGBs formed and began to undermine the system of regulated interest rates. Furthermore, in 1984, after the Japan–US Yen–Dollar Committee recommended that Japan liberalize its financial sector, deposit rates were gradually deregulated.

As a first step, money market certificates (MMCs) were introduced in March 1985; these products feature interest rates based on money market rates, have maturities of one to six months, and require initial deposits of at least ¥50 m. Eventually, MMCs became available with longer maturities and lower initial deposits. Rates on time deposits were completely deregulated by June 1993, and rates on liquid deposits (including ordinary deposits, savings deposits and at-notice deposits but excluding demand deposits) were completely deregulated by October 1994.

During periods of rising interest rates, rates on deregulated time deposits rose more quickly than rates on regulated time deposits

Table 3.1 Changing composition of personal financial assets (¥100bn)

	Mar. 1955		Mar. 1960		Mar. 1965		Mar. 1970		Mar. 1975	
Cash/deposits	2937.9	68%	6895.2	60%	15864.9	58%	38123.9	60%	97536.8	64%
Liquid deposits	1095.3	26%	2014.1	17%	4581.8	17%	10393.8	16%	25347.7	17%
Time deposits	1842.6	43%	4881.1	42%	11283.1	41%	27730.1	44%	72189.1	47%
Trusts	85.7	2%	317.0	3%	1199.6	4%	3503.7	6%	8750.2	6%
Marketable securities	928.2	22%	3076.9	27%	7011.4	26%	14126.4	22%	27335.3	18%
JGBs	73.4	2%	56.7	0%	76.8	0%	364.1	1%	851.8	1%
Municipal bonds	1.0	0%	9.8	0%	18.6	0%	31.3	0%	194.0	0%
Agency bonds	10.0	0%	19.7	0%	195.9	1%	939.9	1%	2009.3	1%
Bank debentures	21.1	0%	164.9	1%	568.4	2%	2012.3	3%	5321.3	3%
Corporate bonds	4.0	0%	41.9	0%	98.5	0%	142.1	0%	1042.2	1%
Investment trusts (beneficiary certificates)	68.5	2%	321.1	3%	1217.7	4%	1041.9	2%	2701.9	2%
Stocks/equity investments	750.2	17%	2462.8	21%	4835.5	18%	9594.8	15%	15214.8	10%
Insurance/annuity reserves	337.8	8%	1250.1	11%	3221.3	12%	7921.2	12%	19003.2	12%
Total (including other)	4289.6	100%	11539.2	100%	27297.2	100%	63675.2	100%	152625.5	100%

Table 3.1 *Continued*

	Mar. 1980		Mar. 1985		Mar. 1990		Mar. 1995		Mar. 2000	
Cash/deposits	199367.3	64%	311987.0	59%	449297.9	49%	600708.6	52%	747917.3	54%
Liquid deposits	42383.0	14%	51366.6	10%	55907.0	6%	66291.3	6%	117050.3	8%
Time deposits	156984.3	50%	260391.7	49%	372936.6	40%	512922.8	45%	592594.4	43%
Trusts	19221.7	6%	36370.4	7%	49844.1	5%	64361.0	6%	35352.9	3%
Marketable securities	52058.2	17%	103159.7	19%	175091.2	19%	136100.1	12%	173109.8	12%
JGBs	7417.3	2%	15625.8	3%	7883.2	1%	7782.9	1%	7182.9	1%
Municipal bonds	441.4	0%	657.8	0%	439.5	0%	769.9	0%	1156.3	0%
Agency bonds	2560.6	1%	4783.7	1%	817.7	0%	926.1	0%	603.9	0%
Bank debentures	11364.9	4%	19110.3	4%	6872.7	1%	16590.3	1%	14532.2	1%
Corporate bonds	1710.4	1%	2177.0	0%	125.6	0%	328.8	0%	998.2	0%
Investment trusts (beneficiary certificates)	5297.6	2%	15831.9	3%	36187.4	4%	22142.5	2%	31917.1	2%
Stocks/equity investments	23266.0	7%	44973.2	8%	122765.1	13%	87559.6	8%	116719.2	8%
Insurance/annuity reserves	40865.1	13%	80021.7	15%	191100.9	21%	298463.5	26%	383684.3	28%
Total (including other)	311512.3	100%	531538.8	100%	925652.0	100%	1150342.0	100%	1389607.3	100%

Note: Figures before and after 1990 are not comparable because of a change in the way the figures were calculated.
Source: Bank of Japan.

(which were linked to the official discount rate). Therefore, in the rising-rate environment that prevailed through 1990, initial deposit requirements declined, thereby contributing to the popularity of deregulated time deposits.

Amid the shift in savings from liquid deposits to time deposits, postal savings started to catch on in the 1980s. The most popular postal savings product is the postal savings certificate, a type of time deposit that can be withdrawn after six months without a penalty and maintained for up to 10 years. The rate is set at the time of the deposit, and interest is compounded every six months. These features contributed to the popularity of postal savings certificates when rates were high. In addition, savers enjoyed the convenience of being able to make deposits at any post office nationwide. The total amount invested in these postal savings certificates soared from the late 1970s to the early 1980s and nearly surpassed the amount of savings in ordinary bank deposits. Not surprisingly, private banks resented the success of the public postal savings system and suffered because of it.

When the BOJ started to ease monetary policy in 1991, huge sums of savings poured into postal savings certificates. The per person cap on the deposits was increased to ¥10 m in 1991, and in that year alone, ¥19 tr. in savings flowed into the postal savings system.

MARKETABLE SECURITIES

In addition to the popularity of liquid and time deposits, another characteristic of the composition of personal financial assets in Japan has been the low proportion of assets in marketable securities, which include stocks and investment trusts, corporate bonds and JGBs.

The proportion of assets in marketable securities has never risen far beyond 20%.

Stocks and investment trusts

The portion of individuals' financial assets in stocks declined steadily in the decades following World War II until the mid-1980s. By the end of fiscal 1989, the share of personal assets in stocks was five percentage points higher than five years earlier. Yet this increase was partially the result of the increase in the market value of stocks during this period.

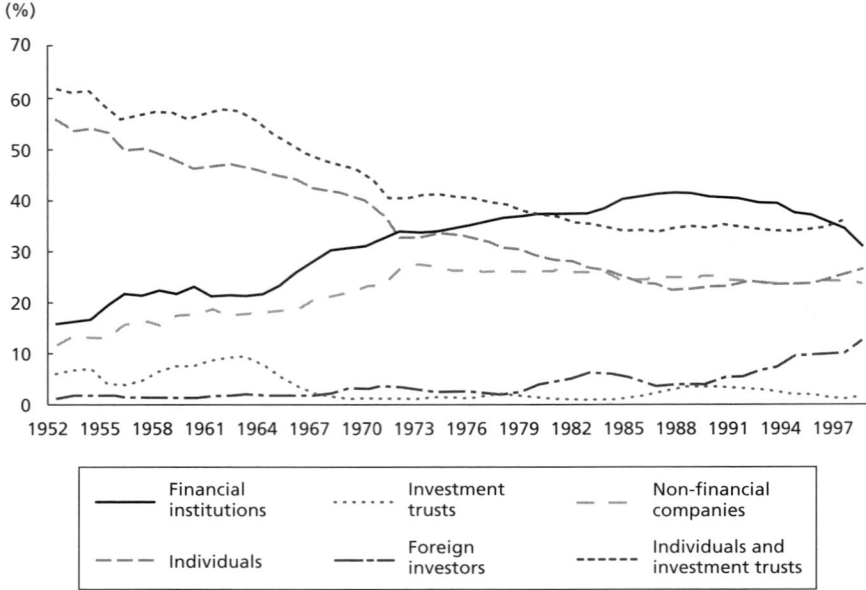

3.3 Ownership of stocks by type of investor.
Source: National Conference of Stock Exchanges, *The Shareownership Survey*.

From 1986 to 1990, individual investors were actually net sellers of stocks by a wide margin, in terms of both number of shares and transaction value.

The diminishing presence of individual investors in the stock market from 1952 to around 1990 is clear in Fig. 3.3, which shows the ownership distribution of stocks by type of investor.

The proportion of stocks owned by individuals (based on total market value) stood at 55% in 1952, when the Supreme Commander of the Allied Powers' (SCAP) Securities Coordinating Liquidation Committee (SCLC) broke up the *zaibatsu* – the large industrial groups from the prewar era. The SCLC sold the shares owned by the *zaibatsu* to employees of the *zaibatsu* companies and the public as part of an effort to democratize the ownership and control of companies after the war. But many people sold their stocks because they had few assets to spare. As a result, individuals' share of stockholdings decreased significantly over the next few years, and continued to decline steadily thereafter. But the combined share of the market accounted for by investment trusts and individuals was largely unchanged until the market crisis of 1965.

In addition to the opportunity to own stocks, a new system of investment trusts, or funds, was created in 1951. A system of investment trusts had existed before the war, but all of them were liquidated when their assets were returned to investors in 1950. The new investment trusts got off to a good start because of favourable market conditions and high expectations that the system would help democratize the ownership of stocks, but the system faced its first test in 1954 and 1955, when stocks fell as a result of the BOJ's tightening stance. Nevertheless, with the help of regulatory reforms that extended the durations of the funds and reduced management fees, the funds recovered and became widely accepted investment vehicles. In fact, they became so popular and carried so much weight in the market that they were considered to be 'the big fish in a small pond', at least until the 1965 market crisis.

The crisis in 1965 was triggered in part by brokerage firms' aggressive sales tactics and the sudden sharp increase in the stock holdings of their funds. Rumours had spread that two brokerages – Yamaichi Securities, which was one of the four leading securities companies at the time, and Oi Securities – were in serious trouble. After investors rushed to cash out of their investment funds and withdraw their other securities, the brokerages had to be rescued by special financing from the BOJ. Massive redemptions dealt a heavy blow to the funds, and the investment trusts never recovered despite reforms to the system.

The share of stock holdings owned by individuals also declined because companies started to acquire other companies' stocks for strategic purposes (cross-shareholdings). Commercial banks bought the stocks held by Kyodo Securities (now the Japan Kyodo Security Foundation) and Japan Security Holding Association (now the Capital Market Promotional Foundation), which were two holding companies established immediately before the 1965 market crisis in an effort to help balance the supply and demand for stocks.

Other mechanisms to promote stable shareholdings were developed in preparation for the liberalization of cross-border capital transactions that was scheduled for 1967.

The lack of participation of individual investors in the market has concerned Japan's Securities and Exchange Council (a part of the Ministry of Finance) for a long time. As early as 1976, the council had begun investigating ways to expand the base of individual shareholders. Investors finally expressed more interest in stocks in the second half of the 1980s, when economic growth was especially strong. With declining interest rates and rising stock prices, individuals increased their purchase of stocks and investment trusts.

The privatization of Nippon Telegraph & Telephone (NTT) in 1986 also significantly contributed to an increase in stock ownership among individuals.

The sharp correction in the market after its peak in late 1989, however, promptly dampened people's enthusiasm and ended the growth in individuals' investment in stocks.

As will be discussed in the last section of this chapter, individual investors in the 1990s worried more about capital preservation than profits and were thus less eager to invest in stocks and investment trusts.

Bonds

Bonds, which have never accounted for more than 10% of personal financial assets in Japan, represent an even smaller portion of personal financial assets than stocks or investment trusts.

JGBs were initially allocated only to banks, but starting in 1975, when the government increased its issuance of JGBs, it sought a way to promote sales to individuals.

One of the government's first moves was to establish preferential tax treatment for individuals who invested in JGBs.

In addition, to promote investment in medium-term JGBs, which were created as part of a plan to diversify JGBs, medium-term government bond funds were developed. Nicknamed *chukoku* funds, these medium-term bond funds helped to put more JGBs in the hands of individual investors but never accounted for more than 3% of household portfolios.

Bank debentures constitute a larger proportion of individual investor bond holdings than JGBs. Bank debentures, which are bonds issued by such special financial institutions as the Long-Term Credit Bank of Japan (LTCB; now known as Shinsei Bank) and the Norin Chukin Bank, are available in two types: one-year zero-coupon bonds and interest-bearing bonds, typically with maturities of five years.

During periods of high interest rates, interest-bearing bank debentures have proven popular; they offer a fixed rate of interest – albeit not as high as that offered by postal savings certificates – over an extended period. One variation of the five-year bank debentures, *Wide*, pays the entire principal and interest (compounded semi-annually) at maturity. They became so popular when rates were falling in 1991 that during so-called 'Wide fever', consumers waited in long lines in front of LTCB branches to buy them.

Recently, however, now that the distinction between short- and long-term financial institutions has been abolished and several of the issuing institutions have collapsed, both the volume of bank debentures issued and the proportion owned by individual investors have decreased.

Given the predominance of indirect financing in Japan, companies have not issued a large amount of bonds. Only in the 1990s – after the eligibility requirements for bond issuances were eased – did the volume of bond issuances increase and the market for bonds start to develop.

Some companies have even issued bonds with short maturities and relatively high coupons that are specially designed to appeal to individual investors.

LIFE INSURANCE ASSETS

Since the end of World War II, the proportion of individuals' financial assets in life insurance policies has grown significantly, from 8% in 1955 to 28% in 2000. Not only have rising incomes allowed individuals to purchase higher-value policies, but a number of attractive products have also become available, including single-premium endowment insurance policies and postal annuity products, of which the latter are readily obtainable at local post offices.

Because Japanese individuals tend to favour life insurance products, Japanese life insurance companies take in considerable sums in premium income, even by international standards. Nevertheless, in the wake of criticism that Japan is overinsured and of the failures of a number of life insurance companies, many consumers are taking another look at their insurance policies.

In a trend that has fuelled the growth of annuity products, people seem more concerned about the risks associated with living longer rather than those of dying sooner.

The financial Big Bang

Japan's economy has been struggling to recover ever since the asset bubble burst in the early 1990s. Interest rates have steadily declined, and in early 1999 the BOJ took the unprecedented step of instituting a zero interest rate policy. As a result, deposit rates have fallen to nearly zero percent and remain at that level. But in spite of the unusually low level of interest rates, the bulk of personal assets remain in deposits and savings and the allocation of personal financial assets remains virtually unchanged.

THE EFFECT OF THE BIG BANG ON THE INVESTMENT SECTOR

Part of the reason for the unchanging investment behaviour of individuals is the continual failure of the stock market to recover, as shown in Fig. 3.4. After the market peaked at the end of 1989, the Nikkei 225 dropped to a low of 14309 in August 1992. Since then, it has managed to climb to 20000 on four occasions, only to fall back to its previous levels and dash the hopes of investors each time.

Because of lingering gloom over the state of the Japanese economy, not to mention the spate of bankruptcies of major companies and financial institutions, individuals have been choosing safety over profits when investing their money. As Fig. 3.5 shows, the proportion of individuals' financial assets held in stocks remained

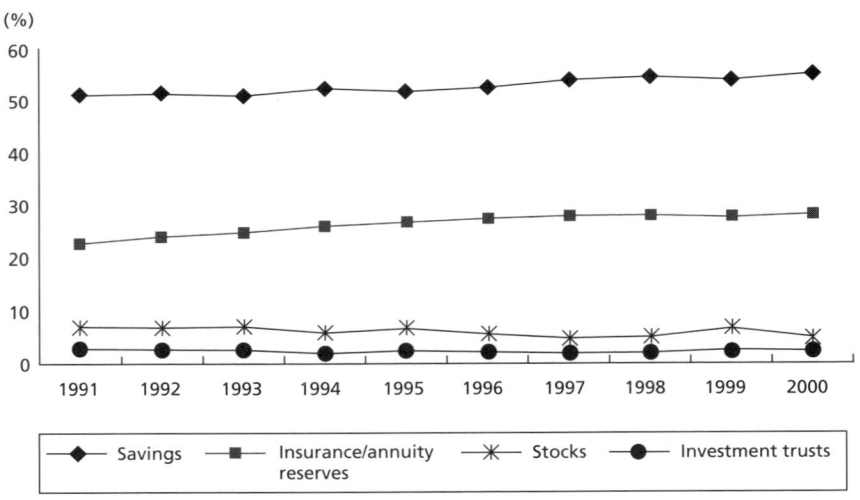

3.4 The composition of personal financial assets in Japan.
Note: The statistics before and after fiscal 1997 differ in format. The fiscal 2000 data are at 31 December 2000.
Source: Bank of Japan, *Financial and Economic Statistics Monthly*.

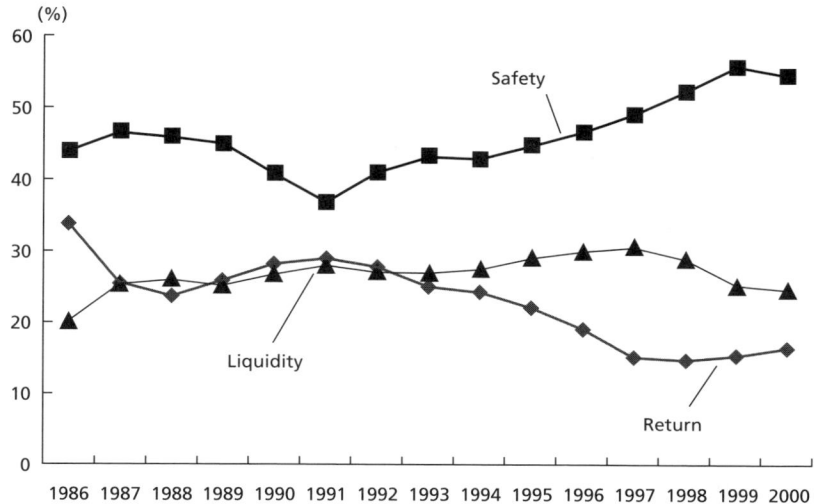

3.5 Allocation of households' financial assets by product characteristic.
Source: The Central Council for Savings Information.

flat at roughly 20% during the 1990s, and the share of assets in investment trusts fell from 15.1% of the market in fiscal 1991 to 8.8% in fiscal 2000.

Nonetheless, signs of positive change have emerged. One of the main objectives of the financial reforms was to alter the tendency of individuals to choose savings and deposits by promoting the establishment of a financial system centred on the securities markets. The Big Bang policy agenda thus included lower commissions for financial services, new products, improved services and expanded options. Accordingly, individuals' savings and investment behaviour has gradually begun to change.

BROKERAGE COMMISSIONS AND THE RISE OF ONLINE TRADING

Stock brokerage commissions were based on a fixed-rate structure for many years. Then, in April 1994, commission fees were partially liberalized, starting with large transactions (of ¥1 bn and above). Commissions were then liberalized for transactions of ¥50 m or more in April 1998. Finally, they were completely deregulated in October 1999. Around this time, a number of discount brokers specializing in online trading entered the market.[2] They began competing to offer the lowest rates in an attempt to win accounts. Whereas brokerages charged a commission of ¥11 500 on trades of ¥1 m under the fixed-rate structure, some online brokers now charge less than ¥1000 for such trades.

Major full-service brokerages have also reduced their commission rates – although not by as much as the discount brokers. Because they want to provide more investment information and better customer service than their discount competitors to attract individuals seeking online brokerage accounts, they have put substantial effort into developing online trading services.

Indeed, the number of individual investors trading online has grown dramatically.[3] By the end of March 2002, about 60 securities firms offered online trading, and the number of online accounts climbed to approximately 3 million, or 15 times the 200 000 accounts that existed at the time commissions were deregulated in October 1999. According to estimates based on a survey by the Japan Securities Dealers Association, individuals placed only about 3% of their stock trades online in October 1999 (based on total transaction value), but by March 2000, approximately 9% were placed online. This proportion continued to increase, to 26% by September 2000 and then 40% by March 2001.

Clearly, online trading appeals to individual investors. Those who trade online are primarily in their 30s and 40s, yet some are in their 20s. Given that most individual stock investors are in their 50s and 60s, the advent of Internet trading has expanded the ranks of investors to include people with little previous investing experience.

But the reduction in commissions brought about by deregulation has not led to an increase in stock trading among individual investors. By March 2000, as the market rebounded slightly, trading activity by individuals was strong. It tapered off again when the market weakened, however, and since March 2000, individual investors have been net sellers of stocks.[4] Figure 3.6 demonstrates that the share of total trading (in value terms) accounted for by individuals peaked in November 1999.

2 A large number of companies entered the brokerage market starting in 1997, in part as a result of a regulatory shift from a licence-based system to a registration-based system in December 1998.

3 The earliest online trading service in Japan began in April 1996.

4 As of April 2001 (the only exception was in February 2001, when individual investors were net buyers).

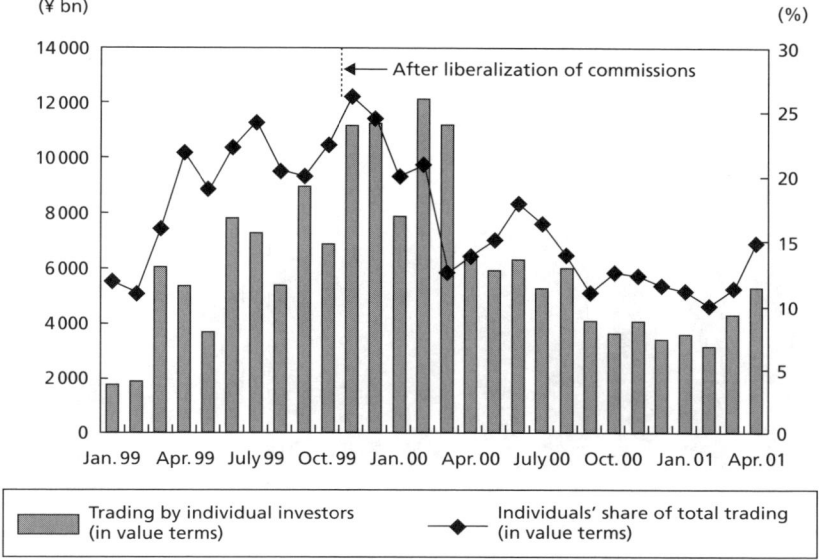

(¥ bn)   (%)

3.6 Trading by individual investors and their share of total trading (in value terms). Source: Tokyo Stock Exchange, *Tosho Tokei Geppo* [TSE Statistics Monthly].

BANKS AND INVESTMENT TRUSTS

Throughout the 1990s, investment trusts accounted for only 2% to 3% of personal financial assets, and even after the financial Big Bang, interest in them remained stagnant. Nevertheless, their assets had increased by the end of 1999, and as of the end of 2000, individuals had invested roughly ¥34 tr. in investment trusts. Including investments from companies, the amount of assets in investment trusts at the end of June 2000 totalled ¥60.5 tr., which is higher than the previous record level of ¥58.6 tr. at the end of 1989, the height of the market bubble. But the amount as of the end of March 2001 decreased to ¥52.8 tr., as companies reduced their holdings of money market funds (MMFs). Of the total investment trust assets, bond funds accounted for more than 70% of them (including 26.5% in MMFs and 46.2% in non-MMF bond funds), and stock funds the remaining 27.4%.[5]

The amount of assets in stock investment trusts peaked at ¥45.5 tr. at the end of 1989 and then steadily declined during the

5 The ban on MMFs was lifted in 1992. Individual investors account for 20–30% of their total assets.

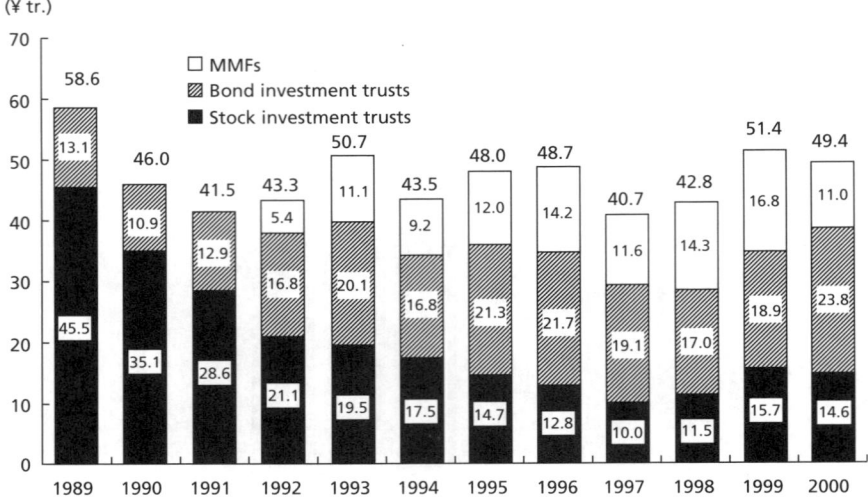

3.7 Net assets of investment trusts.
Source: Investment Trusts Association, Japan.

1990s, falling to as low as ¥10 tr. by the end of 1997. Since 1998, however, the amount of stock fund assets has been increasing again, as shown in Fig. 3.7. Despite continued net selling of stocks by individual investors in conjunction with the decline in the stock market since March 2000, money has continued to flow steadily into stock funds. In the first half of 2000, a number of mega-funds exceeding ¥1 tr. in assets were established, creating quite a stir in the markets. As of the end of May 2001, roughly 20 funds with at least ¥100 bn in net assets existed.

One factor behind the rise in net assets of Japan's investment trusts in recent years has been the dramatic increase in their diversity and the number of ways they are sold. Never before have their products been so readily available to individual investors. Securities firms used to be the only entities allowed to sell investment trusts. Then, in December 1997, banks were permitted to sell the products indirectly by leasing space in their branch offices to investment trust companies; since December 1998, they have been allowed to offer investment trusts directly to the public. Currently, credit unions, life insurance companies, property and casualty insurance companies, and other types of financial services companies are allowed to sell them as well. And investment management companies now sell their funds either directly on the Internet or by phone.

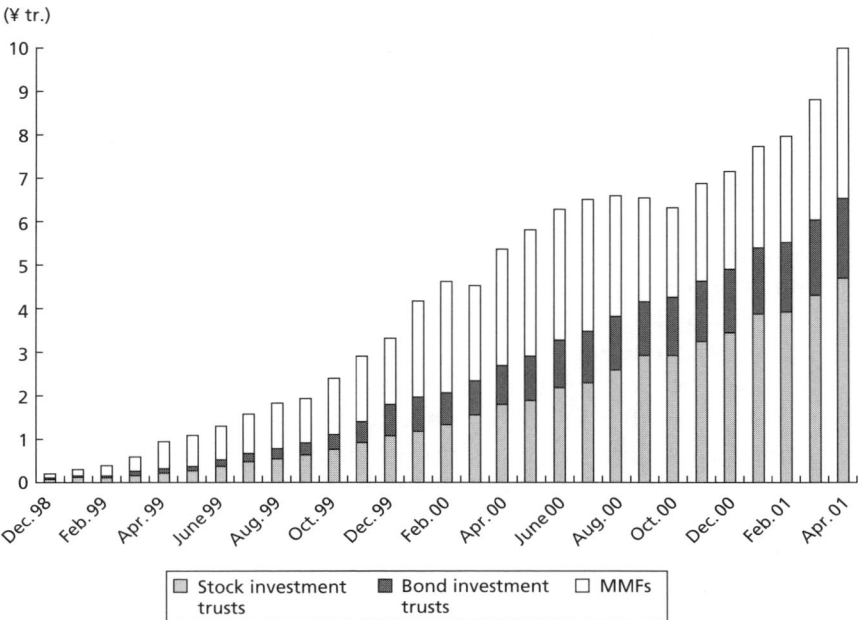

(¥ tr.)

| Stock investment trusts | Bond investment trusts | MMFs |

3.8 Net assets of investment trusts sold through banks and similar financial institutions.
Note: Figures are the totals for publicly and privately offered investment trusts.
Source: Investment Trusts Association, Japan.

Figure 3.8 illustrates that the amount of investment trusts sold through banks and similar financial institutions has been growing steadily since December 1998, topping ¥10 tr. in April 2001. When banks were first allowed to sell the products indirectly, MMFs constituted an overwhelming proportion of the sales, at one point reaching 65%, but as their assets grew, stock funds accounted for an increasing share of sales. By September 2000, stock funds were a greater proportion of banks' fund sales than MMFs. As of the end of March 2001, stock funds accounted for 49.2% of total fund sales by banks; MMFs, 31.1%; and bond funds, 19.7%. By comparison, stock funds accounted for 25.9% of total fund sales by securities firms; MMFs, 24.1%; and bond trusts, 50.0%.

Banks and other registered financial institutions have taken the lead in selling and promoting investment trusts. At the end of March 2001, banks accounted for 12.4% of all investment trust sales and 16.5% of stock investment trust sales. In a survey taken by the Investment Trusts Association Japan in 2000, the largest percentage of investors said they would like to purchase investment trusts from 'banks and similar financial institutions' (31.9%), followed by 'securities companies' (29.2%).[6] If investment trusts become even more popular with individual investors as products become available through a broader variety of sources, the amount of assets in investment trusts is likely to increase even further.

Another noteworthy characteristic of funds sold through banks and similar financial institutions is that the redemption rate for these funds is significantly lower than the average redemption rate for all investment trusts. For example, from November 1999 to October 2000, the annual redemption rate for open-end investment trusts was 77%, while the rate for stock funds sold by banks was 20% to 30%. Perhaps one reason for the low redemption rate in stock funds is that banks and other financial institutions, which are unaccustomed to selling investment products, do not aggressively encourage their customers to switch in and out of funds. No matter what the cause, individual investors are increasingly turning to new entities to purchase investment trusts as long-term investments.

POSTAL SAVINGS

At March 2000, the amount of assets held in postal savings products was roughly ¥260 tr., or about 20% of individuals' total financial assets. Postal savings certificates accounted for ¥212 tr. of the total assets in the postal savings system; postal time deposits, ¥15 tr.; and ordinary postal savings accounts, ¥31 tr. A substantial portion of the postal savings certificates was taken out in fiscal 1990–91, when interest rates were high, and began reaching maturity in April 2000. Given that the total principal and interest of these postal savings certificates is estimated at ¥106 tr., market participants have been keenly interested in forecasting where people will reinvest their maturing postal savings funds.

The Ministry of Public Management, Home Affairs, Posts and Telecommunications (which subsumed the former Ministry of Posts and Telecommunications) projected that 70% of the amount in excess of the ¥10 m initial deposit cap on postal savings certificates and the amount that can be rolled over (which is the amount received at maturity less the taxes on interest) would be reinvested in postal savings certificates and time deposits. The actual reinvest-

---

6 Remarkably, 10.9% of the respondents said they would buy investment trusts on the Internet.

ment rate from April 2000 to April 2001, however, was 72%, slightly higher than the ministry's projection. Given that the rate on 10-year postal savings certificates was only 0.13–0.20% during this time, the high rate of reinvestment of funds in postal savings suggests that the large majority of individuals are extremely risk averse, unwilling to stomach the possibility of losing any capital.

In the private banking sector, an estimated ¥40 tr. in savings are reaching maturity. So far, with the weakness in stock prices, there are no indications of any substantial reinvestment of these funds into either the stock market or stock funds. In contrast, large sums of the maturing private savings apparently flowed into medium-term government bond funds (the *chukoku* funds) and long-term bond funds, which do not offer guarantees on the principal amount but involve very low risk.

From April 2000 to March 2001, the amount of assets in medium-term government bond funds rose by a net ¥3.8 tr., reaching roughly ¥7.6 tr. at the end of March. During the same period, the amount of assets in long-term bond funds increased by a net ¥2.1 tr., reaching ¥10 tr. at the end of March. These products have attracted funds from maturing bank savings products because of their relative safety, not to mention the relatively high yields advertised by some brokerage firms. The attractive yields will stem from gains realized from the use of mark-to-market accounting rules for valuing bond holdings in the funds starting in fiscal 2001 and a related shift from expected yields to actual investment yields for the funds.

In addition to these two bond funds, another popular choice for money coming out of maturing savings products is JGBs. The most preferred JGBs have been those with relatively short maturities: two-year interest-bearing notes and three-year zero-coupon notes. The two-year interest-bearing notes are especially sought after; post offices have sold out of them every month since April 2000. Investors have been drawn to the JGBs with short maturities because of their very low risk and high yields (at least for the recent issues) relative to extremely low deposit rates.

Ease of purchase offers another explanation for the popularity of JGBs. Depositors can conveniently purchase them at post offices if they do not want to reinvest their maturing deposits in postal savings certificates or if they have proceeds in excess of the ¥10 m deposit cap on postal savings certificates. Total sales of JGBs at post offices from April 2000 to March 2001 amounted to roughly ¥2.9 tr., with the most popular being two-year interest-bearing notes.

The postal bureau appears to have anticipated an inflow of funds from postal savings certificates reaching maturity and thus increased its allocation of JGBs for fiscal 2000. JGB sales at post offices averaged only about ¥500 bn each year from 1995 to 1999, and it is clear that part of these maturing postal funds actually have been put into JGBs.

Although many of the depositors who are receiving proceeds from their maturing postal savings products tend to be risk averse, they are not uninterested in actively investing their money. Quite a few of them seem keen on seeking slightly higher returns while minimizing risk as much as possible.

FOREIGN-CURRENCY DEPOSITS AND MMFS

After the Foreign Exchange and Foreign Trade Law (Foreign Exchange Law) was liberalized in April 1998 and restrictions on foreign-exchange transactions and reporting requirements were consequently eased, banks have created a variety of foreign-currency deposits and other products. These deposits are available in US dollars, euros, British pounds, Swiss francs and other major currencies, but dollar deposits and MMFs have been the most popular with Japanese consumers. As of the end of 2000, the amount of individuals' assets in foreign-currency deposits reached about ¥3.8 tr., up 200% in a two-year period. The amount of assets in foreign-currency MMFs increased notably as well, reaching ¥1.3 tr. at the end of 2000, a record level for the seventh successive month since May 2000 (see Fig. 3.9).

These foreign-currency products have become widely accepted for a number of reasons. First, they offer much more attractive yields than yen deposits. For example, 'super' time deposits, one of the main savings products offered by banks, offer a yield of only 0.12–0.15% for a duration of one year, but one-year dollar deposits offer yields of about 4.0–6.0%. Similarly, whereas ordinary MMFs yield a mere 0.1–0.4%, dollar MMFs offer a 6% yield. The BOJ abandoned its zero interest rate policy in August 2000 by raising rates, but deposit rates have still remained very low and encouraged consumers to look for higher-yielding alternatives.

Another factor behind the popularity of these foreign-currency savings products has been the relative stability of exchange rates. After the yen strengthened to ¥104 per dollar in September 1999, investors who believed the yen would weaken started to shift some of their assets to dollar-denominated products. For the rest of 1999

(¥ tr.)

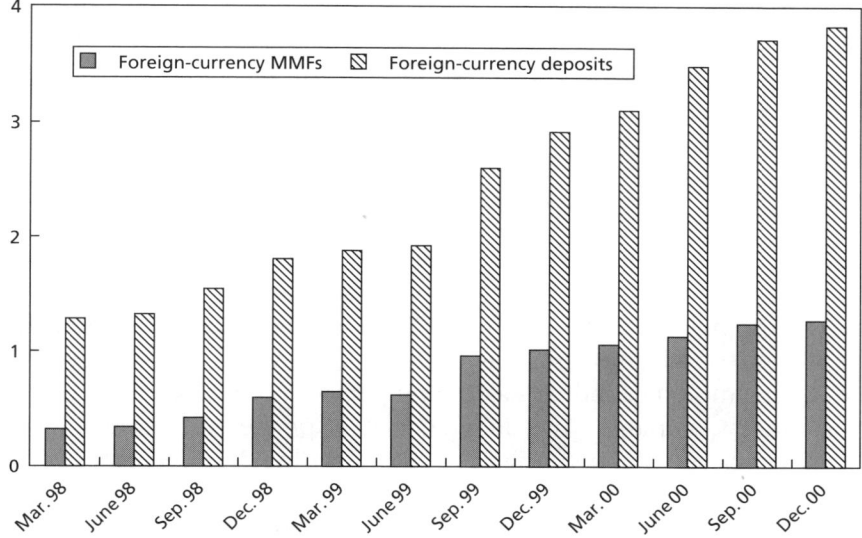

3.9 Foreign-currency MMFs and deposits.
Notes: Figures for foreign-currency MMFs include those owned by companies and individuals, while those for foreign-currency deposits include only those owned by individuals.
Source: Nomura, based on data from the Investments Trusts Association, Japan and the Bank of Japan's *Financial and Economic Statistics Monthly*.

and all of 2000, the yen's value fluctuated between ¥102 and ¥112 per dollar. Believing that the exchange rate risk was relatively low, some consumers seemed to be putting more of their funds into foreign-currency savings products.

Unable to attract savers with low-yielding yen deposits, banks have been heavily promoting foreign-currency alternatives as their core products. Newspapers and magazines now frequently feature advertisements prominently displaying fixed yields that are unheard of in the case of yen deposits. Banks aggressively offer foreign-currency deposits in part because the currency-exchange transaction fees make them more profitable than yen deposits.

Not only has the amount of assets in foreign-currency deposits increased, but the number of accounts has grown as well, from 300 000 at the end of September 1998 to 1.5 million at the end of September 2000, a fourfold increase in two years. The number still does not compare with the number of yen savings accounts, but the growth in accounts indicates that an increasing number of individuals are turning to foreign-currency deposits. The results of a 'Public Opinion Survey on Household Savings and Consumption' conducted by the Central Council for Savings Information show that 12.3% of those with annual incomes of at least ¥10 m are thinking of putting some of their savings into foreign-currency deposits.

LIFE INSURANCE AND RETIREMENT SAVINGS

As illustrated in Fig. 3.4, the share of individuals' financial assets held in insurance and annuity reserves increased from around 1990, when the market collapsed, to 1997. Since then, the proportion has remained steady, hovering at 28% (at the end of 2000). Nevertheless, the amount of individual insurance policies in force from private insurance companies has fallen since it peaked in fiscal 1996 at ¥1496 tr. Sales of new policies have steadily declined since fiscal 1995, while the lapse/cancellation rate gradually increased before jumping to 8.3% in fiscal 1997 (see Fig. 3.10).

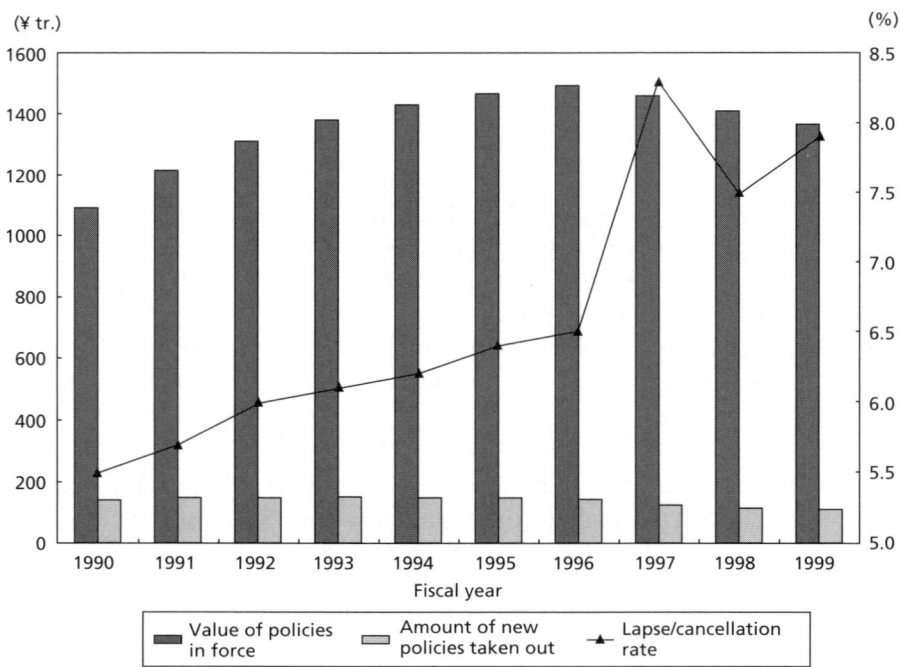

3.10 Individual insurance policies.
Source: Nomura, based on the Japan Institute of Life Insurance, *Life Insurance Handbook*.

Consumers have been turning away from life insurance products in part because of a crisis of confidence in the industry brought about by the financial collapse of six insurers between April 1997 and the end of 2000. Another contributing factor is the prolonged economic downturn in Japan that has compelled consumers to reconsider the financial burden of their life insurance premiums.

Simply put, Japan's life insurance industry has matured. The number of new policies is not likely to increase substantially if consumers continue to choose other financial assets. As a result, the industry has responded in several ways. First, major restructuring has occurred. A number of foreign life insurers have taken control of the collapsed Japanese companies, thereby expanding their operations in the Japanese market. Many of the foreign insurers have managed to buck the industry trend and increase the total value of their outstanding policies.

Meanwhile, Japanese life insurers have been trying to strengthen their businesses by expanding into the so-called third sector (primarily medical, cancer and personal accident insurance) and forging alliances with non-life insurers. Some of these companies have spurred demand and expanded their sales considerably by introducing exciting new products.

The outlook for individual savings in the twenty-first century

One of the key factors affecting the future savings rate of individuals is the increase in the elderly population in Japan. Those over 65 years of age currently account for almost 20% of the population, and this proportion is expected to increase to about 30% by 2010 and 35% by 2020. Because the trend will put pressure on the public pension system, the government may decide to raise the eligibility age for those who can receive benefits or else lower the amount of allowable benefits. According to the previously mentioned 'Public Opinion Survey on Household Savings and Consumption', about 80% of all respondents and roughly 90% of those in their 30s and 40s expressed concern about their financial situation during their retirement years. About 70% of all those who said they were concerned cited insufficient savings or insufficient pension and insurance coverage as the source of their anxiety. In addition, about 70% of those in their 30s and 40s who doubted their pensions would amount to much expected their benefits to be cut.

Because of this uneasiness about financial security during retirement, those in their prime working years – latter 30s to early 50s – face the challenge of building up their own savings to complement any pension they may receive. The amount of money people in this age bracket can invest is limited, however, because most of them put their income toward such major expenses as mortgages and tuition for their children's education.[7] Consequently, households led by seniors account for the bulk of Japan's savings pool. According to a 2000 survey on savings trends compiled by the Statistics Bureau & Statistics Center of the Ministry of Public Management, Home Affairs, Posts and Telecommunications, households headed by someone between the ages of 55 and 64 accounted for 28.9% of total household financial assets in Japan, and those headed by someone over 65 accounted for 37.2%. Meanwhile, those headed by persons between 35 and 44 accounted for only 10.4% of financial assets, and those headed by persons between 45 and 54 accounted for 20.1%. To be financially secure later in life, households headed by those in the latter two age groups will probably have to seek out savings and investment products with higher yields than those offered by conventional savings deposits.

Defined-contribution retirement plans similar to the 401(k) plans offered in the US became available in Japan starting in fiscal 2001. These plans allow plan participants to select from different choices of investment options for their retirement assets. The ultimate amount of money they will have available to them during retirement will depend on the investment performance of their assets, as well as the amount of their additions and withdrawals. If the 401(k)-type plans catch on, individuals will probably become more enticed by and knowledgeable about investment products.

Another factor likely to influence the savings behaviour of individuals is the deposit insurance cap of ¥10 m on time deposits, which

---

7 According to a 2000 survey on savings trends compiled by the Statistics Bureau & Statistics Center of the Ministry of Public Management, Home Affairs, Posts and Telecommunications, mortgage, tuition and other major expenses for those in their 30s averaged ¥6 m a year; for those in their 40s, ¥9.2 m; for those in their 50s, ¥6.7 m; and for those 60s and above, ¥2.3 m.

took effect in April 2002.[8] As this scheduled date for the new deposit insurance ceiling approached, individuals searched for safer places than banks to put their savings and chose to invest in more attractive options. Whether or not the products were covered by product insurance affected investors' decision-making process. A cap on savings and demand deposits is scheduled to be introduced in April 2003.

Surveys indicate that consumers closely follow the developments concerning deposit insurance and the credit risk of banks and similar financial institutions. About one-third of the households in the previously mentioned 'Public Opinion Survey on Household Savings and Consumption' said they had already taken steps to protect their savings. Of this proportion, 45% had moved their savings to creditworthy banks that were on relatively solid financial footing, and another 32% split up their deposits so that they had no more than ¥10 m at any one bank. In addition, 60% of all respondents planned to do something soon about their savings. In a separate survey conducted by the BOJ, about 40% remained wary of banks and other financial institutions. Hence, if private sector banks do not do enough to regain the confidence of consumers, the postal savings system could end up attracting a large proportion of individuals' savings.

A third factor affecting household savings is the development of a whole panoply of new financial products designed to attract the assets of individual investors. Changes to the Law Concerning Securities Investment Trusts and Securities Investment Companies of Japan (the Investment Trust Law) in November 2000 allowed investment trusts to broaden their investments to include real estate, thereby paving the way for the establishment of real estate investment trusts (REITs) in Japan (see Chapter 6). These new products are expected to be fairly popular among individual investors because they can be bought and sold with a minimum of capital and feature moderate risk and return. Also, variable annuities – which are already well established in the US and Europe – were introduced in Japan in April 1999. Whether these insurance-type products will lure Japanese consumers remains to be seen, however.

---

8 The cap on deposit insurance was originally scheduled to take effect in April 2001, but was postponed for one year.

Why people in Japan keep more than half of their financial assets in savings deposits perplexes many in the financial services industry, especially because their low yields continue to persist. Signs of change have started to emerge, but substantial modifications in the savings habits of individuals are not likely until the economy fully recovers and prospects for the stock market brighten.

4 Asset management by the public sector: postal savings, *Kampo* and public pensions

One of the distinguishing characteristics of Japan's financial asset management market is that more than one-third of the ¥1400 tr. in financial assets owned by individual Japanese investors is managed by the public sector. Part of the reason for the significant amount of assets in the public sector is the strong preference among Japanese individual investors for relatively safe investments and the tremendous demand for funds by the public sector during Japan's postwar economic boom. The Japanese public has been willing to invest a significant portion of their savings through the public sector, even though the government entities entrusted with these assets have been criticized for managing the assets in a way that lacks transparency and is inefficient. Japan's version of a financial market Big Bang has led to significant deregulation in the financial system, but nevertheless, the asset management operations of the public sector will probably continue to be a major issue. This chapter takes a look at Japan's postal savings, postal insurance (*Kampo*) and public pension systems – the three main pillars of Japan's public finance system.

The postal savings system

In addition to mail and insurance services, Japan's publicly run postal system offers basic financial services throughout Japan, including savings accounts as well as fund transfer services. A distinguishing characteristic of the Japanese postal savings system is the uniform

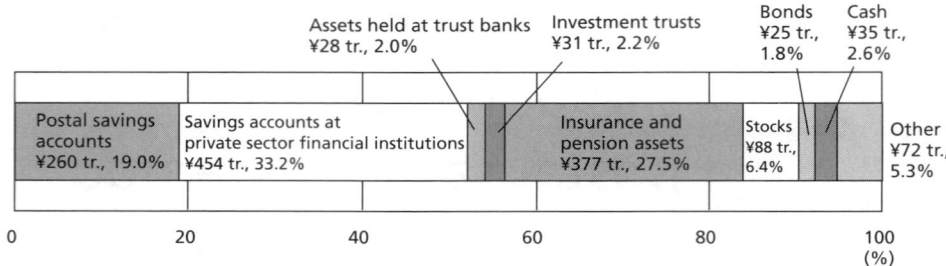

4.1 Breakdown of Japanese households' financial assets by major asset types (end of fiscal 1999).
Source: Nomura Securities, based on data from the former Ministry of Posts and Telecommunications (now the Ministry of Public Management, Home Affairs, Posts and Telecommunications).

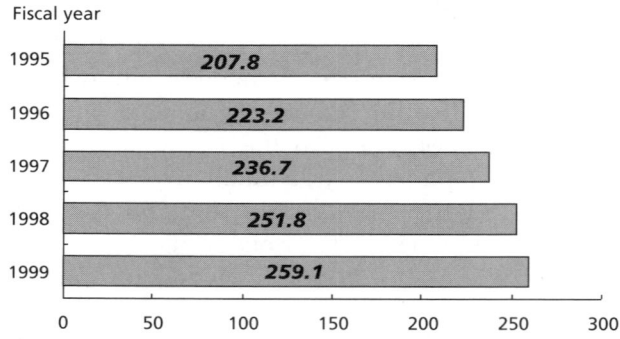

4.2 Aggregate average balance invested in postal savings accounts (¥ tr.).
Source: as Fig. 4.1.

provision of service in approximately 24 000 post offices in all parts of the country, including rural and residential areas where private sector financial institutions do not have many branches. Another defining attribute of the system is that more than 99% of postal savings deposits are relatively small and individually owned because the limit on savings deposits is only ¥10 m.

Figure 4.1 shows a breakdown of the major asset types that are held by Japanese households. At the end of fiscal 1999, total financial assets owned by Japanese households amounted to an estimated ¥1368 tr., of which about ¥260 tr., or roughly 19%, were invested in postal savings deposits. And as shown in Fig. 4.2, the fiscal-year average amount of assets invested in postal savings accounts rose steadily into fiscal 1999.

Postal savings certificates are the core postal savings product. They accounted for about 80% of all assets in postal savings at the end of fiscal 1999. Depositors can earn a fixed yield on their savings for as long as 10 years and withdraw their funds without penalty after six months. In fiscal 2000–2001, a large amount of postal savings certificates – specifically, about ¥106 tr., or about 40% of the total – were due to mature. Depositors were expected to take out of the postal savings system that portion of their savings that exceeded the deposit limit.[1]

In 2001, the organization of the postal savings system and the asset management plan for postal savings began to change significantly. When the integration of central government ministries and agencies occurred in January 2001, the three core functions that were previously administered by the Ministry of Posts and Telecommunications – postal services, postal savings and postal insurance – were reorganized and placed under the Ministry of Public Management, Home Affairs, Posts and Telecommunications. These three functions are now the responsibility of the Postal Services Policy and Planning Bureau and the Postal Services Agency.

In addition, the government decided to shift to a system of discretionary investment of all postal savings assets in April 2001, when major reforms of the Fiscal Investment and Loan Program (FILP) began.[2] An even larger change is in store for 2003, when the Postal Services Agency will be transformed into a new, publicly run corporation. Indeed, despite prolonged debate concerning the possible privatization of Japan's postal system, the government has decided to turn the postal system into a publicly administered company, a move that should lead to a more independently managed postal savings system. If the postal savings system operates entirely on a self-financed basis and manages its assets on a discretionary basis, the system will probably be put on an equal footing with private sector financial institutions. Given the likelihood of increasing competition with private sector financial institutions, then, the postal savings system will need to be managed in a more transparent and efficient manner. The aforementioned changes to the organizational structure of the postal savings system and the new asset management plan will also apply to the postal insurance system.

1 For an in-depth discussion of the potential outflow of funds from the postal savings system, see Chapter 3.

2 For a detailed discussion of FILP reforms, see Chapter 9.

THE ASSET MANAGEMENT SYSTEM

Before 2001, all postal savings assets were entrusted to the Trust Fund Bureau of the Ministry of Finance (MOF). Beginning in April 2001, the management of postal savings was gradually shifted to a system of discretionary investment. Figure 4.3 shows a diagram of how the management of postal savings assets is changing. Because assets are placed with the Trust Fund Bureau for seven-year periods, in principle, the transition to a discretionary investment plan will occur gradually in the next seven to ten years and leave portions of the current plan in place during the transition period.

THE OLD PLAN

Other than funds required for daily deposit withdrawals and loans to depositors, all postal savings assets were deposited with the Trust Fund Bureau of the MOF. The Trust Fund Bureau commingled these funds with premiums for the National Pension Fund (for the self-employed) and Employees' Pension Funds. At the end of March 1999, the amount of funds deposited with the Trust Fund Bureau totalled ¥436 tr., and about 58%, or about ¥251 tr., of these assets were held in the postal savings system. As shown in Fig. 4.3, most of the funds deposited with the Trust Fund Bureau were used to purchase government bonds or to extend loans to local government entities, the national government or FILP agencies. Ultimately, postal savings assets were used to finance public infrastructure investments, such as public housing, roads, hospitals, homes for the elderly and public health centres, as well as private entities, namely, small and medium-sized enterprises and farming, forestry and fishing enterprises. Postal savings clearly played a key role in Japan's system of public finance.

Although the postal savings system was required to deposit its assets with the Trust Fund Bureau, a portion of postal savings assets was self-managed, as part of ongoing efforts to deregulate Japan's financial system. Specifically, the postal savings system borrowed back a portion of the funds deposited with the Trust Fund Bureau and managed the assets on a discretionary basis.

Ever since this system was implemented in fiscal 1987, the amount of assets the postal system independently managed increased each year, as shown in Fig. 4.4. At the end of fiscal 1999, the amount of funds managed independently totalled about ¥61 tr., with most of the funds invested in government and corporate bonds (Fig. 4.5). About 18% of independently managed assets were deposited with trust

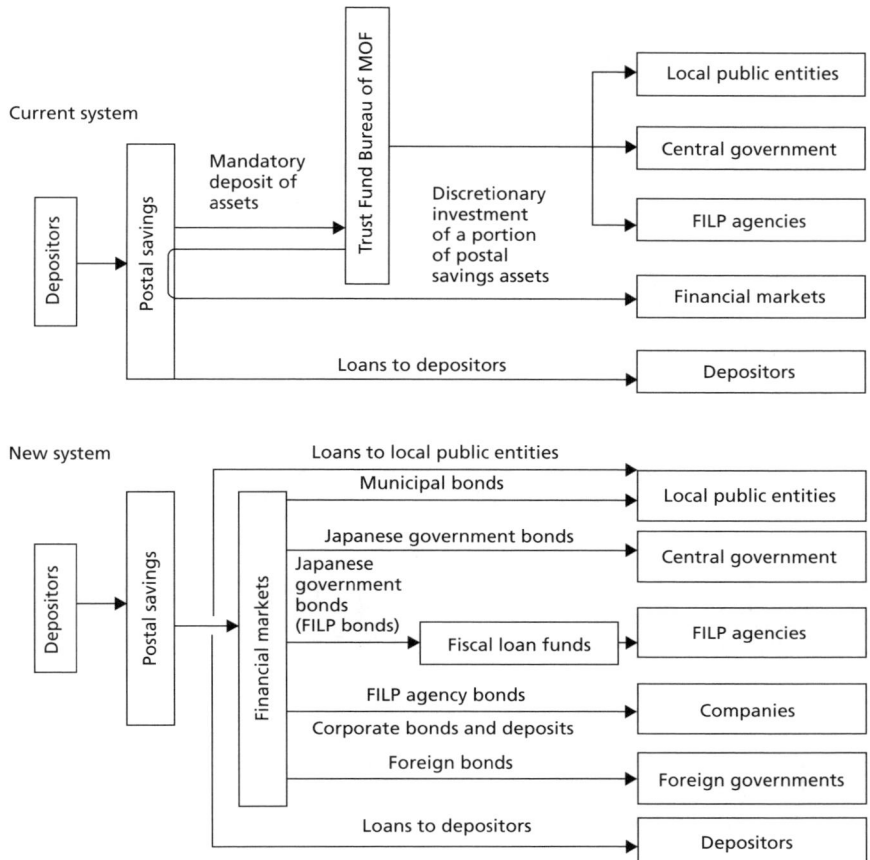

4.3 Comparison of current and new asset management plan for postal savings assets.
Note: In addition to the asset-management channels presented above, some postal savings assets are invested in independently managed designated money trusts (*shiteitan*) through the Postal Life Insurance Welfare Corporation (Fig. 4.6).
Source: as Fig. 4.1.

banks in the form of independently managed, designated money trusts (*shiteitan*), with a portion of these funds invested in equities.[3] Because the postal savings entity could not directly invest in equities, funds were first transferred to the Postal Life Insurance Welfare Corporation, which then invested the funds in *shiteitan* (Fig. 4.6).

3 These *shiteitan*, or independently managed designated money trusts, are invested by trust banks on behalf of investors in stocks, bonds and other securities, separately from other funds.

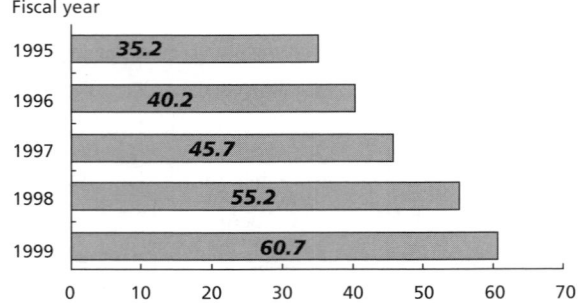

4.4 Amount of independently managed postal savings assets under the current system (¥ tr.).
Source: as Fig. 4.1.

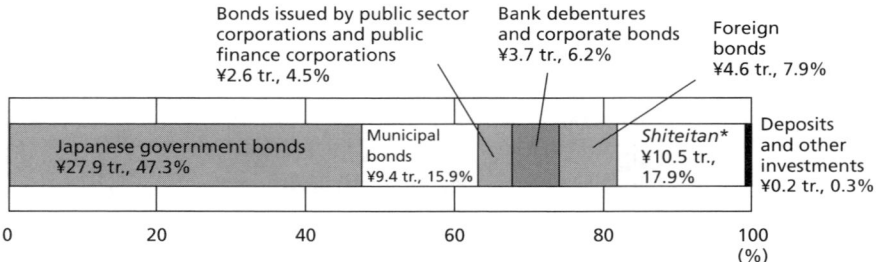

4.5 Asset breakdown of independently managed postal savings assets under current system.
Note: *Independently managed designated money trusts.
Source: as Fig. 4.1.

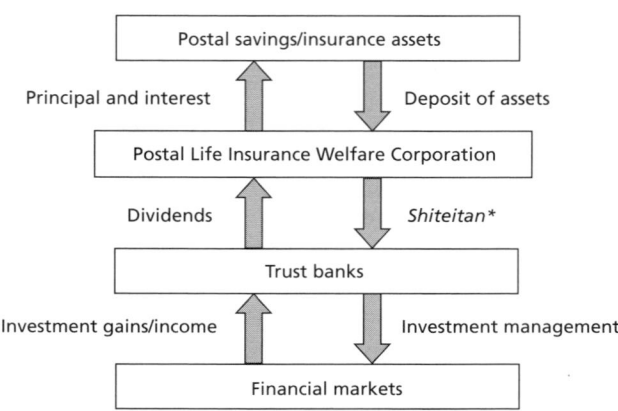

4.6 Postal savings/insurance assets invested in *shiteitan**.
Note: *Independently managed designated money trusts.
Source: as Fig. 4.1.

Table 4.1 Target asset allocations for the core portfolios of postal savings assets (at December 2000)

Asset class	Domestic bonds	Foreign bonds	Domestic stocks	Foreign stocks	Short-term assets
Target allocation	80%	5%	5%	5%	5%
Asset allocation band	+15%~−10%	+3%~−4%	+3%~−4%	+3%~−5%	+4%~−4%

Note: Loans made to local public entities are included in the domestic bond category. Assets invested in domestic and foreign stocks are managed by third parties.
Source: Nomura Securities, based on data from the former Ministry of Posts and Telecommunications (now the Ministry of Public Management, Home Affairs, Posts and Telecommunications).

The postal insurance system also invested indirectly in equities through a similar plan. It was impossible to ascertain the amount of postal savings invested in equities because the types of marketable securities held in the money trusts and the unrealized gains and losses on these securities had not been disclosed.[4]

THE NEW PLAN

As shown in Fig. 4.3, once the transition to an independent asset management system is completed, postal savings assets will no longer be managed through the Trust Fund Bureau. Instead, they will be directly invested in the financial markets. A fiscal 2001 asset management plan for postal savings funds, announced in December 2000, calls for the use of asset–liability management and monitoring of the impact of investment decisions on financial markets. In addition, according to the plan, postal savings assets will be invested primarily in Japanese bonds for stability and safety and secondarily in equities to provide diversification. Postal savings assets may also be invested with the help of the expertise of some entities in the private sector, namely, the trust banks that can offer *shiteitan*. The postal savings entity will continue to purchase FILP bonds for seven years to help ensure that the FILP reforms proceed smoothly.

In addition, part of the fiscal 2001 asset management plan includes establishing medium- to long-term asset allocation target percentages for the core postal savings portfolio. As shown in Table 4.1, according to the plan, 80% of assets will be invested in Japanese bonds; 5% in foreign bonds; 5% in domestic stocks; 5%

4 This information, however, was disclosed in the Postal Service Agency's 'Financial Results of Postal Services for Fiscal 2000' (released in July 2001).

in foreign stocks; and 5% in short-term assets. Compared with the typical asset allocations adopted by Japanese corporate pension plans and life insurance companies, the allocation in the postal savings portfolio to domestic stocks, foreign stocks and bonds, and other risky assets is relatively low. The main reason for such a conservative asset allocation, heavily weighted toward bonds, is the inherently low risk tolerance of the postal savings system; the financial products that have been offered involve no investment risk for depositors, and the postal savings system has maintained an independent budget. The asset allocation band for domestic bonds is relatively wide because the postal savings system will continue to purchase FILP bonds during the transition to a system of discretionary asset management.

Given that the target asset allocation for domestic stocks, foreign bonds and foreign stocks is 5% for each category and that the average amount of postal savings assets invested in fiscal 1999 was ¥259.1 tr., the amount invested in each of these asset classes would equal about ¥13 tr. Yet because the specific amount of postal savings assets currently invested through third parties (i.e., that portion invested in domestic and foreign stocks) had not been disclosed, it was difficult to ascertain the likely extent of fund flows into these assets.

Nonetheless, in 1999, about ¥10.2 tr. in postal savings assets were invested in domestic and foreign stocks through *shiteitan*. No more than 50% of the funds in these money trusts can be invested in domestic stocks, and no more than 30% can be invested in foreign-currency-denominated assets. The 50% constraint does not apply, however, to a certain portion of the *shiteitan* assets. On the basis of all these factors, then, ¥5–13 tr. in postal savings assets will probably be newly invested in domestic stocks and ¥10–13 tr. will flow into foreign stocks in the seven to ten years after 2001. The amount invested in foreign bonds will probably increase as well, considering that in addition to the funds invested through *shiteitan*, the postal savings system had invested about ¥4.6 tr. in foreign bonds on its own at fiscal 1999. In fact, the new inflow into foreign bonds will probably be ¥5–8 tr.

The Ministry of Public Management, Home Affairs, Posts and Telecommunications announced that, starting in fiscal 2001, it will disclose, by asset class, the book and market values of its postal savings and postal insurance assets. Once this information is regularly disclosed, it will be possible to determine the amount of assets invested in the independently managed designated money trusts

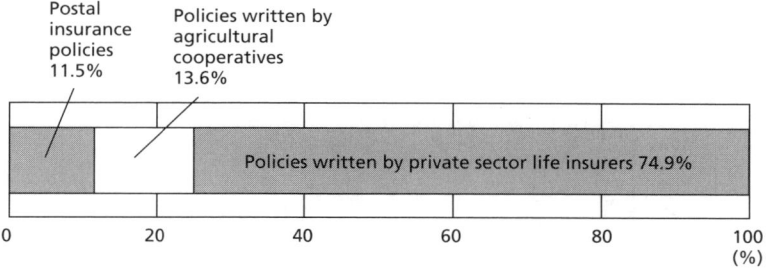

4.7 Market share of postal insurance in individual life insurance policies (fiscal 1999).
Source: as Fig. 4.1.

and, consequently, get a better idea of the extent to which postal savings and insurance assets are likely to be invested in stocks.

The Postal Life Insurance Service

The Postal Life Insurance Service, *Kampo*, a nationally administered insurance programme available at post offices throughout Japan, offers the government a means for providing life insurance as well as other basic forms of security. The unique feature of Japan's postal insurance system is its simple enrolment procedure, which neither requires a medical checkup nor imposes restrictions based on occupation. As shown in Fig. 4.7, at the end of fiscal 1999, there were about 81.3 million postal insurance policyholders, who accounted for roughly 11.5% of the total value of domestic individual life insurance policies. The most common type of postal insurance policy was endowment insurance; 67.01 million of these policies had been taken out, which was 82.4% of all postal insurance policies. Because investment returns on the premiums paid for endowment insurance are not subject to income tax, these policies are a popular savings vehicle among individual investors.

To keep pace with the changes for the postal savings system scheduled for implementation in 2001, some organizational and asset management policy changes were also planned for the Postal Life Insurance Service. Specifically, the organization will be transformed into a public sector corporation, and postal insurance assets will be managed on a discretionary basis, independently of the Trust Fund

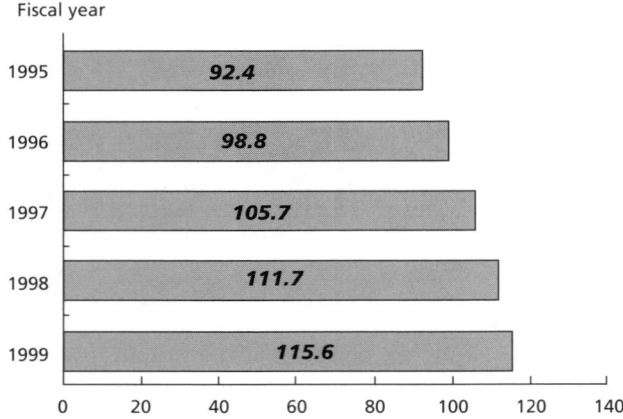

Fiscal year

1995	92.4
1996	98.8
1997	105.7
1998	111.7
1999	115.6

0   20   40   60   80   100   120   140

4.8 Trend in value of postal insurance assets (¥ tr.).
Source: as Fig. 4.1.

Bureau. These modifications will no doubt bring about major changes to the operations of the postal insurance service.

As with postal savings assets, the management of postal insurance assets will be independent of the Trust Fund Bureau. In April 2001, when the government began revamping the FILP system, the transition was implemented, but because the complete transition to an independent asset management system will take seven to ten more years, some elements of the current system will remain in place during the transition phase. As in the preceding section on the postal savings system, it is thus instructive to explain the old asset management system for postal insurance assets.

THE OLD SYSTEM

The assets of the Postal Life Insurance Service consist of premiums paid by policyholders less benefit payments and operating expenses. As these assets accumulated, they were invested to fund future benefit payments. Figure 4.8, which depicts the five-year trend in the value of postal insurance assets, shows that the value of these assets increased each year; by the end of fiscal 1999, the total amount of assets equalled nearly ¥116 tr.

Figure 4.9 illustrates the flow of funds in the postal insurance system. For accounting purposes, premiums received from policyholders are split into a surplus reserve account and a cumulative reserve account. Surplus reserves consist of the excess of fund inflows over fund outflows during a fiscal year and are directly

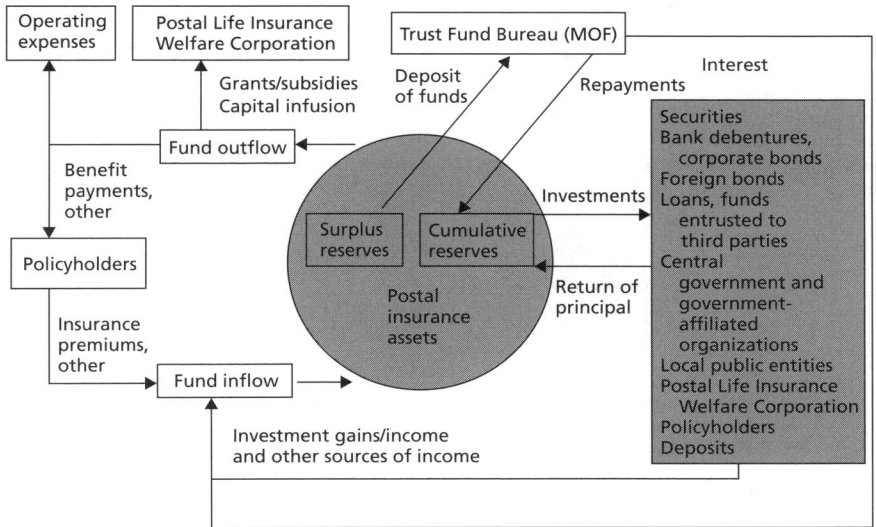

4.9 Flow of funds in the postal insurance system.
Source: as Fig. 4.1.

deposited with the Trust Fund Bureau. At the end of each fiscal year, surplus reserves are transferred to cumulative reserves.

The three core investment principles for postal insurance assets are 'safety', 'advantage' and 'the public interest'. These three principles will also apply when postal insurance assets are managed independently of the Trust Fund Bureau. The major difference between the investment management principles for the Postal Life Insurance Service and those for private life insurance companies is that the public entity manages assets for the public interest. Accordingly, as shown in Fig. 4.10, most postal insurance assets are invested in loans to local public entities, Japanese government bonds and bonds issued by government-affiliated organizations. Also, 10% of postal insurance assets are deposited with trust banks and managed in the form of *shiteitan*. As with postal savings assets, postal insurance premiums cannot be directly invested in equities because of regulatory restrictions. Therefore, premiums are invested indirectly in equities through the Postal Life Insurance Welfare Corporation in the form of *shiteitan*.

THE NEW SYSTEM

As part of the transition to an independent asset management plan, postal insurance premiums are no longer deposited with the Trust

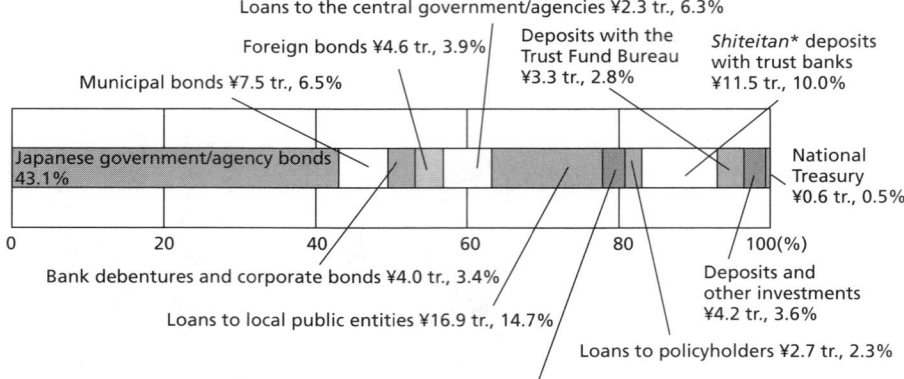

4.10 Asset breakdown of individual insurance assets (fiscal 1999).
Note: *Independently managed designated money trusts.
Source: as Fig. 4.1.

Table 4.2 Target asset allocations for core portfolio of postal insurance assets (at December 2000)

Asset class	Domestic bonds	Foreign bonds	Domestic stocks	Foreign stocks	Short-term assets
Target allocation	80%	5%	6%	6%	3%
Asset allocation band	+10%~−10%	+5%~−5%	+5%~−5%	+5%~−5%	+7%~−7%

Note: Loans made to local public entities are included in the domestic bond category. Assets invested in domestic and foreign stocks are managed by third parties.
Source: as Table 4.1.

Fund Bureau. Instead, they are directly invested in the financial markets. In response to the decision to implement an independent asset management system, the Study Group on Postal Savings and Postal Life Insurance Asset Management issued a final report in June 2000 and announced basic asset management policy guidelines in December 2000. These basic guidelines included instituting asset–liability management and monitoring the impact of investment decisions on financial markets. In addition, medium- to long-term asset allocation target percentages were announced. As shown in Table 4.2, 80% of postal insurance assets will be invested in Japanese bonds; 5% in foreign bonds; 6% in domestic stocks; 6% in foreign stocks; and 3% in short-term assets. As with postal savings assets, the bulk of postal insurance assets are invested in bonds because the insurance products offered involve no investment risk for depositors and the Postal Life Insurance Service has an independent budget.

At the end of fiscal 1999, about ¥11.5 tr. in postal insurance assets was invested indirectly in domestic and foreign stocks through trust banks. But because the details of these investments have not been disclosed, it is unclear how and to what extent a rebalancing of the core portfolio will affect the stock market during the transition to an independent asset management system. Details of the portion of postal insurance assets managed by trust banks are difficult to establish, because these funds are often used to bolster the market through so-called price-keeping operations. Nonetheless, in fiscal 2001, the Ministry of Public Management, Home Affairs, Posts and Telecommunications began to disclose more information on the assets of both the postal savings and insurance services. As a result, the extent to which postal savings and insurance assets are likely to be invested in stocks will become clear, thereby improving the overall transparency of the asset management activities of these entities.

The public pension system

Japan's pension system comprises two core components: a public pension programme and a private pension programme. As shown in Fig. 4.11, the public pension system consists of the National Pension, Employees' Pension and the Mutual Aid Pension. The private pension system consists of individual pension programmes, in which individuals can participate based on their own discretion; the National Pension Fund for the self-employed (including farmers and students); and corporate pension programmes, which are established by companies for their employees (see Chapter 5).

Japan's public pension programme is open to all Japanese nationals, functions as a social safety net and provides financial support to older generations from younger generations. The National Pension system, Japan's most basic public pension programme, is open to all citizens between the ages of 20 and 59 and provides fixed pension benefit payments indexed to prices. At the end of March 1998, the National Pension system covered 70.34 million people.

The National Pension functions as a form of societal insurance by providing pension benefits in the future in return for the payment of premiums today. The programme is supported by younger

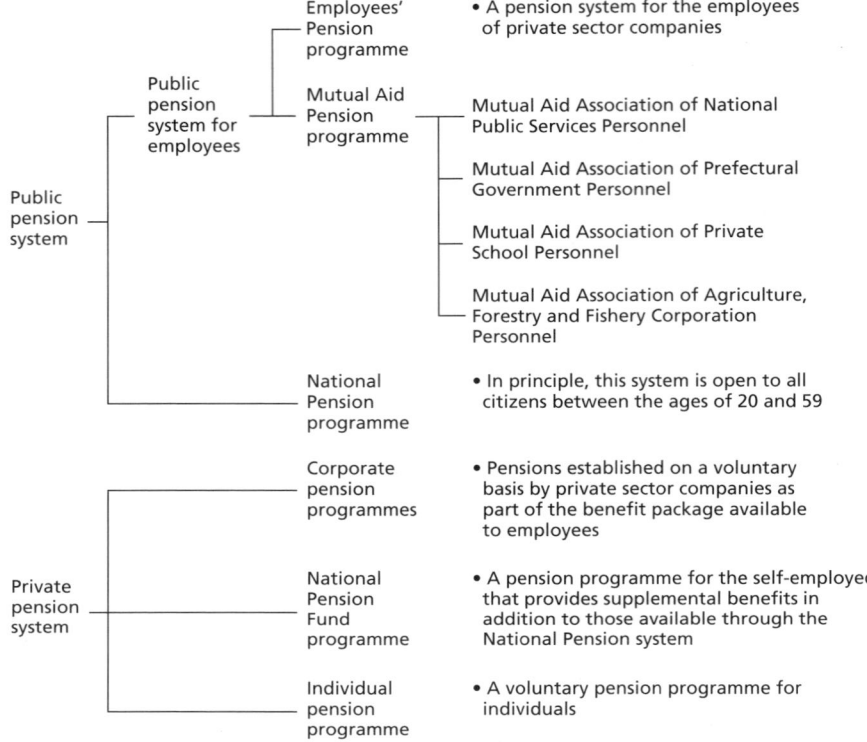

4.11 Japan's pension system.
Source: Nomura Securities.

generations; specifically, a portion of the wealth generated by the younger generations of people who are still working is redistributed to pensioners. In other words, the system is based on a pay-as-you-go method of financing. And even those who are financially unable to pay any premiums are still guaranteed to receive benefits. The public pension programme is funded mainly by premiums and investment returns on pension reserves; however, one-third of public pension benefit payments are covered by the national Treasury.

As a supplement to the benefits paid out by the National Pension programme, the Employees' Pension and Mutual Aid Pension programmes provide pension payments in proportion to each participant's income. As shown in Fig. 4.12, private sector salaried employees are covered by a three-tier pension structure: they participate in both the Employees' Pension and National Pension programmes as well as in corporate pension plans. Those who are

1999 Fiscal year

	Working status of participant	Pension programme	Pension premium
Self-employed, farmers and students		National Pension	¥ 13 300 per month (fixed amount)
Salaried employees	Private sector employees	National Pension and Employees' Pension	17.36% of monthly salary and 1% of bonus payments (payments are evenly split between employers and employees)
	Government employees, persons employed in the forestry, fishery and agricultural sectors, employees of private schools	National Pension and Mutual Aid Pensions	For the mutual aid associations, 13.30–19.49% of monthly salary and 1% of bonus payments (payments are evenly split between employers and employees)
Housewives		National Pension	No premium payments are required

4.12 Public pension premiums paid by major participant groups (fiscal 1999). Source: Nomura Securties, based on data from the *Shakai Hoken Kenkyujo* [Social Insurance Research Institute].

government employees; agricultural, forestry and fishery industry workers; or private school employees are participants in the National Pension and Mutual Aid Pension programmes.

Currently, four Mutual Aid Pension associations are in operation: the Mutual Aid Association of National Public Services Personnel, the Mutual Aid Association of Prefectural Government Personnel, the Mutual Aid Association of Private School Personnel, and the Mutual Aid Association of Agriculture, Forestry and Fishery Corporation Personnel. Table 4.3 outlines these four association pension programmes. In terms of the number of participants and pensioners, the Mutual Aid Association of Prefectural Government Personnel is the largest Mutual Aid Pension programme, and the Mutual Aid Association of Private School Personnel is the smallest programme.

Japan's Mutual Aid Pension programmes have gone through several phases of reorganization. Some programmes have been consolidated, and others have been split into separate organizations. The Mutual Aid Association of Private School Personnel and the Mutual Aid Association of Agriculture, Forestry and Fishery

Table 4.3 Outline of the Employees' Pension and Mutual Aid Pensions systems (at 31 March 1998)

	Employees' Pension system	Mutual Aid pension systems			
		Mutual Aid Association of National Public Services Personnel	Mutual Aid Association of Prefectural Government Personnel	Mutual Aid Association of Private School Personnel	Mutual Aid Association of Agriculture, Forestry and Fishery Corporation Personnel
	Pension programme for salaried employees of private sector companies	Pension programmes for national government employees. Each government agency has its own Mutual Aid Pension programme, but all pension assets are managed under the aegis of the Mutual Aid Association of National Public Services Personnel	Each prefectural government, public school system and police force has its own Mutual Aid Association. The Mutual Aid Association of Prefectural Government Personnel manages a portion of each local entity's pension assets	Pension programme for private school employees	Pension programme for employees in the agriculture, forestry and fishery industries
Number of participants (000)	33 470	1120	3330	400	490
Number of pensioners (000)	7820	580	1320	60	140
Number of pensioners/ Number of participants	23.4%	51.4%	39.8%	14.2%	28.7%
Cumulative pension reserves (¥ tr.)	125.8	7.9	32.2	2.7	2.0
Reserve coverage ratio	5.4	4.5	7.2	11.0	4.6

Notes: **1** Number of participants, number of pensioners and cumulative reserves are at end-March 1998.
2 The reserve coverage ratio is the amount of cumulative pension reserves for the current fiscal year divided by the previous year's total pension payments.
Source: Nomura Securities, based on data from the former Ministry of Health and Welfare (now the Ministry of Health, Labour and Welfare).

Corporation Personnel are now independent of the Employees' Pension Insurance system. In contrast, the former Mutual Aid Pension programmes have been merged with the Employees' Pension programme for the Japan Railway companies, Nippon Telegraph and Telephone and Japan Tobacco, in conjunction with the privatization of these organizations.

NECESSARY REFORMS

Given the decline in pension contributors and the birthrate and the increase in the number of pensioners stemming from the aging of Japan's population, the public pension system is likely to face increasingly difficult financial pressures. The 1999 Pension White Paper contained several projections for future pension premiums. Assuming that the current system is maintained, Employees' Pension insurance premiums will increase to about 35% of an employee's monthly paycheck by 2025, from 17.35% in 1999. In addition, the white paper states that National Pension premiums will increase to about ¥26 000 per month by 2025, from ¥13 300 in 1999. As shown in Table 4.3, the current amount of reserves held by the Mutual Aid Association of National Public Services Personnel and the Mutual Aid Association of Agriculture, Forestry and Fishery Corporation Personnel is lower than the level of reserves at the Employees' Pension programme, which means that the two Mutual Aid Associations are in relatively poor financial shape.

In response to the deteriorating finances of public pension funds, the Japanese government has been taking gradual steps to overhaul the programmes to prevent an inordinate rise in pension premiums. The government is considering increasing the amount of funding provided by the national Treasury (which is currently at one-third of pension payouts), raising the eligible age for receiving payments from the Employees' Pension programme, and reducing the level of benefits. In addition, the authorities may merge the four Mutual Aid Pension programmes with the Employees' Pension system. But because this integration would take a considerable amount of time to implement, the government is considering merging the Mutual Aid Association of Agriculture, Forestry and Fishery Corporation Personnel with the Employees' Pension system first, because of the Association's relatively weak finances. The government is also thinking about establishing a system whereby the Mutual Aid Association of National Public Services Personnel and the Mutual Aid Association of Prefectural Government Personnel would provide support to

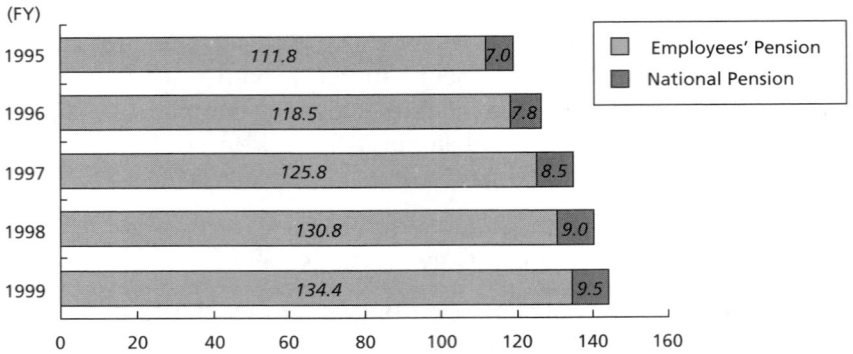

4.13 Trend in reserves for the National Pension and Employees' Pension systems (¥ tr.).
Source: as Fig. 4.12.

each other. If one of the programmes were in better financial shape than the other, then the healthier one would offer some financial support.

INVESTMENT OF PENSION ASSETS

As shown in Fig. 4.13, the cumulative reserves of the Employees' Pension and National Pension programmes increased each year. At the end of fiscal 1999, total reserves for these pension plans exceeded ¥140 tr. Until March 2001, these reserves were deposited with the Trust Fund Bureau of the MOF and used to finance FILP. Since 1986, however, a portion of the funds deposited with the Trust Fund Bureau was loaned to the Pension Welfare Service Public Corporation (a special public sector corporation affiliated with the Ministry of Health and Welfare) and managed independently. The amount of funds managed through the Pension Welfare Service Public Corporation has increased each year; at the end of fiscal 1999, the portion of funds managed by this organization was about ¥27.5 tr.

The Pension Welfare Service Public Corporation has established long-term asset allocation guidelines for its core portfolio of domestic and foreign stocks and bonds. For fiscal 1999, 56.7% of the core portfolio was invested in bonds (including foreign bonds); 26.0% in domestic stocks; 12.3% in foreign stocks; 2.7% in convertible bonds; and 2.4% in short-term assets. Other than the small portion of assets it manages on its own, the Pension Welfare Service Public Corporation hires trust banks, life insurance companies, investment advisory companies and other subadvisors to manage the pension assets. At the end of fiscal 1999, a total of 46 such companies (15 trust banks, 5 life insurance companies and 26 investment advisory companies) divided up the management of the corporation's assets.

Starting in April 2001, in line with the FILP reforms, the management of National Pension and Employees' Pension reserves has steadily moved away from the Trust Fund Bureau. Each year during the succeeding seven to ten years, the Trust Fund Bureau will return about ¥20 tr. in pension assets, thereby sharply increasing the amount of pension assets managed independently of the Trust Fund Bureau. These assets, together with the assets of the Pension Welfare Service Public Corporation, will be managed by the Government Pension Investment Fund, which replaced the Pension Welfare Service Public Corporation in April 2001. After all pension assets are transferred from the Pension Welfare Service Public Corporation to the new Government Pension Investment Fund, total assets under management at the new fund will exceed ¥140 tr.

THE NEW SYSTEM FOR THE MANAGEMENT OF PENSION ASSETS

Figure 4.14 depicts the new, independent asset management system for public pension assets. The Minister of Health, Labour and Welfare, who has full responsibility for and authoritative power over the public pension system, will formulate a basic asset management policy based on a report from a committee set up to study issues related to the operation of the new plan. The Ministry of Health, Labour and Welfare will entrust pension assets to the Government Pension Investment Fund, which will both manage assets internally and entrust asset management to private sector financial institutions based on the basic asset management policies established by the Minister of Health, Labour and Welfare. During the transition period, however, when approximately ¥20 tr. in pension assets are expected to be returned by the Trust Fund Bureau annually, the Government Pension Investment Fund will purchase some FILP bonds to ensure that FILP reforms proceed smoothly.

THE GOVERNMENT PENSION INVESTMENT FUND

A basic asset management policy for public pension assets was disclosed in December 2000. The policy statement discusses the basic concepts for pension asset management, long-term asset allocations

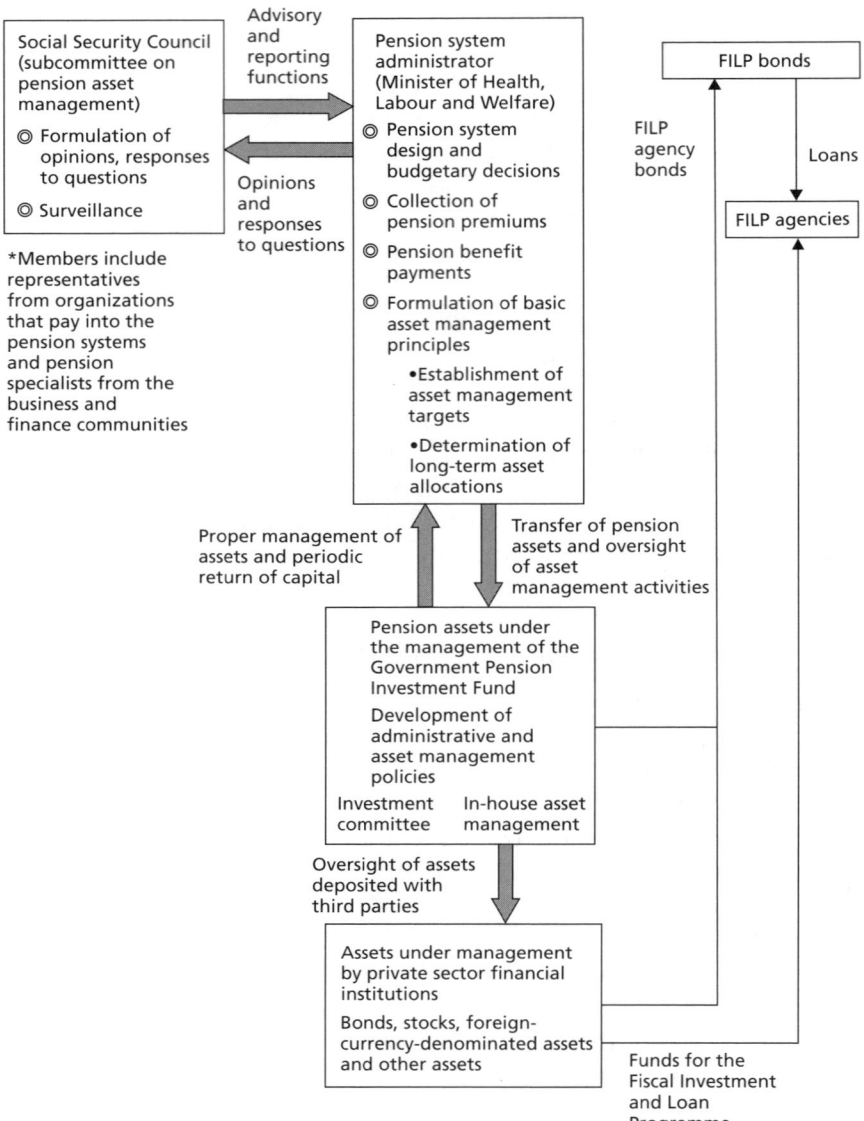

4.14 The new discretionary asset management plan for pension reserves.
Source: Nomura Securities, based on data from the former Ministry of Health and
Welfare (now the Ministry of Health, Labour and Welfare).

Table 4.4 Asset allocations for core portfolio of pension assets (at December 2000)

Asset class	Domestic bonds	Foreign bonds	Domestic stocks	Foreign stocks	Short-term assets
Asset allocation	68%	7%	12%	8%	5%
Asset allocation band	+8%~−8%	+5%~−5%	+6%~−6%	+5%~−5%	−

Source: as Table 4.3.

for the core portfolio, the guiding principles of the Government Pension Investment Fund and evaluation criteria for the Government Pension Investment Fund. The asset allocation for the core portfolio is 68% for domestic bonds, 12% for domestic stocks, 8% for foreign stocks, 7% for foreign bonds and 5% for cash. Compared with the postal savings and postal insurance systems, the asset allocations for stocks and foreign assets are relatively high. Table 4.4 shows the asset allocation bands for the core portfolio. The core portfolio's allocations for each of the asset categories are currently higher than the maximums of the bands listed in Table 4.4. The asset allocations of the core portfolio will be adjusted gradually, however, as assets are transferred from the Trust Fund Bureau. In addition, the basic asset management policy will be reviewed when necessary, but no less frequently than once a year.

Under the new system of independent management of public pension assets, the Government Pension Investment Fund will invest pension reserves in accordance with the basic asset management policy. Because most public pension assets are managed by private sector financial institutions, the Government Pension Investment Fund will mainly focus on selecting the appropriate private sector financial institutions to manage its pension assets, evaluating these institutions, rebalancing the portfolio and managing total portfolio risk. The fund will nevertheless directly manage a portion of the bond portfolio in order to keep expenses down and acquire information and knowledge about asset management.

Given the previously mentioned target asset allocation for domestic stocks in the core portfolio of 12% and total pension reserves at the end of fiscal 1999 of ¥143.9 tr., the value of stock holdings in the core portfolio was then about ¥17.3 tr. And because the actual allocation to domestic stocks at the end of 1999 was about ¥7.1 tr., about ¥10 tr. worth of domestic stocks will have to be purchased for the core portfolio in the seven to ten years following 2001.

Future management of public sector assets

The system of management for public funds in Japan is being revamped at a relatively fast pace, as exemplified by the government's decision to allow the assets of the postal savings, the postal insurance and the public pension systems to be independently managed as part of the FILP reforms and restructuring the postal system into separate government corporations. Yet additional pressure for reform is likely because these reforms do not constitute the privatization of the postal system that market participants expect.

The structural problems related to the massive amount of assets managed by the public sector in Japan will continue to be a major challenge. In particular, some major issues remain unresolved in the assignment of ultimate responsibility for public sector asset management and corporate governance-related areas. Accordingly, the Koizumi administration, which was established in April 2001, declared its intention of implementing further structural reforms and has put privatization of the postal system on its reform agenda.

5 Corporate pension funds

Until 2001, corporate pension plans in Japan consisted mainly of employees' pension fund plans and tax-qualified pension plans. Both are defined-benefit pension plans. In 2001, however, the Defined-Benefit Pension Law and the Defined-Contribution Pension Law were established to expand the types of corporate pension plans available in Japan. These new laws include provisions that apply to both defined-benefit and defined-contribution pension plans, such as rules concerning fiduciary responsibilities and standardized rules for pension contributions. The restructuring of Japan's corporate pension system will probably accelerate as companies increasingly adopt new corporate pension plans allowed by the new laws, and as a result, the investment management industry in Japan should eventually expand.

This chapter discusses the newly established Defined-Benefit Pension Law and the Defined-Contribution Pension Law as well as the outlook for the investment management industry in light of the changing environment of the corporate pension system in Japan.

Defined-benefit pension plans

Employees' pension fund programmes and tax-qualified pension plans in Japan are both defined-benefit pension plans, that is, pension benefits during retirement for each plan beneficiary are guaranteed based on length of service with the company and other factors. At the end of fiscal 2000, the aggregate outstanding value

5.1 Total assets in Japan's employees' pension fund programmes and tax-qualified pension plans.
Source: Nomura Resesarch Institute, *Koushasai youran* [Bond Handbook], 2001 edn.

of assets in employees' pension funds and tax-qualified pension plans was roughly ¥80 tr.

RECENT TRENDS

Figure 5.1 shows the trend in the outstanding value of assets in employees' pension fund plans and tax-qualified pension plans from 1990. The value of assets in employees' pension fund plans rose to about ¥58 tr. by fiscal 2000 from about ¥25 tr. in the early 1990s, while the amount in tax-qualified pension plans increased from about ¥13 tr. to about ¥22 tr. over the same period.

Nonetheless, during the 1990s, deteriorating financial markets and the introduction of new pension accounting standards resulted in various problems for Japan's corporate pension plans. First, because of the prolonged bear market and low interest rates that have endured since the bubble collapsed, it has become increasingly difficult for pension fund managers to achieve investment returns in line with the expected rates of return on pension plan assets. Although Japanese companies typically set the expected rates of return on their plan assets at 5.5%, they are now able to adjust the rate.[1] During the late 1980s, it was common for pension fund

---

1 The 5.5% rate was in line with the deposit rate used by the Ministry of Finance's Fund Operating Division and the expected rate of return used by other social insurance programmes.

managers to achieve returns in excess of their expected rate of return on pension assets. Since the 1990s, however, returns on pension fund assets have been below the expected rates of return, thus forcing companies to make up for the shortfall in the funding of their pension obligations. Quite a number of plan sponsors (as many as 177 in fiscal 2000, according to press reports) have reduced pension benefits in order to offset the increased burdens stemming from the plans' weak investment returns.

Second, the introduction of new pension accounting standards in the fiscal year ended March 2001 has created problems for corporate pension plans. The new standards require companies to recognize the underfunded portion of the pension obligations for their employees' pension fund plans and tax-qualified pension plans as liabilities on their balance sheets and to record pension expenses on their income statements on an accrual basis. Companies experience difficulty, however, controlling pension expenses and the degree to which their pension plans are underfunded because these amounts vary significantly depending on a multitude of factors unrelated to core operations, such as the return on plan assets and the average age of a company's employees.

Because of these problems, the growth rate of assets in tax-qualified pension plans and employees' pension fund programmes has fallen sharply and the number of plans in existence has decreased.

Figure 5.2 depicts the trend in the number of employees' pension funds newly established and the number discontinued since fiscal 1990. During the early 1990s, more than a hundred new funds were established every year. In 1993, however, the number of newly established funds started to decline. Between 1997 and 1999, the number of new funds set up each year fell to fewer than five. Furthermore, although almost no employees' pension funds were liquidated in the early 1990s, an increasing number of funds have been liquidated since 1994. Specifically, the number of employees' pension fund programmes liquidated annually rose steadily from 14 in 1997, 18 in fiscal 1998, 16 in fiscal 1999 and then 29 in fiscal 2000.[2]

Figure 5.3 shows the *net* change in the total number of tax-qualified pension plans since fiscal 1990. As in the case of employees' pension funds, it is clear from the figure that the number of tax-qualified pension plans has been declining in recent years. During the early 1990s, the number of plans increased by more than 3000

---

2 'Nenkin Joho' (Pension Information), *Rating and Investment Information*, April 2001, no. 262.

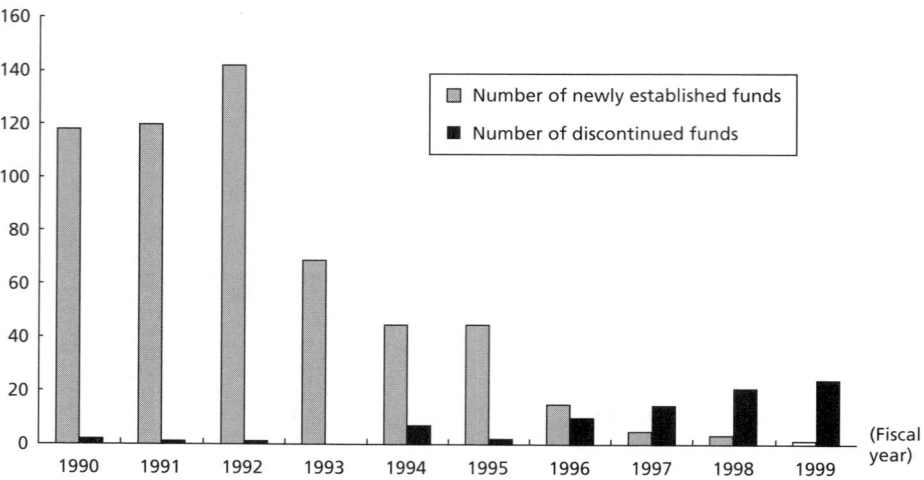

Number of employees' pension funds

5.2 Newly established and discontinued employees' pension funds.
Source: Life Design Institute, *White Paper on Corporate Pensions (Fiscal 2001)*.

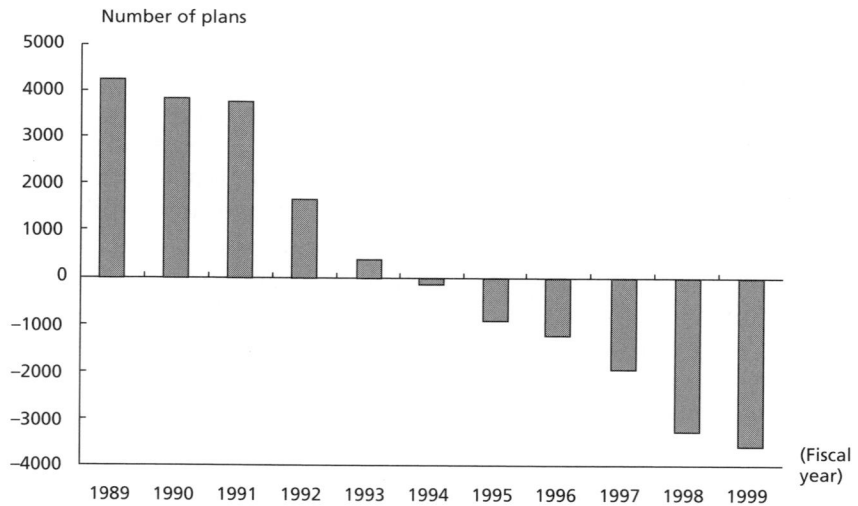

5.3 Net change in number of tax-qualified pension plans.
Source: as Fig. 5.2 and Web site of the Life Insurance Association of Japan.

each year. In 1992, however, the net increase in the number of new plans declined significantly, and in 1994, the net change turned negative. The net decline in the total number of plans was particularly large in fiscal years 1998 and 1999, when the number of con-

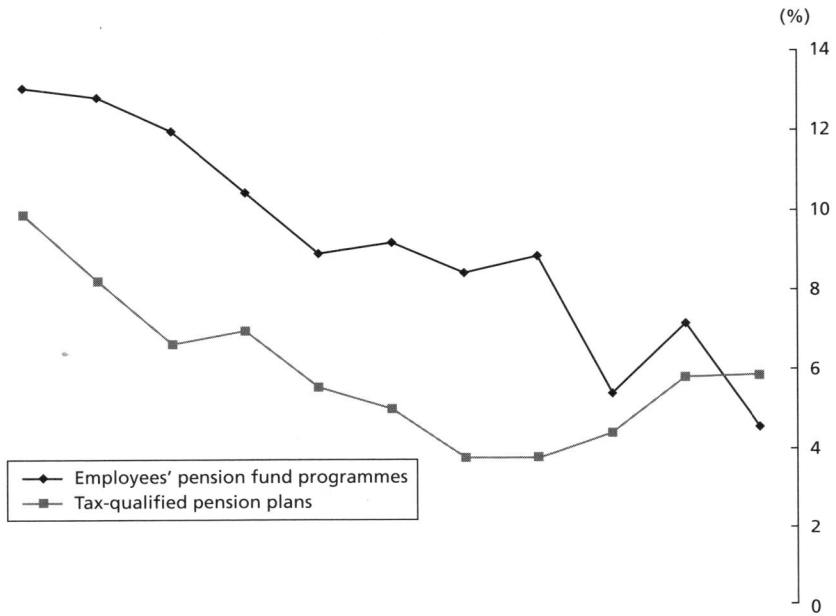

(%)

5.4 Annual growth in assets in employees' pension funds and tax-qualified pension plans.
Source: as Fig. 5.1.

tracts fell by more than 3000 plans each year. At the end of fiscal 1999, the total number of plans in place was 81 466, down 12% from a peak level of 92 467 in fiscal 1993.

As a result of the decline in the number of employees' pension funds and tax-qualified pension plans, the growth in the amount of assets in these plans has also dropped. From the late 1980s to the early 1990s, assets in employees' pension funds grew at an average annual rate of 15.7% while those in tax-qualified pension plans grew at a rate of 12.6%. During the 1990s, however, growth slowed nearly every year, reaching less than 10% for assets in employees' pension funds and below 5% for those in tax-qualified pension plans by the latter half of the 1990s (Fig. 5.4).

IMPACT OF DEREGULATION

Until the 1990s, the management of corporate pension funds in Japan was strictly regulated, with various regulations dictating how and by whom pension assets were managed. Traditionally, for example, only trust banks and life insurance companies were allowed to manage corporate pension funds. In addition, pension fund asset allocations were governed by the so-called '5:3:3:2 rule'. According to this rule, a minimum of 50% of total pension fund assets had to be invested in Japanese government bonds (JGBs) or comparably safe investments; a maximum of 30% could be invested in stocks; a maximum of 30% in foreign-currency-denominated securities; and a maximum of 20% in real estate.[3] Deregulation during the 1990s, however, led to various changes in the corporate pension fund business in Japan (Table 5.1).

For example, after first being allowed to manage corporate pension funds in the 1990s, investment advisory companies have rapidly increased their market share (Figs 5.5 and 5.6). At the end of 2000, investment advisory companies managed about 30% of total assets in employees' pension funds and more than 10% of total assets in tax-qualified pension plans. These market share figures are significant considering that investment advisory companies entered the pension fund business only in recent years.

EMERGENCE OF A MASTER TRUST STRUCTURE

Corporate pension plan sponsors have become able to decide on their own the asset classes for their investments and the asset management companies that fit their particular investment styles. These trends have given rise to financial institutions that offer master trusts.

The master trust structure was first developed in the US in the mid-1970s. Under a master trust structure, a trust bank or the trust division of a commercial bank centrally manages all operational and administrative procedures for those pension assets entrusted to a number of pension fund management firms.

On 9 November 1999, Daiwa Bank and Sumitomo Trust & Banking announced that they would establish Japan Trustee Services Bank, and Nippon Life Insurance and Mitsubishi Trust & Banking announced that they would set up The Master Trust Bank of Japan together with Toyo Trust & Banking, Meiji Life Insurance and Deutsche Bank. Both trust banks are Japanese versions of master trust banks.

As outlined in Fig. 5.7, a master trustee performs three main functions:

---

3 Under this rule, all ratios applied to the book value of the assets.

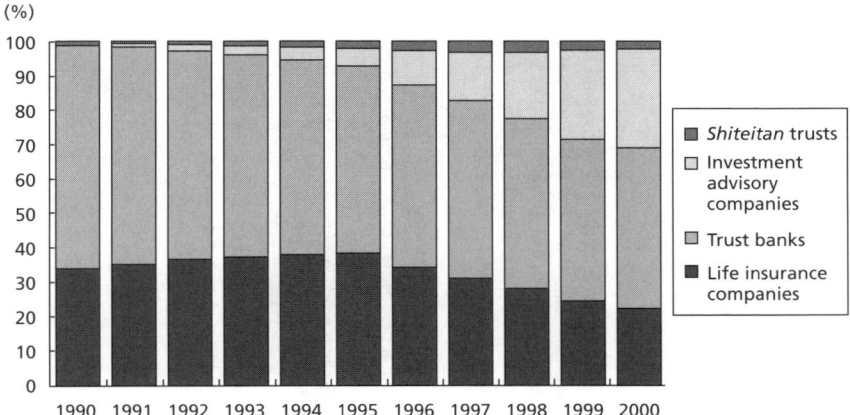

5.5 Share of total employees' pension fund assets managed by key asset management entities.
Source: as Fig. 5.1.

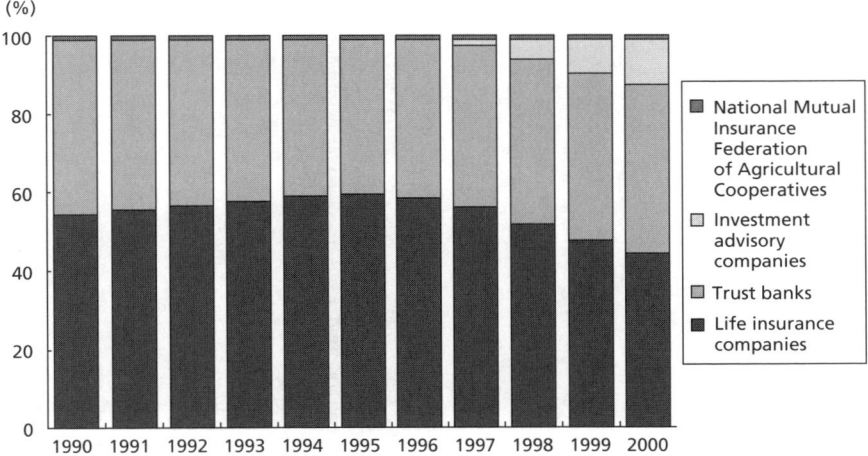

5.6 Share of total pension assets in tax-qualified pension plans managed by key asset management entities.
Source: as Fig. 5.1.

1 Custody, settlement and reporting
This is the fundamental function associated with the centralized management of pension assets. A master trustee is responsible for the custody of securities, transaction settlement and the collection of interest and dividends. The master trustee's functions have recently broadened to include various global custody functions responsibilities, such as custody and

Table 5.1 Deregulation of corporate pension asset management in Japan

Date	Major regulatory changes
April 1990:	Investment advisory companies were allowed to manage corporate pension funds (specifically, they were permitted to manage up to one-third of the total assets in a corporate pension plan). The '5:3:3:2 rule' was adopted for the allocation of pension fund assets managed by investment advisory companies (a minimum of 50% of total pension fund assets [in terms of book value] had to be invested in JGBs or comparably safe investments, and a maximum of 30% could be invested in stocks, a maximum of 30% in foreign-currency-denominated securities, and a maximum of 20% in real estate). In-house asset management was allowed for pension funds with at least ¥50bn in assets; investments for in-house asset management were limited to bonds and deposits
July 1993:	Minimum amount of assets that could be entrusted to investment advisory companies was lowered to ¥100 m
November 1994:	The distinction between 'new money' and 'old money' was eliminated (up to one-third of total plan assets could be managed by investment advisory companies)
April 1995:	The 5:3:3:2 rule for pension fund assets managed by investment advisory companies was eliminated. Investment advisory companies that had been in business for at least three years, instead of the previous eight years, were allowed to manage pension fund assets
April 1996:	Maximum amount of pension assets allowed to be entrusted to investment advisory companies was raised to one-half of total pension fund assets, up from one-third. The 5:3:3:2 rule for pension fund assets managed by trust banks and life insurance companies was eliminated. The 5:3:3:2 rule for corporate pension funds and pension fund associations that meet certain criteria was eliminated

July 1996:	A rule requiring pension funds to allocate pension contributions to trust banks and life insurance companies based on a fixed ratio was eliminated; a rule requiring trust banks and life insurance companies to pay pension benefits based on a fixed ratio was eliminated
December 1997:	The 5:3:3:2 rule was completely eliminated
January 1998:	The rule requiring all pension funds to use the same expected rate of return on plan assets was eliminated
March 1998:	The rule requiring investment advisory companies to have been in business for at least three years before they could manage corporate pension funds assets was eliminated. The rule requiring corporate pension funds to set aside a certain amount of assets for the government's Fiscal Investment and Loan Programme was eliminated
April 1998:	The limit on the amount of employees' pension fund assets that could be managed in-house was eliminated
April 1999:	The rule distinguishing pension fund assets managed by trust banks and life insurance companies from those managed by investment advisory companies was completely eliminated
April 2000:	The ban on the direct transfer of pension assets to pension trusts and separately managed designated monetary trusts (*shiteitan* trusts) was lifted
June 2000:	Restrictions on the amount of pension fund assets that could be managed in-house was eliminated. Restrictions on the direct contribution of listed stocks to pension plans (in addition to pension fund trusts) were eliminated. Restrictions on master trusts specialized in securities custody were lifted

Source: Nomura Research Institute.

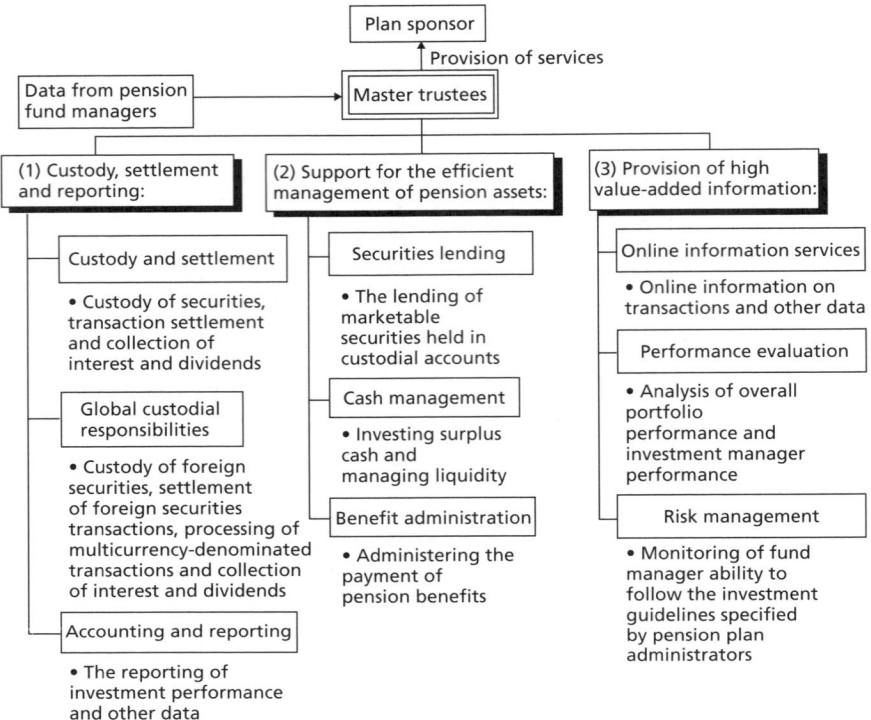

5.7 Master trust services in the US.
Source: Nomura, based on Tatsuji Jyubishi and Seiichiro Yamamoto, *Nenkin kikin ga kaeru shisan un'you bijinesu* (The Impact of Pension Funds on the Asset Management Business), Toyo Keizai Shinposha, 1998.

settlement for foreign securities and consolidated settlement of multicurrency-denominated transactions.

2 Support for the efficient management of pension assets
This function includes securities lending, cash management (i.e., investing excess cash and managing liquidity) and administration of benefits and plan participants. These services are important for corporate pension plans that seek to improve the returns on their pension asset investments by even a few basis points.

3 Provision of high value-added information
Through the Internet and other channels, a master trustee is able to provide corporate pension plan administrators with timely information on the execution of the functions mentioned above, as well as on overall portfolio performance,

the performance of each of the pension fund management firms and the extent to which each of these companies is following specified investment guidelines. A master trustee is therefore the primary entity responsible for administering not only pension assets but also information, through the full use of information technology.

In the US, master trusts are so widely used that they are often referred to as the infrastructure for the pension fund management business. The main reason behind the extensive use of the master trust structure in the US is that pension fund managers and pension plan sponsors need access to timely and accurate information concerning the risk management and investment performance of pension assets. This need has arisen in part because of the strict standards for fiduciary responsibilities imposed on pension plans by the Employee Retirement Income Security Act (ERISA)[4] and the obligation on plans to pay pension insurance premiums to the Pension Benefit Guaranty Corporation (PBGC) in proportion to the degree to which a plan is underfunded. Also, Statement of Financial Accounting Standards (SFAS) 87 mandates the disclosure of the amount of underfunding on a consolidated basis.

PENSION FUND ASSETS MANAGED IN-HOUSE OR BY SUBSIDIARIES

In June 2000, some of the restrictions on the in-house management of pension fund assets of employees' pension funds were either relaxed or eliminated, spurring some Japanese companies to consider managing their pension assets in-house.

Before these restrictions were either lifted or relaxed, the in-house management of pension assets was allowed only for those employees' pension funds that met certain requirements, such as total assets of at least ¥50bn. Accordingly, before the rules were liberalized, no private sector pension plans managed assets in-house. Increasing interest in in-house management of pension assets to improve performance and cost efficiency contributed to the passage

---

4 Sect. 404(a)(1)(B) of the Employee Retirement Income Security Act of 1974 stipulates, in part, that 'a fiduciary shall discharge his duties with respect to a plan with the care, skill, prudence, and diligence under the circumstances then prevailing that a prudent man acting in a like capacity and familiar with such matters would use in the conduct of an enterprise of a like character and with like aims'.

by the Diet of a pension system reform bill on 28 March 2000 that either relaxed or lifted various restrictions on the in-house management of corporate pension assets, starting on 1 June 2000.

The legislative changes mandated several conditions for the in-house management of pension assets, namely, that pension plans establish internal administrative structures and investment performance evaluation methodologies in addition to the conventional core guidelines for pension asset management. Pension plans must also designate a chief investment officer and a fund manager who will be in charge of the in-house management of pension assets. Fund managers must have at least three years of experience managing the types of assets they are responsible for overseeing. For those pension plans that meet the above criteria, the new regulations also expand the array of investment options for in-house asset management to include marketable securities, bond lending and passive stock investments. The new law also allows those pension plans that do not meet all the criteria to invest plan assets in investment trusts. In April 2001, Matsushita Electric Employees' Pension Fund became the first pension plan in Japan to manage assets in-house.

In August 2000, Hitachi established an asset management subsidiary, Hitachi Investment Management, to manage the pension assets of the Hitachi group. Hitachi Investment Management has begun investing the group's pension assets in privately placed investment trusts and other financial products. Other major corporate groups, including Toyota Motor, have also started establishing similar asset management subsidiaries.

In the US, it is relatively common for pension plans to manage assets in-house or for companies to set up asset management subsidiaries. The major characteristics of in-house management of pension assets in the US are as follows:

1 More than half of the large US pension funds (corporate pension plans and public employees' pension funds with more than $5bn in total assets) manage pension assets in-house. Many small and mid-sized pension plans, however, tend to outsource the management of pension assets; only 20% of pension plans with $1bn to $5bn in total assets internally manage pension assets, and only 10% of pension plans with less than $1bn in assets do so.

2 Among the large pension plans that manage assets in-house, the proportion of total assets that are managed in-house varies significantly, ranging between 100% and less than 10%.

Pension assets that are managed in-house are mainly invested in bonds and large-cap US stocks and index funds. Many companies use master trust structures for back-office operations to save on personnel costs.

3 Among the 100 largest corporate pension plans in the US, 16 are run by pension asset management subsidiaries of the plan sponsors. And among these 16 subsidiaries, only three offer asset management services for non-group as well as group companies. Apparently, the asset management subsidiaries that manage a relatively large proportion of their parent company's plan assets tend to be more successful in winning asset management business from non-group companies. Meanwhile, the relatively small asset management subsidiaries, which generally manage only a small proportion of their parent companies' plan assets, tend to have comparatively weak investment performance, mainly because of the relatively small amount of assets they have under management. And because of their relatively poor investment performance, smaller companies have difficulty offering competitive compensation packages to recruit top fund managers. This obstacle tends to further weaken their relative investment performance, which creates a vicious cycle for some smaller asset management subsidiaries.

4 The advantages associated with the in-house management of pension assets include lower asset management fees, reduced costs for monitoring outside asset management companies and potential synergies between plan sponsors and asset management subsidiaries. The disadvantages include the need to establish an organizational structure for managing pension assets in-house and the need to offer competitive compensation packages to hire top fund managers. Many US pension plans that do not manage assets on their own cited the compensation issue as their main reason for not doing so.

5 One of the advantages of establishing an asset management subsidiary is that companies can create compensation arrangements for the subsidiary's fund managers that are independent of the parent company's salary structure. Other advantages are that asset management subsidiaries can focus on the profitability of their core business and expand by managing assets for plan sponsors other than the parent.

Notwithstanding this asset management trend among US pension plans, it is unlikely that many corporate pension plans in Japan will manage their fund assets in-house. Accordingly, any impact on existing independent asset management companies will probably be limited. However, some Japanese corporate pension plans, mainly those with hundreds of billions of yen in assets under management and the confidence to manage their plan assets on their own, may nevertheless try to bring the asset management function in-house by designating some of their finance department employees as fund managers. Attempts to manage assets in-house would be meaningful even if in-house fund managers failed to achieve strong investment performance; the experience itself would be useful in evaluating and selecting outside asset management companies in the future. According to an in-house pension fund manager at Warner-Lambert, the pharmaceuticals company (now a part of Pfizer) decided to manage pension assets internally to better understand the mechanics of outside asset management companies. The manager said that through the experience of directly managing pension assets, the team would be better positioned to understand the asset management process and the underlying reasons outside asset management companies underperform or outperform and, hence, be better able to select outside asset management companies.

The Defined-Benefit Pension Law

The Defined-Benefit Pension Law took effect on 1 April 2002. The passage of this law marks a significant turning point because the legislation establishes a standardized framework for Japan's corporate pension system. With the introduction of the new law, tax-qualified pension plans will be eliminated by 2012, and the administration and management of both existing employees' pension fund programmes and new types of defined-benefit pension plans will be subject to the same set of regulations.

KEY PROVISIONS

The Defined-Benefit Pension Law provides for two new types of corporate pension plans in Japan: contract plans and fund plans. The contract pension plans are not separate corporate entities, whereas fund pension plans are. The new plans incorporate some of the characteristics of the two existing types of pension plans. Specifically, the contract plans offer the flexibility of the tax-qualified pension plans that stems from the mutual agreement between management and employees. In contrast, the fund plans include some of the requirements of employees' pension fund programmes.

With the establishment of the Defined-Benefit Pension Law, companies will be allowed to convert existing employees' pension fund programmes to either contract or fund programmes by returning to the government-run Employees' Pension Fund programme the substitutional component of these plans (which are the salary-linked portion administered by private sector companies). Following the implementation of the new law, four core types of corporate pension plans are likely to become available: contract plans, fund plans, employees' pension funds and defined-contribution plans. The first three plans are defined-benefit pension plans.

The Defined-Benefit Pension Law protects beneficiaries' interests by requiring companies to adequately fund pension obligations and stipulates a common set of rules regarding fiduciary responsibilities and information disclosure. In addition, to encourage the restructuring of corporate pension plans, the law allows companies to switch between employees' pension funds and defined-contribution pension plans.

FIDUCIARY RESPONSIBILITIES AND INFORMATION DISCLOSURE REQUIREMENTS

The new types of corporate pension plans are entities that are legally and physically separate from the plan sponsor in order to shield the pension plans from bankruptcy and other potential problems at the parent companies. Funding obligations, fiduciary responsibilities and information disclosure requirements are also an important part of the new corporate pension structure in terms of helping to protect the rights of pension plan beneficiaries.

The Defined-Benefit Pension Law delineates various responsibilities for companies (in the case of contract corporate pension plans) and pension fund directors (in the case of fund corporate pension plans) pertaining to the establishment of the plans, contributions, management of plan assets and administration of benefits. Both companies and pension fund directors must strictly comply with various laws and ordinances and the decisions made by the

Minister of Health, Labour and Welfare and must prudently fulfil their responsibilities for the benefit of plan beneficiaries (Art. 69 and 70). Fund directors must also abide by decisions made by each fund's board of representatives (Art. 70).

Companies with contract corporate pension funds may neither administer their pension plans for the benefit of themselves or a third party other than plan beneficiaries, nor specify how pension assets are managed or act in any way pertaining to the management of pension assets that is deemed inappropriate according to ordinances enacted by the Minister of Health, Labour and Welfare (Art. 69, Sect. 2). Pension fund directors are also prohibited from acting in any way that may result in a conflict of interest with plan beneficiaries (Art. 70, Sect. 2).

To manage their plan assets, companies with contract plans are required to hire independent entities, namely, trust companies (which would manage the plans based on a trust agreement), life insurance companies (based on an annuity policy) and the National Mutual Insurance Federation of Agricultural Cooperatives (based on an annuity policy) (Art. 65 and 66). Companies are also allowed to use investment advisory companies for managing pension assets that have been entrusted to trust companies (Art. 65, Sect. 2). In the case of fund corporate pension plans, assets can be managed in-house by depositing funds with financial institutions or trading marketable securities through securities companies (Art. 66, Sect. 4). Even if a plan sponsor decides to manage pension assets in-house, it is necessary to sign contracts with financial institutions to administer the assets (Art. 66, Sect. 5). Moreover, the in-house management of pension assets must be conducted with safety and efficiency, as stipulated by ordinance (Art. 67).

In addition to fulfilling fiduciary responsibilities, companies and corporate pension fund directors must provide beneficiaries with pension plan information (Art. 73). Also, because the government has the ability to change its policies on corporate pension plans in ways that may negatively impact on beneficiaries, such as a reduction in benefits, companies and pension fund directors are obligated to make an attempt to provide both plan participants and pensioners with relevant information (Art. 73 of the Defined-Benefit Pension Law and Art. 177, Sect. 2 of the Revised Employees' Pension Insurance Law).

According to the Defined-Benefit Pension Law, fiduciary responsibilities apply not only to companies and pension fund directors, but also to the entities that are entrusted with the management or administration of plan assets.

Asset management companies and investment advisory companies must comply with all relevant laws and abide by pension fund management contracts when managing the assets of contract pension plans and fulfilling their responsibilities for the benefit of plan beneficiaries (Art. 71). Similarly, entities that manage the assets of fund corporate pension plans must comply with all relevant laws and abide by pension asset management contracts in fulfilling their responsibilities for the benefit of plan beneficiaries (Art. 72).

With the revision of the Employees' Pension Insurance Law, fiduciary responsibilities now apply not only to pension fund directors but also to entities that manage the assets of employees' pension funds (Art. 136, Sect. 5 of the Employees' Pension Insurance Law). Specifically, fund management parties that have entered into trust agreements, insurance (including mutual insurance) policies, investment advisory agreements, investment methodology agreements and benefit/asset administration agreements are all required to act with loyalty and prudence for the benefit of plan beneficiaries.

ISSUES AND OUTLOOK FOR CORPORATE PENSION PLANS

The Defined-Benefit Pension Law is significant because it allows a company to structure its pension plan flexibly based on the company's growth phase and employees' various attitudes on employment. Nonetheless, this law remains incomplete insofar as a variety of issues are yet to be resolved. The Upper House approved eight supplementary resolutions on 25 May 2001, when it passed the Defined-Benefit Pension Law. The main supplementary resolutions included the possible adoption of a pension benefit guarantee system, improved enforcement of information disclosure requirements and fiduciary responsibilities on companies as well as entities entrusted with pension assets, and the need for establishing an adequate structure for smoothly switching pension plans from tax-qualified pension plans to other types of plans. Some of the key issues are as follows.

PORTABILITY

In recent years, the need to integrate corporate pension plans has rapidly increased as companies have reorganized to become more competitive on a global scale. Under the current corporate pension system in Japan, if a company with an employees' pension fund programme merges with a company with a tax-qualified pension plan, the tax-qualified pension plan must be discontinued and integrated into the employees' pension fund programme because companies are not allowed to convert employees' pension fund programmes into tax-qualified pension plans. Under the new corporate pension system, however, existing pension plans can be converted into either a contract pension plan or fund plan.

Establishing concrete rules for the restructuring of corporate pension plans in the case of corporate mergers and reorganizations is important. In light of the likelihood that mobility in Japan's labour market will increase as workers' attitudes toward employment become more diverse and corporate restructurings increase, the tax-free portability of pension plans[5] is likely to become a crucial factor. Japan's new corporate pension plans are not portable, and making them portable should be one of the government's top priorities in view of promoting the revitalization of the corporate sector.

MORAL HAZARD

The new Defined-Benefit Pension Law does not provide for the adoption of a pension benefit guarantee system, under which pension benefits would be guaranteed even if a plan sponsor were to go bankrupt. The idea of introducing such a system nevertheless continues to be on the agenda. Under the US system, centred on the PBGC, companies with adequately funded pension plans essentially bail out those with insolvent plans. A pension benefit guarantee system, however, undermines the principle that companies are responsible for meeting pension obligations and may create a moral hazard. Although the UK once considered establishing a similar system, it decided not to because of the significant financial burden that would be imposed on companies and concerns about the possible emergence of a moral hazard.

Japan's new contract and fund corporate pension plans are structured in a way that protects plan beneficiaries. Because contract plans are funded through independent financial institutions and fund plans are legal entities separate from the plan sponsor, creditors of bankrupt companies are unable to claim pension assets. In addition,

---

5 Specifically, portability refers to the ability of individuals to maintain pension assets in their own accounts even if they switch employers.

strict pension funding requirements mean it is possible to prevent corporate pension plans from suddenly becoming insolvent. Therefore, Japan should probably follow the example of the UK and not adopt a pension benefit guarantee system so as to minimize the type of moral hazard that exists in the US pension system as a result of the PBGC. The Japan Federation of Economic Organizations (Keidanren), one of Japan's most powerful business lobbying groups, expressed its opposition to a pension benefit guarantee system in its 24 January 2001 'Reiteration of requests concerning the Corporate Pension Law (tentative name)'.

CONVERSIONS

Under the Defined-Benefit Pension Law, companies will be allowed to convert existing employees' pension fund programmes to either contract or fund plans by returning to the government-run Employees' Pension Fund programme the substitutional component of these plans. One sticking point concerns how plan assets covering this portion – equal to the actuarial reserve – will be returned to the government. The assets can be transferred as cash or in kind, that is, domestic government bonds, stocks or other marketable securities (Art. 114). If stocks are transferred, the government is likely to stipulate, by ordinance, that only a combination of stocks that track the Tokyo Stock Price Index (TOPIX) can be accepted.

The new law also states that companies intending to promptly return the substitutional component of the employees' pension fund programme to the government will be allowed to stop funding that portion if they obtain the consent of the pension funds' board of representatives and the approval of the Ministry of Health, Labour and Welfare. Companies, however, will probably not return the substitutional component of employees' pension funds until the autumn of 2003 because of administrative delays relating to the need to reconcile each company's employees' pension fund records with Social Insurance Agency records to determine the correct amount of benefits for each plan beneficiary.

Although the Defined-Benefit Pension Law will allow companies to convert their existing pension plans to the new plans, the actual procedures necessary to complete conversions will largely depend on various government ordinances, such as those issued by the Ministry of Health, Labour and Welfare. It is important, therefore, for the government to make it easy for companies to promptly return the substitutional component of employees' pension funds.

TAXATION ISSUES

Significant tax benefits are necessary to prompt companies to quickly adopt the new pension plans in Japan. Specifically, pension contributions as well as returns on plan assets should be exempt from taxation, and only benefit distributions should be taxable. Currently, pension contributions are a tax-deductible expense for companies, and income taxes on accrued pension benefits are deferred for participants until they receive the distributions. Pension assets, however, are subject to a special corporate tax in Japan. The argument for this tax is that because taxes on pension benefits are deferred until distributions are made, it is necessary to impose a tax to compensate for the deferred tax revenue on interest income. This special corporate tax rate is quite high, at more than 1% of the amount of pension assets, because the rate was determined when interest rates were relatively high. No other countries impose such a tax on pension assets. Because the tax could serve as a disincentive against the adoption of the new corporate pension plans, the government should eliminate the special corporate tax immediately, starting in fiscal 2002.

The new corporate pension plans are likely to minimize the risk that pension plans will become even more underfunded as a result of companies' returning the substitutional component of their employees' pension funds. In addition, the new programmes will give companies flexibility in designing pension plans, which are one of the main components of employee compensation packages. Specifically, companies can create pension plans based on their growth phase, their employees' increasingly diverse attitudes towards employment and future corporate restructuring plans. To maximize the potential advantages of the new corporate pension plans in Japan, the government must consider the issues mentioned above as well as any other problems that may emerge after the new pension plans are put in place so that they are addressed as promptly as possible.

Defined-contribution pension plans

Having looked in the preceding section at the corporate pension plan business in Japan, including defined-benefit plans, and the changes in the legal framework for pension plans, this section turns to defined-contribution pension plans, which are considered to be Japanese versions of 401(k) plans.

THE DEFINED-CONTRIBUTION PENSION LAW

In response to changes in employees' attitudes toward employment and the increasing diversity of employee compensation packages, the Defined-Contribution Pension Law provides portability for defined-contribution plan assets. With the introduction of defined-contribution pension plans, Japanese companies will be able to choose from three types of pension plan: employees' pension fund programmes, the new defined-benefit pension plans and defined-contribution pension plans. The defined-contribution pension plans are expected to enable companies to flexibly adjust employee compensation packages to achieve various business objectives, such as restructuring their operations and hiring top-notch talent. Under defined-contribution pension plans, corporate contributions are predetermined, and plan participants are fully responsible for deciding how to invest their retirement assets. Consequently, defined-contribution pension plans should help to minimize pension-related burdens for companies that stem from an increase in pension obligations or contributions as a result of changes to the composition of plan participants.

The three main aspects of the Defined-Contribution Pension Law are considered below: the portability of defined-contribution pension plans; the administration and management of corporate pension plans; and the fiduciary responsibilities imposed on companies.

PORTABILITY

Two types of defined-contribution pension plan currently exist in Japan: corporate and individual plans. In corporate pension plans, companies[6] make contributions either independently or together with employees. In individual plans, self-employed workers and other individuals make contributions themselves to the plans, which are administered by the National Pension Fund Association (Art. 2, Sect. 1–4 of the Defined-Contribution Pension Law). Table 5.2 provides

6 'Companies' are those entities to which Art. 6, Sect. 1 of the Employees' Pension Insurance Law applies, and those entities that have been approved as companies under Art. 6, Sect. 3 of the Employees' Pension Insurance Law.

Table 5.2 Outline of defined-contribution pension plans in Japan

	Corporate	Individual
Plan administrator	Companies (business owners)	National Pension Fund Association
Plan agreement	Mutual agreement drafted by company management and employees	Agreement created by the National Pension Fund Association (without the involvement of plan participants)
Contributors	Companies only (plan participants are not allowed to make contributions)	Plan participants
Contribution amounts	Determined based on the method specified in each plan agreement	Can be specified and changed by plan participants based on the plan agreement
Eligibility	Employees of companies with corporate defined-contribution plans who are under 60 years of age (classified as Category 2 participants in the National Pension Fund)	Self-employed individuals (classified as Category 1 participants in the National Pension Fund) and employees of companies who do not have corporate pension plans
Selection of asset managers and plan administrators	Companies select asset managers and plan administrators (companies may decide to manage assets and administer the plans on their own)	National Pension Fund Association selects plan custodians and delegates asset management responsibility to financial institutions (plan participants specify how their retirement assets are managed)
Distribution terms	Distributions are made when plan participants reach 60 years of age, become seriously disabled or pass away	
Distribution options	Lump-sum payment or annuities once plan participants reach 60 years of age; a lump-sum death benefit	Lump-sum payment or annuities if disabled; and
Tax benefits	Contributions are a tax-deductible expense for companies. Limit on the amount of contributions that can be deducted from taxable income per participant per year (corporate): For employees of companies with corporate pension plans: ¥216000. For employees of companies with no corporate pension plans: ¥432000	Limit on the amount of contributions that can be deducted from taxable income per participant per year (individual): Self-employed participants: ¥816000 (this figure includes contributions to the National Pension Fund). For those not eligible to participate in corporate pension plans: ¥180000

an outline of these two defined-contribution pension plans. In both plans, the participants have their own accounts and make investment decisions on their own. Retirement benefits therefore vary depending on the investment performance of each account. Three types of benefit are possible: an old-age pension benefit, once participants reach 60 years of age; a disability benefit; and a lump-sum death benefit (Art. 33–42).

Corporate defined-contribution plans are established and administered by companies with the consent of employees. Individual defined-contribution plans, on the other hand, are open to individuals classified as Category 1 participants in the National Pension Fund, such as self-employed individuals and employees not eligible to participate in their companies' employees' pension fund or other corporate pension plan (Art. 62).[7] To participate in an individual pension plan, individuals must submit applications to the National Pension Fund Association, designate a plan custodian, specify how the pension assets should be managed and make monthly plan contributions.

With defined-contribution pension plans, plan participants have their own accounts, decide how to manage their pension assets, and can roll over pension assets into a different plan, tax free, if a participant changes employers, given that certain criteria are met.[8] Plan participants are allowed to roll over assets from one corporate defined-contribution plan to another, from a corporate plan to an individual plan and from an individual plan to a corporate plan whenever their job situation changes (Art. 25, 73 and 80–85).[9]

---

7 Those groups classified as Category 3 participants under the National Pension Law, such as public servants and full-time homemakers, as well as those participants in corporate pension plans are not eligible to set up individual defined-contribution pension plans. For instance, an employee of a company that has an employees' pension fund programme but has not adopted a defined-contribution pension plan is not allowed to set up an individual defined-contribution pension plan.

8 Employees who have worked at a company for more than three years have the right to receive distributions of their assets when they leave a corporate defined-contribution plan as a result of a job change (Art. 4, Sect. 1, Para. 7).

9 But if a new employer does not have a corporate defined-contribution plan, plan assets must be rolled over to an individual plan. If a new employer has a corporate defined-contribution plan, contributions to an individual plan are not permitted.

MANAGEMENT AND ADMINISTRATION OF CORPORATE
DEFINED-CONTRIBUTION PLANS

Companies are ultimately responsible for managing and administering corporate defined-contribution plans. These responsibilities include not only establishing plan agreements and making contributions on behalf of participants but also helping employees to make their own investment decisions, providing updates on investment performance and administering and reporting plan distributions.[10] Because of the considerable administrative burdens involved and the specialized knowledge needed to manage pension plans, companies are allowed to hire outside firms to manage their plans, specifically, to maintain plan-participant records, send out notifications to plan participants and select investment strategies (these plan custodians are discussed in more detail later) (Art. 2, Sect. 7, and Art. 7, Sect. 1 and 2).[11]

Companies must take the steps shown in Fig. 5.8 to establish and administer corporate pension plans.

Plan agreement

To establish a corporate pension plan, companies are required to obtain the consent of employees (hereafter referred to as 'plan participants'[12]), establish a plan agreement and obtain approval from the Minister of Health, Labour and Welfare. The plan agreement covers a wide range of issues, such as eligibility criteria for participants, the method for calculating contributions, investment options and investment guidelines, distribution amounts and payment methods,

10 Companies must keep plan accounting records and file plan status reports with the Ministry of Health, Labour and Welfare (Art. 49 and 50).
11 The National Pension Fund Association is required to delegate the custodial management of individual defined-contribution plans to outside entities (Art. 60, Sect. 1), which in turn are allowed to outsource part of these functions to other companies (Art. 60, Sect. 3). The National Pension Fund Association can also outsource some operations, such as the administration of plan assets, to outside financial institutions (Art. 61 and 77).
12 'Participants' include full-time homemakers who left the work force before reaching 60 years of age and are not eligible to set up individual defined-contribution plans and individuals who have reached 60 years of age and are therefore ineligible to participate in corporate defined-contribution plans but who still make investment decisions for a portion of their pension assets (Art. 15).

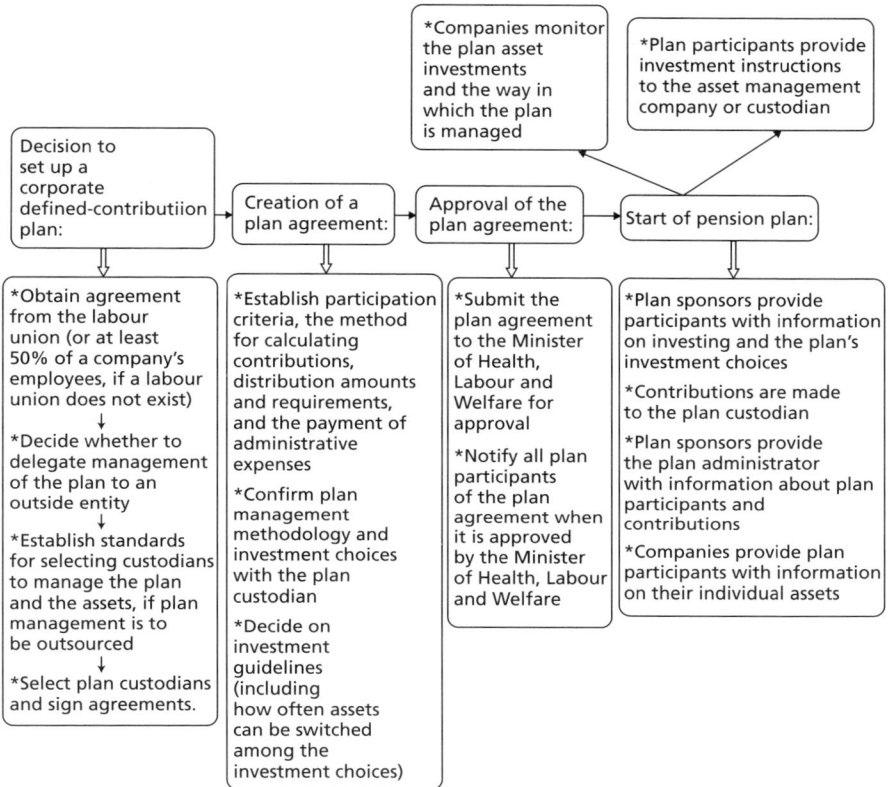

5.8 Procedures for establishing and administering corporate defined-contribution plans.

whether plan management responsibilities are outsourced and the determination of administrative expenses (Art. 3, Sect. 3). In addition, companies must indicate investment options for their plans and decide how frequently plan participants can make changes to their investments.

Companies that decide to use outside entities for pension plan management should establish criteria and procedures for selecting management companies based on their fiduciary responsibility to perform their duties with loyalty (which is discussed in more detail later) prior to finalizing a contract (Art. 43, 44, 99 and 100).

Companies are obligated to make the plan agreement available to plan participants as soon as it is approved by the Minister of Health, Labour and Welfare (Art. 4, Sect. 3).

Investment decisions

In a defined-contribution pension plan, plan participants make their own investment decisions regarding their pension assets.[13] Therefore, companies must provide appropriate support for plan participants with little investment experience. Such support includes educating participants about appropriate investment products and basic investment principles, as well as providing them with sufficient information to help them manage their pension assets. Companies are required by law to help plan participants make sound investment decisions by providing basic information about asset management and considering other similar measures as needed (Art. 22). Although such services are typically not included in plan management responsibilities, companies can have outside firms handle these responsibilities (Art. 97).

As part of the provision of appropriate support for plan participants to make investment decisions on their own, it is very important for companies to offer appropriate investment choices. The Defined-Contribution Pension Law requires plan sponsors and plan custodians to offer at least three of the following investment choices: savings deposits, trusts, investment trusts, stocks, bonds, life insurance policies and non-life insurance policies. In addition, each plan must offer at least one choice for which principal is guaranteed, and plan participants must be allowed to make changes to their investment choices at least once a quarter.[14] The Minister of Health, Labour and Welfare will approve only plan agreements submitted by plan sponsors that meet the above criteria (Art. 23, Sect. 1 and Art. 4, Sect. 1).

Plan sponsors and plan custodians are required to select investment options based on a specialized knowledge of asset management (Art. 23, Sect. 1 and 2). They are also required to educate plan participants about the risk–return characteristics of different types of investment options and to provide them with other information necessary to make appropriate investment decisions (Art. 24). The

---

13 Although plan custodians are allowed to indicate ways to invest assets to plan participants, they are prohibited from recommending specific investments to plan participants (Art. 100, Para. 6).

14 Plan participants specify their investment preferences by choosing at least one of the investment options offered by the plan custodian, determining the amount to be invested in each option and informing the plan administrator about their investment decisions (Art. 25, Sect. 2).

procedures for changing the plan's investment options or modifying the plan agreement are tedious – plan sponsors must obtain the consent of their labour unions (or if a labour union does not exist, the consent of at least 50% of the plan participants) and approval from the Minister of Health, Labour and Welfare. Therefore, when companies initially set up their plans, plan sponsors must carefully choose the plan's investment options, a key factor for participants.

Record-keeping

With defined-contribution pension plans, plan assets need to be tracked for each plan participant. Companies must keep records of plan participants' names, addresses, account balances and other relevant information. They must also notify the plan custodian of the investment decisions made by plan participants and determine which plan participants are eligible to receive pension benefits (Art. 25).

Companies that outsource this function are required to provide record-keeping companies with original documents with information on plan participants, such as name, address, the start or end date of eligibility and account balance. Companies must notify record-keeping firms of any changes in the required information about plan participants and report the amount of plan contributions (Art. 16, Sect. 1 and Art. 18). Plan participants are to receive investment reports from the record-keeping companies at least once a year (Art. 27).

Protection of plan assets

Companies are required to contract with asset management institutions, such as trust banks and life insurance companies, to protect plan assets (Art. 8) from the potential bankruptcy of the plan sponsor and other contingencies by legally and physically separating the assets from the plan sponsors' assets. Asset management companies are typically responsible, based on the contracts with plan sponsors, for a multitude of tasks, such as receiving monthly contributions from the plan sponsor, transferring contributions to the designated financial institutions for management based on plan participants' investment guidelines from the record-keeping firms, and paying pension benefits to retired participants.

In order to eliminate any potential conflicts of interest, companies must establish – and explain to plan participants – objective criteria and procedures for selecting asset management companies similar to those used to choose plan custodians.

FIDUCIARY RESPONSIBILITIES

In these ways, plan sponsors, plan custodians and asset management companies are required to abide by their fiduciary responsibilities of performing their duties with loyalty and prudence based on a familiarity with such matters (Art. 23, Sect. 2, and Art. 43, 44, 99 and 100). The purpose of this requirement is to ensure that the plan sponsors fulfil their responsibility to properly manage the defined-contribution pension plans by making plan participants fully aware that they are responsible for their own investment decisions, and establishing various procedures relating to asset management.

The Defined-Contribution Pension Law specifies rules of conduct for plan sponsors and plan administrators, including a prohibition on activities that may result in conflicts of interest, and stipulates administrative directives in the event of violations.[15] Plan sponsors must strictly comply with the relevant laws, administrative directives and plan agreement, and perform their duties with loyalty to the plan beneficiaries. Some of the rules of conduct stipulated by Art. 43 for ensuring the protection of assets in corporate defined-contribution plans are as follows:

■ companies are not allowed to outsource the management of pension plans and assets for their own benefit or for a third party other than plan beneficiaries;

■ companies that do not outsource asset management cannot select specific investment offerings for their own benefit or for a third party other than plan beneficiaries.

---

15 Companies that manage their pension plans on their own must follow the same principles that apply to outside plan administrators. In addition, they are required to file reports on the operating status of their plans and are subject to inquiries and audits by the Ministry of Health, Labour and Welfare (Art. 51). If such inquiries and audits by the ministry indicate that a company did not comply with the plan agreement or administrative directives, or has improperly managed the plan, the ministry may order the company to make the necessary adjustments or improve plan operations (Art. 52). In extreme cases, the Minister of Health, Labour and Welfare may revoke its approval of the plan agreement (Art. 52, Sect. 2).

Plan custodians[16] are also prohibited from the following types of conduct:[17]

- including in plan custodial agreements provisions for the compensation, in whole or in part, of any losses incurred by plan participants;

- including in plan custodial agreements provisions for special benefits to plan sponsors or participants;

- directly or indirectly offering to plan participants or a third party asset-related profits to compensate, in whole or in part, any losses incurred by plan participants or to enhance any profits of plan participants that arise in the process of the administering of the plan (this prohibition does not apply to cases in which plan custodians are responsible for the losses accidentally incurred);

- making false statements or not properly disclosing factual information concerning matters deemed by ordinances to be important and material to the decision by plan sponsors to hire a plan custodian;

- recommending specific investment options to plan participants with the intention of benefiting themselves or a third party other than plan beneficiaries;

- advising plan participants to select or not select particular investment options (this principle does not apply to investment advisory companies or investment-related companies other than plan custodians).

In these ways, the Defined-Contribution Pension Law also prohibits plan custodians from conduct that may conflict with the

---

16 Defined-contribution pension plan custodians must register with the appropriate ministry (Art. 88). The appropriate ministry regulates these companies by reviewing reports on the status of plan operations and has the right to conduct inquiries and on-site audits of the companies. If deemed necessary, the appropriate ministry can order the plan custodians to halt operations, revoke their registrations and impose other administrative penalties (Art. 102–104).

17 Ministerial ordinances prohibit plan sponsors from conduct that could fail to sufficiently protect the interests of plan beneficiaries, hinder the fair administration of the plans or cause a loss of confidence in the management of the plans. Violations of these ordinances are subject to penalties (Art. 102–104, Para. 7).

interests of plan beneficiaries. The law nevertheless does allow banks and other ordinance-designated financial institutions that can offer investment options to serve as plan custodians (Art. 88, Sect. 2). In addition, it does not prohibit plan custodians from both offering investment products as well as managing plan assets, although the firms must avoid violating their obligation to perform their duties with loyalty to the plan beneficiaries. When financial institutions serve as plan custodians and select investment options in place of the plan sponsor, they must be careful to do so in the interests of plan beneficiaries. If they select their own investment products, the plan custodians must be cautiously aware of potential conflicts of interest arising from their position of receiving management fees from plan participants. Companies, therefore, must receive appropriate explanations from the plan custodian showing not only that the selection of investment options was based on professional expertise but also that no conflicts of interest were involved.

Companies would probably be liable for any unavoidable losses incurred by plan participants as a result of a conflicts of interest stemming from their selection or inadequate monitoring of the plan custodian.

BUSINESS OPPORTUNITIES

In anticipation of the enactment of the Defined-Contribution Pension Law on 1 April 2002, banks, securities companies, insurance companies, asset management companies, consulting firms and other types of financial institution started to develop various financial products and services for the new defined-contribution plans. Some established plan custodial capabilities within their parent operations or as part of group companies, while others focused on developing investment products and consulting services. The entire financial services industry in Japan appeared to be preparing to get involved in the defined-contribution plan business. Some non-financial companies, such as Hitachi, Toyota Motor and Skylark, had already announced plans to establish defined-contribution plans.

These moves are likely to gain momentum, but a number of important factors need to be carefully considered regarding the decision to establish defined-contribution plans. Plan sponsors must offer appropriate support for participants in corporate defined-contribution plans since the participants are responsible for making investment decisions on their own. Specifically, plan sponsors need to educate plan participants about investing and provide them with sufficient investment information. And it is also extremely important for them to carefully select investment choices for the plan because participants can choose, based on the investment-related information provided by the plan sponsor, only from the financial products offered in the plan. Plan custodians (including plan sponsors that opt to handle custodial responsibilities on their own) should thus carefully select investment options based on professional expertise. Japan's Defined-Contribution Pension Law requires plan sponsors to adhere to their duty of loyalty to plan beneficiaries when selecting a plan custodian. But whereas plan sponsors are supposed to select investment products under ERISA, this Japanese law allows financial services companies that provide investment products, either directly or through affiliates, to serve as custodians of defined-contribution plans, either directly or through affiliates. In this case, the plan custodian would provide as well as select investment products, in place of the plan sponsor. Internal controls are thus needed to make sure no conflicts of interest arise.

For a plan custodian to offer investment products from multiple financial services companies would be appropriate, but if it offered only its own financial products or those of its affiliates, it would be highly questionable whether the custodian acted solely for the benefit of plan participants. In the US, a 401(k) plan sponsor can offer a package of investment products from a single financial services company, provided that the plan sponsor – and not the financial services company offering the investment products – makes the decision.

Based on ERISA principles, on which Japan's Defined-Contribution Pension Law is modelled, the best solution for avoiding potential conflicts of interest is for plan sponsors to manage their plans and choose investment options on their own. Yet financial institutions undeniably possess greater expertise in selecting investment products than do Japanese non-financial companies. The second best solution for minimizing potential conflicts of interest is for non-financial companies to outsource the management of their pension plans to companies that are independent of financial service providers. The number of such independent plan custodians, however, is not likely to increase significantly, at least in the near term. Consequently, a practical solution for most Japanese companies at the moment is to hire financial services companies to administer their pension plans and choose the investment products.

Companies must choose plan custodians carefully and recognize the potential conflicts of interest that may arise if they decide on a financial services company that provides as well as selects investment products. A plan sponsor is ultimately responsible for choosing an appropriate plan custodian on behalf of the interests of plan participants, even if the plan custodian is allowed to select the investment products. It is important, therefore, for companies to make clear who is responsible for selecting a plan custodian and what the selection criteria and procedures are. One of the methods for choosing plan custodians is through a request for proposal, by which plan sponsors solicit proposals that include information about the services each custodian can provide.

In the US, the 401(k) business has developed into a major segment of the financial services market. Hundreds of thousands of 401(k) plans have been established, with total plan assets of about $1.7 tr. at the end of 2000, despite the significant fiduciary responsibilities imposed on companies. It is hoped that defined-contribution pension plans will do as well in Japan as they have in the US.

6 Investment trusts

Infrastructure for investment trusts

This chapter summarizes the development of the market for Japanese investment trusts.[1] Major deregulatory measures are reviewed along with other recent developments that either have had or are likely to have a significant impact on the market.

A HISTORY OF INVESTMENT TRUST REFORMS

In 1941, Nomura Securities established the first investment trust for the Japanese market. During World War II, securities companies stopped establishing investment trusts, but with the implementation of the Securities Investment Trust Law in 1951, seven financial institutions, including Nomura Securities, Yamaichi Securities, Nikko Securities and Daiwa Securities, once again began setting up investment trusts. The legal basis regarding offerings, asset management practices and the marketing of investment trusts is stipulated in the Securities Investment Trust Law and the Securities and Exchange Law, as well as in various government and ministerial ordinances and in the self-imposed regulations of the Investment Trusts Association Japan.

Drastic reforms were introduced in 1995 to improve the infrastructure for investment trusts in Japan (see Table 6.1). In that year, the Securities Investment Trust Law was revised to create more

---

1 Investment trusts in Japan are similar to mutual funds in the US but are structured on the basis of trust agreements.

Table 6.1 History of Japanese investment trusts

	Milestones	Major changes
1951	Establishment of Securities Investment Trust Law	
1953	Partial revision of Securities Investment Trust Law	Licensing system replaces registration system
1960	Investment trust management companies spun off from securities companies to become 'independent' entities	
1967	Partial revision of Securities Investment Trust Law	Establishment of rules governing activities of investment trust management companies, including those concerning fiduciary responsibilities
1984	Investment trust management companies permitted to enter investment advisory business	
1990	Foreign companies granted licences for conducting investment trust management business in Japan	
1992	Introduction of money market funds (MMFs)	
1993	Investment trust management companies allowed to directly sell investment trusts	
1995	Major changes to Securities Investment Trust Law	Deregulation of investment trust management business and improvement in disclosure of investment trust information
	Fund management companies allowed to offer both investment trust and discretionary investment management services	
	Introduction of listed Nikkei 300 Stock Index-linked investment trusts	
1997	Investment trust companies begin to sell investment trusts at banks' branch offices (by leasing the space)	
1998	Revision of Securities Investment Trust Law	Introduction of corporation-type and privately placed investment trusts
	Securities Investment Trust Law renamed the Law Concerning Securities Investment Trust and Securities Investment Companies	Notification/approval system replaces licensing system
		Financial institutions allowed to sell investment trusts over the counter
2000	Law Concerning Securities Investment Trust and Securities Investment Companies changed to Law on Investment Trusts and Investment Companies	Investment trusts allowed to include assets other than marketable securities, such as real estate

Source: Nomura, based on *Securities Market in Japan 2000* (Japan Securities Research Institute).

flexible asset management rules for investment trusts and to improve the disclosure of investment trust information. As part of the financial Big Bang programme of deregulation in 1998, the Securities Investment Trust Law was substantially revised and renamed the Law Concerning Securities Investment Trusts and Securities Investment Companies. Then, in 2000, when the law was further revised extensively to allow assets other than marketable securities to be included in investment trusts, it was renamed the Law on Investment Trusts and Investment Companies. The details of the new law will be discussed in a later section.

RECENT INVESTMENT TRUST REFORMS IN JAPAN

Previously, investment trust management companies were required to obtain a licence from the Ministry of Finance. With the revision of the Securities Investment Trust Law in December 1998, however, they are now permitted to offer investment trust management services provided that notification is given to and approval received from the Financial Services Agency (FSA). Other recent regulatory changes include allowing banks and insurance companies to market investment trusts and the introduction of corporate and privately placed investment trusts. In addition, investment trust companies are now allowed to hire investment management subadvisors and to offer wrap accounts. But issues that remained unresolved in 1998 included the possible introduction of an auditing system and the need for even better disclosure.

To improve disclosure, basic fund prospectuses were replaced by more detailed and formal prospectuses in December 2000.[2] Investment trust management companies are now obligated to distribute this new type of prospectus to investors when offering or marketing their funds, but an abridged, easier-to-understand version can also be provided. Moreover, prospectuses can be made available electronically, making it possible for investment trust management companies to market funds more easily over the Internet. In addition to the distribution of prospectuses, the new Securities Investment Trust Law requires investment trust management companies to issue detailed investment reports each fiscal year.

2 Henceforth, unless otherwise noted, 'prospectus' refers to the more recent type of prospectus, which includes much of the same material submitted in securities filings and the complete text of a fund's bylaws.

To improve disclosure, an auditing system was recently introduced whereby third-party certified public accountants audit investment trust management companies. Bond investment trusts used to value their assets at cost but now measure them (including unlisted bonds) at fair value. Furthermore, even though only a portion of the holdings of bond investment trust funds were previously disclosed, complete disclosure is now mandatory. The expected yield for medium-term government bond funds, the most popular type of bond investment trust in Japan, had been relatively high thanks to a large amount of unrealized gains for most funds. With the introduction of mark-to-market accounting, however, yields on medium-term government bond funds will probably be on a par with those for ordinary bond investment trusts. As a result, some medium-term government bond funds are expected to close down and return assets to investors in the near future.

While continuing to deregulate the domestic investment trust industry, securities regulators have been encouraging the industry to establish self-regulatory measures so as to provide protection to investors. In addition, the taxation system for investment trusts has changed. Previously, capital gains for open stock investment trusts were taxed based on the average value of total principal invested in a fund (this average applied to every trust certificate holder). To improve the transparency of the taxation system for investment trusts, this taxation method was replaced in April 2000 with a system whereby gains are taxed based on each trust certificate holder's actual cost basis.

The November 2000 revision of the Securities Investment Trust Law resulted in a number of key changes. First, the revised version of the law allows investment trusts to hold assets other than marketable securities. They can now invest in real estate, property leases, land rights, real estate investment trusts (REITs) and real estate partnerships. Second, investment trust management companies are no longer required to provide specific instructions to trust banks concerning the management of trust assets. Third, fiduciary responsibilities of investment management firms have been clarified. The new law stipulates that important changes to fund bylaws must be approved by a majority of trust beneficiaries. In addition, the law grants beneficiaries who oppose any changes the right to redeem their investments in the fund. The new law also clarifies the meaning of fiduciary responsibility by specifying the duty of care along with the previous duty of loyalty, and requires investment trust management companies to pay damages if they are negligent about their fiduciary responsibilities. Fourth, fund assets must be properly and professionally valued by third-party specialists, such as lawyers, certified public accountants, auditors and real estate appraisers, at the time of acquisition and sale.

THE IMPROVED MARKET ENVIRONMENT FOR INVESTMENT TRUSTS

Reforms of investment trust regulations have encouraged new entrants to participate in the investment trust market, which until 1998 had been limited to investment management companies and trust banks. As noted below, these new entrants have offered investors new ways to buy into funds, and some filter out the large volume of information on investment trusts. Another positive development is the introduction of a defined-contribution pension plan system in Japan (see Chapter 5). Because investment trusts are particularly suitable investment vehicles for these pension plans, the number of investors in investment trusts is likely to increase.

INVESTMENT TRUST MARKET PARTICIPANTS

At October 2000, the Investment Trusts Association Japan had more than 70 member investment trust management companies. To become an investment trust management company, a shareholder-owned corporation must have at least ¥100 m in capital and must obtain approval from the FSA. Recently, an increasing number of overseas financial institutions have been entering Japan's investment trust market. Also, financial institutions are now allowed to provide both investment trust and discretionary investment management services through asset management subsidiaries. These developments have spurred mergers between investment trust management companies and investment advisory companies, as well as mergers between Japanese and overseas financial institutions.

The leading Japanese investment trust management companies (based on net assets under management) are affiliates of Japanese securities firms, such as Nomura, Nikko and Daiwa. Overseas financial institutions, many of which are well known outside Japan but not in Japan, have moved into Japan's investment trust market to take advantage of the expanding market. At the end of 2000, Fidelity Investments was the largest mutual fund company in the world, with about ¥94 tr. in assets under management, followed by the Vanguard Group, with about ¥64 tr. under management, and

Table 6.2 Breakdown of investment trust sales by sales channels, based on outstanding net assets (%)

	Banks	**Securities companies**	**Direct sales by investment trust management companies**
Dec 99	5.5	90.3	4.2
Jun 00	8.8	87.4	3.7
Oct 00	9.5	87.2	3.3

Source: Same as Table 6.1.

Table 6.3 Survey of preferred way of investing in investment trusts, by age of head of household (%)

	Banks	**Securities companies**	**Internet**	**Direct sales by investment trust management companies**	**Other**
Total	31.9	29.2	10.9	8.4	27.9
20–29	24.4	8.9	11.1	11.1	48.9
30–39	28.6	20.1	21.2	9.3	33.1
40–49	35.5	22.6	17.9	7.7	28.5
50–59	32.9	30.9	7.4	9.0	28.3
60–69	32.4	36.2	3.8	7.6	23.2
70 and over	26.9	46.2	2.9	7.0	21.6

Source: Investment Trusts Association Japan survey conducted in November 2000.

Capital Research & Management, with about ¥41 tr. under management. Nomura Asset Management, which has about ¥15 tr. in assets under management, is the largest investment trust management company in Japan and is ranked 13th globally. Nomura Asset Management's Japan Strategic Stock Fund is the largest investment trust in Japan, with net assets of about ¥780 bn at April 2001, followed by the Nikko Japan Open Fund (¥380 bn) and the Fidelity Japan Fund (¥370 bn).

As mentioned before, investment trusts can now be purchased in an increased number of ways. They were previously available only through the branch offices of securities companies, but now investment trust management companies, banks and insurance companies offer them, and some are even available online. Online fund marketers are able to offer funds at reduced or no sales loads by providing customer service through call centres. As shown in Tables 6.2 and 6.3, at October 2000, 87.2% of the outstanding net assets of investment trust funds came from sales by securities companies; only 9.5% from sales by banks; and 3.3% from sales by investment trust management companies.

Nonetheless, a survey conducted by the Investment Trusts Association Japan concerning preferred methods of investing in investment trusts by age group suggests that these trends may change. Overall, respondents expressed a strong preference for investing in investment trusts through banks. Older people, who tend to have relatively high savings rates, expressed a preference for investing through banks and securities companies, but people in their 30s and 40s were inclined to invest in funds online. These survey results suggest that marketing investment trusts through a variety of sales channels may be the best way to meet the needs of investors.

In addition to offering investment trusts through an increased number of venues, securities companies now offer consolidated investment accounts to provide customers with higher value-added services. These accounts enable customers to conveniently trade a wide range of financial products, including investment trusts, and also allow cash to earn interest in money reserve funds (MRFs). Securities companies also offer a dollar-cost averaging programme that allows investors to make systematic, monthly investments of as little as ¥10000 in certain eligible funds. Moreover, to expand their customer bases and promote long-term investing in investment trusts among individual investors, securities companies have been increasingly focused on product development.

In the past, the main sources of information about investment trusts have been basic fund prospectuses and other information from asset management companies, as well as newspaper advertisements and magazine articles about personal finance. Given the many thousands of investment trusts that are available to investors, evaluating and selecting investment trusts would be difficult without uniform standards and the advice of professionals. To make it easier for investors to select investment trusts, the Investment Trusts Association Japan decided in 1997 to set up a centralized source for fund prospectuses and investment reports issued by investment trusts. In addition, it created a database to supply information to organizations that independently evaluate investment trusts. By the end of 2000, several dozen independent rating organizations had become members of the Investment Trusts Association Japan, including Morningstar Japan, Standard & Poor's, Rating and Investment Information and Nomura Research Institute. Other types of member companies and institutions include those that specialize in evaluating investment fund performance, assigning ratings to bond investment trusts and managing wrap accounts. Through both specialized magazines and the Internet, these companies disseminate information to individual investors as well as to companies that market financial products.

THE RELATIONSHIP BETWEEN PENSION FUNDS AND INVESTMENT TRUSTS

In the future, pension assets are more likely to be invested through investment trusts. Two reforms are expected to accelerate this trend. The first is deregulation of the self-management of assets in defined-benefit corporate pension plans. In conjunction with this deregulatory move, corporate pension plan sponsors will have the option of investing the assets in investment trusts, thus giving the sponsors a wide variety of investment choices regardless of the amount of assets in the pension plans. As a result, the sponsors can achieve the same benefits they had when they chose investment management companies. Some small pension plans have taken advantage of the new rules to simplify their asset management operations by using investment trusts that rely on multiple fund managers.

The second major reform that should stimulate growth of the investment trust market is the Defined-Contribution Pension Law, which took effect in October 2001.[3] The law is one of the main pillars of pension-related reform in Japan, and allows for the establishment of defined-contribution pension plans – similar to the 401(k) retirement plans in the US – that will enable employees both to select from a number of investment trusts and variable annuities, including principal-guaranteed financial products, and to trade individual stocks and bonds. The growth of defined-contribution retirement plans in the US and Europe fostered the expansion of the investment trust markets in these countries. Because of the increasing size of Japan's pension assets, the introduction of defined-contribution pension plans should likewise help expand the size of the domestic investment trust market.

Funds of funds, or investment trusts in which a portfolio of funds is selected by experts, are likely to play an increasingly significant role in Japan. These funds are particularly well suited to Japanese investors because many people in Japan are not well informed about investing basics. In general, two types of funds of funds exist: so-called lifestyle funds, for which asset allocations are generally fixed, and life-cycle funds, for which asset allocations are automatically

---

3 See Chapter 5 for details.

adjusted with the passage of time. Life-cycle funds, which are also known as target-year funds, are appropriate for novice investors and for individuals with very little time to spare for managing investments; investors can simply select a fund with a target year close to their anticipated year of retirement and simply hold that same fund to maturity. For the last several years, many investment management companies have introduced funds of funds with various risk–return attributes, based on different mixes of stocks and bonds in the funds, in anticipation of the introduction of defined-contribution pension plans. At the end of April 2001, about 30 funds of funds were in existence, with combined assets of ¥200 bn. Each fund includes several funds with different risk–return attributes. About one-fifth of the funds of funds on the market are life-cycle funds.

Variable annuities, which were first sold in Japan in 1999, are yet another financial product option for defined-contribution pension plans that have been attracting attention recently. These annuities are insurance products with payouts that vary directly with the investment returns on invested premiums. Investors in variable annuities can choose from a number of funds with different risk characteristics and can switch between funds. At April 2002, 16 companies were offering 17 variable annuities products.

The introduction of defined-contribution pension plans should lead to increased awareness of the importance of providing information for evaluating funds and educating ordinary investors about investment trusts. In a defined-contribution pension plan, the administrator selects investment options and presents them to plan participants. Because fund administrators are obligated by fiduciary responsibility to choose plan options in a fair and transparent manner, they are likely to rely on independent institutions for information about funds and then to use this information to help participants select investments. And given the difficult task of educating plan participants with minimal investment experience or expertise, fund management companies are developing informational materials and programmes on investing and investment trusts.

FEE STRUCTURE AND TAXES

When investors put their money into investment trusts, they pay two types of fees: commissions and operating/management fees. The sales commission paid by investors to securities companies when they invest in an open investment trust ranges between 2% and 3% of the initial investment. Some securities companies, however, have recently waived this sales load. In addition to commissions, some fund management companies impose a redemption fee aimed at minimizing the volatility of fund assets as a result of short-term redemptions. Operating/management fees are indirectly paid by investors to the fund management companies, securities companies and trust banks; the fees range between 1% and 2% for actively managed funds and, generally, are less for index funds.

In the case of contractual, publicly offered stock investment trusts, individual investors pay a 5% consumption tax on commissions paid for purchases or redemptions of shares of an investment trust. They are also subject to a 20% withholding tax on fund distributions and a 20% withholding tax on the portion in excess of the initial investment when investors sell shares in these funds (the capital gain). Corporate open-end investment trusts are subject to withholding taxes of 20%, whereas closed-end funds are taxed the same way as individual stocks.

The investment trust market

Many types of investment trusts are available in Japan. As shown in Table 6.4, it is possible to broadly categorize Japanese investment trusts according to organizational structure and the specifics of how they operate.

INVESTMENT TRUST CATEGORIES

Two broad categories of investment trust exist in Japan: contractual and corporate. Contractual investment trusts are securities investment trusts, and corporate investment trusts are set up as corporations for managing investment assets. Contractual investment trusts are established on the basis of a trust agreement specifying the rights and obligations of the trustor (an investment management company in charge of the investment assets), the trustee (a trust bank) and beneficiaries (the investors). Furthermore, contractual investment trusts can be broken down into those in which the trustor specifies the way in which assets are managed and those in which the trustee is entirely responsible for managing the assets. In contrast, corporate investment trusts are set up based on guidelines stipulated in Japan's Commercial Code. Specifically, a planning entity

Table 6.4 Ways to categorize investment trusts

Structure	Contractual	Corporate
Offering method	Public offering	Private placement
Place of establishment	Japan	Overseas
Ability to sell more shares of the fund	Possible (open)	Not possible (unit)
Ability to redeem shares	Possible (open end)	Not possible (closed end)
Listing status	Listed	Unlisted
Core holdings	Stocks	Bonds

Source: Junji Kawahara (*Toushi shintaku no chishiki* (*Basics of Investment Trusts*), Nihon Keizai Shimbunsha, 2000).

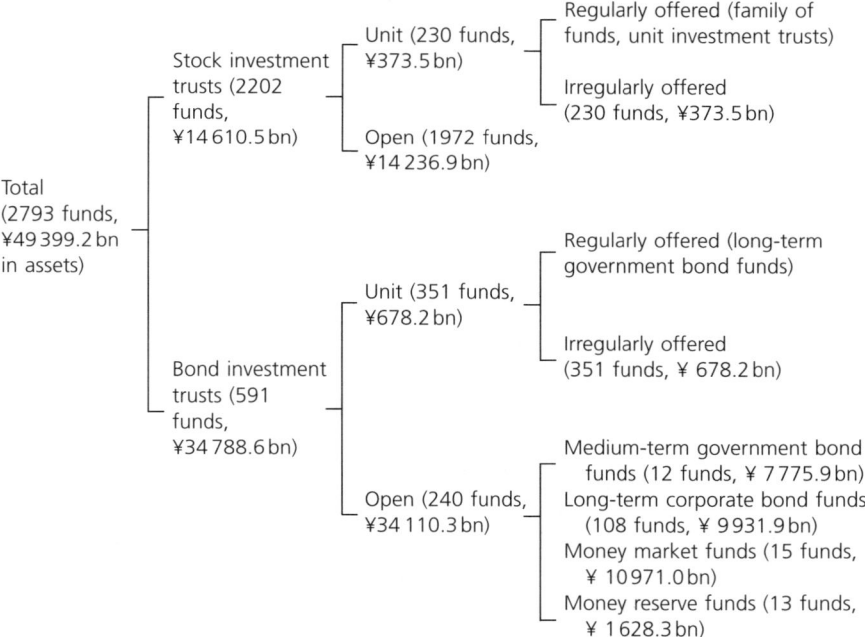

Note: Data are at end-December 2000.
Source: Investment Trusts Association Japan.

forms an investment corporation, which in turn issues securities to investors. There are very few corporate investment trusts in Japan. This investment trust structure, however, is employed for REITs, the first of which was launched in 2001.

Investment trusts can also be categorized as either publicly offered or privately placed funds. Publicly offered funds are those sold to at least 50 general investors, whereas privately placed funds are sold to qualified (professional) investors, as defined by Japan's

Securities and Exchange Law, or to at least two but fewer than 50 general investors. The number of privately placed contractual investment trusts monitored by the Investment Trusts Association Japan has steadily increased each year, from 96 funds, with total assets under management of ¥1.5 tr. at the end of 1999, to 338 funds, with total assets under management of ¥3.6 tr. by the end of 2000. One reason for the sharp growth is that investment management companies with a relatively small amount of assets under management, such as investment advisory companies, have been establishing privately placed investment trusts to improve the efficiency of their asset management operations. Privately placed contractual investment trusts have also been used by funds of funds and hedge funds for creating new types of investment trust products.

Another way of classifying investment trusts is based on whether they were set up in Japan or overseas. Overseas investment trusts are further broken down into those marketed in Japan and those purchased directly from investment management companies outside Japan. Overseas funds marketed in Japan are subject to domestic regulations.

Furthermore, investment trusts can be categorized as either closed-end or open-end funds. The most common type of mutual fund in the US is the corporate open-end fund, and the most common type in the UK is the corporate closed-end fund. In Japan, the main type of investment fund today is the contractual open-end fund.

Another possible subcategorization for Japanese investment trusts concerns the ability to bring in more assets by selling more shares of an existing fund. Fund companies can increase the size of an open investment trust after it has been established, but they cannot do so for unit investment trusts (UIT). A UIT can be more efficiently managed because the amount of assets under management is not affected by fund inflows or outflows. UITs include one type in which shares of a fund with the same product characteristics are offered regularly, such as once a month, and another type that is offered irregularly, in a one-off deal, based on particular sectors or investment themes.

In accordance with Japanese investment trust regulations, investment trusts are classified as either stock or bond investment trusts. Bond investment trusts cannot invest in stocks, but stock investment trusts can own both stocks and bonds. Organizations that analyse and evaluate investment trusts relative to others in the same universe subdivide Japanese investment trusts into various categories. Stock investment trusts include funds that invest mainly in stocks and those that invest mainly in government bonds. In addition, stock investment trusts are classified according to the types of stocks purchased or the investment methodologies employed by the fund. Subcategories include general stock funds (based on conventional investments and strategies), small- and mid-cap stock funds, sector funds, regional funds, balanced funds, index funds and leveraged funds (which also invest in futures contracts).

Some Japanese investment trusts trade on the exchanges. The first such listed investment trust is the Nikkei 300 Index Fund, which began trading in 1995. In addition, various country funds are listed on the Osaka Securities Exchange (OSE) in the form of corporate investment trusts focusing on overseas markets.

NEW TYPES OF INVESTMENT TRUSTS

In response to recent deregulation, fund companies have introduced a variety of new investment trusts in addition to funds of funds. Some of the alternative funds that previously had been available only through private placements but are now publicly offered include hedge funds that take both long and short positions, private-equity funds and REITs. Alternative funds are increasingly catching on with pension funds, foundations, financial institutions and high net worth individuals as vehicles for diversification and achieving higher absolute investment returns.

To date, real estate investments were limited to real estate investment partnerships that required large minimums from investors. The Law on Investment Trusts and Investment Companies, a significant revision in 2000 of the Investment Trust Law, paved the way for the introduction of Japanese REITs (J-REITs), which invest mainly in real estate and mortgage-backed securities. Under Japanese tax law, contractual, publicly offered investment trusts are not taxed at the fund level, and distributions paid by corporate investment trusts can be expensed if at least 90% of earnings are paid out to investors.

Given the lack of liquidity in Japan's real estate market, most fund companies are considering establishing closed-end corporate REITs. Under the corporate investment trust structure, an investment corporation delegates the asset management responsibilities to an investment trust management company and a custodian manages fund assets. Processing and other back-office functions are outsourced to third parties.

A number of J-REITs were expected to be listed on the Tokyo Stock Exchange (TSE) in 2001. To be listed, a J-REIT must have at least 75% of its assets invested in real estate or related assets; at least 4000 trust units; total assets of at least ¥5bn; net assets of at least ¥1bn; and at least 1000 investors. In addition, no more than 75% of the fund's investors can be institutional investors, and at least 50% of the real estate assets must generate income and be expected to be owned for at least a year. So far, most of the real estate investment funds based on the cash flow generated by office buildings and shopping centres and established by major real estate and securities companies have been structured as investment partnerships and other privately placed investment vehicles. Some of these real estate partnerships may be converted into J-REITs and taken public to expand their investor base to include individual investors. By April 2002, three J-REITS were listed on the TSE, and three more were expected by June; their total assets amounted to about ¥600bn combined with ¥350bn net assets.

Another recent fund product innovation is the exchange-traded fund (ETF), which has been made possible by deregulation stemming from financial and economic policies implemented in 2001. In the US, S&P Depositary Receipts (SPDR or 'Spiders'), which track the S&P 500 Index, and the QQQ, the NASDAQ 100 tracking stock, are growing in popularity, primarily among retail investors, because they have lower expenses than traditional index funds. In Japan, regulatory changes and other preparations have paved the way for the creation of ETFs that track major indexes, such as the Nikkei 225 and the Tokyo Stock Price Index (TOPIX). By April 2002, there were 18 such ETFs (four that track the TOPIX, four the Nikkei 225, one the Nikkei Stock Index 300, two the TOPIX Core 30, one the S&P/TOPIX 150 and six sector indexes – two electronics/precision instruments, two transportation equipment and two banking), with a combined market value of about ¥1.3tr. The TOPIX-linked ETFs account for about 52.5% of the total market value of the funds, and the Nikkei-linked ones 45.2%. The TOPIX-linked ETFs have grown in part because of their use by banks as a way to get rid of their cross-shareholdings.

Another new investment product is the wrap account. Whereas funds of funds are standardized products marketed to retail investors, wrap accounts allow for customized mixes of financial products. Some wrap accounts enable investors to choose from different investment trusts, and others are based on investment advisory services. Because wrap accounts allow for greater latitude in choices, fees for these accounts are typically higher than those for funds of funds. Consequently, wrap accounts are marketed to high net worth individuals.

Size of the Japanese investment trust market

This section compares the investment trust market in Japan with that of other major countries and analyses the size of the domestic investment trust market and the types of assets held by domestic investment trusts.

AN INTERNATIONAL COMPARISON OF ASSETS UNDER MANAGEMENT IN INVESTMENT TRUSTS

Figure 6.1 shows a comparison of aggregate net assets under management in open-end investment trusts for selected major countries at the end of September 1999. The amount of assets in open-end investment trusts in Japan was about $472.2bn, or less than 7% of

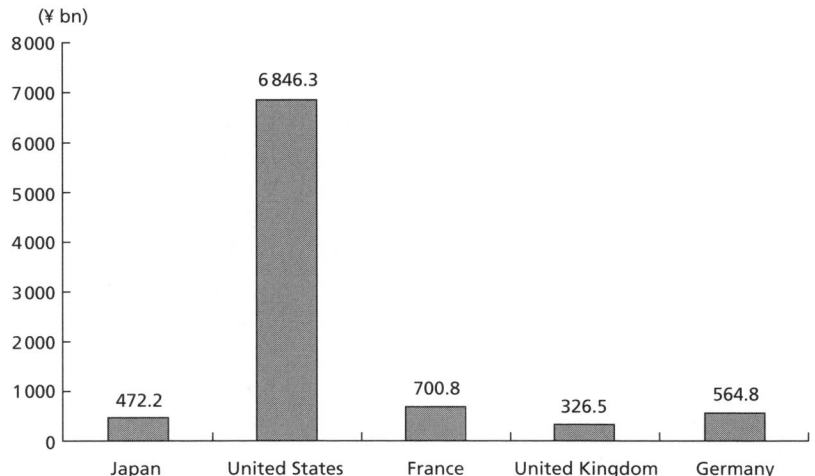

6.1 An international comparison of net assets under management in investment trusts (at September 1999).
Source: Nomura, based on data from the Investment Company Institute and the Bundesbank's *Monthly Report*.

the amount for the US, less than that for France and Germany, and more than that for the UK. The value of net assets in open-end investment trusts as a percentage of GDP (at the end of September 1998) was just under 10% for Japan, almost 70% for the US, about 40% for France, roughly 20% for the UK and approximately 30% for Germany. The amount of assets in open-end investment trusts in Japan exceeds that in the UK in absolute terms but as a ratio of GDP is less than that in the UK.

Factors contributing to the comparatively small size of the Japanese investment trust market include the hesitancy among individual investors to purchase investment trusts, high commissions charged by securities companies, lack of experience among investment management firms, poor investment returns and a general lack of awareness among the populace concerning investment trusts. In addition, above all else, individual investors' preference for safety when investing their savings has kept investors away from investment trusts and other risk assets. Various reforms have been implemented in the past few years that are leading to positive changes in the investment trust market and investment management services, but the risk-averse tendencies of Japanese individual investors remain a significant obstacle.

SIZE OF DIFFERENT TYPES OF INVESTMENT TRUSTS

At the end of 2000, the amount of net assets under management in the 3000 or so investment trusts available in Japan totalled about ¥50 tr. Since their introduction in 1992, money market funds (MMFs) have accounted for an increasing proportion of total investment trust assets (see Fig. 6.2 (a) and (b)). MMFs are a common investment alternative to bank deposits in the US because of their comparatively attractive yields. MMFs have also gained popularity in Japan, given that interest rates have remained extremely low for a prolonged period.

Net assets in stock investment trusts in Japan had been declining since 1990, but in more recent years, they have been increasing. When open investment trusts were first introduced in 1952, they accounted for only 2% of the total amount of assets invested in stock investment trusts, and UITs accounted for 98%. By November 2000, however, open investment trusts came to account for 99% and UITs only 1%, indicating a clear shift in investors' preference toward open investment trusts.

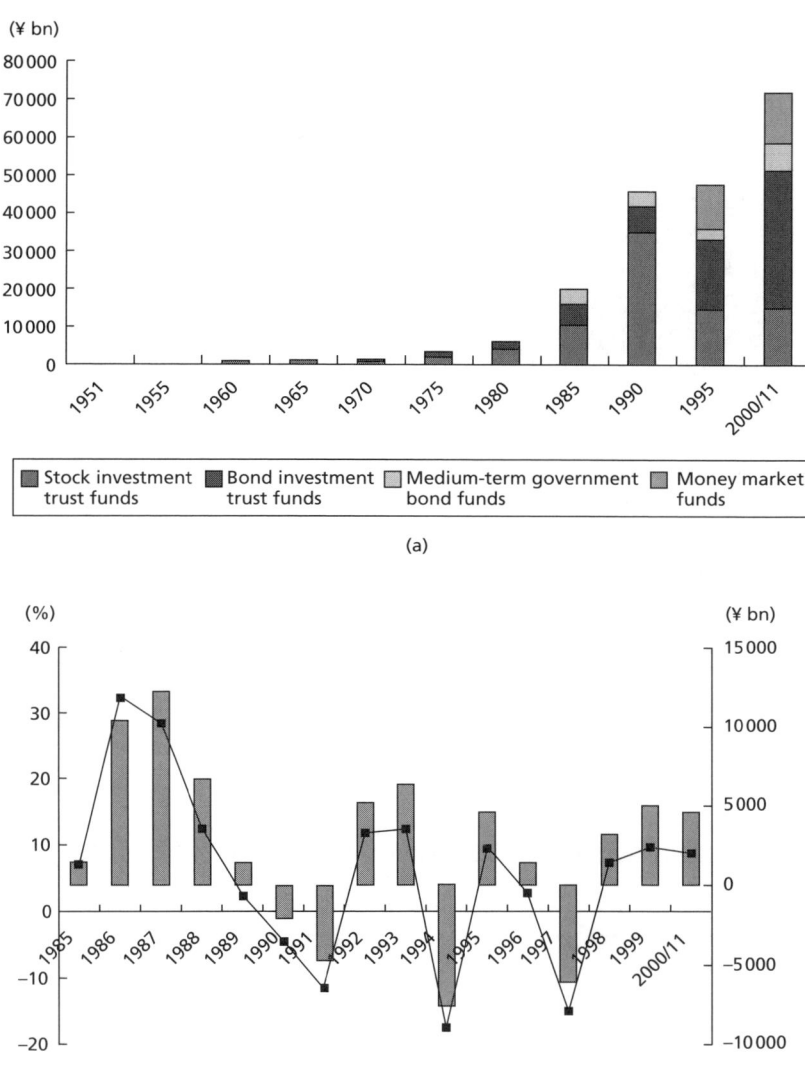

(a)

(b)

6.2 (a) Breakdown of net assets under management by type of investment trust.
(b) Change in assets.
Note: Bond investment trust funds do not include assets invested in medium-term
government bond funds or money market funds; Net change in assets = Purchases
– redemptions.
Source: Nomura, based on data from the Investment Trusts Association, Japan.

After rising sharply during the bubble economy years (the latter half of the 1980s), net assets in investment trusts tended to rise and fall by about 10% from year to year for most of the 1990s (Fig. 6.2). Net assets, however, have been rising gradually since 1998, in part because of a strong stock market in 1999. It is nevertheless too early to conclude that investment trusts have completely caught on with Japanese individual investors. Future trends in demand for investment trusts among Japanese investors will be discussed in the next section.

New types of products are being developed. Investment trusts are typically categorized as either stock or bond investment trusts, but they can also be categorized by many different styles and subclassifications, including large-cap, small-cap, growth and value funds. As we have seen, to meet investor demand, fund companies have also striven to differentiate themselves by offering a wide variety of funds, including sector funds, such as technology and biotech funds; specialty funds, such as mining and natural resource funds; asset-backed securities funds; and leveraged funds, which utilize derivatives. Actively managed stock funds far outnumber passively managed funds in Japan. Passively managed funds include those that track major indexes, such as the Nikkei 225 and the TOPIX, and those that track various sector indexes.

FOREIGN-CURRENCY-DENOMINATED INVESTMENT TRUSTS

Japanese stocks account for less than 20% of the total market value of all stocks worldwide. Given the decline in Japan's market in the 1990s, the importance of global diversification has increased for Japanese investors. Prior to 1995, investment trusts that invested in foreign-currency-denominated assets were subject to various restrictions; for instance, they could invest only in stocks of companies located in industrialized countries with net assets of at least ¥5bn. But after most of these restrictions were eliminated in 1995, the proportion of investment trust assets invested in foreign-currency-denominated assets steadily increased from 6% in 1995 to 12% in 1999. Since then, however, the proportion has fallen, in part because Japan's market performance was strong in 1999. Nevertheless, increasing exposure to foreign-currency-denominated assets remains important for Japanese investors (Fig. 6.3).

One inseparable aspect of investing in assets outside Japan is foreign exchange rates. The appreciation of the yen during the last

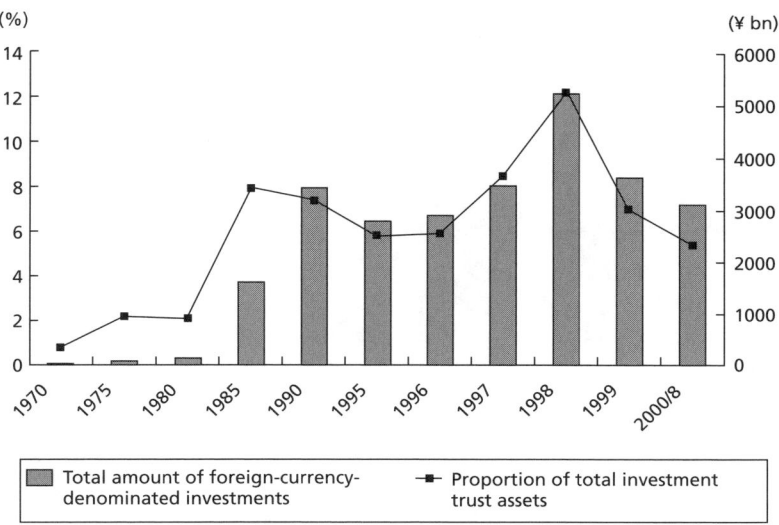

(%)   (¥ bn)

6.3 Investment trust holdings of foreign-currency-denominated assets.
Source: as Fig. 6.2.

several decades has heightened sensitivity to exchange rate fluctuations among domestic investors. Some Japanese investment trusts completely hedge their exposure to foreign-currency-denominated assets, but others dynamically adjust the extent of their hedges. Given that the Japanese market accounts for a smaller proportion of the total market value of stocks worldwide than the US market does, Japanese investors need to consider global investing and currency hedging strategies more seriously. A variety of funds with different hedging strategies – ranging from completely hedged to totally unhedged – are available to meet the particular needs of individual investors.

The current role of investment trusts in Japan

This section looks at investment trusts in the context of individual investors' portfolios and Japan's capital markets. In order for the investment trust market to expand further through increased participation by individual investors, infrastructure improvements are needed along with changes in investors' perception of investment trusts.

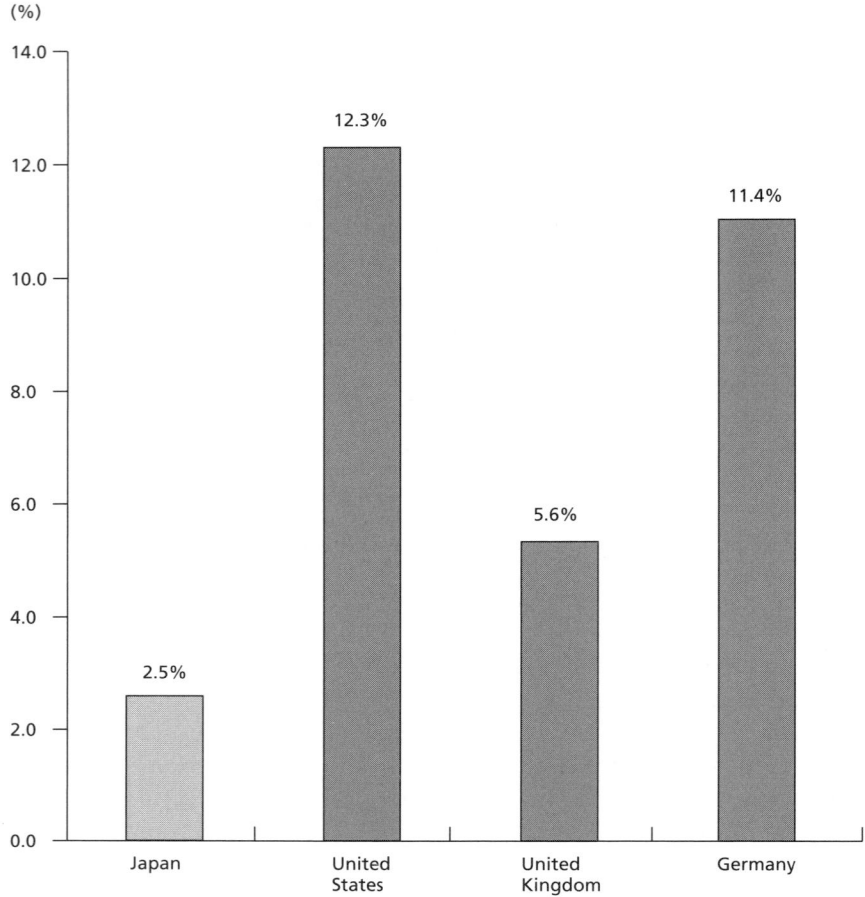

6.4 Investment trust assets as a percentage of total household financial assets (2000).
Note: For the US, investment trust assets include both mutual fund and money market fund assets.
Source: Bank of Japan, *Financial and Economic Statistics Monthly*, and data from the Federal Reserve Board, Office for National Statistics (UK) and the Bundesbank.

INVESTMENT TRUST ASSETS AS A PERCENTAGE OF TOTAL HOUSEHOLD FINANCIAL ASSETS

The value of Japanese household financial assets exceeded ¥1400 tr. at the end of 1999. Of the total figure, over 50% was held in cash and cash equivalents; as shown in Fig. 6.4, only 2% was held in investment trusts, which is significantly lower than in the US, the

UK or Germany. One reason for the low amount of Japanese assets held in investment trusts – in absolute terms, as a proportion of GDP and as a proportion of household financial assets – is that many Japanese individual investors are neither aware of nor very familiar with the products. But with infrastructure improvements and the likelihood that investment trusts will be increasingly available as investment options in pensions plans, the Japanese investment trust market is poised to grow.

The growth of mutual funds in the US was spurred mainly by the development of MMFs and by a heavy inflow of money into stock mutual funds stemming from a strong market and the availability of mutual funds as an investment option in defined-contribution retirement plans. In general, younger retirement plan participants can afford to invest a greater proportion of their retirement assets into stocks because these investors have a relatively long time horizon. In the past, mutual funds in the US had been used by traders for speculation at times, but within retirement plans, they now serve as investment vehicles for steadily building up wealth over the long term. In short, the mutual fund market in the US expanded as investors began perceiving mutual funds as a means of achieving longer-term investment goals rather than as speculative investments and as the public became more interested in investing rather than simply saving. Amid the increasing risks being placed on private- as well as public-sector sponsors of defined-benefit pension plans, the introduction of pension plans in which participants are responsible for their retirement futures can be considered a by-product of the times, but in any event, this development is likely to spur further changes in Japan's investment trust market.

INVESTMENT TRUST ASSETS AS A PERCENTAGE OF THE TOTAL VALUE OF THE STOCK AND BOND MARKETS

The investment trust market in Japan has significant room to grow and can play a much broader role within the equity market. As shown in Fig. 6.5, investment trusts own only 2% of the stocks in Japan by market value, compared with 10–20% in the US and Europe.

According to a survey conducted every three years by the Japan Institute for Securities Information and Public Relations on where individual investors invest their savings, only 8.8% of Japanese households had money in investment trusts in 2000; this number

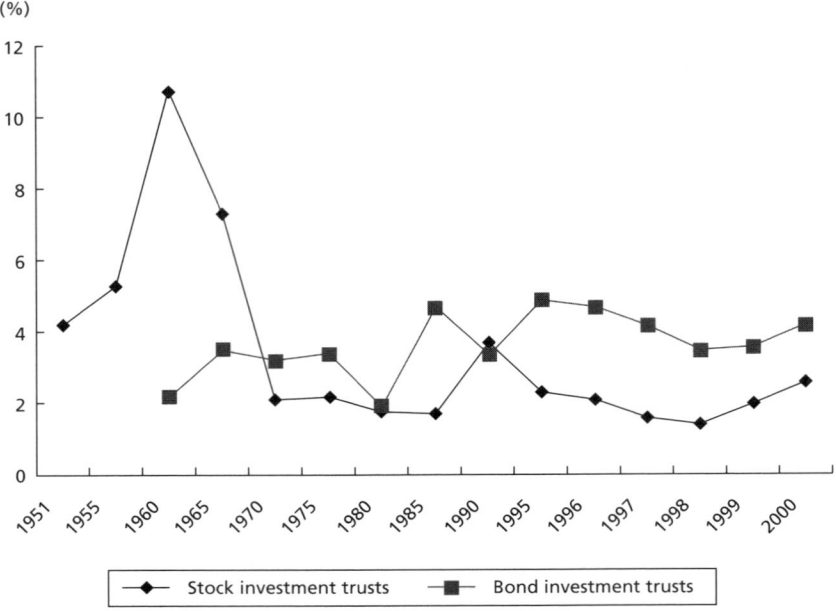

(%)

6.5 Investment trust assets as a percentage of total value of stock and bond markets.
Notes: (1) Total stock market value is the market capitalization of all stocks listed on Japan's stock exchanges. Data are as at August 2000. (2) Total bond market value is the market value of all bonds issued in the domestic bond market and still outstanding. Data are as at February 2000.
Source: Nomura, based on data from the Investment Trusts Association, Japan.

was unchanged from the level in the previous survey in 1997, only marginally up from 6.4% in 1979, and well below its high of 16.7% in 1988. According to the survey, roughly half of the respondents said their most important criteria for investments are safety of principal and liquidity. Of the 8.8% of households (equivalent to roughly 2.87 million households nationwide) with assets in investment trusts in 2000, 68.9% said they had investment trust assets in MMFs, MRFs and medium-term Japanese government bond funds, 23.2% owned domestic bond funds and 21.6% owned domestic stock funds. Of the 83% of households that had never bought investment trusts before, 64% replied that they had no interest and 24.3% said that they did not understand what investment trusts were or how they work. The survey results suggest that the relative inexperience of Japanese individual investors is one of the main barriers to the growth of investment trusts in Japan.

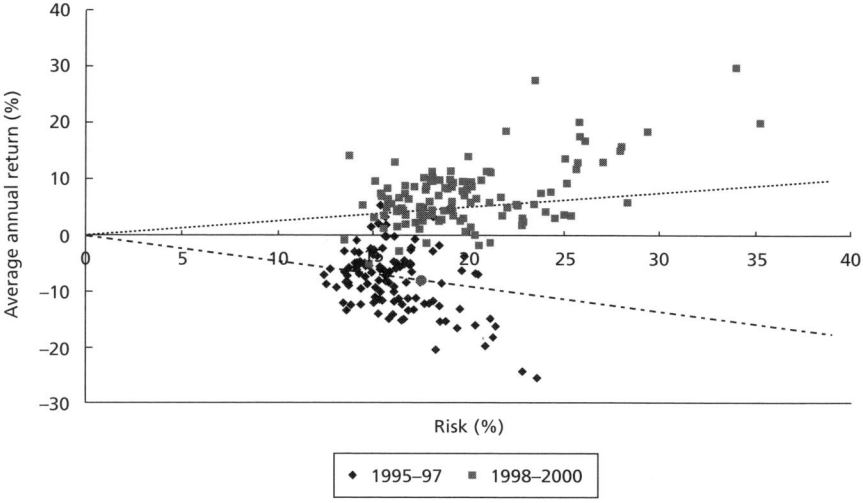

6.6 Risk–return data for domestic stock investment trusts.
Note: The dashed and dotted lines connect the origin with the risk–return plots for the TOPIX index.
Source: as Fig. 6.5.

Performance of stock investment trusts

Figure 6.6 plots risk–return data for 166 domestic, actively managed, open-type diversified stock investment trusts with performance records for the six-year period from 1995 to 2000. Risk and return data are shown relative to the TOPIX and for the 1995–97 and 1998–2000 periods.

For the entire six-year period covered in Fig. 6.6, the overall stock market fell during the 1995–97 period and rose during the 1998–2000 period. Given that each fund has a different risk level relative to the TOPIX, the figure provides an indication of risk-adjusted returns. For each three-year period, a line connects the origin with the risk–return point for the TOPIX. Those stock investment trusts that lie above these lines outperformed the TOPIX, and those below them underperformed the benchmark. During the 1995–97 period, 46% of the stock investment trusts outperformed the TOPIX, and in the 1998–2000 period, 66% outperformed the TOPIX.

Although the funds' performances can be partly attributed to the performance of the overall market, in recent years, deregulation and increased competition between fund companies have probably

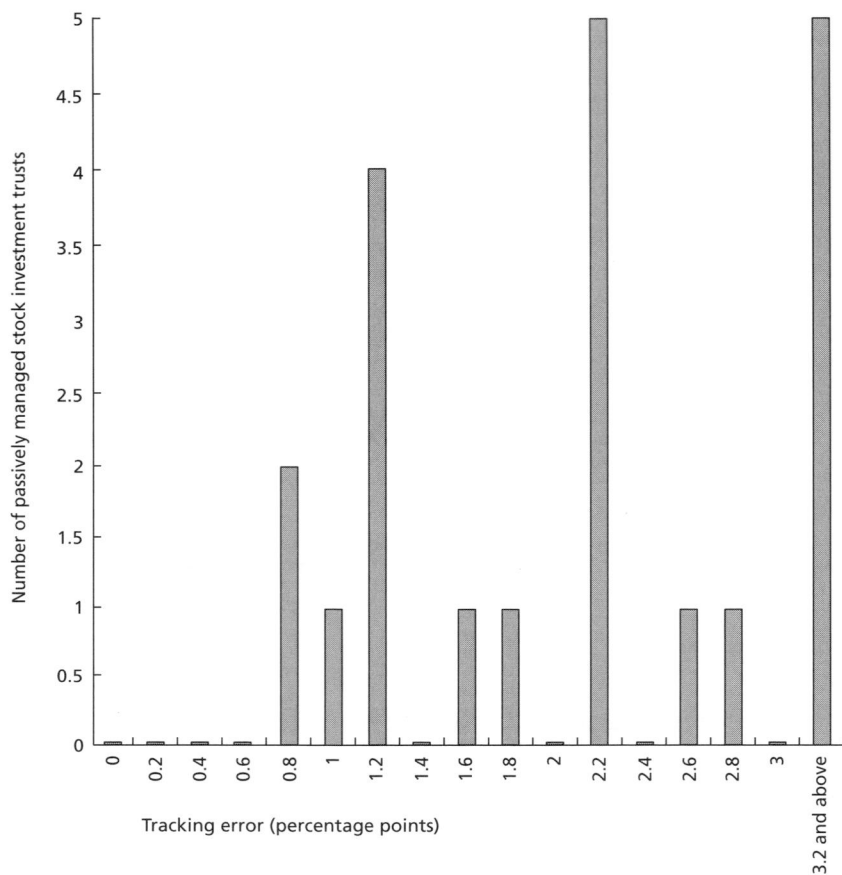

6.7 Distribution of tracking errors (percentage points).
Source: as Fig. 6.5.

resulted in qualitative changes in investment trust funds. The divergence in risk-adjusted returns reflects different product attributes, and the performance of funds in general can be expected to improve as performance data and qualitative fund evaluations become more widely available and lead to intensified competition.

Figure 6.7 shows the distribution of tracking errors relative to the TOPIX for 21 domestic, passively managed, open index funds for which data were available for the six-year period from 1995 to 2000. Tracking error is defined as the annualized standard deviation of the difference between the monthly returns for the investment trusts and the monthly return for the TOPIX.

As shown in Fig. 6.7, the tracking errors for domestic index funds vary widely; however, a large number of funds have tracking errors between 0.8 and 1.2 percentage points, 2.2 pps and 3.0 pps or more. Tracking error can be attributed in part to the amount of assets under management as well as the methodology used to construct a portfolio. To fully replicate the TOPIX, an index fund would need to invest several tens of billions of yen in more than 1000 stocks. Although some funds try to fully replicate the TOPIX, others use sampling methods to create portfolios that mimic the performance of the TOPIX without investing in all the stocks in the index. Still, tracking error often results because of the fund fees and the open-end nature of the index funds, which allows fund inflows and outflows and consequently makes managing the assets more difficult.

7 Banks and insurance companies as institutional investors

This chapter outlines the marketable securities investments of Japanese banks and insurance companies in recent decades, particularly the last few years.

Investments in marketable securities

At the end of fiscal 2000 (March 2001), Japanese bank investments in marketable securities (including ¥22.3 tr. in marketable securities in the non-trust bank accounts of Japanese trust banks) amounted to ¥176.5 tr. These marketable securities investments are the second-largest investment category for Japanese banks after loans, which amounted to ¥474.5 tr. and accounted for 21.9% of the total assets at Japan's 136 banks at the end of fiscal 2000. Investments in Japanese government bonds (JGBs), municipal bonds, corporate bonds and other bonds made up 12.5% of total bank assets; stock-holdings 5.5%; and other marketable securities 4.0%. Compared with banks in the US and Europe, Japanese banks invest a larger proportion of their assets in stocks. Japanese trust banks, meanwhile, had ¥132.9 tr. in marketable securities in their trust accounts, with 28.2% of this total in bonds, 42.7% in domestic stocks and 27.6% in foreign securities.

The 42 Japanese life insurance companies had marketable securities investments totalling ¥110.4 tr. at the end of fiscal 2000, accounting for 57.5% of their total assets. Of the insurers' total marketable securities investments, bonds made up 27.6% of the total; stocks 15.0%; and foreign securities 11.6%.

Japanese banks and life insurance companies are major players in Japan's stock market. In fiscal 2000, banks owned 25.8% of the total shares outstanding, and life insurance companies held 7.6% (Table 7.1). But, as discussed in further detail later in this chapter, Japanese banks and life insurance companies should not be seen as typical cross-shareholding counterparties or strategic institutional investors.

Incidentally, Japanese banks and life insurance companies are major owners of privately placed bonds, including privately placed municipal bonds. These investments are not covered in this chapter because information on these securities is not widely available and because banks and life insurance companies often effectively regard them as substitutes for loans.

Trust banks

Trust banks (including the trust divisions of banks) typically come to mind as one of the major institutional participants in Japan's capital markets. The history of trust banks in Japan since the end of World War II is unique in its evolution.

Prior to World War II, Japanese trust companies managed the assets of wealthy individuals from a long-term perspective, in the form of money trusts. But immediately after the war, the trust business rapidly disappeared for a variety of war-related reasons, including high inflation. By 1948, in part to rescue the trust companies, Japanese trust companies had been transformed into trust banks that were allowed to offer both banking and trust services.

Following this transformation and throughout the first half of the 1950s, the trust divisions of banks primarily administered investor-directed money trusts (*tokkin* trusts) and separately managed designated money trusts (*shiteitan* trusts). Because these products were individually managed and dividends were paid out based on performance, the trust divisions of banks essentially became institutional investors. The trusts they operated, however, were not considered products that were subject to interest rate regulations; therefore, they were suggested to be 'voluntarily restricted'.

In other words, rather than treating the trust operations as institutional investors, regulators increasingly regarded them as financial institutions that provided long-term loans, and in this respect similar

Table 7.1 Percentage of stockholdings held by major investor groups (%, fiscal year-end)

	1975	1980	1985	1989	1990	1995	1996	1997	1998	1999	2000
Financial institutions	36.0	38.8	42.2	46.0	45.2	41.4	41.3	40.2	39.3	36.1	37.0
Banks (including trust banks)	18.0	19.2	21.6	26.7	26.2	25.5	25.9	25.7	25.7	23.7	25.8
Life insurance companies	11.5	12.5	13.5	13.1	13.2	11.2	10.9	10.2	9.4	8.3	7.6
Non-life insurance companies	4.7	4.9	4.5	4.1	4.1	3.6	3.4	3.3	3.2	2.9	2.8
Other	1.9	2.2	2.6	2.1	1.8	1.2	1.0	1.0	1.0	1.2	0.8
Securities companies	1.4	1.7	2.0	2.0	1.7	1.4	1.1	0.8	0.7	0.9	0.8
Non-financial companies	26.3	26.0	24.1	24.8	25.2	23.6	23.8	24.1	24.1	23.7	22.3
Individual investors	33.5	29.2	25.2	22.6	23.1	23.6	23.6	24.6	25.4	26.4	26.3
Foreign investors	2.6	4.0	5.7	3.9	4.2	9.4	9.8	9.8	10.0	12.4	13.2

Source: Nomura, based on the *Shareownership Survey* (National Conference of Stock Exchanges).

to the long-term credit banks and life insurance companies. The core business of Japanese trust banks became the management of commingled designated money trusts, which are principal-guaranteed investment products with attributes similar to those of bank deposits and loan trusts, which are, as the name implies, trusts established to invest primarily in loans. Under this structure, trust banks were limited in their ability to invest in marketable securities.

The trust divisions of Japanese banks nevertheless began to invest in stocks during the economic bubble years of the latter 1980s. During this period, *tokkin* trusts, which were permitted in 1984 to invest in stocks, and fund trusts, which are trusts other than money trusts that are separately managed in accordance with investor guidelines, became the principal conduits for companies' financial engineering activities. During the bubble years, both financial institutions and non-financial companies used these instruments for equity investments and accounted for them separately from long-term investments, such as cross-shareholdings. Because the book value of stocks held in the funds could be treated separately for accounting purposes, these investment trusts offered companies tax advantages. At the end of 1989, investments in *tokkin* trusts and fund trusts amounted to ¥43 tr. of which about 40% was allocated to stocks.

Although official statistics are unavailable, the amount of assets held in *tokkin* trusts and fund trusts has probably declined significantly since the deflation of the economic bubble and the concomitant reluctance of Japanese companies to engage in financial engineering strategies. Currently, the major trust instruments for marketable securities investments include pension trusts, *shiteitan* trusts and money trusts offering dividends based on investment performance (the expected dividend rate is available for the commingled designated money trusts) (Table 7.2). Pension trusts are discussed in Chapter 5, and the government's investments in *shiteitan* trusts are addressed in Chapter 4. Given that the money trusts offering dividends based on investment performance resemble investment trusts and that the amount of funds invested in these trusts is probably relatively small, this chapter mentions them only briefly.[1]

---

1 In addition to investments in marketable securities, Japanese trust banks are increasingly providing custody, book-keeping and other back-office services for pension management and the securitization of assets. These other functions of trust banks are discussed in Chapters 5 and 18.

Table 7.2 Major trust products for marketable securities investment

Type of trust	Outstanding balance at end fiscal 1999 (¥ bn)	Main trust products
Money trusts	93 933.1	Commingled designated money trusts Separately managed designated money trusts (*shiteitan* trusts) other than pension trusts *Tokkin* trusts
Pension trusts	35 225.5	
Trusts other than money trusts	15 756.2	Fund trusts

Source: Trust Companies Association of Japan.

Banks

As noted earlier, Japanese banks invest less than 10% of their total assets in equities and foreign securities. Instead, banks have invested mainly in yen-denominated interest-bearing assets, such as loans and bonds. At the end of fiscal 1999, Japanese banks' investment in JGBs totalled ¥43.3 tr. (equivalent to 31.7% of their total marketable securities holdings); investment in municipal bonds amounted to ¥10.1 tr. (7.4%), and the amount in corporate bonds was ¥17.6 tr. (12.9%). Also, about a half of banks' total funds currently consist of time deposits, which are generally short-term liabilities because more than half of these time deposits are due to mature in less than one year; banks' assets, meanwhile, consist of JGBs and other relatively long-term interest-yielding assets, resulting in a favourable spread between long- and short-term interest rates for banks.

Japanese banks have traditionally invested in bonds as a means of managing the interest rate risks of their assets and liabilities, including loans and deposits, as well as maintaining a certain degree of liquidity. But in response to mounting pressure on banks to improve their profitability and shareholder value, many banks have been trying to improve bond-related gains by focusing more on rate spreads and bond-dealing profits. Therefore, banks' bond divisions are now more inclined to increase their profits through short-term dealing rather than through longer-term active or passive bond investing strategies.

CROSS-SHAREHOLDINGS

Corporate cross-shareholding arrangements are common in Japan. These relationships typically involve a bank owning shares in a non-financial company, which reciprocates by owning shares in the bank. Both the Bank Law and the Anti-monopoly Law prohibit a bank from owning more than 5% of the outstanding shares of any one company, but cross-shareholding relationships are nevertheless prevalent in Japan across all industries. From the mid-1970s, the proportion of shares owned by individual investors has remained between 20% and 29%, while that for financial and non-financial companies has been between 60% and 70%. In general, a high proportion of the total shares outstanding are owned as cross-shareholdings, which is the main reason Japanese banks have a higher proportion of investment assets in equities compared to banks in other countries. In addition, Japanese banks own stocks through *tokkin* trusts, which are managed by trust banks, for investment purposes other than cementing corporate relationships. However, banks' *tokkin* trust investments, including bond holdings, amount to only about ¥2 tr.

The next section considers the significance of cross-shareholdings for banks. For further information on the impact of cross-shareholdings on stock prices, see Chapter 17.

CROSS-SHAREHOLDING RELATIONSHIPS TRANSFORMED

Because Japan's stock market was not well developed in the wake of World War II, the government promoted an industrial recovery through the use of indirect financing. Under an industrial policy that emphasized the allocation of capital to growth industries that were considered to be a priority in terms of national development, the Japanese government adopted very strict interest rate regulations that kept interest rates artificially low, thereby minimizing the cost of capital for Japanese companies. As part of this system, companies forged strong relationships with financial institutions, mainly banks, and banks increased their cross-shareholdings to cement stable long-term lending relationships.

During the market crisis in the mid-1960s, both securities companies and the market suffered as stocks remained anaemic for an extended period. During this time, as the government liberalized Japan's capital markets, Japanese companies also began to forge stable shareholding relationships to prevent takeovers by foreign companies. The leading corporate groups that developed out of these relationships were the former *zaibatsu* conglomerates – Mitsui, Mitsubishi, Sumitomo and Fuyo – and bank-anchored groups, such as the Sanwa and Dai-Ichi Kangyo groups.

In the 1970s, however, particularly following the first oil crisis, the significance of cross-shareholding relationships gradually began to weaken. One of the main reasons for this change was the decline in Japan's economic growth rate during the 1970s, from comparatively high growth to slower, more steady growth. Japanese companies responded by shifting their focus from constant expansion to downsizing their operations by reducing both assets and liabilities. In addition, the Japanese government ran into budget difficulties starting around the mid-1970s because of an increase in public spending aimed at stimulating the economy and because of a decline in tax revenues stemming from an economic slowdown. To cover the deficits, the government issued a massive amount of JGBs, which contributed to the development of a secondary market for JGBs and established the groundwork for the liberalization of interest rates and Japan's capital markets. These developments, together with the globalization of economies worldwide, allowed Japanese companies to reduce their heavy reliance on banks for financing as well as to access global capital markets.

Starting in the 1980s, the US stepped up its criticisms of the *keiretsu* system, an arrangement through which Japanese companies would give the large group companies priority in their business transactions. Japanese companies were thus forced to rethink their cross-shareholding relationships and the *keiretsu* system. During this time, a view that increasingly gained currency was that the large proportion of outstanding shares held as cross-shareholdings hindered mergers and acquisitions, prevented the efficient allocation of resources and hurt Japan's ability to bolster its global competitiveness.

These changes in the economic environment in the 1970s and 1980s brought about a transformation in the main bank system and the practice of cross-shareholding, two factors that had supported the growth of Japanese industry.

NON-PERFORMING LOAN PROBLEM

Although the significance of cross-shareholding relationships has diminished, the proportion of shares held as cross-shareholdings remained relatively high until around 1990. One contributing factor was the July 1987 Basel Agreement, which established uniform standards for international capital-adequacy ratios for banks (capital-adequacy requirements established by the Bank for International Settlements [BIS]). In response to the requirements, Japanese banks raised equity financing, relying on existing cross-shareholding partners to be key buyers of their shares. Japanese companies were in a similar situation and needed to issue equity. In addition, because 45% of unrealized gains on stockholdings are included in the calculation of the BIS capital-adequacy ratio for Japanese banks, unrealized gains on cross-shareholdings were vital for Japanese banks.

Nonetheless, the collapse of the economic bubble resulted in a gradual deterioration in the system of cross-shareholdings. One of the main reasons for its demise was that Japanese banks became saddled with a massive amount of non-performing loans. During the bubble years, banks significantly increased lending to construction firms, real estate companies and non-banks. Most of these loans were collateralized by real estate, but relatively low interest rates and an excess of liquidity fuelled a sharp surge in land prices, which in turn led to more borrowing and thus even higher land prices. After the economic bubble collapsed at the start of the 1990s, Japanese banks ended up with too many non-performing loans.

Starting in fiscal 1992, Japanese banks began to aggressively dispose of these non-performing loans. Since the banks were not able to cover all their credit costs with earnings from operations, they tapped into their unrealized gains on stockholdings, which were massive because they had acquired most of their cross-shareholdings at much lower prices. Even after the collapse of the economic bubble and the resultant sharp decline in the stock market, Japanese banks had about ¥22 tr. in aggregate unrealized gains on securities holdings, mostly stocks, at the end of March 1992 (Fig. 7.1).

Even though banks sold their stockholdings to cover their credit costs, their amount of equity holdings continued to increase; in many cases, banks had simply realized gains on the sales and then bought back the shares. The key factors behind these buybacks were Japanese companies' continued reliance on indirect financing and the lack of stable shareholders other than banks, despite weakening justifications for the main bank system.

Furthermore, in order to maintain lending relationships with their cross-shareholding counterparties, banks had to consult with these corporate customers each time they wanted to sell cross-held shares. As a result, cross-shareholdings on the whole were not significantly

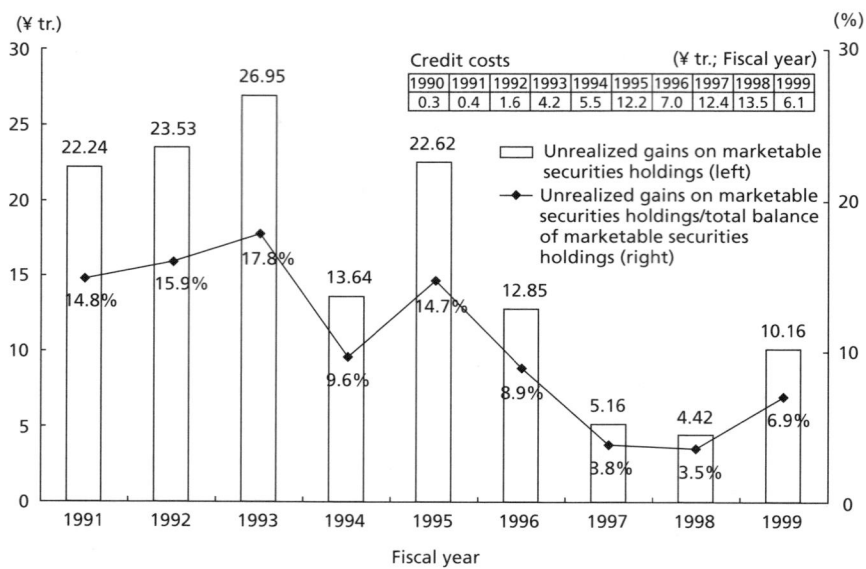

7.1 Japanese banks' unrealized gains on marketable securities holdings.
Note: Credit costs = general loan loss provisions plus loan writedowns.
Source: Nomura, based on data from the Bank of Japan.

unwound, even though cross-shareholdings between financial institutions and those between banks and non-financial companies that were no longer loan customers were gradually unwound.

When the non-performing loan problem first materialized in the early 1990s, banks were able to cover their credit costs with their massive unrealized gains on stockholdings. But as the bad-debt problem worsened, it began to have a detrimental impact on the real economy in several ways. In particular, a credit crunch ensued as Japanese banks tightened their lending policies. Indeed, a vicious cycle was set in motion: a delayed economic recovery led to lower stock prices, which in turn reduced banks' unrealized gains on stockholdings.

During the second half of 1997, fears about the health of the financial system emerged in part as a result of the bankruptcy of Hokkaido Takushoku Bank, one of Japan's city banks. In an attempt to alleviate these concerns, in 1998 the government decided to use public funds to recapitalize banks that had not declared bankruptcy. Nonetheless, concerns about the stability of the financial system re-emerged as a result of delays in establishing an adequate financial regulatory structure and the insufficient amount of recapitalizations provided to the banks. After the government nationalized the Long-

Term Credit Bank of Japan and Nippon Credit Bank, which had both been leading Japanese banks up until then, it stabilized the financial system by developing the financial regulatory framework and using public funds to recapitalize Japanese banks again, this time with ¥7 tr. in March 1999.[2] By the time of this second round of recapitalizations, many Japanese banks no longer had the financial wherewithal to function as main banks, and as a result, it became clear that Japan's main bank system faced a major turning point.

ACCELERATION OF THE UNWINDING OF CROSS-SHAREHOLDINGS

Although some degree of stability has returned to the financial system, no clear signs have emerged of a resolution to the non-performing loan problem that Japanese banks have been struggling with. Between fiscal 1991 and fiscal 1999, Japanese banks took over ¥60 tr. in charges for credit costs. Nevertheless, they are still saddled with a large amount of bad loans, not only because the amount was large to begin with but also because the prolonged recession has resulted in the emergence of new bad loans.

The cross-trades[3] executed for banks to help them offset credit costs led to a deterioration in their financial condition. But these trades increased banks' exposure to stock market volatility because the banks' stockholdings had a higher book value after the trades and, hence, the proportion of banks' capital accounted for by stockholdings increased as well. According to one estimation, a 1000-point change in the value of the Nikkei 225 results in a fluctuation of more than ¥2 tr. in the value of Japanese banks' aggregate unrealized gains on stockholdings.

To reduce their exposure to equities, Japanese banks – the larger ones in particular – need to unwind more of their cross-shareholding relationships. Mark-to-market accounting (valuation at market price rather than at cost), which was introduced in Japan in fiscal 2000, started to apply to cross-shareholdings in fiscal 2001. In that year, banks most likely increasingly sold their cross-held shares without buying them back, because cross-trades have been banned

---

2 For more detail on these developments in the financial system, see Chapter 2.

3 Cross-trades are open-market transactions in which the same securities company simultaneously acts as both the buyer and seller for a particular stock trade. These trades are often used to enable banks to realize gains on stockholdings while maintaining cross-shareholding relationships.

and banks still need to realize gains on stockholdings to offset their credit costs.

Now that cross-shareholdings are marked to market, the balance sheets of Japanese companies are increasingly vulnerable to the moves in the stock market. Banks particularly need to reduce their exposure to the market because their capital-adequacy ratios directly affect their business operations.

In fiscal 1999, Japanese banks unwound more than ¥2.6 tr. worth of cross-shareholdings, and in fiscal 2000, they unwound a similar amount. Moreover, by fiscal 2005, Japan's major banks plan to sell roughly another ¥1 tr. worth of cross-shareholdings. The formation of Mizuho Holdings in September 2000 and the formation of three other mega banking groups – namely, Sumitomo Mitsui Banking Corporation, Mitsubishi Tokyo Financial Group and UFJ Holdings – will probably spur the unwinding of cross-shareholdings in the banking sector. But a rush to sell shares immediately after the establishment of these large groups is unlikely because a financial holding company can own up to 15% of the outstanding shares in any one company.

As they unwind their cross-shareholdings, companies will need to seek out new shareholders. Potential candidates include foreign investors, which have become increasingly influential market participants since the 1990s; pension funds; and individual investors, who may decide to increase the percentage of their financial assets invested in equities. To appeal more to foreign and other investors, Japanese companies urgently need to restructure their businesses to improve profitability and rethink their corporate governance policies.

Although the dissolution of cross-shareholding ties may put downward pressure on equities in the foreseeable future, through a change in the composition of shareholders, the unwinding of these relationships may have a positive impact on stock prices in the long run.

Insurance companies

The main types of insurance policies sold by Japanese life insurance companies (based on the entities to which the products are sold) are individual life insurance policies, individual annuity policies, group life insurance policies and group annuity policies. At the end

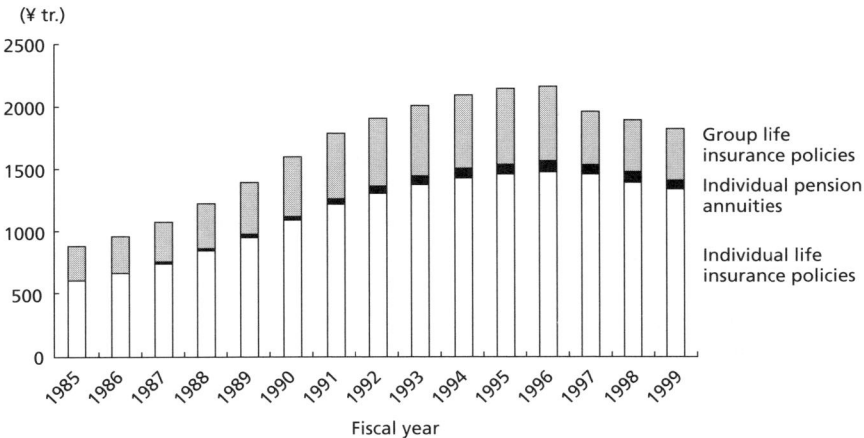

7.2 Value of Japanese life insurance companies' policies in force.
Source: Nomura, based on data from the Life insurance Association of Japan.

of fiscal 1999, the total amount of insurance benefits guaranteed by Japanese life insurance companies to their policyholders was ¥1841 tr. Of this figure, 73.3% was accounted for by individual life insurance policies; 4.0% by individual annuities policies; and 22.6% by group insurance policies (Fig. 7.2).

The duration of the liabilities at Japanese life insurance companies is very long. The average coverage period for individual and group life insurance policies is 20–40 years, while that for individual annuity policies is 20–30 years. To cover future benefit payments, life insurance companies set aside a portion of the premium income they receive from policyholders as liability reserves. At the end of fiscal 1999, the 45 Japanese life insurance companies had total assets of ¥188.4 tr., of which liability reserves accounted for ¥166.5 tr. – equal to 90.6% of the life insurance companies' total liabilities of ¥183.8 tr.[4]

ASSET MANAGEMENT PRACTICES

Because the bulk of their assets are accounted for by liability reserves, the life insurance companies manage their assets in accordance with the following considerations: safety, return, liquidity and the public welfare role of life insurers. Japan's life insurance com-

4 Source: Life Insurance Association of Japan.

panies strive to achieve stable investment returns through appropriate asset allocation and risk diversification. In light of the public and social impact of life insurance companies, safety of principal is a key consideration in how life insurers manage their assets. The Insurance Business Law limits the scope of allowable investments for life insurance companies, and for general account assets, limits exist on the percentage that can be invested in specific asset classes. Specifically, no more than 30% of general account assets can be invested in equities; no more than 30% in foreign-currency-denominated assets; and no more than 20% in real estate. This rule is accordingly referred to as the 3:3:2 rule.

Amid the recent developments in financial liberalization, globalization and asset securitization that have affected Japan's capital markets, Japan's life insurance companies have diversified their investment management practices despite the restrictions on the way they can manage their assets. Specifically, the life insurers can invest in a broader array of assets, utilize more investment management approaches, expand the scope of their financial services and raise funds in a greater number of ways than before.

Currently, Japan's life insurers are striving to achieve guaranteed policy returns by investing primarily in yen-denominated interest-bearing assets, such as bonds and loans. The insurers buy bonds with the intention of holding them for the long term and earning steady investment income. At the end of fiscal 1999, Japan's life insurance companies' bond investments consisted of ¥29.6 tr. in JGBs (28.3% of their total marketable securities investments); ¥6.9 tr. in municipal bonds (6.7%); and ¥15.3 tr. in corporate bonds (14.6%).

The range of available bond investments that have the duration to match the very long duration of life insurers' liabilities is limited. The market at the long end of the yield curve is not very deep; at the end of fiscal 2000, the total amount issued was only about ¥20 tr., even for 20-year JGBs. Accordingly, life insurers invest in a certain amount of risk assets (stocks and foreign-currency-denominated securities) in an effort to cover the cost of their liabilities in the medium to long term. In this sense, the key benchmark for the bond portfolios of the life insurance companies is their 'liabilities'. Given that the insurers must earn returns on their investments that are sufficient to cover the policy returns guaranteed to policyholders over the very long term, they must manage their investments from a long-term perspective.

As it currently stands, the Insurance Business Law, which was passed in 1996, permits Japanese life insurance companies to engage in public bond dealing. Nippon Life Insurance and Dai-ichi Mutual Life Insurance have received approval to serve as public bond dealers and are attempting to increase profits by taking on interest rate risk.

Life insurance companies have had to deal with a rather challenging investment environment in recent years. The next section examines changes that have occurred in the way in which life insurers invest in marketable securities.

1980s: Investment management during the age of the *seiho*

Japanese life insurance companies started to fully embrace their current diversified investment management approach during the 1980s. Until the 1970s, indirect financing dominated in Japan; hence, the main investment choice for Japanese life insurance companies was the extension of loans to domestic companies. Capital was in chronic short supply during the high-growth phase of Japan's economy. During this period, Japanese life insurance companies, along with the long-term credit banks and trust banks, played an important role as steady providers of capital for long-term capital investment projects.

In the 1980s, especially during the latter half of the decade when the economic bubble developed, both domestic and foreign investors closely followed the moves made in capital markets worldwide by Japan's life insurance companies because of the massive amount of investment assets they controlled. The market profile of Japanese life insurance companies became so significant that many global investors became familiar with the abbreviated Japanese term for life insurance companies – *seiho*.

IMPACT ON GLOBAL FINANCIAL MARKETS

Japanese life insurance companies' investments in US Treasuries came to have a pronounced impact on both the bond market and the currency market. It was widely thought that if Japan's life

159

insurance companies significantly reduced their investments in US Treasuries, US bond prices would plunge and the yen would appreciate sharply against the dollar. Indeed, Japanese life insurance companies' presence in capital markets around the world expanded to the extent that their investment moves could potentially have rattled not only the Japanese and US economies but also capital markets in Europe and the US.

A number of important factors led to the rise in the influence of Japan's life insurance companies in global financial markets and the changes in their investment management methodologies.

GROWTH IN ASSETS

During the high-growth phase of the Japanese economy, the marketing might of Japanese insurance companies increased thanks mainly to a huge sales force composed of women, who were hired in increasing numbers in the postwar period. Japanese life insurance products sold well, helped by the rise in personal incomes. According to the fact book published by the Life Insurance Association of Japan, at the end of 1988, the total amount of life insurance policies in force was ¥1200.5 tr., which was equivalent to ¥9.79 m worth of life insurance per person and 426% of Japan's total national income at the time.

Starting around 1965, when term life insurance, whole life insurance with a term rider and other term policies became the dominant type of life insurance product, companies competed by raising their benefits for term policies. In the 1980s, in part because of attractive yields and tax advantages, single-premium endowment insurance and variable-insurance policies for individuals grew in popularity, resulting in continued asset growth for the life insurance companies. By fiscal 1990, Japanese life insurers' total assets increased to around ¥127 tr., a more than tenfold increase from around ¥12 tr. in fiscal 1975.

Japanese life insurance companies increased their assets at a time when other financial institutions experienced a decrease in their total amount of assets. Of the total financial assets at all Japanese financial institutions, the proportion accounted for by life insurance companies rose from only 5.2% in fiscal 1975 to 9.5% by fiscal 1990; the amount peaked at 10.7% in fiscal 1993. In contrast, the proportion of assets accounted for by Japanese banks (not including trust account assets) declined from 44.1% in fiscal 1975 to 38.3% in fiscal 1990 (Fig. 7.3).

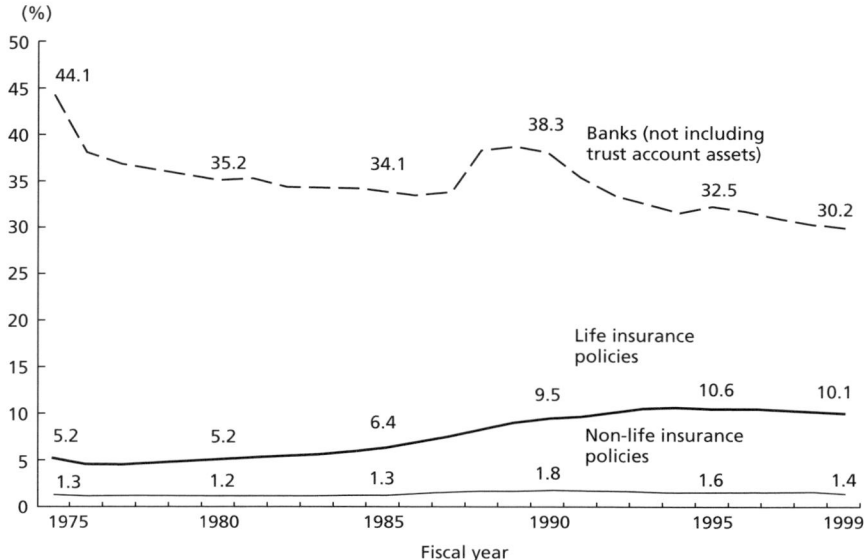

7.3 Life insurers' assets as a proportion of total assets of Japanese financial institutions.
Source: Nomura, based on the Bank of Japan's *Financial and Economics Statistics Monthly* (known as *Economic Statistics Monthly* prior to April 1999).

INDUSTRIAL STRUCTURE CHANGES AND DEREGULATION

Following the first oil crisis in the early 1970s and the resultant spike in energy prices worldwide, Japanese companies implemented various rationalization measures, such as job and production cuts. Primarily old-economy industries continued to restructure, and the base of Japan's industrial structure shifted from manufacturing industries to service industries.

Although the capital shortage in the corporate sector diminished somewhat, the capital shortage in the overall economy continued, mainly because of a lack of funds in the public sector and Japan's trade surplus.

Amid the liberalization of Japan's financial and capital markets (including the 1980 revision of Japan's Foreign Exchange and Foreign Trade Control Law, which liberalized cross-border capital market transactions), further internationalization of the economy and increased securitization of assets, restrictions on Japanese life insurance companies' asset management were relaxed. The types of

161

marketable securities in which life insurance companies could invest were expanded, the maximum allowable allocation for foreign investments was increased, and off-balance-sheet transactions and the use of impact loans[5] were allowed. These changes enabled Japan's life insurance companies to adjust to the changes in Japan's financial and capital markets by being able to raise capital and invest assets more flexibly.

COMPOSITION OF ASSETS

For many years after World War II, life insurance companies invested their assets mainly in the form of loans. Loans were suitable investments because, at the time, life insurance companies were required to pay ordinary dividends to policyholders only with interest income. As Japan's economy downshifted to lower growth, however, Japanese companies began to raise financing in an increasing variety of ways, resulting in a decline in demand for loans. Hence, loans fell from 67.9% of Japanese life insurance companies' total assets under management in fiscal 1975 to 35.4% in fiscal 1989.

Starting in the 1980s, then, life insurers increasingly expanded their investments in risky assets other than loans, mainly by investing in marketable securities, which rose from 21.7% of Japanese life insurance companies' total assets under management in fiscal 1975 to 47.2% in fiscal 1989. In particular, as an alternative to loans as a source of interest income, life insurers turned to corporate bonds and JGBs, the latter of which were being issued in huge volumes. And as JGB issuance terms improved and the secondary market developed further, JGBs accounted for an increasing proportion of life insurance companies' investment portfolios in the 1980s, because the companies not only invested in JGBs for interest income but also actively bought and sold them for capital gains (Table 7.3).

Until the mid-1980s, Japanese life insurance companies had been cautious on equities, as evident in the declining equity weightings in their portfolios. Because Japanese companies maintained constant dividends, higher stock prices resulted in lower dividend yields. Stock dividends were also not particularly attractive to the life insurers because secondary offerings in the 1980s were increasingly done at close to the market value of existing shares rather than at par value.

---

5 Impact loans are foreign-currency loans used by life insurance companies to hedge their investments in foreign-currency-denominated bonds.

Table 7.3 Changes in asset allocations of Japanese life insurance companies over time (%, ¥ bn)

	1975	1980	1985	1989	1990	1991	1992	1993	1994	1995	1996	1997	1998	1999
Call loans, money trusts, cash and deposits	1.7	2.5	11.9	9.4	9.8	9.4	9.5	13.3	10.9	9.5	7.7	9.3	8.0	8.4
Loans	67.9	59.7	45.2	35.4	37.9	39.3	39.2	37.9	37.6	35.9	34.6	33.4	30.8	28.8
Marketable securities	21.7	30.4	35.2	47.2	44.7	43.9	44.2	41.8	44.6	47.8	50.7	50.0	52.2	55.4
Corporate and government bonds	3.4	10.6	11.2	8.5	8.4	9.2	12.3	13.2	18.0	22.5	23.3	23.5	24.7	27.6
Stocks	18.1	17.2	15.1	21.8	22.0	21.5	20.2	19.6	18.6	17.1	16.9	15.7	14.9	15.0
Foreign securities	0.1	2.6	8.9	16.7	14.4	13.2	11.6	9.1	8.0	8.4	10.4	10.9	12.6	12.9
Real estate	7.9	6.4	5.9	5.6	5.5	5.4	5.4	5.3	5.3	5.2	5.2	5.2	5.1	4.8
Other	0.8	1.0	1.7	2.3	2.1	2.1	1.7	1.6	1.6	1.5	1.8	2.1	3.8	2.6
Total assets	12893.0	26257.8	53870.6	116159.7	131618.8	143234.1	156011.1	169122.1	177965.5	187492.5	188659.0	190111.0	191768.4	188417.3

Source: Nomura, based on Life Insurance Association of Japan materials.

Japanese stock prices rose even further in the latter half of the 1980s, fuelled by an excess of liquidity after the Bank of Japan (BOJ) pushed interest rates very low in the wake of the September 1985 Plaza Accord. In this period, Japanese life insurance companies increased their stock investments for two main reasons. First, the insurers bought shares of companies with which they had business relationships to maintain or strengthen ties. Second, they repurchased shares after selling them to offset losses on foreign bond investments stemming from the yen's appreciation in value. As a result, stocks increased from 15.1% of Japanese life insurance companies' total assets under management in fiscal 1985 to 21.8% in fiscal 1989. Furthermore, thanks to the sharp rise in Japanese stock prices, life insurance companies' unrealized gains on stockholdings increased from ¥21 tr. in fiscal 1985 to ¥45 tr. by fiscal 1988.

During the second half of the 1980s, Japan's life insurance companies also dramatically increased their investments in *tokkin* trusts. The *tokkin* trust structure was advantageous because the book value of the stocks in the *tokkin* trust accounts was not included with the book value of the stock investments in the general accounts of the life insurance companies. Thus, stock investments in the *tokkin* trust accounts did not increase the overall book value of insurers' existing stockholdings, and the life insurers could use the income, stemming from capital gains, from their *tokkin* trust accounts to pay dividends to policyholders.

INCREASE IN INVESTMENTS IN FOREIGN SECURITIES

One of the asset classes of which Japanese life insurance companies sharply increased their allocations between fiscal 1975 and fiscal 1990 was foreign securities, especially foreign bonds. A lifting of restrictions on insurers' investments in foreign securities in 1971 contributed to a sharp increase in Japanese life insurance companies' foreign securities allocation from a meagre 0.1% of total assets under management in fiscal 1975 to 16.7% in fiscal 1989. Although the life insurers incurred huge losses in yen terms on their foreign bond holdings as a result of the yen's appreciation following the Plaza Accord, they were able to offset these losses with gains on their domestic stockholdings, which had jumped in value partly because of the BOJ's efforts to stem the appreciating yen by keeping interest rates very low.

During the latter half of the 1980s, the life insurers diversified their foreign investments and increased their yields by adding emerging market funds to their investments in US and Canadian securities. In addition, they set up investment subsidiaries in tax havens and frequently used these units for various investment strategies. The life insurance companies were able to transform capital gains into dividend income because these investment subsidiaries paid their investment gains to the parent companies as dividends. And because the insurers' capital investments in the investment subsidiaries were accounted for at book value, life insurance companies did not have to book currency-related losses on their investments; instead, they could invest through the subsidiaries for the long run.

During the second half of the 1980s, many Japanese life insurance companies also established state-of-the-art trading rooms in their corporate headquarters and monitored global capital markets around the clock. They moved to establish global investment management operations by setting up subsidiaries in major cities in the US and Europe and forging alliances with leading foreign investment management companies.

In short, because of the massive unrealized gains on stockholdings stemming from the strong bull market in Japan in the latter 1980s, Japanese life insurance companies were able to invest in foreign bonds and yet suffered losses on the interest income in yen terms (as a result of the appreciation of the yen); for this reason alone, they grew to be feared as the *seiho* in international capital markets.

1990s: Investment management after the bursting of the economic bubble

After reaching a peak level of 38 915 at the end of 1989, the Nikkei 225 began to decline quickly in 1990. By fiscal 1994, it had fallen to a range of 15000–16000, down more than 50% from the index's all-time high. In addition, Japanese life insurance companies' aggregate unrealized gains on their stock portfolios fell precipitously from ¥45 tr. at the end of fiscal 1989 to ¥5.5 tr. by the end of fiscal 1994 (Fig. 7.4).

During the bubble years, the life insurance companies increased the amount of their policies in force by offering products with relatively high guaranteed yields ranging between 5.75% and 6.25%. The decline in unrealized gains on stockholdings, however, meant

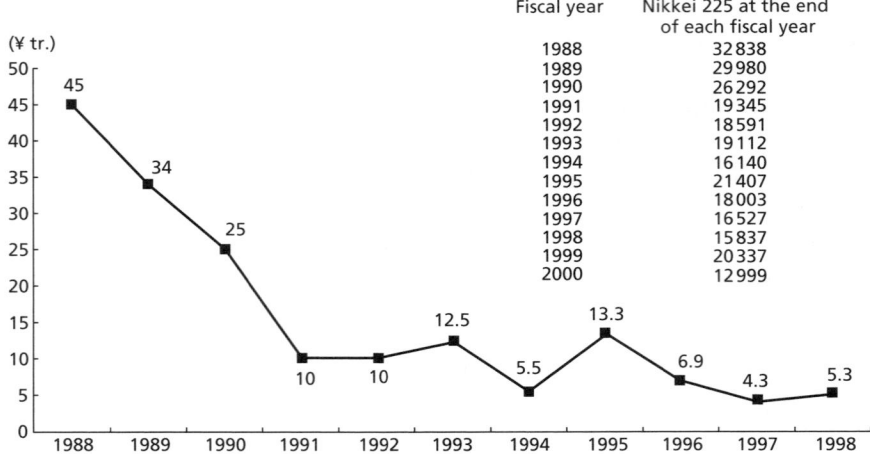

Fiscal year	Nikkei 225 at the end of each fiscal year
1988	32838
1989	29980
1990	26292
1991	19345
1992	18591
1993	19112
1994	16140
1995	21407
1996	18003
1997	16527
1998	15837
1999	20337
2000	12999

7.4 Japanese life insurance companies' aggregate unrealized gains on stockholdings.
© Nihon Keizai Shimbun. Source: as Fig. 7.2.

a drop in the financial resources life insurers had available to offset currency-related losses on their overseas investments as well as raised concerns about whether the insurers had the wherewithal to maintain their stable dividend policies.

In addition, since the bursting of the bubble, interest rates declined as a result of the BOJ's efforts to stimulate the maturing, slowing economy by loosening monetary policy. In September 1995, the central bank lowered the official discount rate to 0.5%, marking the start of a period of ultra-low interest rates. Since life insurers' liabilities have a longer duration than those of banks, the BOJ's loose monetary policy and the resultant decline in interest rates hurt the profitability of Japanese life insurance companies. Since the beginning of the 1990s, many domestic life insurance companies have paid out more in dividends on their policies than they have earned on their investment portfolios. In fact, by the second half of the 1990s, Japan's major life insurers' dividend payments exceeded their investment income by about ¥1.5 tr. per year.

Japan's life insurance companies therefore reduced their holdings of equities and foreign securities to avoid a further sharp drop in unrealized gains on their stockholdings and additional currency-related losses on their foreign securities investments. Stockholdings fell from 21.8% of Japanese life insurance companies' total assets under management in fiscal 1989 to 14.9% in fiscal 1998, and foreign securities dropped from 16.7% to 12.6% over the same period. In contrast, the life insurers increased their allocation of fixed-income investments in order to earn steady investment income. Bond holdings (JGBs, municipal bonds and corporate bonds) rose from 8.5% of total assets under management in fiscal 1989 to 24.7% in fiscal 1998.

Throughout the 1990s, the life insurance companies focused on creating portfolios that could generate stable investment returns. Nonetheless, the investment management divisions of the insurers still faced the challenge of increasing returns to a point that they adequately covered the returns they paid to policyholders. To restore normal spreads quickly, the life insurance companies adopted a two-pronged investment management approach. One portion of the investment assets was dedicated to generating enough interest income from low-risk, yen-denominated interest-yielding instruments to sufficiently cover guaranteed policy yields each year. The remaining portion of the assets, meanwhile, was invested in risky assets in an attempt to enhance total returns within the given risk constraints.

For some of the life insurance companies that sold many high-yield policies during the economic bubble years, policies with guaranteed yields of between 5.75% and 6.25% eventually accounted for 30–40% of their general account assets. To achieve investment returns in excess of 5%, these companies aggressively sold stock and real estate holdings, which weakened their financial strength. At the same time, they also increased their exposure to risky investments. Although most Japanese life insurance companies focused their investments during the early 1990s on relatively low-risk assets, such as loans and JGBs, some insurers stood out for their aggressive investment strategies.

Investment management during the period of bankruptcies

Nissan Mutual Life Insurance, a mid-sized insurance company with ¥2.1 tr. in total assets at the end of fiscal 1995, went bankrupt in April 1997 for two main reasons. First, during the economic bubble years, the company had sold a large number of high-yield individual annuity policies but was unable to generate sufficient investment returns to cover these obligations. Second, the company's attempt to invest in structured derivative products ended in failure. Nissan

Mutual was the first Japanese life insurer to collapse because of losses on high-risk investments intended to boost returns to cover higher-yielding policies.

Then, in June 1999, Toho Mutual Life Insurance, with total assets in fiscal 1997 of ¥3 tr., declared bankruptcy. To meet payments on high-yielding policies underwritten during the economic bubble years, the company realized gains on assets and in the process worsened the quality of its assets. In the end, the company's liabilities exceeded assets by ¥760 bn. By the end of fiscal 2000, six Japanese life insurance companies had become insolvent and gone under, including Nissan Mutual and Toho Mutual. Most of the bankruptcies were the result of the insurers' inability to generate investment returns sufficient to cover guaranteed yields and a deterioration in asset quality (Table 7.4).

OUTFLOW OF PENSION ASSETS AND EFFORTS TO STRENGTHEN ASSET MANAGEMENT CAPABILITIES

After the bankruptcy of Nissan Mutual, policyholders became extremely concerned about the creditworthiness of life insurance companies. This heightened sensitivity led to a decline in the amount of group pension fund assets entrusted to the life insurers. In April 1996, the guaranteed yield on group pension insurance assets was lowered to 2.5% from 4.5%, a move that sparked an outflow of pension fund assets from the general accounts of the life insurance companies. One of the major policy cancellations, by the Pension Welfare Service Public Corporation, involved ¥5 tr. in pension assets. This outflow accelerated as a number of life insurance companies went bankrupt. The amount of group pension assets entrusted to the 14 large and mid-sized life insurance companies (including Chiyoda Mutual Life Insurance and Kyoei Life Insurance) fell by ¥1.5 tr. in fiscal 1998 from the previous fiscal year and by ¥2.5 tr. in fiscal 1999.

Some of the assets from cancelled insurance policies were transferred to the investment advisory affiliates and special accounts of life insurance companies. These moves were part of some life insurance companies' strategic efforts to increase the amount of pension assets under management at their investment advisory affiliates, where investment returns were directly related to the performance of the advisor. For the same reason, some life insurance companies, mainly the leading ones, transferred several hundreds of billions of yen in assets from special accounts to their investment advisory

Table 7.4 Summary of major bankruptcies among Japanese life insurers (¥ bn)

	Nissan Mutual Life Insurance	Toho Mutual Life Insurance	Daihyaku Mutual Life Insurance	Taisho Life Insurance	Chiyoda Mutual Life Insurance	Kyoei Life Insurance
Date ordered to cease operations	1997.4.25	1999.6.4	2000.5.31	2000.8.28	2000.10.9	2000.10.20
Total assets for fiscal year prior to bankruptcy	2 167.4	2 804.6	1 721.7	204.5	3 501.9	4 610.0
Publicly disclosed amount of net liabilities	200.0	200.0	122.2	1.2	34.3	about 4.5
Final amount of net liabilities	310.0–320.0	760.0	320.0	?	595.0	689.5
Amount covered by the life insurance industry	200.0	380.0	145.0	?	0	0
Residual funds after bankruptcy proceedings	–	580.0	435.0	?	435.0	435.0
Applicable law	Insurance Business Law	Insurance Business Law	Insurance Business Law	Insurance Business Law	A special law for the rehabilitation of financial institutions	A special law for the rehabilitation of financial institutions
Source of bailout financing	Insurance Policyholder Protection Fund	Life Insurance Policyholders' Protection Corporation of Japan	Life Insurance Policyholders' Protection Corporation of Japan	Life Insurance Policyholders' Protection Corporation of Japan	Life Insurance Policyholders' Protection Corporation of Japan	Life Insurance Policyholders' Protection Corporation of Japan
New owner	Artemis (France)	GE Capital (US)	–	–	AIG (US)	Prudential (US)

Note: The publicly disclosed amount of net liabilities is the figure reported in the press.
Source: Nomura, based on Life Insurance Association of Japan materials.

affiliates. In addition, they implemented several measures to improve the investment management capabilities of the firms, such as introducing performance-based compensation systems for fund managers.

The investment management divisions of life insurance companies also became more cognizant of asset–liability management in the mid-1990s. Starting in April 1996, the life insurers adopted separate-account management systems, one after another. Under these systems, liabilities were categorized on the basis of product type, such as individual policies and group policies, and assets matching the unique attributes of each product group were managed separately, thereby allowing a transition to flexible risk management. In this way, the life insurers' system of investment management gradually improved from the days when assets were all lumped together.

INSURANCE POLICIES AND ASSET MANAGEMENT

The bankruptcies among Japanese life insurance companies raised concerns about the viability of some insurers and led to individual policy cancellations and sluggish growth in new policy underwritings. Solvency margin ratios, a kind of capital-adequacy ratio for life insurers, were disclosed starting in fiscal 1997. Policy cancellations were especially high for life insurance companies with relatively low solvency margin ratios (Table 7.5). With a rise in cancellations and lower growth in the amount of new policies underwritten, the life insurance companies faced even greater difficulties in closing the gap between their investment returns and guaranteed returns to policyholders. A decline in the amount of policies in force meant a drop in premium income and, consequently, a decline in funds for covering future dividend payments to policyholders.

The total amount of individual insurance and individual annuity policies in force for Japan's mid-sized and large life insurance companies declined year on year in fiscal 1997 and continued to fall below previous year levels for the two following fiscal years. Consequently, the role and responsibilities of the investment management divisions of the life insurance companies have become even more important.

In fiscal 1999, the prospects for insurance policy sales brightened somewhat, thanks to the introduction of insurance products with discounted premiums. Nonetheless, the average guaranteed yield on insurance policies remained high, at 3.5% to 3.9%, making

Table 7.5 Solvency margin ratios in Japanese life insurance companies (%)

	1997	1998	1999	2000
Nippon Life Insurance	939.9	849.9	1095.8	778.1
Dai-ichi Mutual Life Insurance	632.1	662.1	865.6	682.3
Sumitomo Life Insurance	526.2	589.5	675.7	551.3
Meiji Mutual Life Insurance	720.0	706.0	731.0	667.0
Asahi Mutual Life Insurance	654.8	688.8	732.7	543.4
Mitsui Mutual Life Insurance	491.6	519.6	676.7	492.7
Yasuda Mutual Life Insurance	648.1	727.2	808.5	602.6
Chiyoda Mutual Life Insurance	314.2	396.1	236.1	—
Taiyo Mutual Life Insurance	873.0	869.1	1050.3	806.8
Kyoei Life Insurance	300.7	343.2	210.6	—
Daido Mutual Life Insurance	1016.8	998.0	1004.2	757.6
Nichidan Life Insurance (formerly Nippon Dantai Life)	308.6	377.5	425.9	464.7
Fukoku Mutual Life Insurance	722.4	820.6	906.5	779.3
Tokyo Mutual Life Insurance	431.6	478.7	446.7	—
Sony Life Insurance	1545.5	1429.1	1437.1	1905.9

Note: Solvency margin ratio = solvency margin amounts divided by total risk.
Source: Nomura, based on Life Insurance Association of Japan materials.

it highly unlikely that investment returns would improve quickly. For those life insurers that had realized gains on stockholdings again and again to help close the negative spread between investment returns and guaranteed yields to policyholders, it has become increasingly difficult to continue to do so because the book value of their stockholdings has increased while the overall market has fallen. Another investment management issue confronting Japan's life insurance companies is increased interest rate risk because they shifted to longer-term bonds in the second half of the 1990s.

Japan's life insurance companies need to restructure their portfolios so that they are less vulnerable to a decline in stock prices and a rise in interest rates. Specifically, they need to adopt new portfolio strategies, such as reducing the amount of strategically owned shares, investing flexibly in equities and investing new assets in shorter-duration bonds. The insurers should also rethink their product strategies. For example, they could consider increasing sales of group insurance policies that need to be renewed each year.

In fiscal 1999, Japanese life insurance companies started to forge alliances with other insurance companies. Partnerships between life insurance and non-life insurance companies can be regarded as a constructive effort to bolster stagnant sales of insurance policies because they have led to more marketable products and an increase in the number of products each company is able to offer. In general, the alliances have been part of strategies aimed at maintaining and expanding customer bases and the value of insurance policies in force.

If these alliances turn out to be successful and industry sales improve, life insurers' investment returns are likely to improve as well. Such a development, coupled with efforts to restructure investment portfolios and revamp business operations, should lead to stronger Japanese life insurance companies later in the twenty-first century.

8 Cross-border money flows and the exchange rate

Japan, which has been the world's foremost creditor country for a good number of years, continues to run a current account surplus in excess of ¥10 tr. every year. This incessant accumulation of ever more external assets in one form or another means that the Japanese, whether they like it or not, have a growing need to diversify their international investments. So, from a macroeconomic objective of protecting the wealth of the nation, Japan has had a paramount need to understand the mechanisms behind exchange rate fluctuations. The revised Foreign Exchange and Foreign Trade Law, which took effect in April 1998, relaxed the controls on capital transactions between Japan and other countries even further, thereby making it easier for Japanese companies to diversify their international investments and contributing to a broadening of interest in exchange rates from the world of importers, exporters and institutional investors to the level of individual investors.

The direct determinant of exchange rate fluctuations is the international flow of capital, which is, in turn, affected by a complex web of factors. Differences in countries' business cycles, price levels, macroeconomic policies and short- and long-term interest rates, along with market participants' readings of the exchange rate policy stances of the financial authorities of relevant countries, interact to establish capital flows. Rarely do these factors simultaneously point in the same direction; in fact, they generally counteract each other to some degree, and the extent of their impact changes with time to reflect both the degree to which these various factors have been discounted by the market and the focus of the market at the time.

These basic points about the international flow of capital form the foundation of this chapter, which reviews the shifting pattern of international capital flows between Japan and the rest of the world since the latter half of the 1980s, when Japanese investors started seriously diversifying their assets internationally. The factors that determine cross-border money flows and the linkages between them and the actual yen–dollar exchange rate will also be discussed.

Trends in the current account surplus

The present series of yen-based statistics on the balance of international payments released by the Bank of Japan (BOJ) goes back as far as 1985 (previously the bank released these statistics in dollar terms). These statistics serve as the basis for this review of the trends in capital flows between Japan and the rest of the world since the latter half of the 1980s.

THE CURRENT ACCOUNT SURPLUS AND NET TOTAL INVESTMENTS

For Japan as well as other countries, the balance of payments, which equals the sum of the current account balance, the capital account balance, changes in the official reserve account, and net errors and omissions, must equal zero. Given the consistency of Japan's current account surplus, it follows that, on an *ex post* basis, it has had a net outflow of funds in its capital account in some form or another. An amount on par with that of the current account surplus has been recycled from Japan to other countries in a variety of forms, including direct investment, portfolio investment, remittances and lending by banks, trade credits and net changes in official reserves.

Figure 8.1 illustrates the continuity of Japan's current account surplus throughout the period under review. Only slight cyclical variation is evident. And for the most part, the trends in net total investments, which account for the bulk of the capital account, have been a mirror image of the trends in the current account surplus.

International portfolio investment from Japan increased dramatically in the latter part of the 1980s as a result of the appreciation of the yen in the wake of the Plaza Accord of September 1985, the relaxation of regulations on foreign investment by institutional investors and the loose monetary policy adopted by the BOJ. In fact, the sum of the net outflows of direct investment and portfolio investment exceeded the current account surplus, and the difference was made up by other investments. In other words, the massive

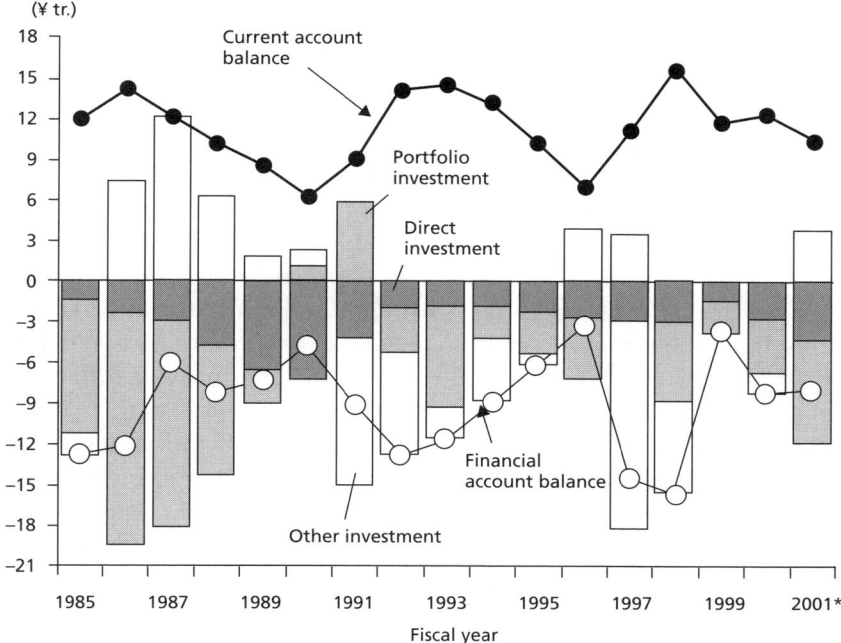

8.1 The current account balance and the financial account balance.
Notes: Figures for direct investment, portfolio investment and other investment are net. Negative values indicate capital inflows. *Figures to 2001 are annualized, based on data to September.
Source: Bank of Japan, *Balance of Payments Monthly*.

growth in Japan's investments abroad during these years was financed by a combination of the current account surplus and funds raised abroad by Japanese banks.

With the bursting of the economic bubble at the beginning of the 1990s, Japanese companies and investors began repatriating some of their funds from overseas, resulting in a net inflow of portfolio investments in both 1990 and 1991. During the remainder of the early 1990s, the diminishing capacity of domestic businesses and financial institutions to take on risk caused the net outflow of direct and portfolio investments to fall below the level of the current account surplus. The difference was made up by other investments, which swung to a net outflow; Japanese banks, facing stricter capital-adequacy requirements, had started paying back the funds they had borrowed earlier from overseas.

In contrast, the second half of the 1990s reveals no clear pattern in the balance of payments. The current account surplus shrank in

175

1996, but this was accompanied by a decline in net outflows of total investments. In particular, the move by Japanese banks to collect on their overseas loans created a large net inflow of other investments. Then in the following two years, the current account surplus actually widened. The flows of portfolio investments to and from Japan varied, but the net outflow of total investments roughly corresponded in scale to the current account surplus.

One major constituent element in this net outflow of funds was the large amount of other investments, which were primarily fund transfers from Japanese banks to their international branches. The banks had been running into a hefty 'Japan premium' when they borrowed in overseas interbank markets. Then in 1999 and 2000, the deficit in total investments fell below the level of the current account surplus. The difference was made up by a sharp increase in Japan's official reserve assets when the monetary authorities intervened in the foreign exchange market to sell yen and buy foreign currencies on a record-breaking scale. In 2001, capital outflows were on a par with the size of the current account surplus, mainly as a result of an expanded net outflow of direct investments and hedged investments in foreign bonds.

TRENDS IN DIRECT INVESTMENT

Foreign direct investment from Japan grew throughout the latter part of the 1980s. The strength of the yen and trade friction with the US had prompted Japanese manufacturers to shift their production offshore. Strong overseas investment by insurers and other financial institutions, including real estate companies flush with funds from the economic bubble, had also compounded the growth in investment abroad.

The outflow of direct investment peaked in 1990, which marked the high point of the domestic financial and real estate bubble. Then, from 1991 to 1993, investment abroad declined. As domestic businesses and financial institutions saw their profits shrink and their balance sheets deteriorate, they generally lost their enthusiasm for overseas investment projects. The flow of outward direct investment has been growing again since 1994, albeit at an extremely slow rate.

For example, until 1996, Japan's investment in other Asian countries increased. At that time, businesses were seeking both to lower their production costs by shifting operations offshore and to get in early on what they thought would be promising markets for the future. Unfortunately, the Asian currency crisis of 1997 dashed this hope. Overall investment in the region declined for a while, but

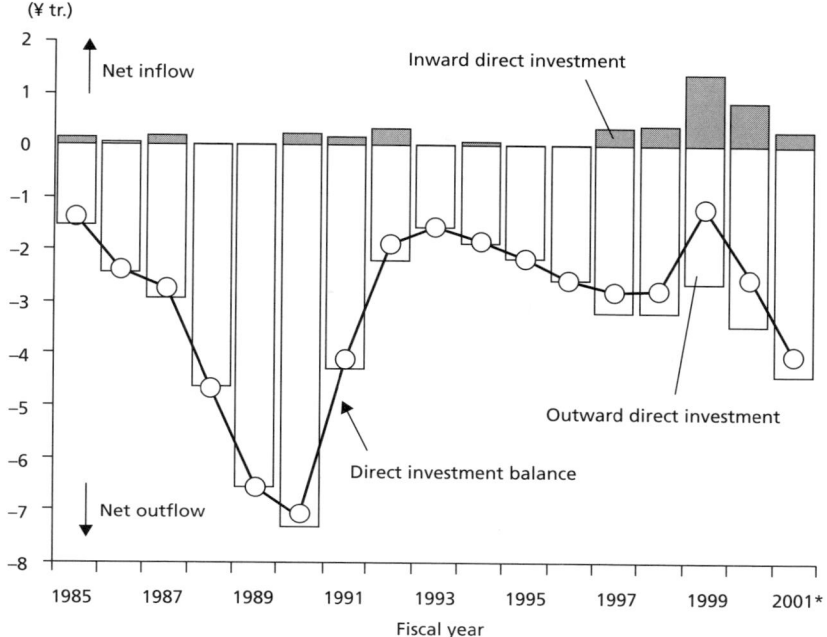

8.2 Inward and outward direct investment.
Note: *Figures for 2001 are annualized, based on data to September.
Source: as Fig. 8.1.

shows signs of having picked up again as Japanese companies try to remain globally competitive in light of China's accession to the World Trade Organization. Nonetheless, amid an environment of increased corporate regrouping and mergers and acquisitions on a global level, some Japanese telecommunications companies and other businesses have been either acquiring companies in industrialized countries outright or taking equity stakes in them.

Meanwhile, foreign direct investment in Japan continues to run at a low level, at least by comparison with Japan's direct investments in other countries. Reflecting this discrepancy, Japan's direct investment balance has consistently recorded a net outflow, as shown in Fig. 8.2. By international standards, Japan's ratio of inward to outward direct investment is extremely low. Reasons for this low level of inward direct investment vary. Some people cite the closed nature of the Japanese market and the conservative culture of Japanese business; another rationale contends that the relatively high level of wages and the entry barrier posed by Japan's difficult language markedly discourage foreign investors.

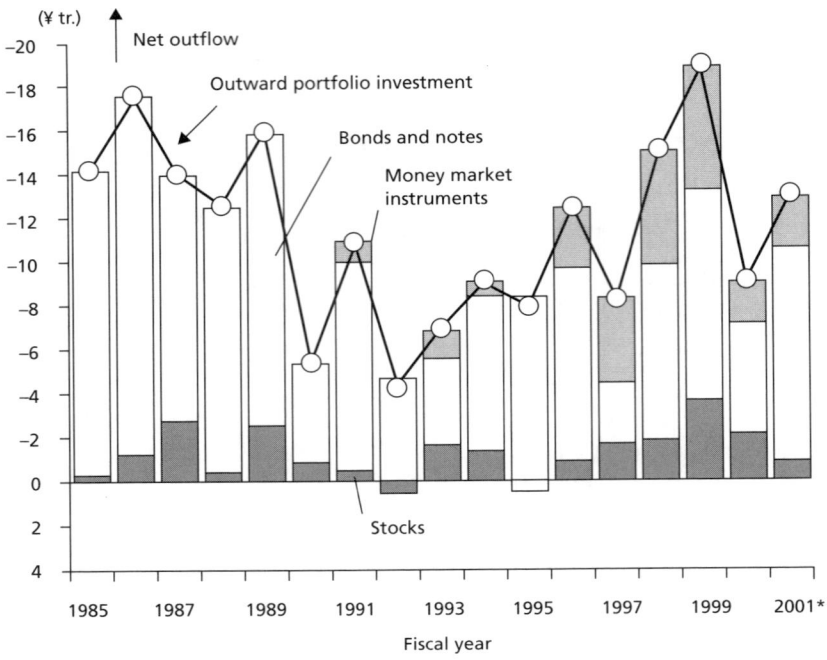

8.3 Outward portfolio investment.
Notes: Money market instruments include derivatives. For 1990 and before, figures
are based on the statistics for equity and debt securities in the old data series for
the long-term capital balance. Debt securities are presented in the graph as 'bonds
and notes'. *Figures for 2001 are annualized, based on data to September.
Source: as Fig. 8.1.

But in recent years, the situation has been gradually changing.
Since 1997, a stream of foreign investment has flowed into a variety
of sectors in Japan, particularly financial services, automobiles and
telecommunications. Foreign corporations have been either acquiring equity stakes in or simply taking over Japanese companies outright. Because of the global regrouping of businesses in these fields,
corporate governance in Japan has been shifting toward placing a
greater emphasis on shareholders' interests; domestic companies that
are financially struggling or on the brink of collapsing have also
become more willing to accept foreign ownership as part of their
business restructuring processes.

TRENDS IN PORTFOLIO INVESTMENT

Figure 8.3 shows Japan's external portfolio investment by type of
security. Clearly, the largest share of investment continues to be in

medium- and long-term bonds, although the share of investment in equities has gradually increased over the years.

During the latter half of the 1980s, Japanese institutional investors – particularly life insurance companies – were very interested in investing in foreign bonds. The pace of their investment in bonds slowed somewhat in the early 1990s, however. The losses investors experienced from the earlier rise of the yen and the reduced risk tolerance of financial institutions following the collapse of the economic bubble made investing in bonds less attractive.

Toward the end of the decade, a renewed surge in net purchases of foreign bonds became apparent. The extraordinarily low level of domestic interest rates and optimism surrounding the prospects of the newly launched euro, as well as the lifting of restrictions on investment in foreign-currency-denominated securities by domestic pension funds, favourably influenced bond purchasers. The level of these net investments was especially high in 1999, when purchases of Euroyen bonds increased along with those of US and European issues.

Japanese investments in foreign bonds then contracted sharply in 2000. First, the plunge in Japan's stock market once again reduced the risk tolerance of institutional investors. Second, mark-to-market accounting rules were adopted for financial instruments; these rules have the effect of making the value of assets on companies' balance sheets more volatile than before. And third, regulators imposed stricter standards on the way life insurance companies are able to calculate their solvency margins. But in 2001, a bullish steepening of the yield curve in the US contributed to an increase in hedged Japanese investments in foreign bonds.

In broad terms, Japan's investment in foreign equities has been much smaller in scale than its investment in foreign bonds. Except for 1992, the net flow has been outward – in other words, Japanese investors have been net buyers of foreign stocks. The size of the outflow grew from 1996 to 1999, an increase that reflects the efforts of trust banks and life insurance companies to diversify their portfolios by increasing their investments in the US and European markets, which were setting new record highs. Another factor contributing to the growth in Japan's foreign equity investments was the strong fund inflows in these years from pension plans to trust banks, which manage pension plan assets. But the amount of the equity investment outflow has contracted considerably since 2000, when a sharp correction in the prices of telecommunications, media and technology stocks started in the US and spread to other markets.

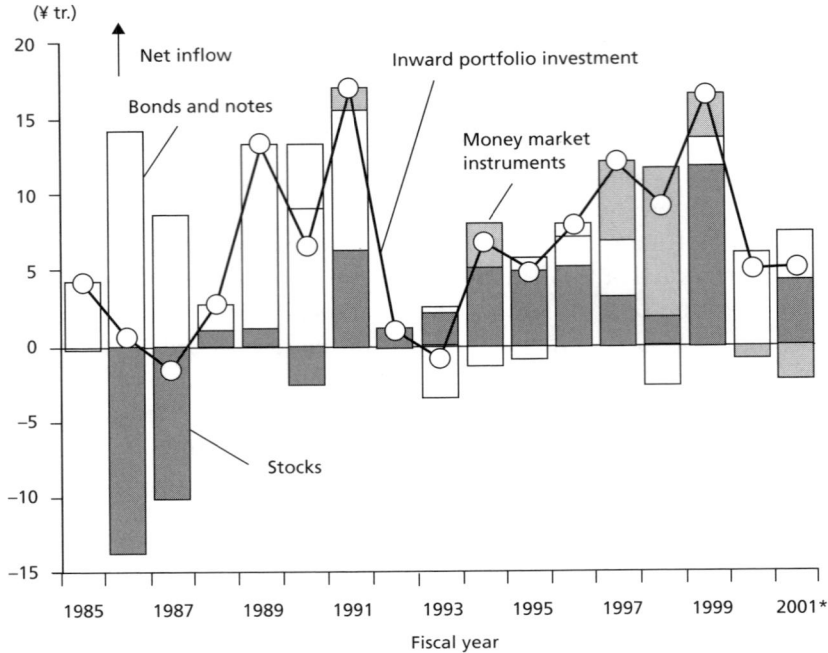

8.4 Inward portfolio investment.
Notes: Money market instruments include derivatives. For 1990 and before, figures are based on the statistics for equity and debt securities in the old data series for the long-term capital balance. Debt securities are presented in the graph as 'bonds and notes'. *Figures for 2001 are annualized, based on data to September.
Source: as Fig. 8.1.

Japanese investment in money market instruments registered an increase in the latter part of the 1990s. Part of this increase reflects purchases by Japanese financial institutions of the yen-denominated commercial paper that was issued by special-purpose subsidiaries set up in tax havens. Investments in various Euroyen structured bonds also rose. These trends, along with the increased complexity of alternative investments, have made tracking the patterns in cross-border capital flows and their impact on the foreign exchange market more difficult than before.

Trends in overseas investment in Japanese securities, meanwhile, are indicated in Fig. 8.4. From the time of the 1985 Plaza Accord to the early 1990s, there were net inflows of investments in Japanese medium- and long-term bonds. In part, the rising value of the yen had made Japanese government bonds (JGBs) attractive to foreign investors. In addition, because of the strong demand for funds during these economic bubble years, Japanese and non-Japanese companies located in Japan were actively issuing foreign currency bonds. From 1992 to 1995, however, the net flow of bond investments turned outward. This change followed the redemption of foreign-currency bonds by Japan-resident companies and foreign investors' profit-taking on JGB holdings.

In 1996, the pattern once again reversed to a net inflow of bond investments. And as prospects for the Japanese economy became clouded by a consumption tax rise in April of that year, the amount of the net inflow expanded in 1997. Bond purchases were driven up by investors' flight to safety in the wake of declines in stock markets around the world.

Then, in 1998, with Japanese government bonds trading at record-high price levels and because of growing concerns about Japan's fiscal health arising from the government's string of economic stimulus packages, investments in Japanese bonds turned into a net outflow. But the direction of the flow reversed again in 1999, and the scale of the net inflow of investment in bonds has expanded since 2000, as investors turned once again to fixed-income securities against a backdrop of receding hopes for further increases in stock prices on bourses around the world.

On the equity side, foreign investors were net sellers of stocks from 1985 to 1987, the year of Wall Street's Black Monday. They became net buyers in 1988 and 1989 but resumed their net sales in 1990, when Japan's economic bubble burst. During the 1990s, foreign investors increased their investment in Japanese equities, and have tended to be net buyers since 1991. Part of the reason is that Japanese shares have been relatively inexpensive, at least compared with US and European stocks. In 1999, expectations of an economic recovery in Japan and the strengthening of the yen's value combined to push foreigners' net purchases of Japanese stocks up to a record high, topping the ¥10 tr. mark. But in 2000, the amount of foreign investments in Japanese stocks declined because of sales by international investors seeking to make up for losses incurred in the weakening US market and fears that the Japanese economy would suffer another slowdown. The trend reversed in 2001, on expectations for the structural reform programme initiated by the new prime minister, Junichiro Koizumi.

OFFICIAL RESERVE ASSETS

Japan's official reserve assets (consisting largely of foreign currency reserves) fluctuate mainly as the result of intervention in the

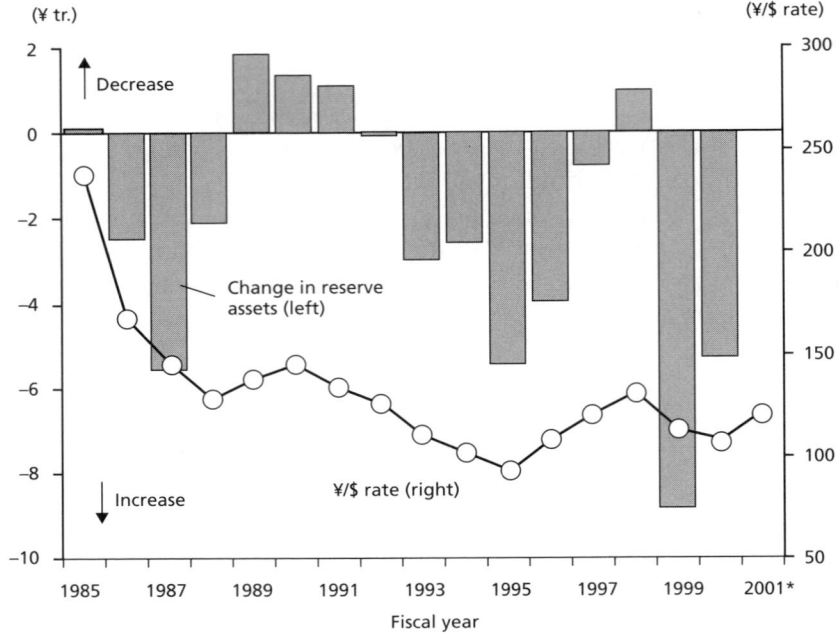

(¥ tr.)

(¥/$ rate)

8.5 Changes in reserve assets and the yen–dollar rate.
Notes: The yen–dollar rate is the annual average of daily closings on the Tokyo forex market. *Figures for 2001 are annualized, based on data to September.
Source: as Fig. 8.1.

currency market. As shown in Fig. 8.5, during the latter part of the 1980s, these reserves rose sharply. The principal cause of the increase was the BOJ's selling of yen and buying of dollars to ease the strong upward pressure on the yen in the wake of the Plaza Accord. From 1989 to 1991, the BOJ then intervened in the other direction; it purchased yen to counter the downward pressure that resulted from the outflow of direct investment funds and then from the bursting of the economic bubble.

Since 1992, the current account surplus has grown, and Japanese corporations have become less enthusiastic about directly investing overseas. These developments have pushed up the value of the yen, and so the BOJ responded by again selling yen for dollars, thereby pushing the official reserves up once more. The central bank bought an especially large amount of foreign currency in 1995, when, at one point, the dollar fell below ¥80, its lowest level ever against the yen since the move to a floating-rate regime.

The dollar eventually recovered against the yen, and in 1998, it traded for a while at a level approaching ¥150 to a dollar. This rise

182

was powered in part by so-called carry trades, in which US hedge funds inexpensively borrowed short-term funds in yen and purchased dollars. In response, the BOJ and the US Federal Reserve jointly intervened to buy up yen, which led to a decline in Japan's official reserves. Yet in 1999, the BOJ sold yen for dollars on an unprecedented scale to lessen the upward pressure on the yen. The active buying of Japanese shares by foreign investors, who were attracted by the prospects of an economic recovery, prompted the BOJ's move. Since 2000, the central bank has intervened by continuing to sell yen to minimize the upward pressures on the yen, amid another economic slowdown and deflation in Japan.

For the most part, the BOJ has intervened in the currency market by selling yen and buying dollars in response to the long-term upward trend in the yen's value, which will be discussed in the following section. What distinguishes this recent intervention is the high frequency and volume. Partly because Japan has steadily run a current account surplus, the level of foreign currency reserves has generally risen over the years. And when Japan intervenes in the currency market, it usually does so on a scale larger than that of Western countries. In recent years, Japanese intervention amounting to more than $10bn in a single day has not been unusual. On average, the estimated value of the Japanese authorities' intervention is about 10 times that of their US counterparts.

No one knows exactly why the BOJ has chosen to intervene on such a large scale. One interpretation is that it shows the strength of the Japanese authorities' commitment to stabilizing the value of the yen. But another view maintains that such intervention has been vital to achieving the desired results because of the relatively low level of credibility of the BOJ among currency market participants. At any rate, since the second quarter of 2000, the Ministry of Finance (MOF) has been publishing reports on the foreign exchange intervention operations that were implemented during the course of the quarter. The information, which is released slightly over a month after the end of the quarter and is posted on the ministry's Web site, includes the dates, currencies and amounts of the authorities' foreign exchange operations.

The long-term uptrend in the yen's value

Ever since the shift from a fixed exchange rate system to a managed float, the value of the yen has generally increased against the dollar

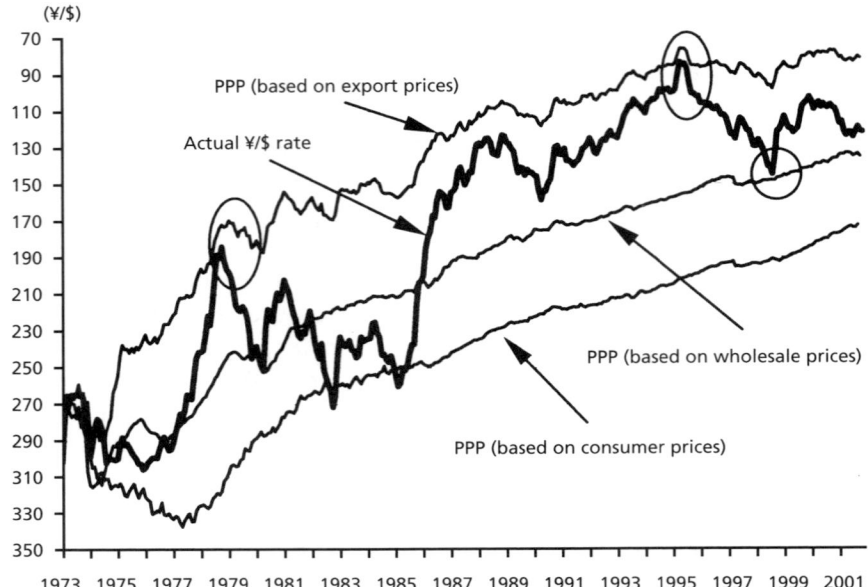

8.6 Yen–dollar rate and purchasing power parity.
Notes: March 1973 is the base month. Export price levels for Japan use the BOJ's export price index (WPI-based). Actual ¥/$ rates are the mid rates.
Source: Nomura.

over the long term, even though it has been volatile over the short and medium term. This long-term uptrend can be analysed in terms of two major factors, namely, purchasing power parity (PPP) and the Japan–US cumulative current account balances.

PURCHASING POWER PARITY

Figure 8.6 traces the course of the actual yen–dollar exchange rate and of PPP as calculated from three sets of price indexes in Japan and the US – export prices, wholesale prices and consumer prices – since 1973. The base month for the calculations is March 1973, the month following the shift to a floating-rate system for the yen.

One important point highlighted in this figure is that since the latter part of the 1970s, the purchasing power of the yen has steadily strengthened relative to the dollar in terms of any of the three price indexes, because the rate of inflation as measured by all three indexes has been consistently higher in the US than in Japan. A relatively higher rate of inflation translates into a depreciation of a currency's value. Since inflation in Japan has been relatively low, the yen has tended to rise over the long term, not only against the dollar but also against other major currencies, such as the German mark (and more recently its successor, the euro) and the British pound.

With March 1973 as the base month, the actual yen–dollar exchange rate moves within a range whose upper boundary (where 'upper' refers to a stronger yen) is the PPP curve based on export prices and whose lower boundary is the PPP curve based on consumer prices. Furthermore, the actual rate has come close to the PPP curve based on export prices only twice in the course of the past quarter-century. The first time occurred during the dollar crisis in 1978, when the greenback fell so far that the Carter administration was forced to come up with a policy to defend it, and the second happened in 1995, when Lloyd Bentsen, President Clinton's first Treasury secretary, moved to push the yen up against the dollar. And the actual rate only tested the lower boundary – the PPP curve based on consumer prices – during the first half of the 1980s, when the Reagan administration was promoting a strong-dollar policy as part of its Reaganomics agenda.

Notably, the link of causation between the trend in PPP and the upward trend in the actual exchange rate is not clear. Although to some extent it may be true that the rising purchasing power of the yen, resulting from Japan's relatively low inflation rates, has tended to push the value of the yen up, the upward trend in the yen's value could also be keeping Japan's prices down – and pushing up the purchasing power of the yen.

CUMULATIVE CURRENT ACCOUNT BALANCES

The set of trends presented by the Japanese and US current account balances are worth examining as well. Since the latter part of the 1980s in particular, the US has consistently tended to run a current account deficit, in the process becoming the world's foremost debtor nation, whereas Japan, which has consistently run a current account surplus, has become the world's greatest creditor. These parallel but contrasting developments are often cited as the main factors behind the yen's long-term rise against the dollar.

Figure 8.7 presents the trends in the cumulative current account balances of Japan and the US as percentages of nominal GDP in tandem with the yen–dollar exchange rate since 1970. As this figure shows, the basic direction of all three curves is similar. The growth of US external liabilities tends, over the medium to long term, to

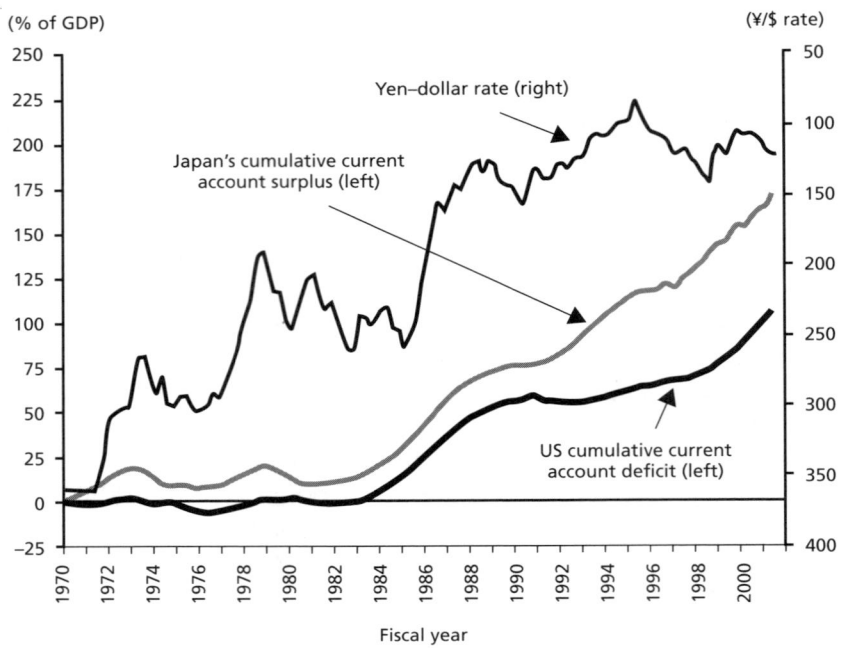

8.7 Japan–US cumulative current account balances and yen–dollar rate.
Note: Cumulative current account balances are calculated from the first quarter of 1970.
Source: Nomura.

increase the risk faced by foreigners investing there. Therefore, in order to sustain a smooth inflow of funds from abroad, the US has found it necessary to accept a certain degree of dollar depreciation as a way of making its assets appear more attractively priced.

Also, as is well known, Japan's consistently huge surplus trade with the US has been the source of frequent trade disputes between the two countries. The fact that this huge Japanese surplus has persisted may be taken as a sign of imbalance in the price competitiveness of the two countries' tradable goods; indeed, one viable conclusion is that the dollar's depreciation against the yen is required as an adjustment mechanism. Although it seems impossible to pinpoint precisely what sort of cause-and-effect relationship is at work, most academic, government and private-sector studies have found Japan's cumulative current account surplus and the United States' external indebtedness to be significant determinants of the very long-term trends in the yen–dollar rate.

CHANGES IN EXCHANGE RATES

The key determinants of the yen–dollar exchange rate in the short and medium term are said to be changes in the market's consensus view of interest rate trends and economic growth prospects in Japan and the US. As a practical matter, however, finding a set of financial and economic indicators that show a stable correlation with the exchange rate over time is extremely difficult. Among a wide range of indicators, two in particular appear to have a relatively strong correlation with short- and medium-term trends in the yen–dollar rate: the spread in nominal short-term rates and the difference in leading economic indicators between the two countries.

THE SPREAD IN NOMINAL SHORT-TERM RATES

Figure 8.8 plots the actual yen–dollar exchange rate against the spread between the three-month Eurodollar and Euroyen interest rates (based on month-end values) since January 1980. The graph shows that when the spread exceeds 350 basis points, the dollar tends to start rising against the yen after a certain time interval. Throughout the entire period of slightly more than 20 years, the spread exceeded 350 basis points in 135 months; in 88 of these months, or 62% of the total, the dollar rose against the yen in the following three months. And if the exceptional 18-month period when the yen strengthened from July 1998 to December 1999 is excluded, then in 67 of the remaining 99 months when the rate spread exceeded 350 basis points (roughly two-thirds of the cases), the dollar rose against the yen in the following three-month period. Hence, an investor who mechanically bought dollars whenever the rate spread topped 350 basis points would have made money in the following three months roughly two times out of three.

Conversely, in 84 of the 124 cases in which the rate spread was less than 350 basis points – or slightly over two-thirds of these cases – the yen rose against the dollar during the subsequent three-month period. Empirically, then, a spread of 350 basis points in nominal short-term rates appears to be a significant indicator of short-term trends in the yen–dollar exchange rate.

One hypothesis for this correlation between short-term rate spreads and short-term yen–dollar trends is that because the long-term trend in the value of the yen against the dollar has been upward, Japanese investors require a relatively high yield on liquid dollar-denominated assets to compensate for risk. Or, rather, the

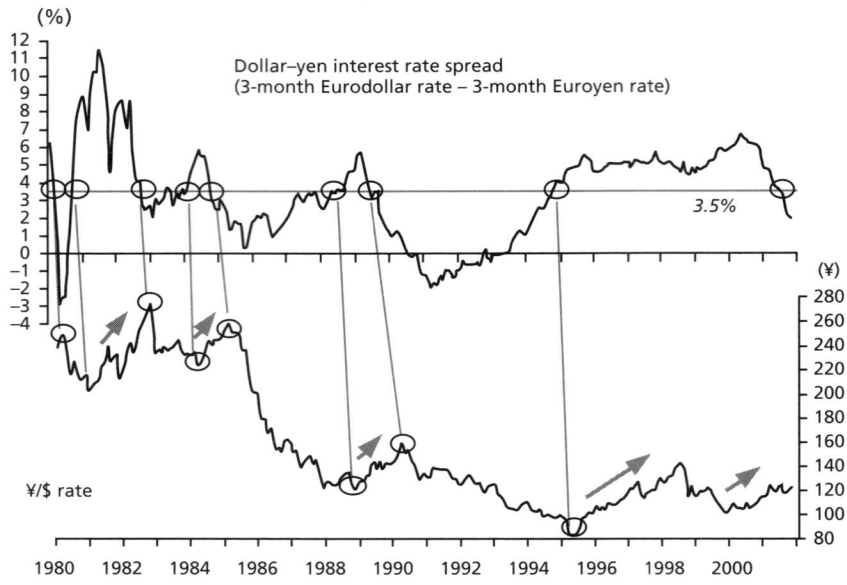

Dollar–yen interest rate spread (3-month Eurodollar rate – 3-month Euroyen rate)	Period	No. of months	¥/$ rate 3 months later	
			Stronger dollar	Stronger yen
350 bp or above	Jan. 80–July 01	135 months (100%)	88 months (62%)	51 months (38%)
	Jan. 80–July 98	99 months (100%)	67 months (68%)	32 months (32%)
Below 350 bp	Jan. 80–July 01	124 months (100%)	40 months (32%)	84 months (68%)

8.8 Short-term interest rate spread and yen–dollar rate.
Note: Rates are at month-end.
Source: Nomura, based on various materials.

currency market may be discounting an average difference of about 3.5 percentage points in the two countries' long-term inflation rates (see the previous discussion of purchasing power parity).

In any case, an analysis of the spreads between various types of interest rates in Japan and the US indicates that one factor that appeared to have a relatively significant correlation with changes in exchange rates was the spread in nominal short-term rates. Other differences, such as those in nominal long-term rates and in real rates, show some correlation at times but fail to show a consistent relationship with the yen–dollar rate over the long term.

LEADING INDICATOR DIFFERENCES

Ever since the beginning of the 1990s, the difference between the economic growth prospects of Japan and the US has started to have a stronger impact than before on the yen–dollar rate. Figure 8.9 presents the difference between the two countries' normalized year-on-year changes in their indexes of leading economic indicators since 1992, along with the changes in the yen–dollar rate for the same period. The two countries' leading indexes were chosen because the currency market is particularly focused on future economic trends. Also, the difference in normalized year-on-year changes was used because of the significant differences in the volatility of the changes stemming from the differences in the time series used for the two countries' leading indexes.

As the panel in the lower part of Fig. 8.9 shows, a very strong positive correlation exists between the difference in leading indexes

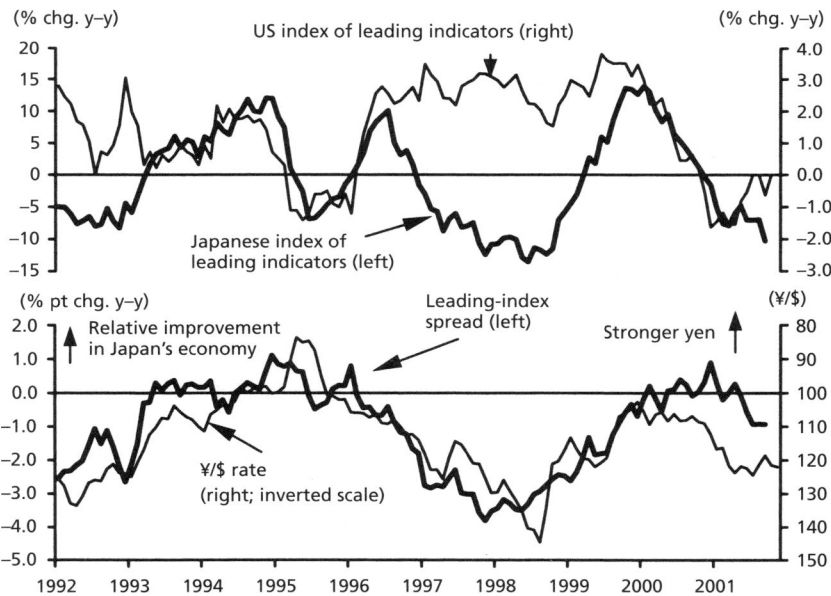

8.9 Leading index spread and yen–dollar rate.
Notes: The leading index spread is the normalized difference in the year-on-year changes for the Japanese and US composite leading indexes (Japan – US). Data are adjusted for stock prices and interest-rate spreads. Specifically, the TOPIX index and the long-/short-term rate spread are factored into the Japanese composite leading index. The leading index in the US case is for October, and in the Japan case September. Exchange rates are based on monthly averages in the New York market.
Source: Nomura, based on various materials.

and the actual yen–dollar rate. When the outlook for the Japanese economy is stronger than that for the US economy, the yen tends to rise against the dollar, and conversely, when the outlook for the US economy is stronger than that for the Japanese economy, the dollar tends to rise against the yen. Based on a simple regression analysis of the two variables for the period since 1992, the coefficient of determination is 0.78.

The preceding section noted that the 18-month period from July 1998 to December 1999 was an exception to the correlation between the spread in short-term interest rates and changes in the yen–dollar rate. The difference in leading indexes can account for the yen's rise during this period, but this correlation seems to have emerged only in the early 1990s; it does not appear to hold for the 1980s.

Three reasons for this recent increase in correlation between the two countries can be found. First, during the 1980s the Japanese economy was dependent on the US economy, so a close correlation between the two countries' business cycles could be expected. Hence, the difference in the economic outlooks tended to be too insignificant to attract much interest from currency market participants. But during the 1990s, the degree of economic dependency lessened. That Japan had to face its own particular financial problems in the wake of the collapse of its asset bubble contributed to a divergence in economic trends in the two countries.

Second, during the 1980s, before the bubble burst, Japan's potential growth rate was by far the highest of any major industrial nation. Comparing Japan's economic conditions with those of other countries using an indicator such as the growth rate was thus uncommon. Since then, the relative decline of Japan's potential growth rate to a level comparable to that of other industrial nations has likely made such comparisons more meaningful. (Nevertheless, the correlation between the differences in leading indexes and the yen–dollar rate that emerged during the 1990s could fade away in the years ahead. One threat is Japan's declining birthrate and aging population, which could cause the country's potential growth rate to plunge, as is generally feared; and in contrast, the US could manage to sustain the high growth rate predicted by the adherents of the 'new economy' school of thought.)

Third, equity investments have begun to account for a larger share of Japan's international capital flows, as noted in the first section of this chapter. Perhaps in part because cross-border equity investments are more sensitive to differences in economic outlook than to differences in interest rates, the difference in leading indexes has become a significant determinant of changes in exchange rates.

Political factors and the yen–dollar exchange rate

An analysis of the historical trend in the yen–dollar exchange rate shows that in many cases, the decisions by the US or the establishment of international regimes under US leadership marked turning points in the yen–dollar exchange rate. The trend began with the August 1971 'Nixon shock' (the decision by the US to abandon the convertibility of dollars into gold, which led to the end of the Bretton Woods system of fixed parities). Then, after the shift to floating exchange rates, other notable event-driven turning points included the Carter administration's attempt to defend the dollar, starting in November 1978; the Reagan administration's stringent adoption of a strong-dollar policy as part of the Reaganomics agenda; the switch to a policy of promoting a weakening of the dollar under the September 1985 Plaza Accord; the moves in 1987 to stabilize the dollar under the Louvre Accord and then to prop up the slumping dollar in December of that year through a coordinated intervention among G7 central banks; a 1990 Paris meeting at which G7 finance ministers and central bank governors agreed to monitor the yen's depreciation; the Clinton administration's use of a stronger yen to apply market-opening pressure on Japan soon after Clinton took office in 1993; and finally, the 'orderly reversal' declaration and switch to a strong-dollar policy orchestrated by Treasury Secretary Robert Rubin in 1995. These examples highlight how the yen–dollar exchange rate has been significantly affected by the exchange rate policy of the US, either directly or through international regimes.

THE PRESIDENTIAL ELECTION CYCLE

The timing of the changes in the yen–dollar exchange rate displays all the workings of a political cycle, given that the rate has been significantly affected by US policy on the value of the dollar. The cycle, however, does not influence the direction of the exchange rate, which varies according to the economic conditions of the times. Instead, the cycle tends to affect the volatility of the yen–dollar rate.

Table 8.1 demonstrates the volatility of the yen–dollar rate since 1984, as measured by the difference between the annual high and

Table 8.1 Volatility in yen–dollar rate

Year	Avg. closing rate for the year	High (¥/$ rate)	Low (¥/$ rate)	Difference (¥)	As % of avg. rate for the year
1984	237.61	251.70	220.00	31.70	13.3
1985	238.03	263.65	199.80	63.85	26.8
1986	168.04	203.30	152.55	50.75	30.2
1987	144.51	159.20	121.85	37.35	25.8
1988	128.18	136.80	120.45	16.35	12.8
1989	138.14	148.03	123.80	24.23	17.5
1990	144.88	160.35	124.05	36.30	25.1
1991	134.56	142.02	125.10	16.92	12.6
1992	126.64	134.95	118.60	16.35	12.9
1993	111.06	125.95	100.40	25.55	23.0
1994	102.18	113.60	96.35	17.25	16.9
1995	93.97	104.70	79.75	24.95	26.6
1996	108.79	116.18	103.97	12.21	11.2
1997	120.95	131.60	110.68	20.92	17.3
1998	131.00	147.64	113.81	33.83	25.8
1999	113.87	124.75	101.35	23.40	20.6
2000	107.75	114.98	101.46	13.52	*12.5*
Avg. (1988–2000)				21.68	19.5
Avg. for election years (1988–2000)				14.61	12.6
Avg. for non-election years (1988–2000)				24.82	22.3

Note: Rates are for the Tokyo forex market.
Source: Nomura.

low for the yen–dollar rate divided by the average closing rate for the year. As the data show, the volatility has clearly been consistently lower in presidential election years (the years that are evenly divisible by four). The lowest volatility in 17 years was in 1996, when the difference between the yen–dollar rate's high and low for the year was only ¥12.21. The next lowest range was ¥13.52 in 2000, followed by ¥16.35 in both 1988 and 1992. All of these periods of lower volatility occurred during presidential election years. The high–low range was somewhat higher, at ¥31.70, in 1984 – the year before the Plaza Accord – and the yen was trading at around ¥240 to the dollar. But the volatility in 1984 was still only 13.39%, the sixth lowest in the period under review. In general, the volatility of the yen–dollar rate tends to contract and expand in a four-year cycle that happens to correspond to the four-year cycle of presidential elections: can this finding be merely a coincidence?

The presidential election campaign process in the US is quite prolonged, starting late in January and running through election day in early November. It also coincides with campaigning for all the seats in the House of Representatives and roughly one-third of the seats in the Senate. So, during election years, although candidates advance various policy proposals, the government rarely goes out on a limb to make any major changes in its economic or dollar policy.

Another point to note is that the financial services sector favours a strong dollar, even though business and labour favour a weak dollar. These conflicting demands may lead the government to seek to keep the dollar from moving too far in either direction in election years. Perhaps not surprisingly, then, the volatility of the yen–dollar rate tends to increase in the year after a presidential election.

This pattern, however, appears to be particular to the yen–dollar rate and is not apparent in the exchange rates of the German mark or other currencies against the dollar. This peculiarity is probably related to the fact that the trade negotiations between Washington and Tokyo have also concerned macroeconomic and currency issues. In contrast, Washington's negotiations with its other trade partners, for example with the European Union, have generally been politically managed to revolve around issues involving specific industries.

THE TREASURY SECRETARY AND THE DOLLAR

Another important political factor emerges upon examination of the trends in the yen–dollar rate since the 1980s – the identity of the key players who have set US policy on the dollar. The Department of the Treasury is responsible for managing the dollar policy of the US, so the Treasury secretary has traditionally wielded tremendous influence in this area. In fact, in the 1980s and 1990s, there were two instances in which a new incoming Treasury secretary led to a 180-degree reversal in US policy regarding the dollar.

The first case took place during the Reagan administration. President Ronald Reagan's Treasury secretary during his first term was Donald Regan, a Wall Street veteran who had served as chairman of Merrill Lynch. Under Regan's leadership, the Treasury adopted a strong-dollar policy to comply with Reagan's economic agenda. During Reagan's second term, however, Regan was succeeded by a lawyer, James Baker, who orchestrated the Plaza

Accord, the historic agreement between the Group of Five industrial nations to push the value of the dollar down; the dollar subsequently lost about half of its value against the yen.

The second about-face came during the Clinton administration. President Clinton's first Treasury secretary was Lloyd Bentsen, a former chairman of the Senate Finance Committee. In February 1993, soon after taking office, Bentsen informed Congress that he favoured a stronger yen. Consequently, during the next several years, the Japanese currency rose to a record high against the dollar. But just two years later, he was replaced by Robert Rubin, another Wall Street veteran. Rubin quickly moved to strengthen the dollar; he arranged for the April 1995 statement from the G7 nations calling for the 'orderly reversal' of the yen's rise.

Interestingly, the Treasury secretaries with Wall Street backgrounds both adopted strong-dollar policies, whereas the lawyer and former senator sought to push the value of the dollar down. The financial services sector in the US tends to favour a strong dollar both as a way of controlling inflation, which is an enemy of the financial markets, and as a way to attract foreign investment to the US. And because lawyers and legislators tend to be more attuned to the concerns of business, they are more likely to favour a weak dollar as a means of bolstering the competitiveness of US manufacturers and protecting American jobs.

What the US, now burdened with a record-high current account deficit, will try to do for the dollar in the early years of the twenty-first century remains to be seen: will it seek to strengthen the dollar so as to help secure a steady inflow of funds to finance the current account deficit? Or will it seek to weaken the dollar so as to help reduce the deficit?

During the latter part of the 1990s, Washington's priority seemed to be strengthening the dollar. But a strong dollar is a double-edged sword. Although a strong dollar could make financing the current account deficit easier, at the same time it could also sap the competitive strength of American manufacturers, thereby causing the deficit to swell. For the US to continue indefinitely with a policy that includes both a widening current account deficit and a strong dollar would be difficult. In this light, it is possible that the George W. Bush administration may choose to move away from a short-term focus on deficit financing and instead look for ways to reduce the current account deficit, perhaps by trying to engineer a second Plaza Accord.

The government and the public bond primary market

More than ever before, the fiscal crisis confronting the Japanese government is the subject of intense debate. The key issues concern not only Japan's budget deficit, which as a percentage of GDP is the largest of any developed country, but also reforms associated with related areas, such as the special accounts, the Fiscal Investment and Loan Program (FILP) and public sector corporations. This chapter reviews some of the causes for the deterioration in Japan's public finance during the 1990s, particularly regarding the interdependence of the general account, the FILP and the Japanese government bond (JGB) market. The chapter also considers the outlook for the state of the country's public finance in the twenty-first century.[1]

State of crisis

Japan's public finances are in a state of crisis. They are in their worst condition since the end of World War II, in terms of both budget deficits and the amount of outstanding government debt. At the end of fiscal 1999, the country's long-term debt (the projected actual amount, including that for supplemental budgets) at the national and local government levels was an estimated ¥600 tr., amounting to 117% of GDP. By the end of fiscal 2001, this figure was projected to reach about ¥666 tr., or 128.5% of GDP (Table 9.1).

In light of the deterioration in the government's finances, the government adopted a policy of fiscal austerity. It reduced general-

1 Local government finance is also an important subject but is beyond the scope of this book.

Table 9.1 Long-term debt at national and regional government levels (¥ tr.)

National government debt	209	325	449	484	506
Japanese government bonds	172	245	332	365	389
Local government debt	70	139	174	184	188
Overlapping portion of national and regional government debt	−1	−14	−22	−26	−28
Total national and local debt	278	449	600	642	666
As percentage of GDP	58.6%	87.2%	116.9%	125.0%	128.5%

Notes: GDP for fiscal 2000 is the government's estimated actual figure, and the figure for fiscal 2001 is the government's estimate. At the end of fiscal 2001, about ¥44 tr. in government bonds had been issued for the Fiscal Loan Fund Special Account.
Source: Ministry of Finance.

account expenditures to ¥82.7 tr. for the draft fiscal 2001 budget, which is 2.7% lower than the ¥85.0 tr. in spending for fiscal 2000. The government also cut the amount of public bond issuances to ¥28.3 tr. for fiscal 2001, which was down from ¥32.6 tr. in fiscal 2000 (Fig. 9.1). The government's reliance on JGBs, however, did not substantively change between fiscal 2000 and 2001; indeed, the fiscal 2000 figure was boosted by ¥4.5 tr. in expenditures that arose as a result of funds not being needed to redeem JGBs to support the financial system in case of the bankruptcy of financial institutions.

The government's ability to adjust its spending has become progressively more limited. General expenditures, which are discretionary, amounted to 79.8% of total general-account expenditures in fiscal 1965, but fell to 62.0% by fiscal 1985 and then to 58.9% by fiscal 2001. Furthermore, in a February 2001 'Medium-Term Fiscal Projection', the Ministry of Finance projected that this ratio would fall to 51.3% by fiscal 2004 (Fig. 9.2). The main reason for the projected decline is a rise in interest expense. This cost as a percentage of total general-account expenditures has increased to nearly 20%, from 0.6% in fiscal 1965, 4.9% in fiscal 1975 and 19.5% in fiscal 1985. Because of low interest rates in Japan, the ratio has not risen sharply in recent years. Nonetheless, the cost of debt servicing has greatly limited the government's ability to flexibly manage spending.

The extent of the deterioration in Japan's public finances becomes even more evident when the situation is compared with that of other countries. After suffering massive budget deficits during the 1990s, in fiscal 2001, the US, UK and Italy either reported budget surpluses (excluding social security) or roughly broke even. In contrast, Japan's budget deficit for fiscal 2001 amounted to 7.7% of GDP. In fact, Japan now has more government debt outstanding as

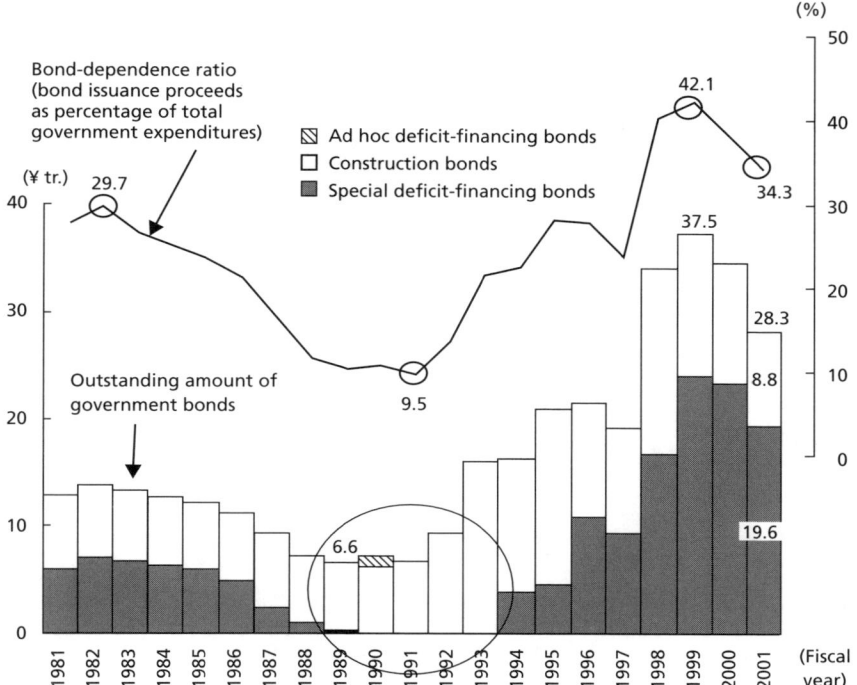

9.1 Trend in government bond issuance.
Note: Figures to fiscal 1999 are actual amounts for each fiscal year; fiscal 2000 figures are based on amounts that include supplemental budgets; fiscal 2001 figures are based on the amounts of the initial budget.
Source: Ministry of Finance.

a percentage of GDP than does Italy, which throughout the 1990s was well known for its high levels of indebtedness (Fig. 9.3).

The interdependence of the general account, the special accounts and FILP

This section examines some of the factors behind the deterioration of Japan's public finances. But first, a brief review of the structure of Japan's system of public finance is in order. As shown in Fig. 9.4, Japan's system of public finance can be broadly divided into three complementary segments: the general account, special accounts and FILP.

The general account, which is often mentioned in the press, is for Japan's general expenditures and revenues. Revenues in the

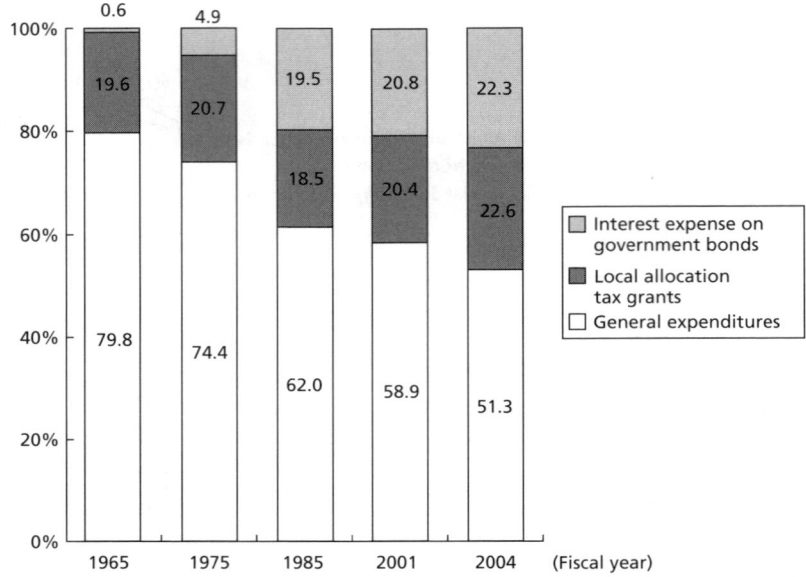

9.2 General expenditures as a percentage of total general account expenditures.
Note: All figures are based on initial budgets. Fiscal 2004 figures are from the
Ministry of Finance's 'Medium-Term Fiscal Projection' (February 2001).
Source: Ministry of Finance.

account consist mainly of personal and corporate income taxes, and
expenditures comprise those for the nation's basic needs, such as
social security and education.

In contrast, the special accounts are for items that should be
accounted for separately from general revenues and expenditures,
such as for-profit ventures and special items. For fiscal 2001, 37
special accounts were established. They covered costs for such areas
as road improvements, welfare insurance and apportionment of local
allocation and transfer taxes.

FILP augments the core system of public finance. FILP funds come
from sources that are backed by the creditworthiness of the Japanese
government, such as postal savings and premiums for postal life insurance (*Kampo*), the National Pension and Employees' Pension. Most
FILP funds passed through the Ministry of Finance's Trust Fund Bureau
to government-affiliated financial institutions and public sector corporations and organizations, which in turn provided funds to the private
sector.[2] In fiscal 2000, the amount of planned FILP spending was

2 April 2001 reforms, described in detail later, resulted in changes in the sources
of funds and the distribution mechanism.

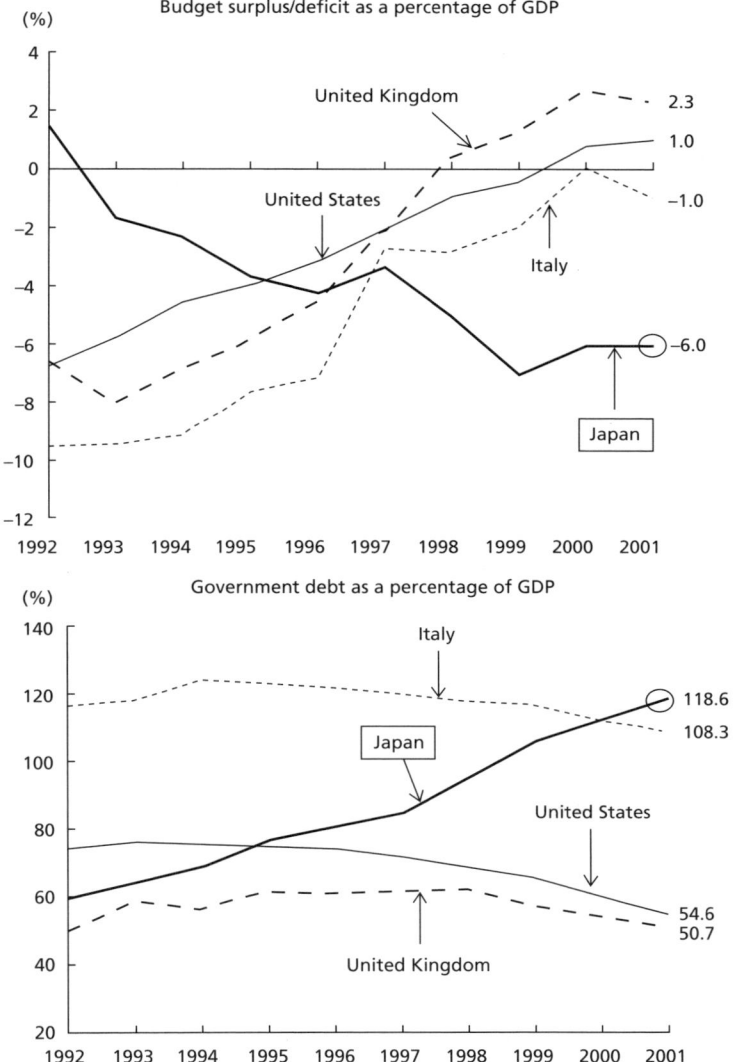

9.3 The public finances of Japan, the US, the UK and Italy.
Note: Figures for Japan and the US do not include social security expenditures.
Source: Nomura, based on data from the Organization for Economic Cooperation and Development's *Economic Outlook*, no. 68, December 2000.

¥43.7 tr., or about half of the amount of expenditures for the general account. Given the relatively large size of the FILP plan, the programme is often referred to as Japan's 'secondary budget'. Of the three primary functions of public finance – the allocation of resources, fiscal policy

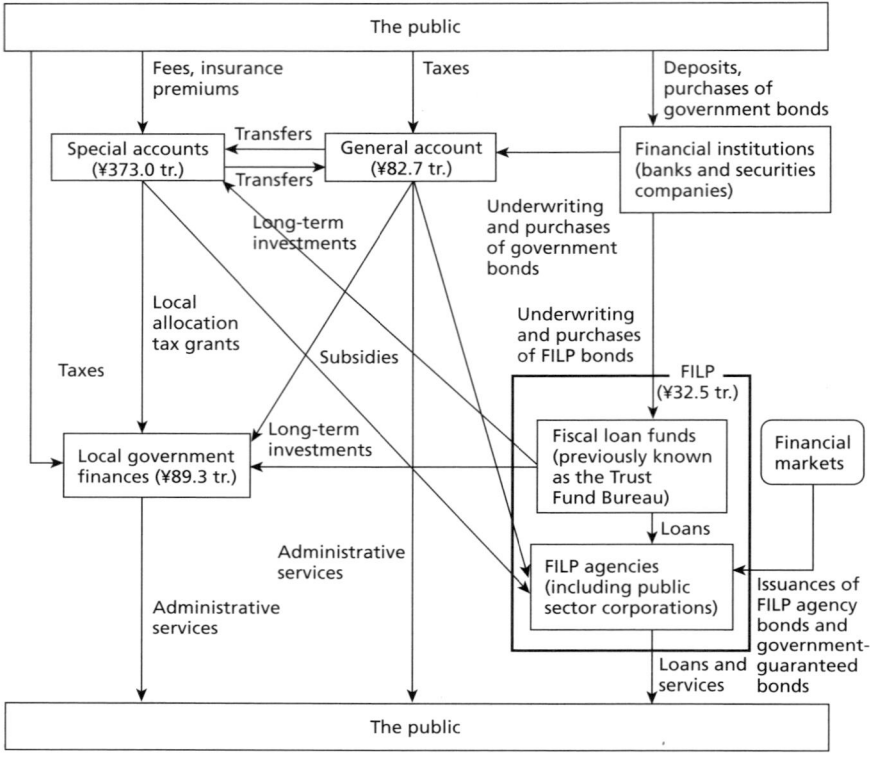

9.4 The general account, special accounts and FILP.
Note: Figures for the general account, special accounts, FILP and local governments are based on the initial budget for fiscal 2001. Some overlap occurs in the expenditures for these entities.
Source: Nomura.

and the redistribution of income – FILP plays a role in the allocation of resources and fiscal policy (Fig. 9.5).

For fiscal 2001, ¥82.7 tr. was initially earmarked for general-account expenditures; ¥373.0 tr. for special accounts; and ¥32.5 tr. for FILP. Actual net expenditures are significantly less than the gross amount because of the flow of funds among the three accounts. For example, funds in the general account may be transferred into special accounts and FILP.

PROMISE OF ECONOMIC GROWTH

The Japanese government attempted to reform the nation's budget without increasing taxes during the 1980s, and in fiscal 1990, it suc-

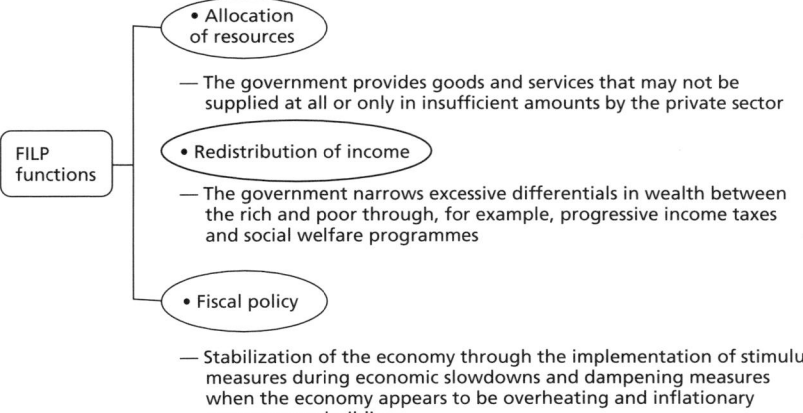

9.5 FILP and the three primary functions of public finance.
Source: *Zusetsu Nihon no Zaisei* [Japan's Public Finances Illustrated], Haruhiko Kato ed., Toyo Keizai Shinposha (annual).

ceeded in not issuing any deficit-financing bonds. Full-fledged budget reform started in 1980, amid a deterioration in public finances following the second oil crisis. To control government expenditures, in fiscal 1982, the government imposed a 'zero-ceiling' policy that mandated that the year-on-year increase in nominal budget requests from all ministries be set at zero. Furthermore, the government adopted a 'negative-ceiling' policy between fiscal 1983 and fiscal 1987, which resulted in year-on-year declines in annual general-account spending during this period. Thanks to this reduction in expenditures and an increase in tax revenues stemming from strong economic growth in the economic bubble years, in fiscal 1990, for the first time in 15 years, the Japanese government did not need to issue deficit-financing bonds (Fig. 9.1).

The budget reforms of the 1980s were successful because across-the-board ceilings were imposed on expenditures in the initial budgets, and tax revenues were estimated conservatively. In addition, supplemental budgets were used to adjust expenditures in order to stimulate the economy. This budget reform mechanism worked because of steady economic growth and the corresponding increases in tax revenues. Japan thereby managed to free itself from having to issue deficit-financing bonds, at least until the economic bubble collapsed.

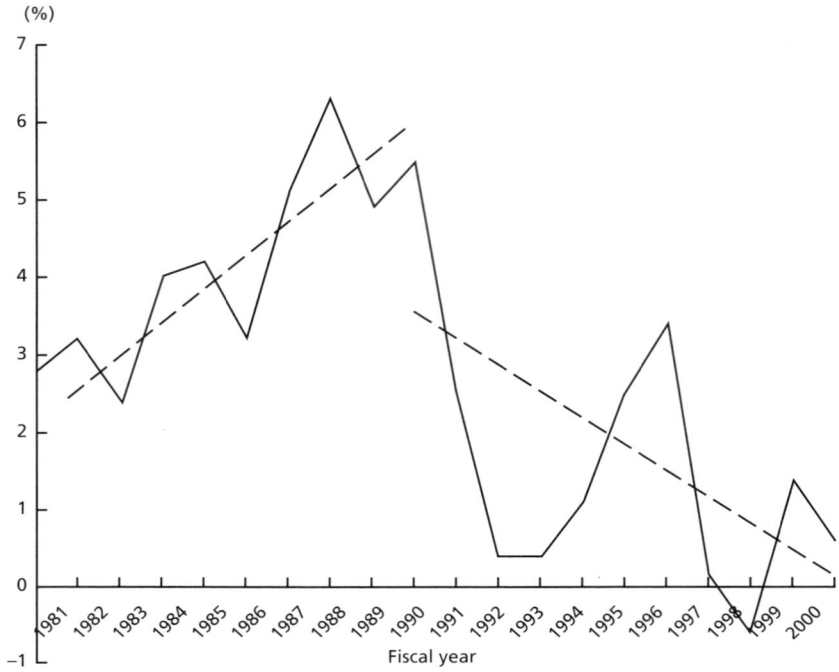

9.6 Trend in Japan's real GDP growth.
Source: Nomura, based on data from the Cabinet Office's Economic and Social
Research Institute.

LIMITATIONS OF JAPAN'S PUBLIC FINANCE SYSTEM

How Japan's public finances came to deteriorate following the
achievement of the reforms in the 1980s is attributable to a number
of factors. When the Japanese economy began to slow starting in
fiscal 1991, it went into an extended slump as the economic bubble
came to an end and the yen appreciated (Fig. 9.6). The problem
was that throughout the 1990s the Japanese government continued
to manage the nation's finances based on the assumption of steady
economic growth, even as it became clear that the economy would
not continue to expand as much as it had in the 1980s.

In an attempt to stimulate the economy in the early 1990s, the
government implemented a series of economic stimulus packages.
Between August 1992 and September 1995, the government put
together six economic stimulus packages that centred on public
works spending and amounted to about ¥67 tr. (Table 9.2). Tax
revenues, however, did not increase as much as the government
expected. In fact, the government's projections of tax revenues fell

Table 9.2 Economic stimulus packages during the 1990s (¥ tr.)

(¥ tr.)

Type of package	Cabinet meeting approval date	Total spending	Public works spending (real spending)	Public bond issuance (deficit-financing bonds)
The first comprehensive economic stimulus package	Aug. 1992	10.7	6.3 (5.0)	2.3 (0.0)
The second comprehensive economic stimulus package	Apr. 1993	13.2	7.2 (5.8)	2.2 (0.0)
Emergency economic stimulus package	Sep. 1993	6.2	2.0 (1.6)	3.6 (0.0)
New comprehensive economic stimulus package	Feb. 1994	15.3	3.7 (3.0)	2.2 (0.0)
Emergency economic stimulus package to cope with the yen's appreciation	Apr. 1995	7.3	3.2 (2.6)	2.8 (0.6)
Economic stimulus package	Sep. 1995	14.2	9.0 (7.0)	4.7 (0.2)
Supplemental budget for fiscal 1997	Feb. 1998	4.5	0.7 (0.6)	1.8 (1.0)
Comprehensive economic stimulus package	Apr. 1998	16.0	7.7 (3.6–5.2)	N.A. (N.A.)
Total spending		87.4	39.8 (29.1–30.8)	19.6 (1.8)

Note: Real spending (spending that has a direct impact on aggregate demand) = public works spending × 0.8. The ratio of the cost of land for public works projects to total public works spending is estimated at 20%.
Source: Nomura.

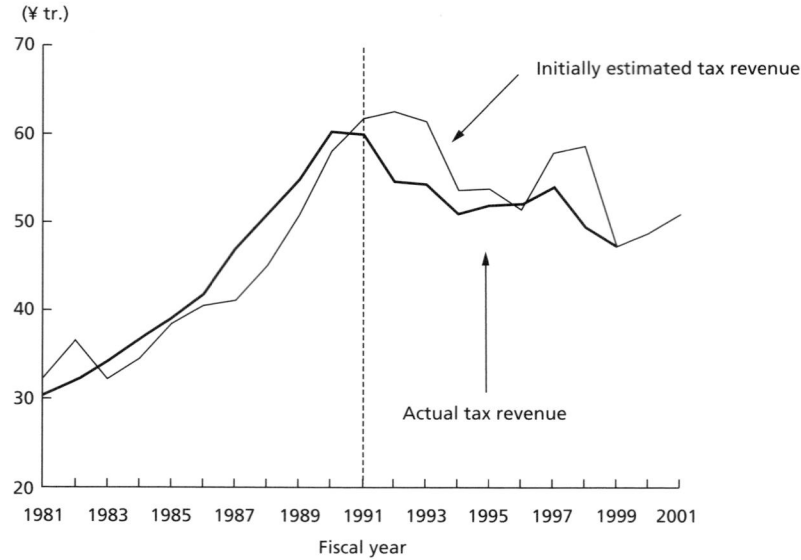

9.7 Trend in general-account tax revenues.
Note: Tax revenues consist of general tax and stamp tax revenues.
Source: Nomura, based on data from the Ministry of Finance.

short in almost every year since fiscal 1991 (Fig. 9.7). A steady deterioration of the nation's budget was the inevitable result.

The failure of Japan's fiscal reforms

The government's economic stimulus packages led to a sharp deterioration in Japan's fiscal health. In fiscal 1996, when the government issued a total of ¥21 tr. worth of public bonds (¥12 tr. in deficit-financing bonds and ¥9 tr. in construction bonds), the Ministry of Finance declared that, as from November 1995, Japan was in a state of fiscal crisis.

The government then conducted a complete review of fiscal expenditures in fiscal 1997, which was earmarked as the first year of fiscal reform. After raising the consumption tax to 5% from 3% in April 1997, the cabinet put together a fiscal reform plan in June 1997. The key objectives of the plan included a reduction of the budget deficit to less than 3% of GDP by fiscal 2003 and a halt in the issuance of special deficit-financing bonds by the same year (Table 9.3).

Table 9.3 Japan's fiscal reform: timeline of major initiatives

19 December 1996	Fiscal objectives decided on by the cabinet: • A reduction of the budget deficit to less than 3% of GDP and a halt in the issuance of special deficit-financing bonds as soon as possible, but no later than fiscal 2005. • Principles for improving Japan's fiscal soundness, including a thorough review of all expenditures, with no exceptions.
18 March 1997	At the fourth meeting of the Conference on Fiscal Structural Reform, Prime Minister Ryutaro Hashimoto presented five principles for reforming Japan's public finances, including: • A reduction of the budget deficit to less than 3% of GDP and a halt in the issuance of special deficit-financing bonds by fiscal 2003, rather than fiscal 2005. • Establishment of specific numerical targets for the reduction of major expenditures during the intensive reform period of fiscal 1998–2000.
3 June 1997	At its eighth meeting, the Conference on Fiscal Structural Reform compiled Measures for the Promotion of Fiscal Structural Reform: • In accordance with the Conference on Fiscal Structural Reform's Measures for the Promotion of Fiscal Structural Reform, the cabinet approved a framework for the Promotion of Fiscal Structural Reform.
28 November 1997	The Fiscal Structural Reform Act was enacted: • The act mandated the reduction of the budget deficit to less than 3% of GDP and a halt in the issuance of special deficit-financing bonds by fiscal 2003. • The act also required specific numerical targets for the reduction of major expenditures, such as social security and public investments, during the intensive reform period of fiscal 1998–2000.
29 May 1998	Revision of the Fiscal Structural Reform Act: • Allowed for flexibility in the issuance amount of special deficit-financing bonds. • Postponed the target year for achieving fiscal soundness to fiscal 2005 from fiscal 2003. • Changed the target reduction for social security expenditures for the fiscal 1999 initial budget from 'around 2%' to 'as much as possible'.
11 December 1998	Freeze on the Fiscal Structural Reform Act: • Temporary freeze on the enforcement of the Fiscal Structural Reform Act. • Time frame for removing the freeze to be determined based on such factors as economic and fiscal conditions once Japan's economy recovers. • Measures necessary for putting the Fiscal Structural Reform Act into force again to be based on economic and fiscal conditions following the suspension of the Act.

Source: Haruhiko Kato, ed., *Zusetsu Nihon no Zaisei (Japan's Public Finances Illustrated)*, Toyo Keizai Shinposha (annual).

But starting in the second half of 1997, the economy rapidly worsened. Increasing instability in the financial system led the government to shift its focus to fiscal reform. The government accordingly revised the Fiscal Structural Reform Act in May 1998 to allow for flexibility in the issuance amount of special deficit-financing bonds and to postpone the target year for achieving fiscal soundness to fiscal 2005 from fiscal 2003. This revision significantly watered down the Fiscal Structural Reform Act, and in late 1998, the government temporarily suspended the Act. The government then included a large amount of spending in the fiscal 1999 budget to stimulate the economy, thereby further dimming the prospects for Japan's fiscal reform efforts.

FILP reforms

The Fiscal Investment and Loan Program, or FILP, is often referred to as Japan's 'secondary budget'. FILP financing, which is limited to certain types of projects and enterprises, takes the form of interest-bearing loans rather than taxpayer money, in the belief that interest-bearing loans should contribute to the efficient and effective use of the funds. FILP-financed projects can be categorized as: 1) projects that should be partially funded by those that benefit from the particular projects; 2) projects in which self-discipline and self-motivation are expected; 3) projects that may not be adequately financed or appropriately managed by the private sector; and 4) policy-related projects to support and complement the private sector. Over the years, the focus of FILP has shifted from the establishment of Japan's industrial, technological and social infrastructure to quality-of-life improvements (Table 9.4).

Although FILP spending must be approved by the Diet, 'the general provisions of the budget stipulate that even in the middle of a fiscal year, the FILP plan can be increased up to 50% from its initial plan to meet changes in economic conditions unpredicted or for other such unavoidable reasons, by usage of the "flexible management clause"'.

THE 1990s

During the 1990s, the flexible management clause was often employed to increase FILP budgets considerably compared with initial budgets, and FILP's role as a fiscal policy tool (with its cyclical adjustment function) was emphasized over its intended function as a 'secondary budget' for developing the country's infrastructure. The government used FILP funds to help finance the previously

Table 9.4 Major programmes financed by FILP (%)

Fiscal year	1955	1965	1975	1985	1995	2001
Quality-of-life improvements	**45.1**	52.8	64.1	69.8	76.0	**75.0**
Housing	13.8	13.9	21.4	25.4	35.3	29.9
Living environment	7.7	12.4	16.7	15.7	16.4	19.9
Social welfare	2.1	3.6	3.4	2.8	4.0	3.9
Education and culture	4.5	3.1	2.9	3.6	2.0	2.8
Small and medium-sized enterprises	8.1	12.6	15.6	18.0	15.3	16.1
Agriculture, forestry and fisheries	8.9	7.2	4.1	4.3	3.0	2.4
Social infrastructure	**32.1**	31.9	25.2	21.9	16.2	**19.2**
National land preservation and disaster relief and recovery	7.7	3.1	1.2	2.3	1.3	2.3
Road construction	3.7	7.9	8.0	8.8	7.7	11.2
Transportation/communications	12.2	13.9	12.7	8.4	4.6	2.3
Regional development	8.5	7.0	3.3	2.4	2.6	3.4
Industrial infrastructure	**22.8**	15.3	10.7	8.3	7.8	**5.8**
Industry/technology	15.8	7.8	3.0	2.9	3.1	1.0
Trade/economic cooperation	7.0	7.5	7.7	5.4	4.7	4.8
Total	100.0	100.0	100.0	100.0	100.0	100.0

Note: Figures are based on initial budgets per fiscal year.
Source: Nomura, based on data from the Ministry of Finance.

mentioned economic stimulus packages; ¥29 tr. in additional spending was added to initial FILP plans between fiscal 1992 and fiscal 1998 (Fig. 9.8). The massive increase in FILP expenditures generated criticism of public sector corporations and raised concerns about the potential crowding out of the private sector. This criticism eventually led to a reform of the FILP system.

The government's Fund Operation Council began deliberations on FILP reforms in February 1997 and then released a final report on the issue at the end of 1997. The report included proposals for abolishing the requirement that postal savings and other public funds be deposited with the Trust Fund Bureau and for encouraging FILP agencies to raise funds directly from the capital markets. The goal was to improve FILP agency operations by subjecting them to market forces.

In June 1998, the Fundamental Law on the Reform of the Governmental Ministries and Agencies, which included provisions pertaining to the implementation of FILP reforms, was passed by the Diet. The Fund Operation Council finalized its proposals for reforming FILP in August 1999, and a broad framework for FILP reform was announced in December 1999.

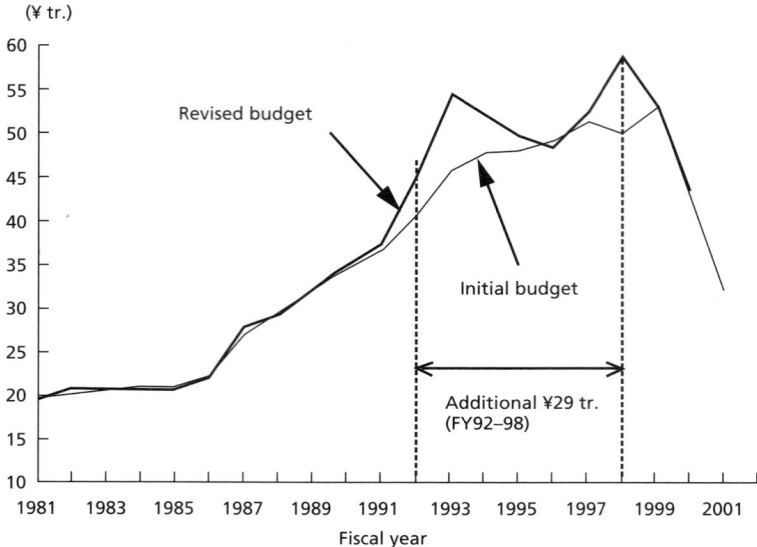

9.8 Expansion of FILP through the flexible management clause.
Note: Figures are for general FILP funds, excluding the postal savings and pension reserves that are self-managed.
Source: Nomura, based on data from the Ministry of Finance.

The Fund Operation Council reviewed two main problems concerning FILP, namely, its source of funds and investments. One council member pointed out that the government's fiscal discipline was weakening because funds simply went into FILP through deposits of postal savings and pension reserves with the Trust Fund Bureau. In this vein, a possible solution to the problem would be to sever the link between the sources and uses of FILP funds. Some argued that the FILP system was adequately based on the demand for and supply of FILP funds and, therefore, the availability of funds was not a given.

The council eventually decided to eliminate the requirement that postal savings and pension reserves be deposited with the Trust Fund Bureau.

2001 REFORMS

On 24 May 2000, the Bill for the Amendment to the Trust Fund Bureau Fund Act and Others passed the Diet, paving the way for the implementation of FILP reforms in April 2001. As a result of these reforms, all postal savings and pension reserves are no longer to be deposited with the Trust Fund Bureau; instead, they are to be invested in the capital markets.[3] Second, in principle, FILP agencies are to raise funds directly from the capital markets for FILP projects by issuing FILP agency bonds. Third, FILP projects are to be reviewed on cost analysis and other measures of efficiency (Table 9.5). The reforms significantly changed the structure of FILP (Fig. 9.9).

The most significant FILP reform was allowing the issuance of three types of bond to fund FILP spending: FILP agency bonds, government-guaranteed bonds and FILP bonds. FILP agency bonds, which are not guaranteed by the government, are bonds issued directly in the capital markets by FILP agencies, such as public sector corporations. Government-guaranteed bonds are bonds backed by the Japanese government, and FILP bonds are issued to finance FILP projects. FILP bonds are backed by the Japanese government and thus have the same creditworthiness as that of JGBs.

Under the new FILP structure, public sector corporations are primarily required to issue FILP agency bonds. The new structure, however, also allows for the issuance of government-guaranteed bonds by 'agencies that are unable to immediately issue agency bonds without government guarantees'. In addition, 'funds raised collectively by the government through the issuance of FILP bonds in accordance with market conditions can be appropriated to FILP agencies implementing required policies or to projects requiring very long-term financing that face difficulty or higher costs issuing FILP agency bonds or government-guaranteed bonds'. In other words, the issuance of FILP bonds under the new structure is limited to improve fiscal discipline.

Despite the implementation of these FILP reforms, the FILP plan for fiscal 2001 does not appear to have been based on the fundamental principles reflected in the reforms. Specifically, although the new system primarily requires FILP agencies to raise funds by issuing agency bonds, according to the initial budget for fiscal 2001, just 20 agencies planned to issue FILP agency bonds, and aggregate agency bond issuance was only about ¥1105.8 bn (Table 9.6). On the other hand, the total issuance of FILP bonds was nearly ¥43.9 tr., consisting of ¥10.5 tr. in bonds to be sold directly through the capital markets, ¥17.9 tr. to be sold through the postal savings system, ¥11.9 tr. for sale through the national pension system and ¥3.6 tr. for sale through the postal life insurance (*Kampo*) system. The government intends to gradually increase the amount of FILP bonds sold in the capital markets, but some concerns have been raised about whether the sales will go smoothly. Although the government says

3 See Chapter 4 for a detailed discussion of this subject.

Table 9.5 Outline of FILP reforms

1) Elimination of the mandatory deposit of postal savings and pension reserves with the Trust Fund Bureau:
- Compulsory deposit of postal savings and pension reserves to be abolished, and these funds invested in the capital markets from 1 April 2001.
- Loans from postal life insurance (*Kampo*) reserves to FILP agencies to be eliminated, and these reserves invested in the capital markets.

2) Market-based fund-raising:
- The FILP agencies will raise capital directly from the capital markets by issuing FILP agency bonds.
- Government guarantees may be provided for some agencies that are unable to immediately issue agency bonds without government guarantees. Guarantees will be subject to rigorous, individual screening and strict ceilings in order to maintain fiscal discipline.
- Funds raised collectively by the government through the issuance of FILP bonds in accordance with market conditions can be appropriated to FILP agencies implementing required policies or to projects requiring very long-term financing that face difficulty or higher costs issuing FILP agency bonds or government-guaranteed bonds.

3) Review of FILP target areas and projects using policy (subsidy) cost analysis and other measures:
- Hypertrophied FILP projects to be avoided by examining FILP target areas and projects in terms of their complementary role to private business and their financial soundness thereof in the future.

4) Other issues:
- The abolition of the compulsory deposit of postal savings and pension reserves to be accompanied by appropriate transitional measures to sustain forgone loans and avoid detrimental effects on the market for the smooth enforcement of FILP reform.
- Some provisions have been made to ensure funding for financially weak local governments. Even after discretionary investment begins, postal savings and postal life insurance reserves can be lent directly to local governments with uniform lending conditions and under simplified procedures, provided loans are within the scope of the municipal bond plan and the FILP plan and within a lending ceiling determined by the Diet during the budgeting process as a special exception for local governments.
- The reformed FILP shall also be approved by the Diet as part of the national budget.
- Disclosure by each FILP agency, as well as of the entire FILP system, will be improved.
- The Trust Fund Bureau is to be abolished, and an appropriate framework for the new FILP system is to be established (Fiscal Loan Fund Special Account).

Source: Nomura, based on Ministry of Finance information on the FILP reform.

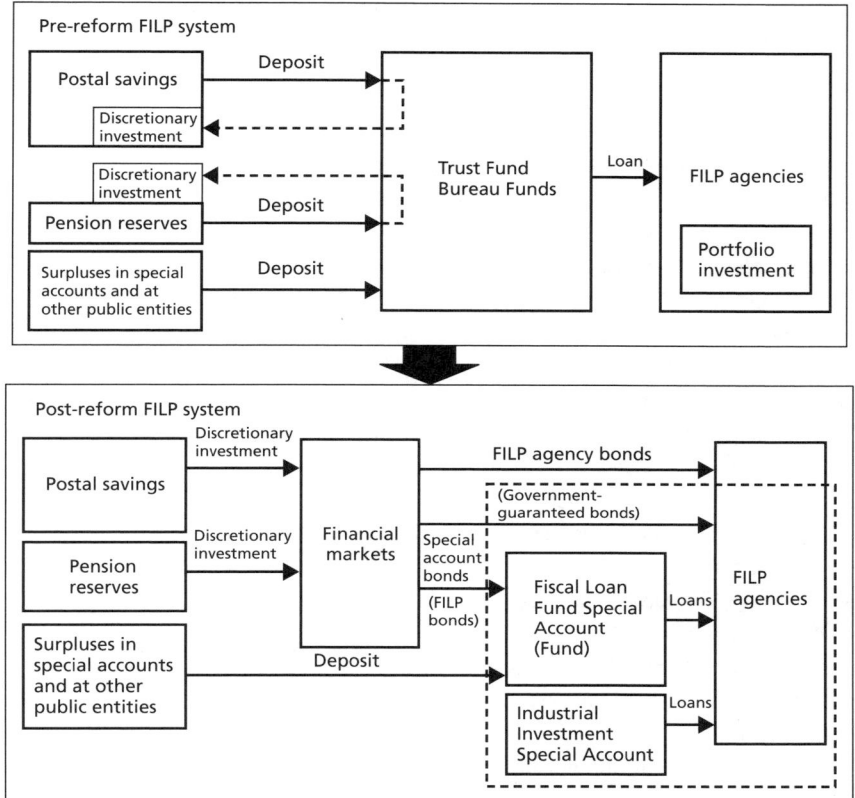

9.9 Comparison of the old and new FILP systems.
Note: In addition to the Trust Fund Bureau Fund mentioned above, FILP also receives financial resources from postal life insurance (*Kampo*) funds, the Industrial Investment Special Account, and by issuing government-guaranteed bonds; (1) In addition to the above, FILP also includes loans to local governments using postal savings and postal life insurance (*Kampo*) funds. (2) Special account bonds refer to government bonds issued to raise funds for the Fiscal Loan Fund Special Account (i.e., FILP bonds).
Source: Ministry of Finance, *FILP Report 2000*, August 2000.

that it will gradually increase the amount of FILP bonds issued directly to the market, some are sceptical that adequate demand for FILP bonds exists among investors.

The government bond market

Japan's government bond market has grown since 1990, particularly after the issuance of government bonds increased rapidly starting in

Table 9.6 Scheduled issuance of FILP agency bonds and FILP bonds according to fiscal 2001 initial budget

FILP agency bonds:	¥ bn
The Housing Loan Corporation	200.0
Agriculture, Forestry and Fisheries Finance Corporation	15.0
Japan Finance Corporation for Municipal Enterprises	100.0
Development Bank of Japan	100.0
Japan Bank for International Cooperation	200.0
Urban Development Corporation	30.0
Teito Rapid Transit Authority	43.9
Japan Regional Development Corporation	10.0
Social Welfare and Medical Service Corporation	10.0
The Promotion and Mutual Aid Corporation for Private Schools of Japan	6.0
Japan Scholarship Foundation	10.0
Japan Highway Public Corporation	150.0
Metropolitan Expressway Public Corporation	10.0
Hanshin Expressway Public Corporation	10.0
Japan Railway Construction Public Corporation	10.0
New Tokyo International Airport Authority	50.0
Corporation for Advanced Transport & Technology	6.0
Water Resources Development Public Corporation	10.0
Shoko Chukin Bank	224.9
Electric Power Development Company	10.0
Total	1105.8
FILP bonds:	**¥ tr**
(a) Amount to be issued directly to the market	10.5
(b) Amount to be issued as a transitional measure	33.4
Amount to be sold through the postal saving system	17.9
Amount to be sold through the national pension system	11.9
Amount to be sold through the postal life insurance system	3.6
Total (a + b)	43.9

Source: Ministry of Finance.

fiscal 1998, when fiscal reform plans were temporarily shelved (Fig. 9.1). Some of the improvements in the JGB market included the regular issuance of 3-month financing bills (FBs) through competitive auctions and the public offering of 2-year Treasury bills (TBs) starting in April 1999 (Table 9.7). In addition, the government began to issue bonds with a wider range of maturities. Specifically, the public offering of 30-year government bonds commenced in

Table 9.7 Improvements to Japanese government bond market

	Bond structure/auction developments	Developments in the secondary market	Individual investors and other developments
1990:	*July* Start of bimonthly Treasury bill issuance	*April* Relaxation of rules limiting packaging of new government bonds with existing government bonds with same coupon rate and maturity	
	Immediate announcement of auction results for 20-year bonds, medium-term government notes and Treasury bills	Reduction in face value of Treasury bills	
	October Increase in ratio of 10-year notes underwritten by syndicates from 40% to 60%	*May* Start of market for options on government bond futures	
1991:	*January* Start of online auction system for 10-year notes	*March* Securities lending companies allowed to participate in Treasury bill lending business	
	April Immediate announcement of auction results for 10-year notes		
	Standardization of monthly amount of 10-year notes issued to syndicates		
1992:		*January* Increase in number of bond issues for which OTC bid and ask prices are published daily	*January* Cabinet approves outline of tax reform to exempt foreign companies from taxes on profits on Treasury bill transactions
1993:	*April* Schedule for auctioning 10-year government notes shortened		*April* Introduction of cumulative investment programmes by banks

213

Table 9.7 *Continued*

	Bond structure/auction developments	Developments in the secondary market	Individual investors and other developments
1994:	*February* Start of public offerings for 6-year notes		*January* Increase in amount eligible for *maruyu* tax-exempt savings system
1995:		*September* Abolition of self-regulations on the sale of government bonds underwritten by financial institutions	
1996:	*April* Change in schedule for fixed-percentage public auctions New method for determining issuance terms for 5-year discount notes Introduction of quarterly funding cycle for 20-year bonds	*February* Start of trading of futures on 5-year notes *April* Changes in bond-lending rules (limit on interest rates on collateral lifted) *October* Start of rolling settlement (transactions settled seven business days after the trade date)	*February* BOJ starts up JGB registration system on BOJ-NET *December* Establishment of targets for improving Japan's public finances
1997:		*April* Settlement period shortened from seven business days to three business days Increase in number of bond issues for which OTC bid and ask prices are published	*October* Maximum period between issue date and first coupon payment date for 20-year government bonds shortened from 11 months to five months *December* Fiscal Structural Reform Act takes effect
1998:	*April* Introduction of a non-competitive auction for medium-term notes (2-, 4- and 6-year notes)	*December* Abolition of requirement that all securities trades must be conducted on an exchange	*June* Revision of Fiscal Structural Reform Act

1999:	*March* Start of pre-announcement of bond auction dates and related information	*April* Elimination of withholding tax on original issue discount for Treasury bills and financing bills	*October* Issuance of refunding bonds for debt transfer from Japanese National Railways Settlement Corporation and the National Forest Service
	April Start of public offerings of 1-year Treasury bills	*September* Elimination of withholding tax on JGB interest income for non-residents	*December* Temporary freeze of the Fiscal Structural Reform Act
	September Start of public offerings of 30-year bonds		
2000:	*February* Introduction of 5-year coupon notes		
	June Start of public offerings of 15-year floating-rate bonds		
	September Start of public offerings of 3-year discount notes		
2001:		*March* Introduction of reopening method (immediate packaging of new government bonds with existing government bonds with the same coupon rate and maturity) and a method of calculating accrued interest for these JGBs	*April* Higher tax exemptions for non-residents on interest income from shelf-registered government bonds

Source: *Zaimu Detabukku: Zaisei no Genjo to Tenbo (Public finance data book: The current state and outlook for Japan's public finance)*, Okura Zaimu Kyoukai, 2001.

September 1999, followed by the first issuance of 5-year government coupon notes in February 2000, and the first public offering of 3-year discount government notes in September 2000.

For fiscal 2001, the government planned to issue a total of ¥98.6 tr. worth of bonds, consisting of ¥28.3 tr. in new financial resource bonds, ¥59.7 tr. in refunding bonds and ¥10.5 tr. in new Fiscal Loan Fund Special Account bonds (FILP bonds), to be publicly offered to the market (Table 9.8). The total amount of planned government bond issuance rises to ¥131.9 tr. if ¥33.4 tr. in FILP bonds that are to be sold as a transitional measure to the postal savings and pension insurance systems are taken into consideration.

Public finance and the government bond market: The outlook for the twenty-first century

This section examines the outlook for Japan's public finance system and public bond market from the perspective of the supply and demand for bonds.

ON THE SUPPLY SIDE

Fiscal reform, which was essentially abandoned in 1997, has once again become the subject of debate under the current administration of Prime Minister Junichiro Koizumi. Given current economic conditions in Japan, however, a significant improvement in the general-account balance is highly unlikely. One of the major factors that will probably hamper any improvement in the state of Japan's public finance system is high social security expenditures for pensions, health care and welfare. In the general account, social security expenditures were ¥17.5 tr. in the initial budget for fiscal 2001, or 21.2% of total government expenditures, representing the largest expenditure category in the budget. The Ministry of Health, Labour and Welfare projects social security expenditures will reach ¥207 tr. by fiscal 2025, which is nearly triple the amount in fiscal 2000 and 31.5% of national income (versus 20.5% in fiscal 2000 (Table 9.9)).

Pensions account for the largest portion of Japan's social security expenditures. The public pension system was reformed in the spring of 2000, and further reform is expected in 2004. Nonetheless, the government will most probably have to implement changes

Table 9.8 Recent government bond issuance in Japan (¥ tr.)

	FY98 initial budget	FY99 initial budget	FY00 initial budget	FY00 revised budget	FY01 initial budget
Issuance to the private sector					
Syndicate underwriting	13.4	20.2	16.4	16.4	20.4
10-year notes	13.2	20.0	16.3	16.3	20.4
5-year discount notes	0.2	20.0	0.1	0.1	–
Public offerings	24.0	40.8	62.7	64.7	69.5
30-year bonds	–	0.4	0.7	0.7	0.6
20-year bonds	2.4	2.4	2.4	2.4	3.0
15-year floating-rate bonds	–	–	2.4	2.8	3.2
6-year notes	3.0	5.0	2.5	2.5	–
5-year coupon notes	–	–	9.1	9.9	18.9
4-year notes	3.0	5.0	2.5	2.5	–
3-year discount notes	–	–	0.3	0.3	0.6
2-year notes	1.4	5.2	12.8	13.6	16.8
Treasury bills	14.1	22.8	30.0	30.0	26.4
Total issuance to the private sector	37.4	61.0	79.1	81.1	89.9
Issuance to the public sector					
Trust Fund Bureau	12.0	2.8	–	–	–
Postal savings system (for discretionary investment)	2.8	2.8	–	–	–
Postal savings system (for over-the-counter sales at post offices)	0.7	0.8	2.5	2.5	2.5
Bank of Japan	5.1	3.7	4.2	4.2	6.2
Total issuance to the public sector	20.5	10.1	6.7	6.7	8.6
Total	57.9	71.1	85.9	87.9	98.5
New financial resource bonds	15.6	31.1	32.6	34.6	28.3
Refunding bonds	42.4	40.1	53.3	53.3	59.7
Fiscal Loan Fund Special Account bonds	–	–	–	–	10.5

Source: Ministry of Finance.

Table 9.9 Projections for Japan's social security expenditure (¥ tr.)

	FY 2000 (based on budget)	As % of national income	FY 2005	As % of national income	FY 2010	As % of national income	FY 2025	As % of national income
Total social security benefit payments	78	20.5	100	23.0	127	26.0	207	32.5
Pensions	41	11.0	53	12.0	67	13.5	99	15.0
Medical care	24	6.5	32	7.5	40	8.0	71	11.0
Welfare and other	12	3.0	16	3.5	21	4.5	36	5.5
(Nursing care)	4	1.0	7	1.5	10	2.0	21	3.0

Source: The Ministry of Health, Labour and Welfare.

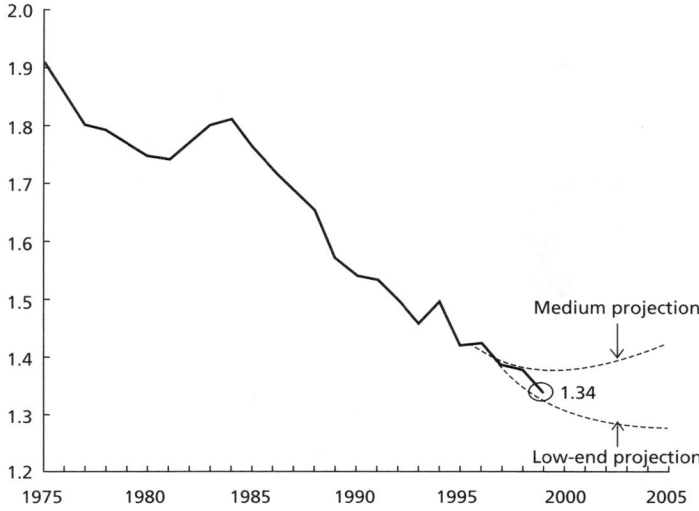

9.10 Total fertility rate in Japan.
Source: Ministry of Health, Labour and Welfare.

that go beyond current expectations. One of the biggest problems confronting the nation is that Japan's fertility rate – the total number of children a woman bears in her lifetime – has been declining at a faster pace than the government's reform plan had assumed (Fig. 9.10). Moreover, the government has not yet implemented a plan to increase the ratio of basic pension benefits paid by the national Treasury from one-third to one-half of total basic pension obligations, even though this plan was one of the objectives of the pension reforms established in 2000. Further delays in this increase could lead to heavier financial burdens on the national Treasury. To minimize the potential negative impact on Japan's public finances from an underfunded public pension system, drastic changes, such as partial privatization of the system, will probably be necessary.

A number of other factors are likely to put additional pressure on Japan's public finances. Radical tax reform measures, such as a sharp rise in the consumption tax, may be necessary to increase government revenues since the existing tax base is unlikely to provide a significant increase in tax revenues in the short run. The number of entities receiving FILP funds, such as government-affiliated financial institutions and public sector corporations, is unlikely to decline in the near term. And finally, the issuance of government bonds is likely to increase further over the medium to long term because the flexible management clause allows for an increase in FILP spending.

219

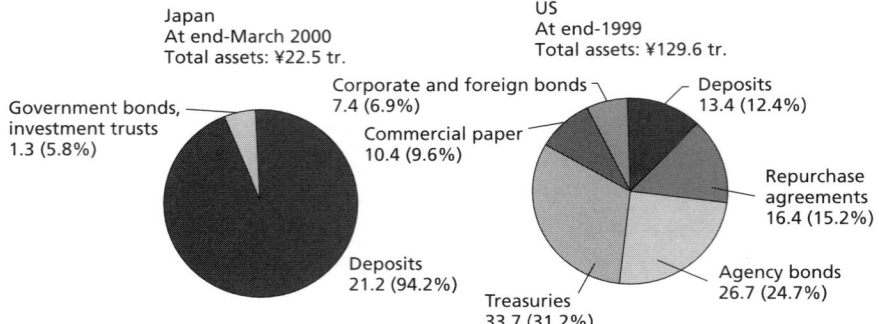

9.11 Comparison of asset allocations for local governments in Japan and the US.
Note: The breakdown for Japan does not include loans. US dollar amounts were converted into yen based on an exchange rate of ¥120.
Source: Nomura, based on Bank of Japan, *Flow of Funds Accounts Statistics* and the Federal Reserve Board, *Flow of Fund Accounts*.

ON THE DEMAND SIDE

Although reducing the issuance of government bonds through fiscal and FILP reforms is important, the government should also continue efforts to stabilize demand for government bonds. As discussed earlier, various reforms intended to stimulate demand have gradually been implemented, such as the issuance of bonds with a wider range of maturities, tax exemptions on bond interest for foreign investors and the creation of zero-coupon bonds. In addition, the government should attempt to increase demand from major bond investors.

Although some Japanese institutional investors, such as pension funds and insurance companies, invest in marketable securities, much like their US counterparts, other large Japanese investors, such as local governments, universities, foundations and associations, place their funds primarily in savings deposits. A comparison of the asset allocations for local governments in the US and Japan reveals that most US institutions invest in fixed-income securities, mainly Treasuries and agency bonds, whereas more than 90% of local governments in Japan keep their funds in deposits (Fig. 9.11). These local governments have increasing opportunities to raise their asset allocations for marketable securities in light of the introduction of deposit insurance caps in April 2002, but whether these funds will contribute significantly to total demand for JGBs remains to be seen.

CHAPTER 10

Corporate finance in Japan

Because of ongoing structural changes in the financial system, corporate finance in Japan has now reached a major turning point. Generally speaking, corporate finance has been affected by trends in economic growth.

The period up to 1973 was characterized by strong economic growth and a shortage of capital. From 1973 to 1979, however, the capital shortage abated somewhat as companies reduced output and scaled back their operations. Then, during the first half of the 1980s, the shortage of capital stabilized as economic growth became more stable. During the economic bubble years of the latter half of the 1980s, corporate financing activity expanded at an unprecedented rate as corporate investment increased. In the 1990s, after the collapse of the economic bubble, many Japanese companies retrenched and streamlined their operations for the first time since the oil crises of the 1970s. After suffering a shortage of capital for many years, the corporate sector had a surplus of capital by the latter half of the 1990s (Fig. 10.1).

Over these decades, Japanese companies increasingly shifted away from indirect financing (through banks) and toward direct financing (from capital markets). They also increasingly relied on debt, particularly straight bonds, rather than equity for financing. The bursting of the economic bubble made it apparent by the middle of the 1990s that Japanese companies needed to change their management and financing strategies because their returns on capital were too low. Finally, in the latter half of the 1990s, while Japanese companies were increasingly turning to the capital markets for their financing needs, corporate earnings deteriorated and credit risks rose when a number of listed companies went bankrupt.

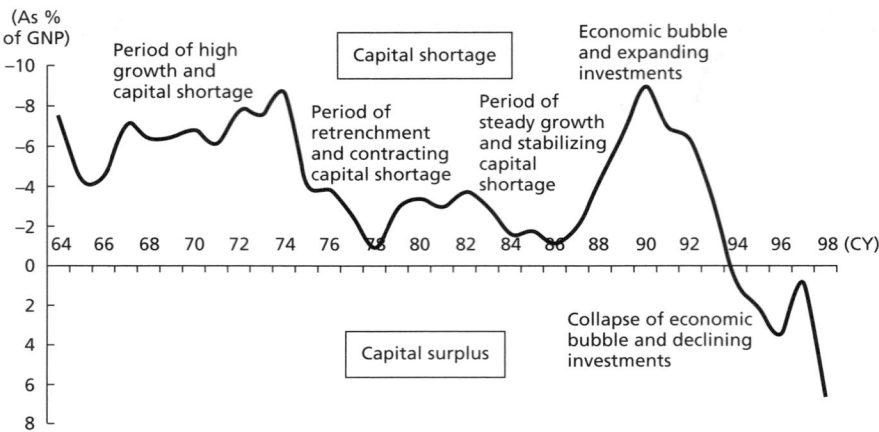

10.1 Trend in capital surpluses/shortages for private non-financial companies.
Source: Bank of Japan, *Flow of Funds Account Statistics*.

Japanese companies have thus been facing increasing pressure from the financial markets to revamp their corporate management and financial strategies. The average ROA (the ratio of operating profit on a parent, pretax basis to total assets) in fiscal 1999 for approximately 2000 listed Japanese companies was 3.7%, and the average ROE (the ratio of net profit to shareholders' equity) was nearly 0%. The low level of these financial ratios can be attributed mainly to the massive extraordinary losses stemming from the disposal of surplus or non-performing assets as companies attempted to restructure, but low profitability has remained a pervasive problem.

Corporate finance and changes in the economic structure

During the strong economic growth phase from 1960 to 1974, when sales grew nearly 20% a year (see Fig. 10.2), companies expanded aggressively. During this high-growth period, companies lacked sufficient capital to meet their tremendous demand for funds. Therefore, the main issue in corporate finance was procuring adequate capital to finance the many investment opportunities that were available. Given that the capital markets were still undeveloped at this time, Japanese companies tried to meet their strong financing needs

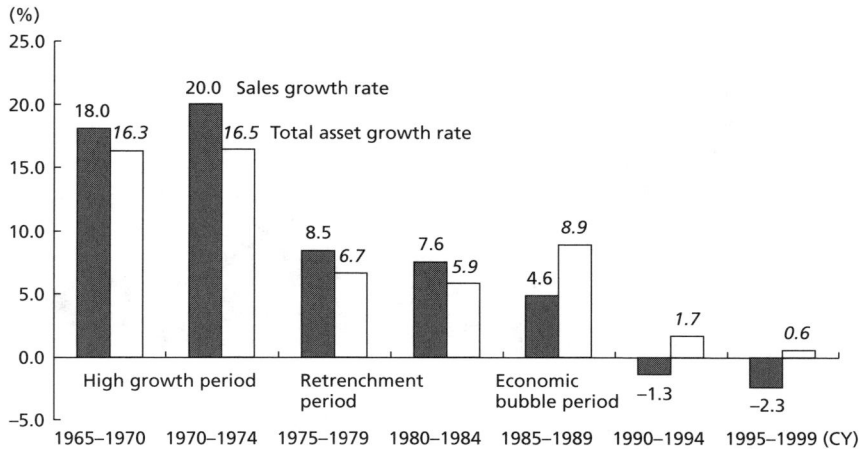

10.2 Key growth rates for Japanese companies (five-year averages).
Source: Data are for manufacturing companies included in Bank of Japan, *Analysis of the Financial Statements of Principal Enterprises in Japan* for 1965–1970 and the Nomura Industrial 350 for 1970 onward.

by borrowing from banks and other financial institutions. The amount of borrowing contributed to a sharp decline in the average ratio of shareholders' equity to total assets (the shareholders' equity ratio) for Japanese companies to around 15%, which, based on current criteria, is the level for a BB credit rating.[1]

EQUITY FINANCING

As bank borrowings became the main source of financing, the ability to generate more than enough profit to service debt began to serve as an important financial benchmark for companies. As a result, Japanese companies naturally began to focus on recurring profits. Although the long-term prime rate remained high at 8% during the high-growth period, companies grew while maintaining an average ROA of around 10%, which was rather high, especially compared with current levels.

Following the first oil crisis in 1973 and until 1979, Japanese companies retrenched and scaled back their operations, which helped to alleviate the capital shortage they faced. Because the ROA

1 If a company has two or more different ratings from credit rating agencies, the higher or highest rating is used (details are discussed later in the chapter).

223

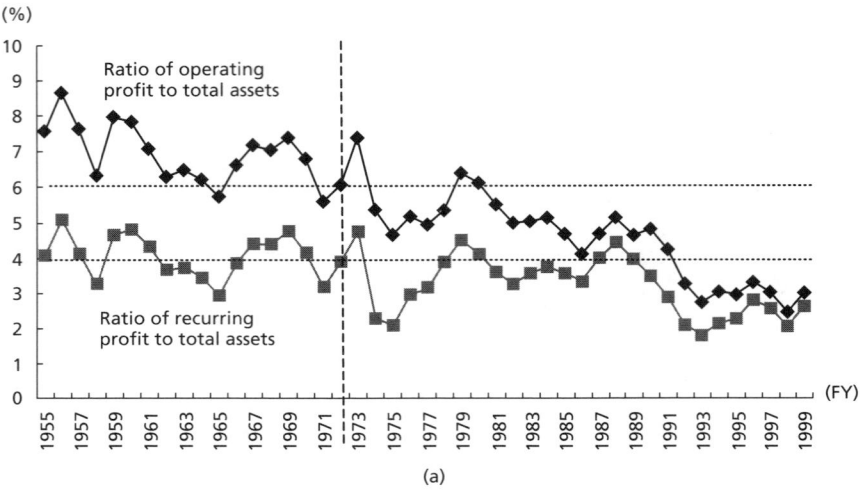

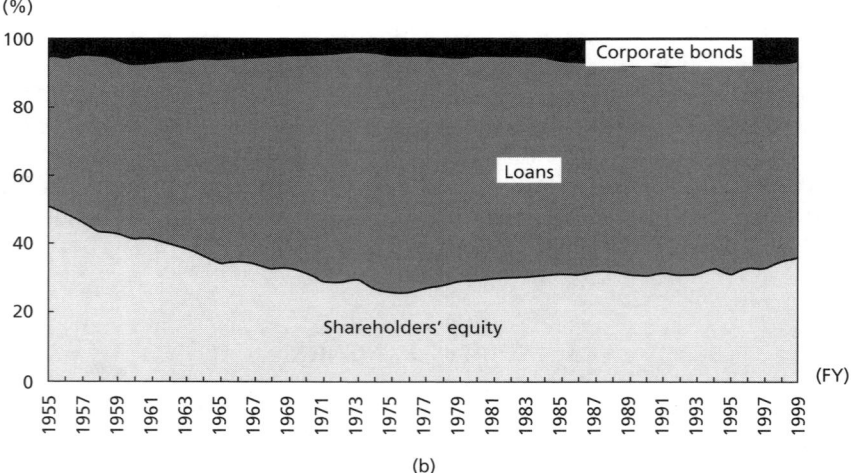

10.3 (a) ROA for Japanese companies, 1955–1999. (b) Capital structure of Japanese companies, 1955–1999.
Source: Ministry of Finance, *Financial Statements Statistics of Corporations by Industry*.

of Japanese companies in this period declined to 4–5%, companies were compelled to restructure their unprofitable operations and sell off underutilized assets (Fig. 10.3). Shareholders' equity ratios then began to improve by fiscal 1976, when companies started to scale down their debt.

After the two oil crises in the 1970s, the Japanese economy moved into a phase of low growth. During the first half of the 1980s, economic growth stabilized and corporate demand for capital continued to exceed supply, but the imbalance stabilized (Fig. 10.1). Companies aggressively expanded overseas in order to seek new growth opportunities in response to the yen's strong appreciation. This move, in turn, led to an increase in business risk and currency risk that encouraged companies to focus on strengthening their balance sheets. Toward this end, Japanese companies increasingly turned to equity-linked financing, including the issuance of new shares, convertible bonds and bonds with warrants. The market environment for issuing equity was favourable at the time – interest rates had remained at record low levels since the Plaza Accord in the autumn of 1985, stocks were in a bull market and corporate earnings were relatively strong.

The composition of funds raised by Japanese companies changed drastically during this period. The proportions of debt and equity changed, partly because companies issued equity to finance their capital investments, other long-term investments and financial investments. As discussed later in the chapter, this trend ultimately contributed to the current low levels of ROA and ROE among Japanese companies. Also, during this period, many companies established finance subsidiaries both in Japan and overseas; the overseas subsidiaries helped to raise capital, and all of them played a role in expanding the companies' sophisticated financial investment operations.

Starting in the mid-1980s, companies stepped up their equity and equity-linked financing (Fig. 10.4). The amount they raised in this manner from fiscal 1980 to fiscal 1984 totalled about ¥15.3 tr. Then, from fiscal 1985 to fiscal 1989, when the Nikkei Average hit an all-time high, the amount companies raised by issuing equity or equity-linked securities more than quadrupled to ¥66.6 tr.

Convertible bonds were the main type of security issued by Japanese companies during the latter half of the 1980s; total convertibles issued over this period amounted to ¥30 tr., or about 45% of the ¥66.6 tr. in total equity financing. Of the remainder, ¥20 tr. was accounted for by bonds with warrants and ¥16 tr. by other types of securities, such as publicly offered shares. For companies listed on the Tokyo Stock Exchange (TSE), the issuance of convertibles and bonds with warrants resulted in a more than ¥20 tr. increase in aggregate shareholders' equity, in the form of stock and additional paid-in capital. The increase represents almost twice the comparable growth related to publicly offered shares and about 40% of the ¥50 tr. in aggregate shareholders' equity of TSE-listed companies as

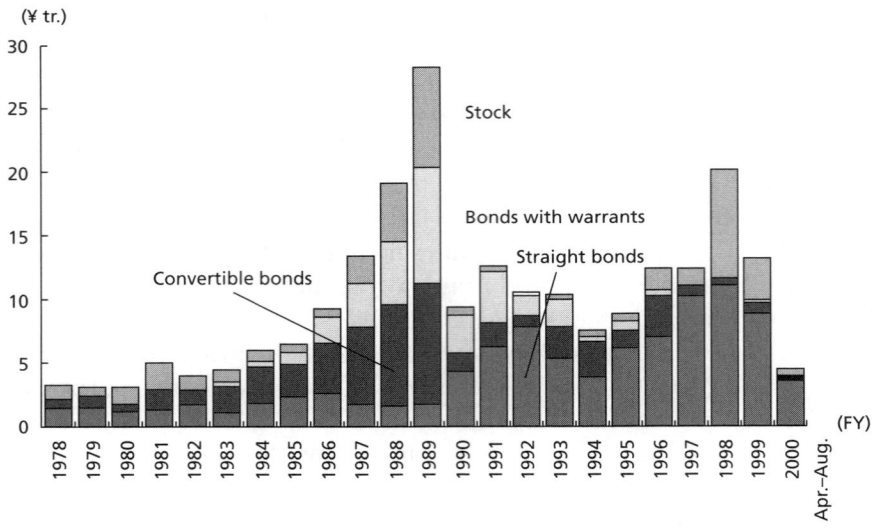

(¥ tr.)

10.4 Trends in fund-raising by Japanese companies.
Source: Japan Securities Dealers Association, *Shoken Gyoho*.

of the end of fiscal 1984. By comparison, issuances of straight bonds amounted to only ¥7 tr. during the first half of the 1980s and ¥10 tr. in the second half.

The average shareholders' equity ratio rose to about 30% in the second half of the 1980s, which was roughly in line with the ratio for US companies. This percentage, however, is an average for two contrasting groups of companies – only the major Japanese companies, which were able to easily tap the capital markets, had high shareholders' equity ratios; most of the other companies were in much weaker financial shape.

DEBT FINANCING

Another major turning point in Japanese corporate finance occurred in 1990, when issuances of equity and equity-linked securities rapidly fell off because of the correction in the stock market, the establishment of capital-adequacy requirements by the Bank for International Settlements (BIS) and a rise in interest rates. From the time the Plaza Accord was signed in 1985 until 1989, equities benefited from relatively low interest rates.

Between fiscal 1990 and fiscal 1994, equity-linked financing fell about 66% from its peak level to ¥22 tr.; from April 1990 to early

1993, the market for public stock offerings was practically closed off. Public stock offerings started up again in 1993, but companies had to meet various criteria, such as a minimum ROE and dividend payout ratio. In the five years to fiscal 1999, equity-linked financing totalled about ¥23.5 tr. But a large portion of this funding – ¥7.7 tr. – was accounted for by banks' issuance of preferred stock to the government in fiscal 1998 to shore up their capital. Excluding this special factor, the amount of equity-linked financing in this five-year period came to ¥15.8 tr.

The conversion of convertible bonds and the exercise of warrants attached to bonds issued during the 1980s slowed down. During the first half of the 1990s, the outstanding balance of convertibles and bonds with warrants trading below parity[2] totalled ¥22 tr., which led companies to refinance by issuing debt and redeeming these equity-linked securities. The rapid shift to issuance of straight bonds was also prompted in part because banks had been reducing their lending in order to meet BIS capital-adequacy requirements. Initially, Japanese companies had issued mostly Eurobonds, such as Euroyen bonds, but later, they began to issue an increasing amount of domestic straight bonds.

For many years, Japanese corporations had to meet various criteria before they could issue corporate straight bonds. Moreover, most corporate bonds have had to be backed by collateral since the prewar era, as a legacy of efforts that were first made around 1933 to improve the quality of corporate bonds. These bonds, except for electric utility bonds, have thus been considered to be a limited source of financing. In the postwar era, companies did not issue unsecured corporate bonds until 1979, when Matsushita Electric Industrial issued an unsecured convertible bond; TDK Corporation followed suit in 1985 with the first unsecured straight bond.

Commercial Code restrictions on the amount of corporate bonds that a company could issue were abolished in 1993. Other types of numerical eligibility criteria for bond issuance gradually gave way to credit-rating criteria. The rating requirements for corporate bond issuance were gradually relaxed, with the minimum eventually lowered to BBB. Ultimately, eligibility criteria were completely eliminated in 1996, and restrictive covenants pertaining to a company's financial condition were also liberalized. These changes,

---

2 The price of the bond is less than the stock's market price times the conversion ratio.

which made issuing bonds easier for companies, contributed to a gradual rise in the amount of straight bonds issued – from ¥1 tr. in 1989 to ¥4.4 tr. in 1990 and then about ¥10 tr. in 1998.

Commercial paper has not been a widely used choice for raising short-term funds. The amount of commercial paper outstanding in Japan totalled ¥15.8 tr. at the end of September 2000, compared with about ¥100 tr. in the US. Non-financial companies became eligible to issue commercial paper in Japan in 1987, and ever since, securities companies, non-banks and insurance companies have been allowed to tap the commercial paper market. Furthermore, maturity restrictions and eligibility standards were relaxed in 1996.

Nevertheless, because of lingering sundry problems concerning issuance procedures and costs, commercial paper currently accounts for only about 1% of total corporate financing in Japan. Previously, non-financial companies issued commercial paper and invested the proceeds in higher-yielding, large time deposits. Because of the elimination of this arbitrage opportunity, however, the outstanding balance of commercial paper has not increased significantly following the deregulation of commercial paper issuance. Thus, despite expectations that commercial paper would become a standard short-term financing instrument, companies have not fully embraced it.

Many of the finance subsidiaries mentioned earlier have been either restructured or liquidated. In recent years, as Japanese companies have expanded in the US, Europe and Asia in conjunction with the broader trend of the internationalization of business, the role of these finance subsidiaries has changed. They now focus more on cash management, such as raising and pooling funds for group companies around the world, and net settlement and reinvoicing to streamline the management of multicurrency transactions.

The rise in credit risk

In addition to changes in the environment surrounding corporate finance, another important development has been the increase in corporate credit risk. Accordingly, credit ratings have risen in importance; in fact, they have become widely recognized as a key issue in corporate finance.

Unlike in the US, credit ratings have played a limited role in Japan, in part because they were introduced in conjunction with various regulations during the 1980s. Nevertheless, to some extent, the rating system in Japan has played an important role in increasing the number of companies able to issue bonds. For example, credit ratings were used as issuance eligibility criteria for samurai bonds (yen-denominated bonds issued in Japan by non-residents) in 1981, which resulted in an increase in the number of companies eligible to issue the bonds, and for domestic corporate straight bonds in 1990 (alongside existing numerical eligibility criteria).

Until 1990, credit ratings in Japan did not fully serve as an indication of credit risk – which is supposed to be their primary function – since the basic assumption in the capital markets during this time was that only companies that would not default were able to issue corporate bonds. But by November 1990, issuance eligibility criteria were no longer based on numerical standards and instead were uniformly based on credit rating (the minimum rating at the time was A or higher). Consequently, the number of companies that became eligible to issue bonds increased by more than three times those eligible based on the previous numerical standards. The elimination of all issuance standards meant that companies with credit ratings of BB or lower were no longer restricted from issuing high-yield bonds. But even five years after the restriction was lifted, only one company – a regional general merchandise store – had issued a BB-rated convertible bond.

Banks also introduced their own internal quantitative credit risk rating systems in an attempt to set appropriate lending rates. Because of the difficulty involved in linking ratings to loan terms in practice, however, the cost of funds for bank loans is still lower than that for corporate bonds. Before the issuance of bonds by companies with lower credit ratings expanded, a noticeable rise in the number of major bankruptcies in 1995, followed by a string of failures of financial institutions, caused investors to become more risk averse than before. Ironically, the importance of credit ratings became increasingly recognized not so much because of the lifting of restrictions on high-yield bond issuances but, rather, because of a deterioration in earnings and a rise in bankruptcies among listed companies, which were generally thought to have low credit risk.

Starting around 1995, an increasing number of listed companies and small and medium-sized financial institutions went bankrupt. In 1997, the collapse of major financial institutions, including Yamaichi Securities and Hokkaido Takushoku Bank, made the securities markets extremely sensitive to corporate credit risk. Japanese companies were no longer able to issue BBB-rated bonds, and banks cut back on lending, resulting in a credit crunch. Amid this difficult

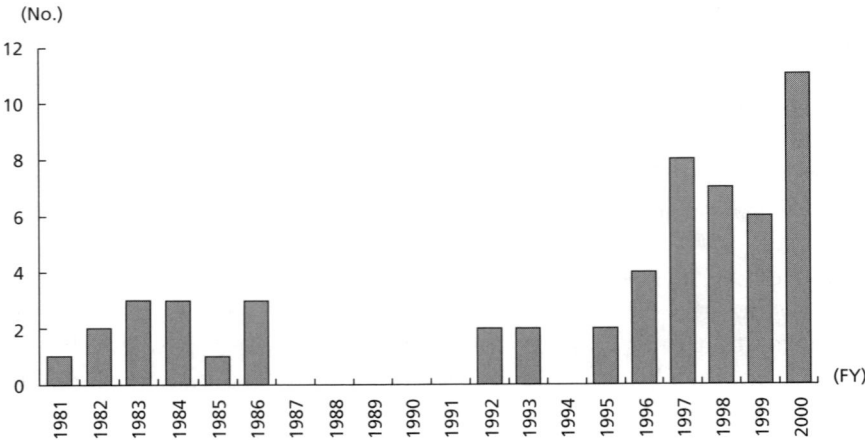

10.5 Bankruptcies of listed Japanese companies.
Source: Teikoku Databank.

environment, major companies with strong credit ratings rushed to raise funds by issuing debt.

Figure 10.5 shows the trend in bankruptcies among listed Japanese companies. Those companies that went under defaulted on their corporate bonds. Although earlier bankruptcies had led to a number of defaults on outstanding bonds, including convertible bonds privately placed overseas, a common practice was for main banks to purchase bonds in default at par, thereby averting losses among investors. This uniquely Japanese practice eventually disappeared, however, because banks lost their ability to prevent defaults. Banks stopped acting as de facto guarantors for corporations and ceased purchasing bonds in default in 1993, when Muramoto Construction went bankrupt and defaulted on its privately placed domestic bonds. Subsequently, a number of companies defaulted on their publicly offered bonds: Olympic Sports on its overseas convertibles, Daito Kogyo on its overseas straight bonds, Yaohan Japan on its domestic convertibles and JDC on its domestic straight bonds. Investors ultimately suffered losses as a result of these defaults (Table 10.1).

Defaults on bonds by major Japanese companies are typically dealt with in accordance with the Corporate Reorganization Law. Specifically, unsecured bonds in default rank *pari passu* with all other obligations. The collection period for these claims is usually long, and only about 5% (20% at the most) of the outstanding amount is typically collectible, which is significantly lower than

Table 10.1 Bankruptcies of publicly traded companies and corporate bond defaults

Date	Company	Bankruptcy procedure	Amount of liabilities (¥ m)	Reduction	Type of bonds issued	Straight-bond disposal
Aug. 1991	Maruko	Corporate Rehabilitation Law	285 837	79%	Swiss franc-denominated privately placed convertible bond	–
May 1992	Lec	Corporate Rehabilitation Law	25 344	65%	Swiss franc-denominated privately placed convertible bond	–
Jul. 1993	Nikkatsu	Corporate Rehabilitation Law	49 700	90%	Swiss franc-denominated privately placed straight bond	Bank guarantees
Nov. 1993	TSD	Bankruptcy	9 239	–	Swiss franc-denominated privately placed convertible bond	–
Dec. 1993	KYC Machine Industry	Corporate Rehabilitation Law	97 000	89%	Swiss franc-denominated privately placed straight bond and other issues	–
Jan. 1995	Nippon Data Kiki	Composition Law, bankruptcy	41 500	–	Swiss franc-denominated privately placed convertible bond	–
Sep. 1996	Olympic Sports	Composition Law, bankruptcy	35 506	–	Euroyen-denominated convertible bond	–
Jan. 1997	Kyotaru	Corporate Rehabilitation Law	101 332	80%	–	–
Jul. 1997	Tokai Kogyo	Corporate Rehabilitation Law	511 007	98%	–	–
Jul. 1997	Tada Construction	Corporate Rehabilitation Law	171 400	87%	–	–

Table 10.1 *Continued*

Date	Company	Bankruptcy procedure	Amount of liabilities (¥ m)	Reduction	Type of bonds issued	Straight-bond disposal
Aug. 1997	Daito Kogyo	Corporate Rehabilitation Law	159 221	92%	Swiss franc-denominated privately placed straight bond	–
Sep. 1997	Yaohan Japan	Corporate Rehabilitation Law	161 383	97%	Domestic convertible bond and other issues	Purchase of domestic convertible bonds at 10% of par value (¥100) prior to approval of restructuring plans
Dec. 1997	Toshoku	Corporate Rehabilitation Law	639 700	92%	–	–
Jul. 1998	Asakawagumi	Corporate Rehabilitation Law	60 300	95%	–	–
Sep. 1998	Longchamp	Corporate Rehabilitation Law	8 758	91%	–	–
Oct. 1998	Morisho	Bankruptcy	16 121	–	Swiss franc-denominated privately placed convertible bond	All privately placed bonds secured with deposits
Oct. 1998	Tescon	Company rehabilitation under the Commercial Code	11 700	60%	Euroyen-denominated convertible bond	–
Dec. 1998	JDC	Corporate Rehabilitation Law	406 717	91%	Domestic straight bond and other issues	Value of bonds reduced by 90%
Jul. 2000	Sogo	Civil Rehabilitation Law	1 870 000	95%	–	–

Notes: Reductions are for bonds in default (which rank *pari passu* with all other obligations).
– = Not applicable.
Source: Nomura, based on various newspaper reports.

the 40% that is collectible in the US. As in the case of Muramoto Construction, even secured bonds can rank *pari passu* with all other obligations if the value of the collateral declines. Although defaults on bonds by major Japanese companies are not common, recent trends suggest that a deterioration in earnings can quickly lead to defaults and a relatively low probability of loan recovery. These trends have had a major impact on credit ratings in Japan.

The introduction of the Civil Reorganization Law as the new law on corporate bankruptcies has made it easier for insolvent companies to initiate reorganization procedures promptly. In addition, the introduction of debt-equity swaps could lead to higher recovery rates for corporate bond investors.

Credit ratings

About 1000 Japanese companies have credit ratings. Based on the higher or highest rating for companies with two or more credit ratings, the bulk of the ratings range between A and BBB. Although an increasing number of companies have speculative BB or lower ratings, this group still accounts for only 8% of all companies with credit ratings. Most of these companies are 'fallen angels' whose bond ratings have been downgraded. As discussed later in the chapter, 20–30% of Japanese companies have ratings of BB or lower from non-Japanese rating agencies.

Corporate bonds issued by companies with ratings of AA or higher account for almost 40% of the outstanding amount of corporate bonds, even excluding electric utility bonds. Although a BBB rating is the most common rating for Japanese companies, less than 20% of the outstanding amount of corporate bonds are rated BBB. Therefore, Japan's corporate bond market consists mainly of bonds with relatively high credit ratings, with the average rating based on the outstanding amount being A+ (Table 10.2). As in the case of equity financing, direct debt financing increased primarily among major corporations.

Credit ratings play an important role in debt financing. As the internationalization of the securities markets progresses, the divergence between the ratings assigned by domestic rating agencies and overseas agencies has become an issue. Credit ratings in Japan are provided by several domestic rating agencies as well as nationally recognized statistical rating organizations (NRSROs), which are designated as such by the Securities and Exchange Commission (SEC)

Table 10.2 Distribution of credit ratings

FY1999 outstanding bond issuance amount by credit rating

Credit rating		Number of companies				Credit ratings and outstanding corporate bonds					
		Highest rating		Lowest rating		Highest rating			Lowest rating		
						Number of companies	Outstanding corporate bonds (¥ bn)		Number of companies	Outstanding corporate bonds (¥ bn)	
AAA	(Aaa)	32	3.2%	9	0.9%	9	2 347.2	5.7%	0	0	0.0%
AA	(Aa)	147	14.9%	82	8.3%	66	13 373.0	32.3%	27	5 256.9	12.7%
A	(A)	373	37.9%	262	26.6%	236	17 272.5	41.8%	143	7 866.4	19.0%
BBB	(Baa)	349	35.4%	441	44.8%	287	7 316.5	17.7%	334	14 118.8	34.1%
BB	(Ba)	62	6.3%	141	14.3%	54	841.8	2.0%	123	10 062.6	24.3%
B and below	(B and below)	22	2.2%	50	5.1%	11	207.1	0.5%	36	4 053.4	9.8%
Total		985	100.0%	985	100.0%	663	41 358.2	100.0%	663	41 358.2	100.0%
Average rating		A relatively weak		BBB relatively strong		A+ relatively weak			BBB relatively weak		

Notes: Fiscal 1999 outstanding bond amounts are for companies that were assigned credit ratings (excluding financial institutions, electric power/gas utilities and unlisted companies); the highest and lowest ratings are used for companies that were rated by more than one credit rating agency.
Source: Nomura, based on rating agency data.

of the US. The four major agencies in Japan are Rating and Investment Information (R&I), Japan Credit Rating Agency (JCR), Standard & Poor's (S&P) and Moody's Investors Service (Moody's). Although domestic rating agencies have the largest market share in Japan, S&P and Moody's have been increasing their coverage by assigning ratings to companies even if they do not receive a formal request from the company.

The average gap between the ratings assigned by Japanese and US agencies has for some time been three notches, which is equivalent to one grade (Table 10.3). Among the credit ratings assigned to Japanese companies by Japanese rating agencies and their US counterparts, only about 3% are the same, and a gap of more than two grades, such as that between A and BB, is not uncommon.

The trend in credit ratings for Japanese companies has been changing drastically. From fiscal 1997 to fiscal 1998, when corporate earnings growth turned negative, more than half of the companies with credit ratings were downgraded (Fig. 10.6). Credit ratings for major companies (the 126 that are included in the Nikkei Average and which have been rated regularly since 1991) were downgraded to around A, after having remained stable between A+ and AA− for a number of years.

The main reasons for the downgrades were a weak economy and a deterioration in corporate earnings. Compared with previous downgrades, one key difference was that the credit ratings for some companies were lowered in response to the deregulation of certain industries, such as non-life insurance and utilities, transportation and related sectors. Another difference was changes in the rating policies among rating agencies. In 1998, S&P and Moody's lowered their credit ratings on various Japanese companies, but in 1999 the number of downgrades by the US agencies fell slightly. In contrast, Japan's R&I downgraded a number of Japanese companies, apparently as part of a shift to a new rating system in response to worsening corporate fundamentals in Japan. As the downgrades by R&I accelerated, the gap between the ratings issued by Moody's and R&I narrowed, albeit slightly. Conversely, the gap between ratings assigned by R&I and JCR widened to 0.7 notches, the largest spread ever. The Japanese credit-rating agencies have been increasingly assigning different ratings to the same bonds, with the percentage of identical ratings assigned by the Japanese agencies falling to 40% from 60%. These trends suggest that credit-rating differences are no longer simply along Japanese and US lines.

Table 10.3 Credit rating gaps among rating agencies

Number of notches	Japanese rating agencies		Japanese rating agencies vs US rating agencies								US rating agencies	
	R&I-JCR		MDY-R&I		MDY-JCR		S&P-R&I		S&P-JCR		S&P-MDY	
4 notches (higher)									1	2%		
3 notches (higher)											5	5%
2 notches (higher)	1	0%									11	12%
1 notch (higher)	11	3%	2	1%	1	1%	3	3%	1	2%	20	21%
Same rating	142	41%	8	3%	1	1%	19	22%	6	11%	31	33%
1 notch (lower)	152	44%	32	12%	6	4%	13	15%	12	21%	23	24%
2 notches (lower)	38	11%	84	33%	23	16%	15	17%	8	14%	4	4%
3 notches (lower)	5	1%	74	29%	36	26%	27	31%	11	20%		
4 notches (lower)			38	15%	37	26%	9	10%	7	13%		
5 notches (lower)			17	7%	21	15%	2	2%	8	14%		
6 notches (lower)			2	1%	13	9%			2	4%		
7 notches (lower)					1	1%						
8 notches (lower)					1	1%						
9 notches (lower)												
Total	349	100%	257	100%	140	100%	88	100%	56	100%	94	100%

Example: For R&I–JCR, of the 349 companies that were rated by both R&I and JCR, compared with the rating assigned by JCR, one company was given a rating 2 notches higher by R&I, while 135 companies were assigned a rating 1 notch lower by R&I.

Notes: R&I: Rating and Investment Information; JCR: Japan Credit Rating Agency; MDY: Moody's Investors Service; S&P: Standard & Poor's; credit ratings are at the end of March 2001; data do not include JCR's p-ratings and S&P's financial institution pi-ratings, which cannot be converted into notches.

Source: Nomura, based on rating agency data.

236

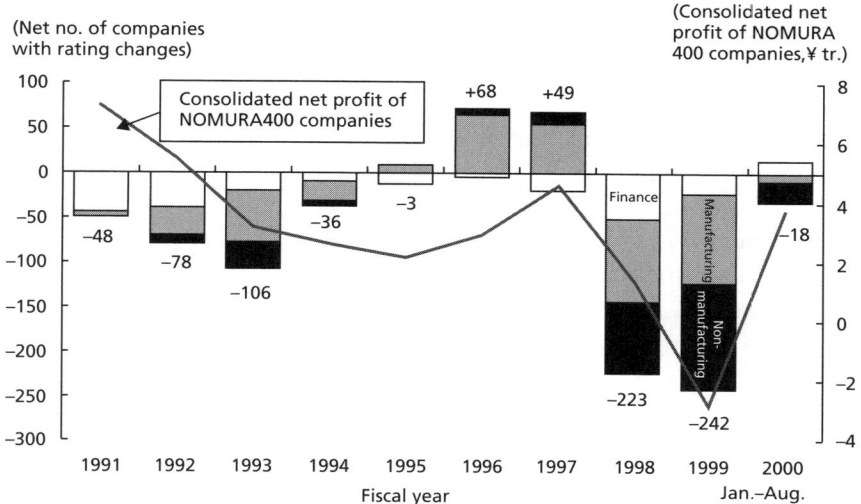

(Net no. of companies with rating changes)

(Consolidated net profit of NOMURA 400 companies,¥ tr.)

10.6 Corporate earnings and credit rating changes (by Japanese rating agencies). Note: The net number of companies with rating changes is the number of companies with rating upgrades minus the number with rating downgrades; credit-rating change data are on a calendar year basis; consolidated net profit for the NOMURA400 companies is on a fiscal year basis (e.g., 2000 = FY3/2000); in cases where more than one credit rating agency changed ratings for a company within the same year, only one change is counted; credit ratings are those assigned by Japanese agencies (the former Japan Bond Research Institute, the former Nippon Investors Service, Rating and Investment Information and Japan Credit Rating Agency).
Source: Nomura, based on data from credit rating agencies.

To alleviate the credit crunch in 1997–98, the government recapitalized financial institutions with public funds to help bolster lending to the corporate sector, including small and medium-sized companies. In addition, in March 1999 restrictions on credit lines were lifted, and collateralized bond obligations (CBOs) were introduced as a way to provide financing to BBB-rated companies. The adoption of these measures helped to ease the credit crunch somewhat.

Yet the relationship between non-financial companies and financial institutions has changed drastically and has generally been weakening; it is highly unlikely that companies will rely upon financial institutions for support as much as they used to in the past. Financial institutions now have a less prominent role in the economy, and the market has less confidence in the ability of the Japanese financial system to be flexible in meeting the funding requirements of the corporate sector. In 1996, the disclosure of

237

dealer quotations for bonds traded over the counter was extended to cover all issues. Because market participants have become extremely sensitive to credit risk, bond issuance terms now more fully reflect credit ratings.

With debt financing, including the refinancing of maturing debt, becoming the main choice for raising capital in Japan, it is increasingly important for companies to carefully manage their balance sheets, including their ratios of debt to equity, so that they can adequately raise financing at favourable costs.

Trends in the financial condition of Japanese companies

This section looks at various financial indicators of Japanese companies. As mentioned earlier, the ROA (based on operating profit) of Japanese companies has declined sharply since fiscal 1973. According to the Ministry of Finance's Financial Statements Statistics of Corporations by Industry, the average ROA remained stable at around 7% until fiscal 1973 but then fell over the next 10 years, until it levelled off at 4–5%. In the mid-1980s, ROA declined temporarily as a result of a recession brought on by a strong yen, but later recovered. During the 1990s, ROA fell to a record low of about 3%.

NET INTEREST/DIVIDEND INCOME AND ROE LEVELS

For about 2000 exchange-listed Japanese companies, the average net non-operating (or financial) income remained negative for many years, because of a heavy reliance on bank loans, but then approached zero in fiscal 1986. In the second half of the 1980s, the average recurring profit margin exceeded the average operating profit margin, thanks in part to financial investment-related gains and income. During this period, ROA declined 1.6 percentage points to 4.5%. But because the ratio of net interest/dividend income to total assets increased 1.8 percentage points, the average recurring profit margin stayed at around 4.5%.

This improvement is attributable to favourable interest rate changes, improved debt-to-equity ratios and gains from investments in financial assets, which helped to partially offset a deterioration in operating margin. The biggest factor was a decline in interest expense stemming from lower market interest rates. Even though

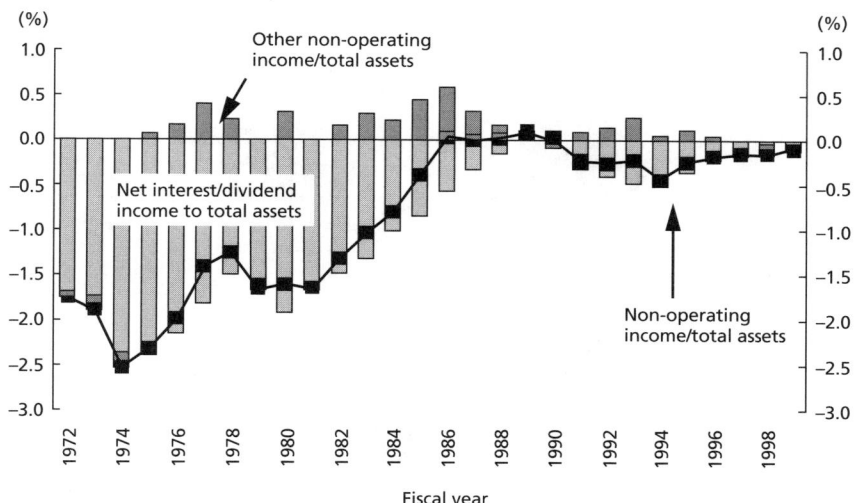

10.7 Net interest/dividend income as percentage of total assets for 2000 listed companies (parent basis).
Source: Nomura.

companies carried 40% more interest-bearing debt in fiscal 1988 than in fiscal 1980, interest expense actually declined, because the long-term prime rate declined to around 5% in 1988 from 10% in the early 1980s and because companies issued more equity-linked bonds, which have relatively low coupons. Although net interest/dividend income stopped improving in the early 1990s, when interest rates rose and stock prices fell, it has remained relatively stable since then because interest rates have been at record low levels (Fig. 10.7).

Since the cost of debt for Japanese companies has been low, corporations have been less focused on the cost of equity, which has been relatively high. The primary reason for the decline in ROA and ROE has been excess investments financed for the most part by equity capital that cost more than the returns that were generated. Another source of the problem was the continued use of recurring profit as a performance benchmark.

During the last 20 years, the average ROE of Japanese companies has declined significantly. ROE declined between fiscal 1979 and fiscal 1989 mainly because of a sharp decrease in leverage accompanied by lower ROA. Lower ROA was the primary reason for the decline in ROE between fiscal 1989 and fiscal 1999, given that leverage during this period did not decrease significantly (Fig. 10.8).

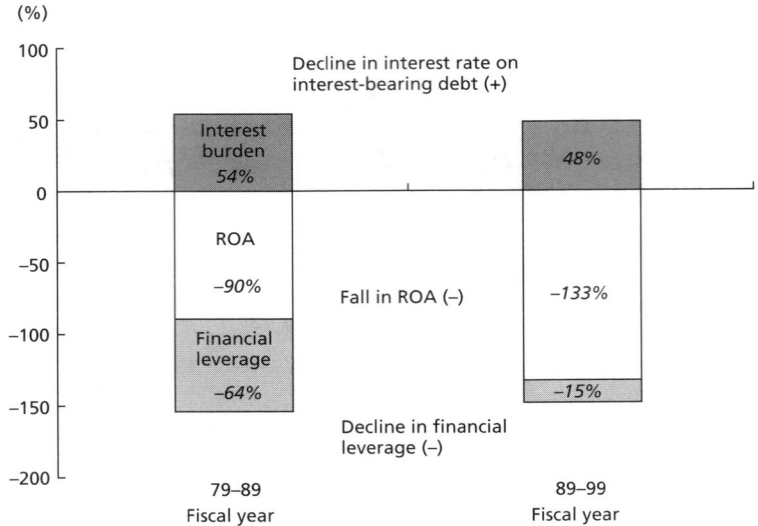

10.8 Analysis of factors behind decline in ROE.
Note: The above shows a decomposition of ROE (based on recurring profit) for listed companies for fiscal 1979–1989 and fiscal 1989–1999; ROE has been decomposed into ROA, interest expense and the debt-to-equity ratio.
Source: Nomura.

SUPPLY AND DEMAND FOR CAPITAL AND CORPORATE BALANCE SHEETS

During the retrenchment period between the two oil crises in the 1970s, asset turnover and profitability improved as companies reduced their investments and used their working capital more efficiently. Asset turnover and profitability began to deteriorate again, however, in the late 1980s because capital spending, loans and investments significantly exceeded cash flow.

As shown in Fig. 10.9, a graph of the supply and demand balance for capital, demand for investment capital has consistently exceeded retained earnings. During the second half of the 1980s in particular, not only capital spending but also investments and loans and liquid assets, including short-term marketable securities, increased. When returns on financial assets fell considerably in the 1990s, they became a drag on overall profitability because returns on operating assets also deteriorated.

Higher levels of equity financing have contributed to the strengthening of cross-shareholding relationships between companies and financial institutions in Japan. Since fiscal 1986, the amount of stock and additional paid-in capital on corporate balance sheets has increased by ¥36 tr., while marketable securities and investment

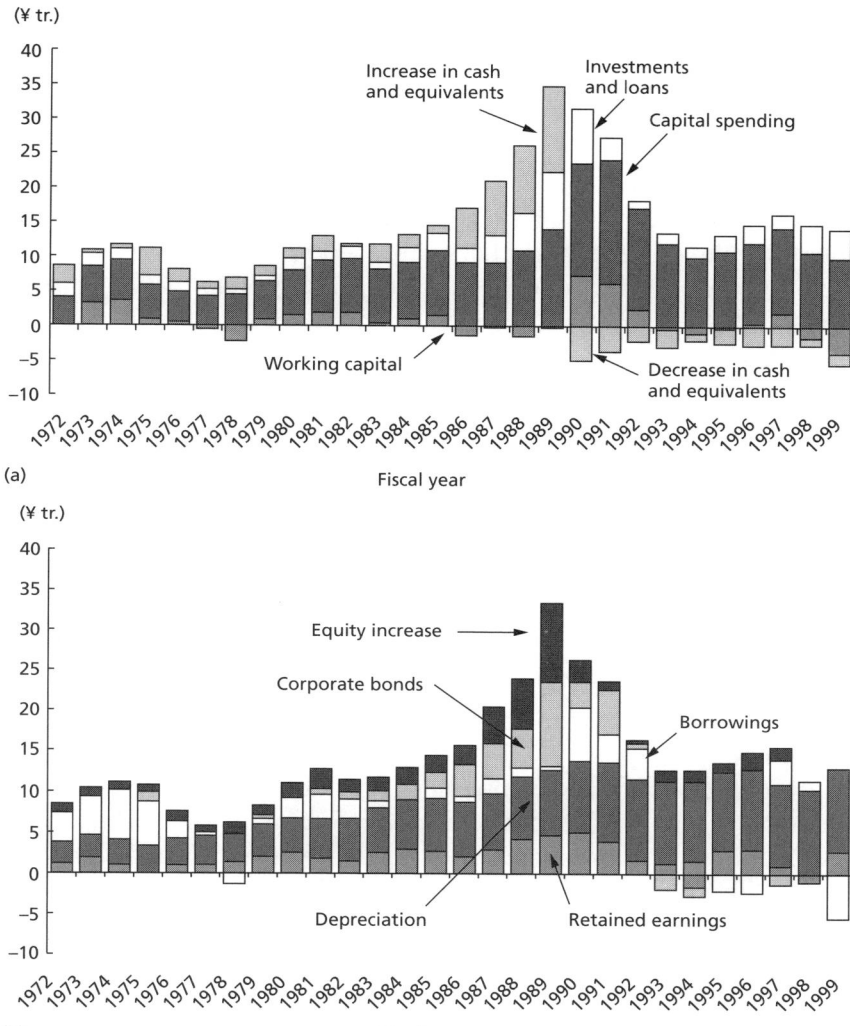

10.9 (a) Demand for capital among listed companies. (b) Sources of capital for listed companies.
Note: External sources of financing include the new issuance of equity and corporate bonds, and borrowings.
Source: Nomura.

securities have risen by ¥40 tr. Most likely, a significant portion of these shares – even after adjusting for those shares held by institutional investors and financial institutions and for investments in affiliated companies – are held in the form of cross-shareholdings.

In terms of market value, listed companies owned between 30%

and 40% of other listed companies' shares in 1990. This figure declined to 20% at the end of 2000, an indication that banks and companies have been steadily unwinding their cross-shareholdings. Facing pressures to shrink their bloated balance sheets, companies stopped increasing their total assets during the second half of the 1990s. Japanese companies have 15% of their total assets in liquid assets (cash and short-term marketable securities), which is a considerably higher ratio than that for US companies. Given the relatively low returns on these cash holdings, corporate managers need to re-evaluate their cash levels and their cross-shareholdings.

STABLE DIVIDEND POLICIES

Although Japanese companies consider their profit trends when determining dividends, for the most part, they pay a stable amount of dividends per share as their main method of passing on profits to shareholders. Some companies establish target dividend-payout ratios and pay dividends based on actual profits, but most prefer to make stable dividend payments. Since 1990, the dividend-payout ratio for Japanese companies has soared because dividends have remained stable even though profits have declined. This trend reflects Japanese companies' reluctance to lower dividends even if profits fall.

Compared with US companies, dividend-payout ratios among Japanese companies tend to be lower for companies with higher ROE. Among US companies with an ROE of 10%, many pay out more than 40% of profits as dividends, whereas very few Japanese companies pay out such a high percentage. By generally paying out dividends that have a more direct relation to the level of their profits, US companies thus tend to have more flexible dividend policies than Japanese companies do.

CONSOLIDATED VERSUS PARENT COMPANY ACCOUNTING

Companies reported financial results primarily on a parent basis for many years, but recently, consolidated information has become increasingly widespread for valuing companies and reporting results. The prevailing view is that companies should be assessed on a groupwide basis and that because many companies have expanded their operations through affiliates, the gap between parent and consolidated earnings has widened to such an extent that it cannot be ignored. The preference for consolidated financial data is understandable, especially given the increasing difficulty in properly assessing a company's profitability and asset quality based solely on parent data.

Ratios of consolidated revenues or assets to parent revenues or assets range between about 1.4x and 1.5x, and these ratios have been increasing over the last few years. Moreover, the ratio of consolidated interest-bearing debt to parent interest-bearing debt is about 1.8x; the ratio of net consolidated profit to net parent profit has ranged between 0.7x and 1.3x, with the average at 1.0x. Consolidated and parent ROEs are approximately the same because subsidiaries contribute little to group profits or shareholders' equity. Indicators of a company's financial condition, such as the debt-to-equity ratio, tend to be much lower at the consolidated level.

Trends in financial ratios and credit ratings differ significantly between companies, depending on the financial condition of group companies. Figure 10.10 shows the relationship between credit ratings and key financial metrics, such as total assets and shareholders' equity. These metrics are directly related to credit ratings at both the consolidated and parent levels. In contrast, measures of financial condition, such as shareholders' equity ratios and debt-to-equity ratios, tend to be lower on a consolidated basis for companies with poorer credit ratings, which suggests that problems at companies with low credit ratings exist not only at the parent level but also on a groupwide basis. Therefore, disclosure of consolidated financial figures tends to be advantageous for blue-chip companies but disadvantageous for poorly performing companies.

The changing environment for corporate finance

As already mentioned, Japanese companies borrowed heavily from banks during the postwar, high-growth period, which resulted in higher debt ratios, but their financial condition began to improve significantly starting around the mid-1970s. After aggressively issuing equity during the second half of the 1980s, major companies saw their shareholders' equity ratios improve enough to nearly match those of US companies.

STRUCTURAL REFORMS

An increasing amount of investments with comparatively low returns, however, resulted in significantly lower ROEs. To address

243

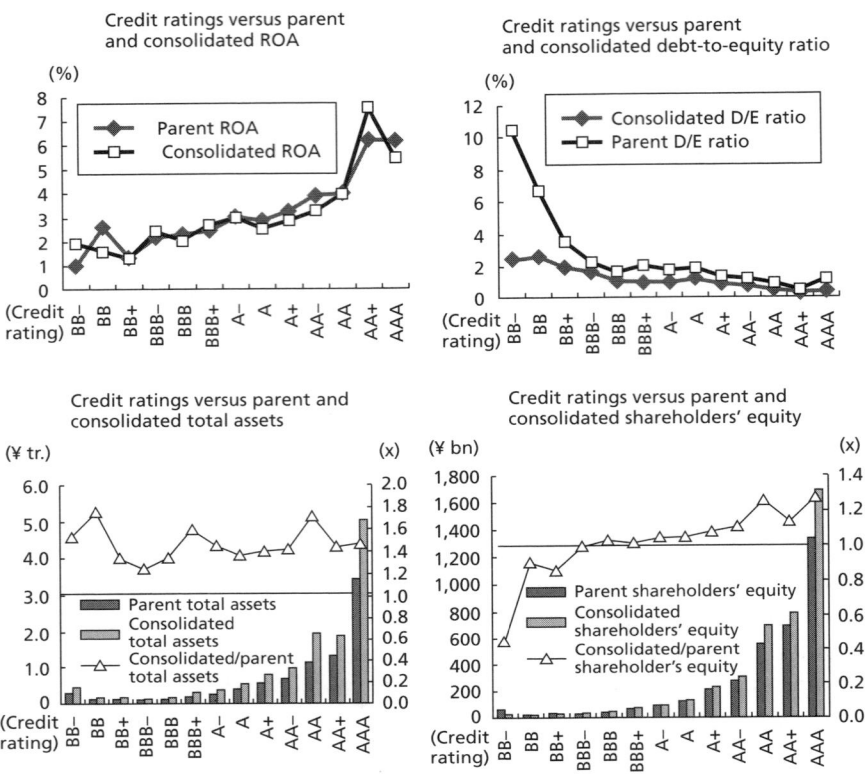

10.10 Credit ratings versus key financial metrics on a parent and consolidated basis.
Note: Credit ratings are the highest ratings for each company in 1999; all financial data are for fiscal 1998.
Source: Nomura, based on credit rating data and company financial statements.

this problem, companies have tried to revamp and shrink their balance sheets over recent years by reducing their high levels of cash, financial assets and business investments. From a corporate finance perspective, the problem was an excess of equity that had been issued to finance many of these investments. Although some companies restructured in the wake of the oil crises by selling off or discontinuing poorly performing operations and reducing assets, Japanese companies today face a different environment than in previous periods. Specifically, the role of banks as both lenders and shareholders has changed as the capital markets are increasingly used for financing. In turn, the base of investors has been changing. Moreover, the securities markets have been deregulated and liberalized, and new accounting, legal and tax frameworks have been established. Amid these changes, Japanese companies have become increasingly market-oriented in their financial and management strategies by focusing on their market value and credit ratings.

In addition to low returns on capital, another factor contributing to corporate management reform has been structural changes in the stock market. Foreign investors' share of the value of trading of Japanese stocks has grown to about 50%. In addition, pension funds and other purely investment-oriented investors that emphasize fundamentals and seek capital gains are increasing their presence and becoming the leading market participants; they are taking the place of strategic investors that seek to cement corporate relationships in the form of cross-shareholdings.

Moreover, an increasingly widespread notion since 1997 has been that the survival of a company could depend upon its market valuation and its credit rating. Driven by these concerns, top executives have been participating more actively in activities having to do with investor relations. Through dialogue with institutional investors and securities analysts, corporate executives have been able to gain a better understanding of the views held by market participants. This communication, in turn, often brings about additional managerial reforms. Furthermore, companies must deal with the dramatic changes in the legal and regulatory infrastructure, including the Commercial Code, taxes and the accounting system. Often, these systemic changes have provided companies with new tools to accomplish significant managerial reforms.

THE ACCOUNTING BIG BANG: THE TRANSITION TO CONSOLIDATED ACCOUNTING

Since fiscal 1999, consolidated financial results have become increasingly prominent. In addition, various new accounting standards have been adopted, such as classifications of subsidiaries based on the degree of control the parent company exerts, mark-to-market accounting of financial products and pension-accounting rules. Other moves that are part of an ongoing comprehensive review of accounting standards to bring Japan's accounting standards in line with the Statements of Financial Accounting Standards (SFAS) and the International Accounting Standards (IAS) include consideration of accounting standards for impaired assets and business combinations (Table 10.4).

For many years, most Japanese companies reported only parent

Table 10.4 Major changes in accounting standards

Year of change	Details
2000	Focus on reporting earnings results on a consolidated basis, degree-of-control standard used to determine whether a subsidiary is consolidated, tax-allocation accounting, cash flow statements
2001	Mark-to-market accounting for financial instruments, new pension accounting standards
2002	Mark-to-market accounting for cross-shareholdings
2003	Plan to introduce impaired-asset accounting standards

Legal and tax reforms to spur business reorganizations

Year of change	Details
1997	Reform of antitrust laws to allow the establishment of holding companies
1999	Industrial Revitalization Law
2000	Reform of the Commercial Code; introduction of stock swap and stock transfer schemes
	Civil Rehabilitation Law
2001	Reform of the Commercial Code; introduction of corporate split-up system
	(starting 2001) Plan to overhaul the Commercial Code
2002	Plan to introduce consolidated taxation system

Legal and regulatory reforms for improving corporate finance flexibility

Year of change	Details
1994	Reform of the Commercial Code to allow share buybacks
1995	Freeze on tax regulation that treated share buyback proceeds as dividends
1996	Elimination of corporate bond issuance standards and liberalization of financial criteria for issuance of corporate bonds
1997	Establishment of a special provision of the Commercial Law to allow companies to buy back their shares more flexibly
	Reform of the Commercial Code to allow the establishment of stock-option programmes
1998	Reform of the Commercial Code to allow companies to use additional paid-in capital to purchase their own shares (law expires in 2002); revision of the Foreign Exchange and Foreign Trade Control Law
1999	Elimination of restrictions on credit lines
2001	Elimination of tax regulations that treated share buyback proceeds as dividends
2001	Plan to revise the Commercial Code to remove restrictions on treasury stock, ease regulations on stock options and allow companies to issue tracking stocks

results. Currently, only about 30 companies present their financial results based on SFAS; all others do so in accordance with Japanese accounting standards. Consolidated financial results first appeared in Japan in 1977, but the Commercial Code, which includes provisions on the payment of dividends, and the taxation system remain centred on parent financial results. Corporate management has thus traditionally focused on financial issues from a parent perspective.

In the late 1980s, when many companies diversified into new business areas, interest in the concept of consolidated or group-based management grew among Japanese companies. This interest, however, led to the development of corporate cultures that contributed to excessive group expansion. Furthermore, valuations of companies still relied on parent financial results because of inadequate disclosure of consolidated information.

The trend toward harmonizing Japan's accounting standards with internationally accepted standards stems in part from pressure for financial information that is comparable on a global basis and in part from mounting concerns that current financial results may be concealing corporate liabilities or losses, such as unrealized losses on assets and parent-company losses that have intentionally been shifted to affiliates. Some critics argue that Japan is merely passively adopting international accounting standards. Nonetheless, significant changes in Japan's accounting framework, including a shift toward reporting financial results on a consolidated basis, are fostering changes in the way Japanese companies are managed.

DEVELOPMENT OF A LEGAL FRAMEWORK

The government has developed relatively flexible laws and regulations regarding corporate reorganizations and taxation that are likely to support management reforms. For the most part, regulations concerning the capital markets have been relaxed or eliminated, and because many believed that some commercial and tax laws prevented Japanese companies from more drastic restructuring, various steps have been taken to improve the ability of Japanese companies to restructure their operations; specifically, restrictions on the establishment of holding companies have been lifted, stock swaps and transfers have been permitted and corporate split-ups are now allowed. Although a system of taxing companies on a consolidated basis will not be introduced until sometime in 2003 at the earliest, the elimination of various restrictions relevant to corporate management has progressed considerably.

Furthermore, the first sweeping revisions of the Commercial Code in about 50 years are coming into effect during 2001–2002. These changes are due to include measures that should give companies greater flexibility in managing their businesses. For example, to speed up decision-making, the number of required attendees and issues to be voted on at general shareholders' meetings will be reduced. In addition, a broadened range of people will be eligible for stock options. Other expected changes involve the minimum number of shares constituting a round lot (the figure can be determined by companies), the introduction of a paperless settlement system for commercial paper and improvements in the settlement system for corporate bonds.

Consolidated operations

The aforementioned systemic changes have significantly affected the way Japanese companies manage their consolidated operations. In order to incorporate the evolving corporate management perspectives into our analysis, the discussion of the impact of the changes that follows is based on interviews with executives of major companies and other relevant data.

MANAGING ON A CONSOLIDATED BASIS

Many Japanese companies recognize the importance of managing their operations on a group rather than parent basis, and the concept has caught on in quite a number of companies. But some companies are not yet at that stage in the decision-making process – they still focus on parent operations when making key decisions, such as those related to capital spending and budgeting. Companies that have been managing operations primarily on a consolidated basis are electronics and automobile companies, which have operated globally through overseas subsidiaries and spun off production and sales subsidiaries. One problematic issue peculiar to Japan involves the case of a parent company that owns a publicly traded subsidiary. The subsidiary is independent from the parent but is nevertheless classified as a consolidated subsidiary under Japanese accounting rules, which complicates efforts to manage operations on an integrated basis.

The shift toward consolidated accounting has also been having a significant impact on companies' financial targets. In the past,

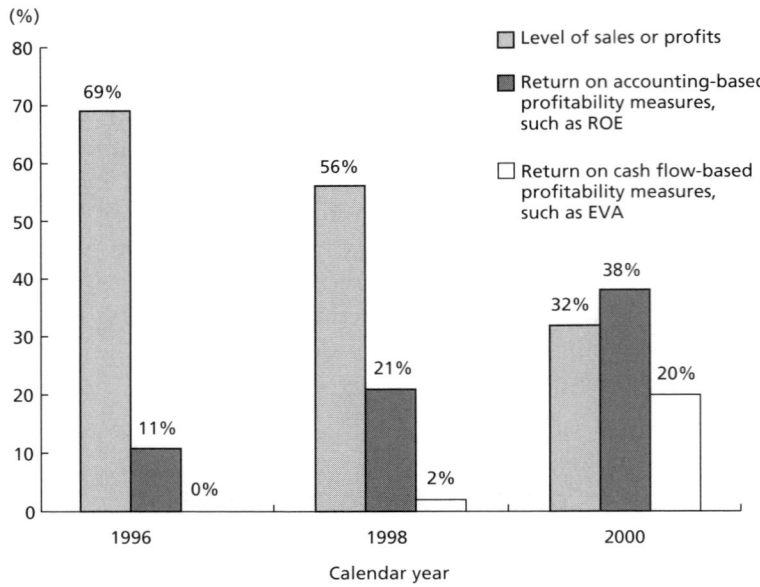

10.11 Comparison of the major financial targets of Japanese companies. Source: Nomura, based on surveys of large corporations.

companies focused on the parent company's recurring profit, but many now consider consolidated ROE and ROA to be the most important financial targets (Fig. 10.11). More than half of all major Japanese companies now establish ROE targets, and about half of these companies disclose these targets. Japanese companies no longer casually establish ROE targets – a large number have set targets of 8–10%, which is consistent with their medium-term business plans and appropriate levels of the cost of capital. This practice of establishing profitability targets has now become fairly well established.

More companies are embracing the concept of cash flow management. For instance, it is now common for medium-term management plans to include target cash flow levels. Companies that are focusing on reducing their outstanding debt often attempt to achieve positive free cash flow through such measures as selling assets – a strategy that is typical in retrenchment periods. In any event, more and more companies are setting free cash flow targets. An increasing number of companies focus the most on cash flow-based profitability measures, such as EVA[3] and cash flow return on investment (CFROI). Indeed, most Japanese companies now consider some type

3 EVA, or economic value added, is a registered trademark of Stern Stewart & Co.

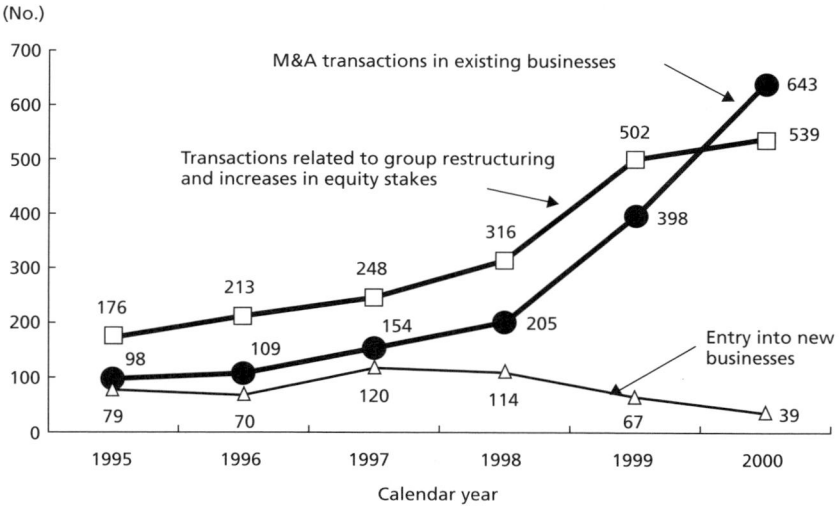

(No.)

10.12 Number of M&A transactions among domestic corporations.
Source: Nomura.

of return on capital as their most important performance benchmark, a sign that major changes are under way in the framework of corporate finance in Japan.

ACCELERATED RESTRUCTURING

Japanese companies are making progress in restructuring on a groupwide basis and improving the quality of their balance sheets. Mergers and acquisitions are becoming a common method for reorganizing subsidiaries. The number of M&A deals involving Japanese companies has jumped sharply in recent years. In 2000, more than 1300 M&A deals involved only Japanese companies, a 40% increase year on year (Fig. 10.12).

The first stage of corporate reorganization in Japan typically centres on corporate groups and involves the merging of existing business divisions, realigning group companies and increasing the equity stake in group companies. Although this phase sometimes includes measures to deal with existing problems, such as the discontinuation of struggling subsidiaries, it is clear that companies are aiming to improve their competitiveness by focusing on core businesses and getting rid of non-core operations.

During the second stage, the emphasis is on a full-scale strengthening of core businesses. Realignments and deals with outside

251

companies, in an effort to focus and strengthen existing businesses, typically significantly exceed consolidations among group companies. An example of such a deal is Nissan Motors' sale of its aerospace division in 2000.

Stock swaps and transfers have been used so far to transform group companies into wholly owned subsidiaries, but in the future, they could be used for acquisitions involving companies outside the group and aimed at business reorganizations. M&A activity is likely to continue at a strong pace for some time, partly because companies have a greater choice than before of ways to reorganize. One such option is a corporate split-up, which has become easier since 2001. One of the consequences of an increase in M&As is that companies now pay more heed to their market value, an important factor in acquiring another company or in defending against a takeover attempt.

CHANGES IN POLICIES ON GROUP EQUITY

The conventional reasons for taking a subsidiary public used to be that the move would increase employee morale, put pressure on management to improve performance and ultimately lead to improved growth for the business as a whole. Yet this point of view has become less prevalent recently. An increasing number of major companies in Japan and overseas are not interested in taking subsidiaries public, in the belief that the fundamentally correct strategy from a consolidated management perspective is to keep a subsidiary private and maintain control over what could turn into a core business. Even though on average more than 30 Japanese subsidiaries go public each year, at the same time publicly traded subsidiaries are being taken private in the wake of the introduction of a stock swap system. So far, nearly 40 formerly public subsidiaries – including those of Sony, Matsushita Electric Industrial and Canon – have been taken private.

Still, some companies recognize the benefits of taking subsidiaries public. Some companies are interested in considering initial public offerings (IPOs) of subsidiaries on a case-by-case basis, with the strongest candidates being non-core subsidiaries that generate few synergies with the parent's main business and technology subsidiaries with strong growth potential that the stock market is likely to recognize and value appropriately. Some other companies, meanwhile, believe the IPO option provides incentives for overseas subsidiaries. As the importance of eliminating the discounts on the values of businesses within a conglomerate becomes more widely recognized, Japanese companies have also begun to consider issuing tracking stocks as an alternative means of raising capital for growth businesses and, at the same time, being able to maintain managerial control over the business and obtain a high market valuation for the business. In June 2001, Sony issued Japan's first tracking stock, for its Internet service provider subsidiary.

For spinning off non-core businesses and cutting off their equity ties to the group, companies now have a number of options to choose from that are based on the characteristics of each subsidiary's business. An important consideration for companies is to select a technique that enhances the competitiveness of the subsidiary yet minimizes any negative effect on employees. If a subsidiary is considered to have strong profit and growth potential, an IPO is a possible option. Other choices include establishing joint ventures with or selling subsidiaries to other companies in the same industry and implementing a management buyout, which would maintain the independence of the unit. Such moves have already been made, although there have been only a few cases. More companies are likely to consider these types of reorganization measures, some of which will lead to IPOs.

THE QUALITY OF BALANCE SHEETS

For many years, improving the quality of balance sheets has been the most important issue confronting Japanese companies. Most companies, however, appear to believe more work needs to be done and are determined to continue reducing their assets, ranging from cash to cross-shareholdings (Fig. 10.13). In addition to the perennial working capital, particular assets companies are focusing on include real estate and other types of property, plant and equipment.

With the pending introduction of impaired-asset accounting, it is becoming increasingly imperative for companies – and not just those in the construction and real estate sectors – to reassess their production facilities and idle assets. As evidenced by recent sales and securitizations of head office buildings, companies have begun to restructure their real estate holdings. Moreover, Japanese real estate investment trusts (J-REITs) can now be established, a change that should add liquidity to the real estate market and help companies to reconfigure their property holdings.

The introduction of new pension accounting standards in fiscal 1999 led to the problem of how to treat several tens of trillions of

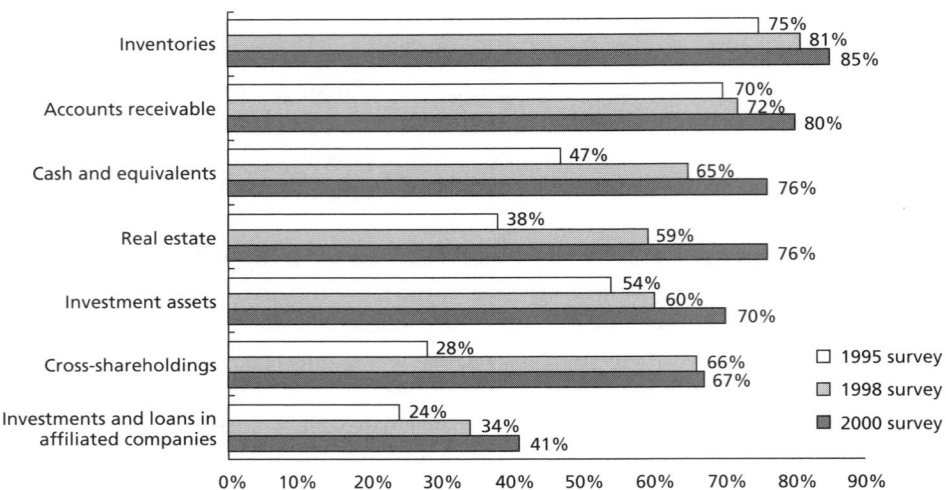

10.13 Major categories of asset reductions by large Japanese companies.
Note: The above percentages indicate the ratio of respondents that are in the
process of reducing assets or plan on reducing assets in the categories listed.
Source: Nomura, based on surveys of large corporations.

yen in aggregate unfunded pension liabilities (based on the projected benefit obligation), an amount that until then had been un-
disclosed. Most companies elected to establish pension trust funds,
to which the companies contribute stockholdings. This move enables
companies to remove cross-shareholdings from the asset side of their
balance sheets and pension liabilities from the liabilities side. In
addition, given that marketable securities and investment assets are
now subject to mark-to-market accounting rules, it reduces the exposure of companies' balance sheets to price risk. But the exposure to
the market has been shifted to companies' pension assets and liabilities. Even though many companies took care of their transition
liabilities that arose in the first fiscal year of the new accounting
rules, the subsequent decline in the stock market resulted in underfunding of pension obligations and an increase in service costs for
some companies. Hence, stock market fluctuations remain a major
risk for companies.

THE UNWINDING OF CROSS-SHAREHOLDINGS AND CHANGING VIEWS TOWARD STABLE SHAREHOLDERS

Based on Nomura surveys of major companies, the average proportion of shareholders that companies recognize as stable share-

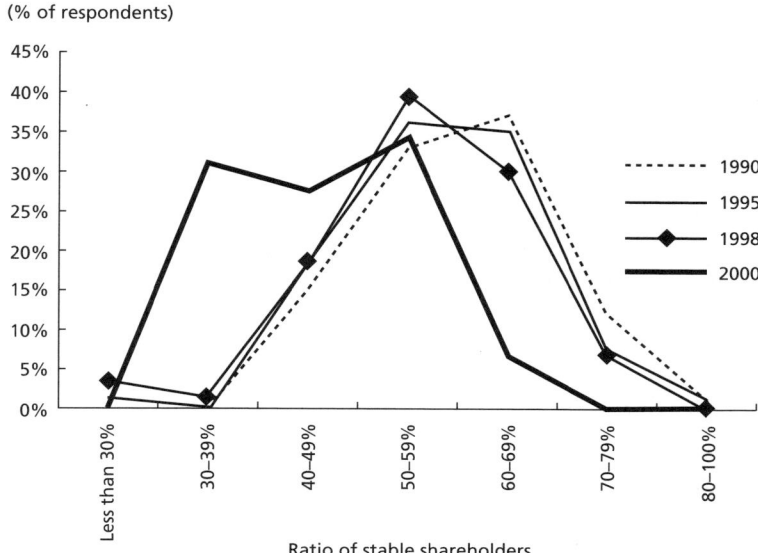

(% of respondents)

- - - - - - - 1990
————— 1995
—◆— 1998
——— 2000

Ratio of stable shareholders

10.14 Distribution of ratio of stable shareholders.
Source: Nomura, based on surveys of large corporations.

holders has fallen to less than 50% (Fig. 10.14). As shown in the figure, the greatest number of companies have a current strategic shareholder ratio of about 50% (the mean is still 50%).

It is worth noting, however, that an increasing number of companies have a strategic shareholder ratio of only about 30%. This trend does not necessarily mean that the composition of shareholders is changing drastically, but it does suggest that the concept of a strategic shareholder for some companies is evolving. In other words, companies are increasingly aware of the uncertainty of whether their traditional stable shareholders, such as insurance companies and banks, will continue to hold their shares for strategic purposes. According to a Nomura survey, about 70% of companies intend to maintain or increase their proportion of stable shareholders, but quite a large number of companies recognize that a decline in the ratio is all but certain.

Shareholders that Japanese companies would like to have, in addition to existing stable shareholders, include foreign, individual and institutional investors with long-term investment horizons. Recognizing that finding more traditional stable shareholders and buying back shares are not likely to be sufficient to minimize the impact of sales of cross-shareholdings, many companies are leaning toward a management focus on cash flow and other financial metrics to maintain or boost their stock prices.

LIFTING OF RESTRICTIONS ON SHARE BUYBACKS AND THE STRENGTHENING OF BALANCE SHEETS

In 1995, restrictions imposed by both the Commercial Code and tax laws on share buybacks were lifted. At first, most companies considered share buybacks – which reduce excess equity and cash holdings – as a means of using capital more efficiently. At the end of March 2002, a total of 970 public companies had bought back more than an aggregate ¥4 tr. of their own shares. This amount pales in comparison with the nearly ¥70 tr. in equity and equity-linked securities that public companies issued during the second half of the 1980s. In Japan, although share buybacks using retained earnings as well as additional paid-in capital are allowed, shares worth only about ¥300 bn were actually bought back in this manner.

Not even 20% of Japanese companies have bought back their shares. Of those that have, only about 20% did so with the stated intention of passing on profits to shareholders, which is a significantly lower proportion than the 60% for US companies. Some argue that the framework for share buybacks in Japan is less flexible than that in the US because Japanese companies are restricted from holding treasury stock. Japanese companies are likely to buy back shares as a way to use proceeds from their sales of cross-shareholdings as well as to return effectively to shareholders the surplus cash stemming from the improved use of capital.

MANAGEMENT VIEWS ON RAISING CAPITAL

Given the prolonged low level of interest rates and lack of demand for funds to finance business expansion, corporate financing activity has been relatively quiet. Instead, companies are highly focused on improving the quality of their balance sheets to maintain or improve their credit ratings. They are thus concentrating on reducing debt and financial leverage to minimize their financial risk.

Although companies are likely to increasingly tap the capital markets directly for financing, this trend does not mean that companies consider their relationships with banks unimportant. As major Japanese banks continue to reorganize, companies are becoming more selective about the banks with which they do business. Many companies intend to reduce the amount of outstanding bank loans, but at the same time, in an attempt to maintain business relationships to some extent with main banks, companies want to maintain a certain amount of credit through lines of credit and overdraft privileges. Japanese companies have traditionally relied on their main banks for deposits, loans, cross-shareholdings and services stemming from long-standing business relationships. As a result, companies are likely to unwind their cross-shareholding relationships with those banks with which they do not have close business ties.

Companies remain reluctant to issue new equity because many believe they should focus on increasing shareholder value and because they have a limited need for new financing. After having been criticized for not focusing enough on shareholder value, companies are now more sensitive to their market valuations. Nonetheless, companies appear interested in raising capital to finance growth businesses within their groups, such as Internet and biotechnology businesses, and to strengthen their financial condition.

Japanese companies' levels of cash and equivalents have fallen, in part because of the adoption of groupwide cash management policies. But given the difficulties of flexibly issuing commercial paper in Japan today, companies find they need to hold a relatively large amount of cash, by managing short-term bank borrowings and retained earnings, to maintain adequate liquidity. Companies now have improved access to lines of credit from banks, which serve as an alternative to commercial paper issuance. Longer term, improvements in the commercial paper market are likely to be an important issue in terms of alleviating the liquidity problems of companies. Starting in April 2002, bank time deposits are insured only up to ¥10m, a modification that encourages companies to reassess their deposit accounts.

Japan's outlook for corporate finance

Corporate finance in Japan has been undergoing dramatic changes. Many Japanese companies are strengthening corporate governance by appointing board members who are not executive officers. Further evidence of the broadening extent of management reforms is the increasing adoption of stock option programmes. An increasing number of companies – not just the bold, forward-looking ones – have put into place frameworks for developing management and financial strategies that are closely tied to the capital markets and global financial trends.

Future issues for Japanese companies are likely to include thorough reviews of their capital structure policies and implementation of the new management and financial frameworks that have been established. For instance, companies should adopt widely accepted financial performance benchmarks, such as EVA, as criteria for determining whether to exit businesses or for calculating employee compensation and other incentives. Moreover, management needs to reassess the value added by the head offices – which have become noticeably bloated in terms of function and payroll in Japan as well as other countries – and consider introducing internal profit centre structures and establishing holding companies.

Financial strategies that major companies are increasingly accepting include the use of positive cash flow to benefit shareholders through dividends and share buybacks and the adoption of dividend policies based on group profits. The focus of management is likely to be not only on strengthening the balance sheet, where the priority is on debt reduction, but also on improving the returns to shareholders based on consolidated profits and the efficient use of cash.

Even if the economy recovers, the extent of corporate debt and equity financing for investment projects is likely to remain modest, because Japanese companies will continue to focus on improving the quality of their balance sheets. Equity and equity-linked securities are likely to be used for financing major M&A deals and investments in growth businesses. But unlike before, such financing deals may be difficult because of the challenge of coming up with an attractive story for the equity. Hence, refinancing by issuing new debt will probably be the most common way to raise capital.

But to ensure that companies can raise capital smoothly and regularly, not only do companies need to manage their balance sheets carefully; the capital markets must also be improved to enhance their depth. The secondary market for bonds should be further developed, and changes should be made to facilitate the issuance of commercial paper for short-term financing needs. With the appropriate additional systemic reforms, Japanese companies can be expected to show positive results from their management focus on consolidated operations in the next several years.

11 The Bank of Japan's monetary policy

The Bank of Japan's (BOJ) monetary policy attracted widespread attention during the 1990s and became the subject of fervent debate in 2000 in particular. After reaching a peak of intensity in August 2000, scrutiny of the central bank and its policies subsided somewhat when the BOJ abandoned the zero interest rate policy that it implemented in February 1999. Then on 19 March 2001, amid increasing uncertainty over the economy and a sharply growing chorus of calls for further monetary easing, the BOJ shifted its stance on monetary policy management by adopting a policy of quantitative easing. This pressure on the central bank to ease further will no doubt continue.

The range of the debate and the intensity of the discord in 2000 and 2001 regarding the BOJ's monetary policy was not wholly unpredictable. It was the result of several important changes in the operating environment of the BOJ. First, the new Bank of Japan Law, passed in April 1998, has given the central bank greater independence and full authority over monetary policy, both in theory and in practice. But the law also requires the BOJ to make its monetary policy decision-making process more transparent by fully disclosing its policy intentions to the public and to the markets.

Another crucial change has come about because the central bank has found itself mired in a set of extraordinary circumstances, as BOJ Governor Masaru Hayami once said. After a decade-long recession that contributed to a massive amount of non-performing loans and related side effects that have effectively hobbled the banking sector, the BOJ essentially had little choice but to adopt a zero interest rate policy. As the economy continued to run into unprecedented difficulties, various viewpoints emerged regarding the appropriate role of monetary policy. Indeed, the BOJ's decision to institute a zero interest rate policy was a move that had no precedent in any other country. Even so, the policy's impact on the economy, as measured by conventional standards, was so minimal that doubts arose about the effectiveness of using monetary policy to control the economy at all. These circumstances made it more difficult for the BOJ to manage monetary policy and for outsiders to assess the impact of policy decisions. In short, these changes in the operating environment of the BOJ in the late 1990s heightened interest in how the bank plans to conduct monetary policy, not only among government officials, market participants and private sector economists but also politicians, academics, reporters and overseas observers.

This chapter examines the structure of the BOJ as an organization and analyses its monetary policy in light of the new conditions in which the bank must now operate. The first section further explains the effect of the new Bank of Japan Law on the structure and character of the current environment under which the BOJ conducts monetary policy. To provide a better understanding of the bank's role in establishing monetary policy, the second section of this chapter looks at the specific operating principles and key factors the BOJ considers in determining monetary policy. In addition, recent changes in the methods the central bank uses to implement monetary policy are examined. The third section provides a discussion of some of the critical issues facing the BOJ, namely, the possible adoption of an inflation-targeting policy and the relationship between monetary and fiscal policy; and the final section outlines some of the remaining issues the central bank faces and the probable direction of BOJ policy.

The new Bank of Japan Law

To understand the BOJ and its policies, it is necessary to examine the new Bank of Japan Law, which was passed in April 1998. The new law was established in response to the realization that the BOJ's independence in managing monetary policy had been strongly compromised by government influence, resulting in a negative impact on Japan's economic performance. In the latter half of the 1980s, the BOJ was burdened with the responsibility of having to use monetary policy to stimulate domestic demand, partly because the Japanese government's priorities were on fixing the ailing national budget and cooperating with foreign partners. The central bank's policy of keeping interest rates low contributed to the inflation of asset values, consequent sharp deflation, and ultimately, stagnant economic growth and instability in the financial sector when banks became stuck with non-performing loans. It is this backdrop – the bank's role in creating a low interest rate environment that contributed to the economic bubble – that gave rise to the new BOJ Law. Another impetus behind the new law was the worldwide trend toward giving central banks greater independence in order to improve economic performance. For example, the European Central Bank (ECB), which was granted a relatively strong degree of autonomy similar to the Bundesbank's, was established with this hope in mind.

THE BOJ'S INCREASED INDEPENDENCE

As clearly noted in Art. 2 of the new BOJ Law, one of the guiding principles of the BOJ's management of monetary policy is that 'currency and monetary control shall be aimed at, through the pursuit of price stability, contributing to the sound development of the national economy'. Article 3 explicitly stipulates the extent of the bank's independence: 'The Bank of Japan's autonomy regarding currency and monetary control shall be respected.' The word 'autonomy' is used instead of 'independence' in Art. 3 apparently to maintain consistency with the provision in Art. 4 that '[the BOJ's] currency and monetary control and the basic stance of the government's economic policy shall be mutually harmonious' and with Art. 65 of the Japanese Constitution, which states that 'executive power shall be vested in the Cabinet'. To classify the BOJ's role as independent would be problematic because, according to constitutional law, the bank could then be regarded as an institution with executive powers.

Notwithstanding the specific wording of the provisions, the new BOJ Law differs from the previous version of the law in a fundamental way. According to Art. 1 of the old law, which was established in 1942, in the midst of World War II, the objectives of the central bank were spelled out as being limited to 'the regulation of the currency, control and facilitation of credit and finance, and the maintenance and fostering of the credit system, pursuant to national policy, in order that the general economic activities of the nation might adequately be enhanced'.

Although the word 'independent' is not used in association with the BOJ's role, the provisions in the new BOJ Law concerning the government's supervision of the central bank and the Policy Board members clearly strengthen the BOJ's independence. Article 43 of the Bank of Japan Law of 1942 gave the Minister of Finance the authority to command the BOJ to act, if it was deemed necessary to do so in order for the BOJ to fulfil the government's objectives. In addition, the original law gave the cabinet the authority to demand the resignation of the Governor and the Deputy Governor of the BOJ, and the Minister of Finance wielded the same authority over the BOJ's Policy Board members. Under the new law, however, the wide-ranging authority of the Ministry of Finance over the central bank has been eliminated, and the government's power over the BOJ's Policy Board members has been significantly restricted. Specifically, the government cannot dismiss BOJ directors in the absence of extraordinary circumstances, such as when 'an executive is adjudicated bankrupt' or 'an executive is sentenced to imprisonment or given heavier punishment'.

When the new BOJ Law was being drafted, one of the major points of contention was the degree to which the government could participate in the process of determining monetary policy. To the dismay of the BOJ, the government was allotted a participating role in the formulation of monetary policy. Specifically, Art. 19, Para. 1 of the new law states that 'the Minister of Finance and the minister who is in charge of economic and fiscal policy . . . may, when necessary, attend and express views at Board meetings for monetary control matters' (details concerning the BOJ Policy Board will be discussed later in the chapter). In addition, according to Art. 19, Para. 2 of the new law, these government officials 'may submit proposals regarding monetary control matters, or request that the Board postpone a vote on monetary control matters until the next Board meeting of this type'.

This provision allowing government officials to postpone a Policy Board vote was a major source of disagreement at the drafting stage, even though the Policy Board maintained the power to 'decide whether or not to accommodate the request' to postpone a board vote. Apparently, few believed that the government would actually exercise its new right to delay a vote. Many thought that the clause was inserted merely as a formality to create the impression that the government still had some influence over the BOJ; the government was not actually expected to follow through on any move that would otherwise be considered to be against the spirit of the law. Indeed, even though the laws concerning the operations of the Bundesbank include a similar provision on the postponement of board decisions, the German government has never exercised its power in this regard. When the BOJ considered lifting its zero interest rate policy in August 2000, however, the government did exercise its right to request postponement of the decision. The Policy Board nevertheless rejected the request and decided by a majority vote to raise interest rates. In accordance with the new BOJ Law, the minutes of the board deliberations on the rate decision were made public, which perhaps contributed to the level of intensity in the debate on the decision.

The BOJ's decision to abandon its zero interest rate policy in spite of opposition from the government confirmed the central bank's strengthened independence and its role as the primary institution responsible for managing Japan's monetary policy. Thus, the most important effect of the new BOJ Law has been to clear up the confusion that had existed to March 1998 over which part of the government had the ultimate say in Japan's monetary policy. Given the BOJ's newly found status as the ultimate decision-making authority, then, monitoring the BOJ to ascertain the direction of Japan's monetary policy has become increasingly relevant.

IMPROVED TRANSPARENCY

The 1998 law not only provides strengthened independence for the central bank but also requires more transparency. In other words, the BOJ must assume more responsibility in explaining its policy decisions to the public. Art. 3, Para. 2 stipulates that 'the Bank shall endeavour to clarify to the public the details of its decisions, as well as its decision-making process, regarding currency and monetary control'. Since the passage of the new law, the BOJ has been working to establish various measures to improve the transparency of its policy decision-making process.

One measure seeks to improve how the monetary Policy Board functions. The Policy Board consists of nine members: the Governor of the BOJ, two Deputy Governors and six other 'deliberative members [who] shall be appointed by the Cabinet, subject to the consent of the House of Representatives and the House of Councillors, from among those with academic expertise or experience including experts on the economy or finance' (Art. 23, Para. 2).

Under the old BOJ Law, the Policy Board was only nominally in charge of monetary policy. Actual monetary policy decisions were made at meetings of the top BOJ officials – the Governor, the Deputy Governor and the seven executive directors. The Policy Board's role

Table 11.1 Schedule of monetary policy meetings (first half of 2000)

Date of monetary policy meeting	Publication date of monthly report	Publication date of monetary policy meeting minutes
19 Jan.	22 Jan.	5 Mar.
9 Feb.	13 Feb.	23 Mar.
28 Feb.	–	18 Apr.
19 Mar.	21 Mar.	1 May
12, 13 Apr.	16 Apr.	23 May
25 Apr.	–	20 Jun.
17, 18 May	21 May	20 Jun.
14, 15 Jun.	18 Jun.	18 Jul.
28 Jun.	–	17 Aug.

Source: Bank of Japan.

was limited to rubberstamping decisions. Because it was unclear who was ultimately determining monetary policy, the Policy Board was considered a 'sleeping board'. Under the new law, however, these directors' meetings have been done away with, and all decision-making authority and final responsibility for monetary policy rests with the Policy Board.

Another change in the law, included in Articles 14 and 15, establishes a regular monetary policy meeting format as a platform for disclosing deliberations on monetary policy (Table 11.1). Policy meetings must be held on a regular basis, and matters regarding monetary policy must be determined by a majority vote of the members who are present (votes require the presence of at least two-thirds of the members). A vital aspect of the new structure is that all decisions, including those for emergency situations, must be made at these monetary policy meetings. Furthermore, because these decisions must now be officially disclosed to the public, no uncertainty will exist about whether the BOJ has actually changed its monetary policy stance, as was the case under the previous version of the law. Now that all monetary policy decisions are made at the policy meetings and that these decisions must be disclosed to the public, the intense type of BOJ watching that used to occur has become unnecessary.

To keep the public apprised of its actions, about six weeks after each monetary policy meeting, the BOJ is also required to release a summary of that meeting's minutes. This summary has been nicknamed the 'green paper'. The complete details of each meeting are then made available to the public 10 years following a meeting. As a result of these updated disclosure requirements, it is now possible to gain a fuller understanding of the Policy Board's assessments of the economic and financial circumstances that play a role in determining the nation's monetary policy. And although the opinions in the summaries are not directly linked with any particular Policy Board member in order to maintain anonymity, the summaries have proven to be useful for discerning the direction of the BOJ's monetary policy; they provide insight into the consensus and minority opinions of the Policy Board and reveal the extent to which its opinions have changed over time.

Another measure requires the BOJ Governor to hold a press conference once a month. The Governor must convey the central bank's views on the current economic and financial environment and explain its management of monetary policy. This press conference should take place on the day after the release of the BOJ's 'Monthly Report for Recent Economic and Financial Developments', which comes out two business days following the first monetary policy meeting of each month (sometimes the Policy Board meets twice a month). The press conference comes at a crucial time – after the release of both the BOJ's 'Monthly Report' and the results of the latest policy meeting but before the release of the summary of the minutes of the meeting – and thus often provides new information that can surprise the market.

To improve transparency still more, in October 2000, the central bank started issuing a report called the 'Outlook and Risk Assessment of the Economy and Prices'. In this report, the BOJ discusses its longer-term outlook for the economic and financial landscape and provides the bank's assessment of the upside potential and downside risk in the economy for the next one to two years. The report includes the ranges of the nine board members' forecasts for prices and other economic indicators, including real GDP, the domestic wholesale price index and the consumer price index (CPI) (excluding perishables) (see Table 11.2). These forecasts, which are referred to as the 'Forecasts of Policy Board Members', appear in the form of high–low ranges, with the highest and the lowest figures of the group excluded. At April 2001, the range for real GDP growth was between +0.3 percent and +0.8 percent; for the domestic wholesale price index between −0.9 percent and −0.6 percent; and for the CPI (excluding perishables) between −0.8 percent and −0.4 percent. The bank's 'Outlook and Risk Assessment of the Economy and Prices' is currently released twice a year in April and October,

Table 11.2 Consumer price index, Japan (year on year, %)

		Composite (excluding perishables)	Durable goods	Semi-durable goods	Non-durable goods	Private sector services	Utility charges	Housing
96	1Q	−0.07	−0.24	0.01	−0.28	0.12	0.11	0.25
	2Q	0.13	−0.23	0.02	−0.19	0.13	0.13	0.26
	3Q	0.23	−0.22	0.02	−0.18	0.18	0.16	0.24
	4Q	0.30	−0.20	0.05	−0.05	0.15	0.11	0.25
97	1Q	0.47	−0.19	0.00	0.10	0.11	0.17	0.26
	2Q	2.03	−0.05	0.21	0.65	0.65	0.31	0.27
	3Q	2.16	−0.03	0.22	0.63	0.65	0.44	0.26
	4Q	2.25	−0.03	0.27	0.43	0.71	0.68	0.23
98	1Q	1.86	−0.01	0.25	0.23	0.59	0.57	0.24
	2Q	0.07	−0.12	0.09	−0.36	0.02	0.33	0.12
	3Q	−0.23	−0.11	0.04	−0.33	−0.04	0.16	0.08
	4Q	−0.32	−0.10	−0.02	−0.08	−0.08	−0.14	0.03
99	1Q	−0.10	−0.08	−0.01	0.05	0.02	−0.05	−0.05
	2Q	−0.03	−0.07	−0.05	0.07	0.00	−0.04	0.01
	3Q	0.00	−0.07	−0.06	0.12	0.07	−0.12	0.02
	4Q	−0.13	−0.09	−0.06	0.02	0.04	−0.07	0.04
00	1Q	−0.23	−0.13	−0.07	−0.06	−0.01	−0.04	0.06
	2Q	−0.29	−0.16	−0.10	−0.01	−0.11	0.05	0.06
	3Q	−0.36	−0.18	−0.12	−0.07	−0.17	0.16	0.06
	4Q	−0.55	−0.17	−0.19	−0.09	−0.20	0.05	0.08
01	1Q	−0.56	−0.16	−0.20	−0.07	−0.21	0.09	0.05
	2Q	−0.59	−0.15	−0.23	−0.17	−0.19	0.07	0.08

Notes: The CPI is on a nationwide basis, with 1995 as the base year. Figures for 'composite (excluding perishables)' are year-on-year changes, while those for other categories are contributions to the change in the 'composite (excluding perishables)' category. 'Non-durable goods', 'private sector services' and 'utility charges' are Nomura-devised categories, and correspond to the Ministry of Public Management, Home Affairs, Posts and Telecommunications' categories as follows: 'non-durable goods' = 'consumer non-durables − fresh foods − electricity/gas/water charges; 'private sector services' = services − rent − (public service expenses − public housing rent − communications expenses and air transportation costs); 'utility charges' = public service expenses − public housing rent − communications expenses and air transportation costs + electricity/gas/water charges.
Figures may not add up because of rounding.
Source: Nomura; Ministry of Public Management, Home Affairs, Posts and Telecommunications.

as part of the BOJ's 'Monthly Report for Recent Economic and Financial Developments'.

The decision to release the report 'Outlook and Risk Assessment of the Economy and Prices' came in response to criticism that there were few, if any, indicators of the central bank's medium- to long-term outlook and policy objectives. By contrast, the BOJ's short-term outlook had become relatively transparent with the disclosure of the summaries of the monetary policy meetings and the BOJ's statements on monetary policy changes. This improved transparency of the BOJ's outlook on the economy and its assessment of the major concerns it faces in managing monetary policy should make for better assessment of the results of the BOJ's monetary policy.

The BOJ's Web site has also enhanced its ability to make its actions more transparent by providing a vast amount of information (www.boj.or.jp). Even as recently as 1998 or so, those who wanted information on the BOJ had to visit the central bank's headquarters in Nihonbashi in person and often had to wait in line. The new Web site allows the public to easily obtain whatever information it needs from offices and homes.

A large number of essays published by BOJ staff are also accessible through the BOJ's Web site. These essays, which are published under the names of BOJ staff members and do not represent the official views of the BOJ, often provide valuable insights. At the beginning of each essay, a disclaimer appears, stating that 'the opinions presented herein are the personal views of the authors, and do not represent the official opinion of the Bank of Japan or of the [authors'] Department'. Even so, the essays are often quite revealing regarding monetary policy and, at times, they offer a better reflection of the BOJ's true views on monetary policy than its official statements and reports. Therefore, the essays are a valuable resource, for both gaining an understanding of the ongoing debates within the BOJ and forecasting monetary policy.

The management of monetary policy

This section discusses the bases for the BOJ's decisions on monetary policy and the principles the central bank uses to justify its policies. The sole reference in the new BOJ Law to the principles and objectives of monetary policy can be found in Art. 2: 'Currency and monetary control shall be aimed at, through the pursuit of price stability, contributing to the sound development of the national economy.' This section of the law, however, is too abstract and needs more specific details regarding actual implementation. The following sections outline some of the practical implications for the BOJ that stem from Art. 2. To gain a fuller understanding of the BOJ's role, it is useful to study the summaries of the Policy Board meetings, the official statements regarding changes in the central bank's monetary policy and the speeches made by Policy Board members.

PRICE STABILITY

It can be inferred from Art. 2 that the most important variable on which the BOJ bases its monetary policy is the level of prices in the Japanese economy. Achieving price stability is a common objective of central banks because of the shared belief that monetary policy can contribute to stable economic growth through the stabilization of prices.

Nevertheless, although there is a broad consensus on price stability as a goal, the concept of price stability is ambiguous. The BOJ explains its view of price stability in a report titled 'On Price Stability', which was released in Japanese in October 2000. This report is an excellent reference for better understanding which price trends the BOJ focuses on when determining monetary policy. The following are the key elements of the report:

1 Price stability can be defined as 'a situation [that is] neither inflationary nor deflationary' from the perspective of the Japanese public.

2 'The conduct of monetary policy may change depending on whether price fluctuation is due to demand-side or supply-side factors.'

3 'Low inflation in the 1990s largely reflected weak demand amid the economic slowdown, and . . . such supply-side factors as technological innovation, deregulation, intensification of global competition and the distribution revolution have more recently put additional downward pressure on prices.'

4 'It is difficult to assign specific numerical values to the definition of price stability that are consistent with the sound development of the economy. . . . Even if certain numerical values were assigned, they would not serve as a reliable guidepost in the conduct of monetary policy, and the exercise would not be likely to contribute to enhancing transparency of the conduct of monetary policy.'

According to this report, the BOJ's ideas about price stability markedly differ from those of some other market participants and economists. Specifically, the difference lies in the BOJ differentiation between 'good' and 'bad' price deflation. The BOJ defines 'good price deflation' as a condition that is brought about by technological innovation, deregulation, the distribution revolution and other factors that improve supply-side efficiencies and result in higher levels of production, improved corporate profitability and increases in income for workers. In contrast, 'bad price deflation' is defined as deflation that results from a lack of demand; it can lead to lower corporate profits and decreased incomes and is often accompanied by the risk of the emergence of a deflationary spiral. The BOJ believes that rather than focusing on 'good price deflation', it should instead be on guard for 'bad price deflation'. Thus, when the BOJ formulates its monetary policy by assessing price trends, it does not focus on specific price indexes; it attempts to make an overall assessment of the state of the economy.

In other words, the BOJ cannot be expected either to loosen or tighten monetary policy simply on the basis of a decrease or increase in price indexes or an acceleration in price changes. The corollary of this difficulty, then, is that trying to forecast the BOJ's monetary policy by looking only at headline price index figures is not meaningful. In the words of the BOJ, it is important to ascertain the 'characteristics of price fluctuations in light of various indexes related to prices'.

THE IMPORTANCE OF THE GDP GAP

If understanding the 'characteristics of price fluctuations' is more important than simply looking at price changes, then the way in which the BOJ examines the 'characteristics of price fluctuations' must be analysed and understood. In essence, the BOJ believes that it is critical to assess the direction of the trend in the GDP gap, which is the gap between actual GDP and the country's potential GDP when all factors of production are fully utilized. To fully grasp the BOJ's thinking in relation to the GDP gap, examining the minutes of the monetary policy meetings can be instructive. For example, the minutes of the November 1999 policy meeting, which was held nine months after the BOJ's decision to adopt a zero interest rate policy, include the following discussion about the GDP gap:

> *(A member) raised the question of how the judgement [sic] would be made whether deflationary concern had or had not been dispelled, which was the basis for terminating the zero interest rate policy. Specifically, the member questioned whether the judgment should be based on (1) price developments, or rather, (2) real economic activity measured by the difference between the actual growth rate*

and the potential growth rate or by the output gap. On this point, a few members commented that price developments would be the main element, and in judging the outlook for prices, underlying factors such as the supply and demand balance and downward pressure on wages would also be examined thoroughly. Another member added that the prospect of a self-sustained recovery in private demand was a very important criterion at this stage in view of the aforementioned points of concern, and therefore required careful attention.

An analysis of this excerpt provides insight into the main factors behind the BOJ's decision to lift its zero interest rate policy. The BOJ was not focusing on price levels alone but also on the GDP gap and the extent of the possibility of a self-sustaining recovery in domestic demand, which is a key determinant of the GDP gap. The same reasoning appears in the aforementioned report, 'Outlook and Risk Assessment of the Economy and Prices':

Regarding prices, evaluation of the output gap is of critical importance. Taking into account a decline in the economic value of capital stock and widening mismatching in the labour market reflecting recent rapid structural changes in the economy, potential supply growth is likely slowing down. Considering the slower growth in potential supply and the outlook for demand described above, the output gap is expected to narrow moderately.

Careful examination of this statement provides further insight into the BOJ's mindset. The BOJ was not focusing on supply and demand levels in isolation but rather on whether the GDP gap was widening or narrowing. Therefore, although supply–demand levels are often the key variables used to ascertain whether price trends are deflationary, the BOJ believes that the critical factor to monitor – in determining whether the GDP gap is likely to narrow – is whether the mechanisms for sustainable economic growth are in place in the private sector.

A theoretical framework called the Taylor Rule links the GDP gap to monetary policy and says that the optimal fed funds rate should be adjusted on the basis of the rate of inflation and the GDP gap. The following commonly used formula stems from the Taylor Rule:

*Optimal fed funds rate = Rate of increase in the core CPI +
(0.5 × GDP gap) + 0.5 × (Rate of increase in the core CPI −
Target rate of increase in the core CPI) + potential GDP
growth rate.*

To calculate the optimal fed funds rate, the GDP gap must be estimated, which is not easy, partly because of technical difficulties. The application of the above equation to Japan, based on a multitude of scenarios, suggests that the BOJ's target overnight call rate should be negative because of the current large GDP gap; hence, the lifting of the zero interest rate policy was not justifiable. But if the focus is placed on the *change* in the GDP gap – which has been narrowing – then the abandonment of the zero interest rate policy was appropriate. In essence, then, different assumptions lead to entirely different conclusions about the proper way to conduct monetary policy.

The following extract from a speech by Kazuo Ueda, a Policy Board member who voted against the lifting of the zero interest rate policy, helps to explain the confusion surrounding the application of the Taylor Rule:

> *Uncertainties about the size of output gap have important implications for the Taylor Rule. Orphanides, Porter, Reifschneider, Tetlow & Finan (1999) report interesting simulation results. They suggest policy attenuation, i.e., to decrease the response of the interest rate to the gap in the presence of large measurement errors with respect to output gap. Moreover, when measurement errors are very large, it is better to respond to the difference between the growth rate of actual and that of potential output rather than to output gap. In other words, the interest rate now responds to the change in the output gap rather than its level. They call this the growth rate rule.*
>
> *Most of the board members now believe that, assuming that no major negative shocks hit the economy, the economy will grow in fiscal 2000 at a higher rate than some of the largest, but reasonable estimates of the growth rate of potential output. Then, the growth rate rule, assuming that its usefulness carries over in the neighbourhood of the zero bound on the interest rate, seems to give us a positive interest rate under a wide range of assumptions.*

Again, if the change in the GDP gap rather than the absolute value of the GDP gap is employed, the lifting of the zero interest rate policy can be justified. Thus, it can be inferred from the BOJ's abandonment of its zero interest rate policy that the bank considered the change in the GDP gap to be an important factor in determining monetary policy.

But a major problem in estimating the GDP gap is ascertaining the potential GDP growth rate, which must be somehow reliably calculated. If, for example, the potential growth rate is 1% and the actual growth rate is 2%, then the GDP gap narrows. In contrast, if the potential growth rate is 2.5% and the actual growth rate is 2%, then the GDP gap widens. These examples show that the BOJ's estimates for Japan's potential economic growth rate are a key determinant of the central bank's monetary policy.

In another October 2000 BOJ report, titled 'Price Developments in Japan: A Review Focusing on the 1990s', the central bank suggests that the potential growth rate of Japan's economy may have declined to about 1%. This figure is considerably lower than the estimates of private sector economists, which range between 1.5% and 2.5%. The lower BOJ estimate suggests that the central bank may have a tightening bias. That said, one should bear in mind the risks associated with inferring too much from BOJ forecasts.

LONG-TERM INTEREST RATES, FOREIGN EXCHANGE RATES AND MONETARY POLICY

As discussed earlier, economic fundamentals, such as price levels and the GDP gap, are the most important determinants of BOJ policy. Fundamentals alone, however, cannot fully explain the rationale behind the BOJ's decisions concerning monetary policy. To some extent, trends in the financial markets also have an undeniable influence on monetary policy.

Before looking in detail at how trends in the financial markets can affect Policy Board decisions, it is instructive to examine the background leading up to the BOJ's decision in February 1999 to guide short-term rates to zero. The decision was highly unusual in that it came at a time when the BOJ was revising its economic outlook upward. At the time, long-term interest rates were rising sharply because of heightened concerns about a worsening supply–demand balance for JGBs. What triggered the concerns was an announcement by the Ministry of Finance in late 1998 that, through the Trust Fund Bureau, it would no longer buy JGBs on the open market or purchase newly issued JGBs. In early February 1999, the yield on 10-year JGBs rose to 2.4%, up almost 1.5 percentage points in about two months. This increase, in turn, caused nervousness about the possible negative effects of a further increase in interest rates on the economy. Consequently, the government and politicians demanded an increase in the BOJ's outright purchases of long-term JGBs or monetization of the government debt as a means to hold down the rise in long-term rates. Pressure came from the US as well for a relaxation of Japan's monetary policy, as fears were mounting that the US economy could be negatively affected by higher interest rates in Japan. In light of these pressures, the BOJ opted to ease monetary policy.

The BOJ will not admit that the main reason behind its decision to ease its stance was rising long-term interest rates. The official point of view is that the central bank is unable to control long-term interest rates. Yet clearly, as explained previously, the higher long-term interest rates and related pressure on the BOJ to act were indeed the key determinants of the central bank's move to loosen monetary policy. Apparently, the central bank chose to lower its target for the uncollateralized overnight call rate rather than resort to such measures as increasing outright purchases of long-term JGBs and monetizing the government debt, which the BOJ wanted to avoid.

In contrast to the above situation in which the BOJ seems to have submitted to pressures to ease, in other cases the central bank has remained steadfast in its resistance to mounting pressures to act. In September 1999, for instance, as the yen appreciated against the dollar, the BOJ faced intense pressure to ease monetary policy further. The bank had almost no other conventional monetary policy measures to rely on, however, because short-term interest rates were already near zero. The BOJ believed the most appropriate policy option at the time was 'unsterilized' currency market intervention, which involves increasing the supply of yen by selling yen for dollars without subsequently taking the supply back out of the market through open-market operations. Indeed, with a G7 meeting close at hand, some even speculated that unsterilized intervention by the BOJ was a prerequisite for a coordinated intervention by the main G7 members.

Nonetheless, the BOJ has elected not to adopt any new policies. After this decision, the BOJ issued a statement, which is excerpted below:

The foreign exchange rate in itself is not a direct objective of monetary policy. One of the precious lessons we learned from the experience of policy operations during the bubble period is that monetary policy operations linked with control of the foreign exchange rate runs a risk of leading to erroneous policy decisions. Having said this, it does not mean that monetary policy is pursued without any consideration to the development of the foreign exchange rate. The Bank considers it important to carefully monitor the development of the foreign exchange rate from the viewpoint of how it affects the economy and prices.

In short, if the BOJ is concerned about the value of the yen against the dollar and other major currencies, it is apprehensive because of the potential effects of the yen's exchange rate on Japan's economy, not because it wants to control the exchange rate itself. Before being named BOJ Governor, Masaru Hayami expressed his personal opposition to the idea of directly linking monetary policy with the exchange rate. It is therefore safe to assume that the BOJ will not act solely on the basis of trends in the currency market. Generally speaking, the BOJ wants to try to distance its policy-making decisions from any trends in the financial markets, but when it believes that its independence may be compromised, it will act relatively flexibly.

MONEY SUPPLY AND MONETARY POLICY

With its target rate for the uncollateralized overnight call loan rate down to virtually zero, thus leaving no room for further easing, the BOJ faced increasing pressure in the spring of 1999 to switch the focus of its policy from interest rates to the supply of money. In particular, the government, politicians and some economists have pressured the BOJ to resort to quantitative easing, which involves increasing the rate of growth in the monetary base (cash and banks' current account deposits held at the BOJ) in an effort to expand the money supply. The BOJ has nevertheless maintained a cautious stance on making such a move. Its disagreement with the government stems from a major difference in opinion concerning the way in which monetary policy affects the economy and how money supply is determined. Because these subjects have been debated for some time and because the disagreements are likely to carry into the future, the following discussion attempts to dissect the key issues in the debate.

Some economists, monetarists in particular, hold the view that the money supply is more important than interest rates as a determinant of real economic activity and that money supply, as apparent from the term, is determined by the amount of funds supplied by the central bank. Specifically, economists in this camp argue that the money supply rises in proportion to any increase in the monetary base supplied by the central bank. From the perspective of monetarists, any decrease in the rate of growth in Japan's monetary base suggests that the BOJ has been neglecting one of its primary responsibilities.

The BOJ, however, disagrees with the view of the monetarists. That is, the BOJ believes that controlling the money supply is impossible even if it can control the monetary base. The foundation of the BOJ's argument flows from its tendency to attach greater importance to the demand for funds than to the money supply – that is, even if the monetary base rises, the money supply will not expand and bank lending will not increase if the demand for funds in the private sector (excluding the financial sector) is weak. This argument seems justifiable considering that the additional funds supplied by the BOJ under its zero interest rate policy are piling up in excess reserves at financial institutions and in money market brokers' current accounts at the BOJ, which are not subject to reserve requirements.

Again, because the BOJ considers the demand for money to be important in determining its policy on the money supply, it is not inclined to shape its monetary policy solely on the basis of controlling the money supply. This approach contrasts with that of the Bundesbank, which appears to pursue a monetarist style of monetary policy.

MONETARY POLICY TOOLS

This final section summarizes the monetary policy tools used by the BOJ. One significant change in this regard occurred in March 2001 – specifically, the central bank shifted to a policy of quantitative easing, targeting the outstanding balance of the current accounts for its money market operations rather than the uncollateralized overnight call loan rate.

Before the shift to quantitative easing, the BOJ's primary monetary policy tool was implementing a change in the official discount rate, which is the interest rate the BOJ charges to financial institutions for loans. It is no exaggeration to say that until the mid-1990s, changing monetary policy was analogous to raising or lowering the official discount rate. But from the mid-1990s to the spring of 2001, the BOJ primarily relied on guiding the uncollateralized overnight call loan rate by adjusting the amount of funds supplied to the short-term money market. In fact, the policy guidelines compiled by the Policy Board state that 'the target for the uncollateralized overnight call loan rate should be around 0.25% on average', which suggests that the uncollateralized overnight call loan rate was the BOJ's preferred monetary policy tool and thus that the central bank is now more focused on the market mechanism.

Further evidence of the BOJ's new focus is that, ever since July 1995, the official discount rate has exceeded the uncollateralized overnight call loan rate and thus become considerably less important for monetary policy. When the official discount rate is lower than the uncollateralized overnight call loan rate, financial institutions tend to rely on loans from the BOJ. Accordingly, the BOJ used to manage its monetary policy by adjusting the official discount rate. When the official discount rate is higher than the uncollateralized overnight call loan rate, however, financial institutions tend to raise funds in the short-term money market. As a result, rather than focusing on lending to financial institutions, the BOJ had decided to make open market operations the primary method by which it adjusts liquidity in the financial system.

The BOJ abandoned the uncollateralized overnight call loan rate as its main target for money market operations in March 2001, and shifted to the outstanding balance of current accounts maintained at the central bank by private sector financial institutions. The target balance at the end of June 2001 was ¥5 tr., up ¥1 tr. from the average outstanding balance of ¥4 tr. before the shift in policy approach.

The quantitative easing policy appears at first glance to be a complete shift in the BOJ's stance on monetary policy, but really is not. This point becomes more apparent in a comparison of the zero interest rate policy and the current quantitative easing policy. Under the former policy, the central bank supplied an amount of funds to the market that exceeded the amount of legally required reserves in order to keep short-term interest rates near zero. Under the quantitative easing policy, by contrast, the BOJ guides the balance of current accounts above the amount of required reserves in an effort to keep short-term interest rates near zero. The similarities between the two approaches are clear. The target balance of current accounts as of July 2001 was ¥5tr., which matched the average balance during the time the BOJ had adopted the zero interest rate policy. Hence, for now we can characterize the quantitative easing policy as effectively the same as the zero interest rate policy.

But the BOJ shifted to quantitative easing in March 2001 not to revert to the zero interest rate policy but rather to avoid having to publicly acknowledge the central bank's policy failure of retreating on the zero interest rate policy in August 2000, which the BOJ would have done had it simply just gone back to the zero interest rate policy. The move may have been intended to avoid making BOJ Governor Hayami look bad. Another factor behind the central bank's move to a quantitative easing policy was perhaps a desire to disarm those at home and abroad who had been critical of the BOJ and its monetary policy.

Of the several aspects of the March 2001 monetary easing, one that was more important than the quantitative easing policy was the clear linkage between market operations and inflation indicators, in an effort to lower long-term interest rates through a commitment or policy duration effect. Specifically, the BOJ said that 'the new procedures for money-market operations [will] continue to be in place until the consumer price index (excluding perishables, on a nationwide statistics [*sic*]) registers stably a zero percent or an increase year on year'. This statement represents a more specific commitment to monetary easing than the central bank's previous statements under the zero interest rate policy to 'continue the . . . policy until deflationary concern is dispelled'. And, as a result, the impact of the BOJ's policy move on the yield curve was that much greater.

The role of the official discount rate has changed since 2001. The BOJ announced in February 2001 improvements in the way of liquidity provision, including the establishment of a standby lending facility ('Lombard-type' lending facility). Through this facility, the central bank lends at the official discount rate at the request of private sector banks. In other words, whereas the BOJ used to extend loans on its own initiative, financial institutions could now receive loans from the BOJ just by applying. In so doing, the central bank aims to help stabilize the financial positions of financial institutions and hold down short-term interest rates. The official discount rate thus effectively lost its previous role and took on a new one, as an interest rate for the new standby lending facility.

The quantitative easing policy is an experiment. The central bank appears to have been pressured to adopt the policy by critics at home and abroad, even as it seemed sceptical about – rather than not having enough confidence in – the likely impact of the move. It is unlikely that the BOJ changed its view on the transmission mechanism of monetary policy, specifically the relationship between base money and the money supply, and it is highly uncertain whether the central bank will flexibly turn to increases in the balance of current accounts as a way to further ease monetary policy. Quantitative easing, again, is an experiment whose impact only time will tell.

Key issues and future directions

The April 1998 passage of the new Bank of Japan Law, which has strengthened the BOJ's independence and transparency, should foster enhanced confidence in the bank's monetary policy in the intermediate to long term and lead to improvements in Japan's economy. The central bank certainly deserves strong praise for its efforts to disclose more fully to the public its policy-making process.

Nevertheless, during the late 1990s, the BOJ's role in establishing monetary policy has neither been fully understood nor well received. Both in Japan and abroad, the bank bore the brunt of severe criticism when it abandoned its zero interest rate policy, and faced strong demands that it ease monetary policy further. Much of the misunderstanding and related criticisms of the BOJ's zero interest rate policy can be attributed to the extraordinariness of the policy – never before had any central bank taken such a drastic step. Such strident criticism of the BOJ thus seems unfair.

In light of the criticism and problems confronting the BOJ, however, the issues that the central bank must deal with in the future are clear. First, the BOJ needs to make its management of monetary policy even more transparent. One possible way to promote transparency of its procedures is through the adoption of an inflation-targeting policy. Inflation targeting was the subject of heated policy debate in 1999, when nominal short-term interest rates were approaching zero. Some argued that the BOJ could contribute to an economic recovery by increasing the expected inflation rate, which, in turn, would lower real short-term interest rates. In other words, these advocates regarded inflation targeting as a way to further ease monetary policy when short-term interest rates are near zero. Perhaps more important, however, is that inflation targeting can be a tool for enhancing the transparency of monetary policy management.

Monetary policy based on inflation targeting attempts to achieve a target inflation rate that is linked to a certain price index (typically the consumer price index). Inflation targeting can reduce the uncertainty and vagueness surrounding monetary policy because specific numerical values are assigned to the objective of price stability.

Despite the advantages of an inflation-targeting policy, the BOJ is currently opposed to its adoption and the assignment of specific values to price stability. The BOJ's reasoning begins with the assumption that in an environment where supply and demand factors are exerting downward pressure on prices, the short-run 'rate of inflation that is in line with the sound development of the national economy' is lower than the long-run 'rate of inflation that is in line with the sound development of the national economy'. In addition, the quantified targets for price stability must be reasonable for an extended period of time, but are unlikely to be, given the nature of the current deflationary environment. Therefore, these targets are unlikely to serve as reliable guidelines for monetary policy or improve the transparency of monetary policy management, and thus resorting to inflation targeting is neither realistic nor appropriate.

Yet because central banks in other developed nations face similar, if not identical, problems, using the aforementioned factors as reasons to justify not introducing an inflation-targeting policy does not necessarily make sense. In addition, because it is highly unlikely that price declines stemming from supply-side factors will continue for several decades, the BOJ could still use inflation targeting as a rough guide for its monetary policy over the medium to long term. The real reasons behind the BOJ's opposition to inflation targeting could be the difficulty of finding monetary policy measures for definitively attaining the targets and the central bank's concern that politicians and others may attempt to interfere with its monetary policy decisions if the target inflation rate is not achieved.

The other major issue confronting the BOJ is the coordination of monetary and fiscal policy. Around the world, while fiscal policy has become less effective as a measure for stimulating the economy, using monetary policy as a tool for fine-tuning the economy has grown in importance. In accordance with this trend, the BOJ's monetary policy is likely to play a greater role in the management of Japan's economy. In addition, greater expectations for an accommodative monetary policy could result from Japan's globally unprecedented fiscal problems.[1] Specifically, the BOJ could face

---

1 See Chapter 9 for details.

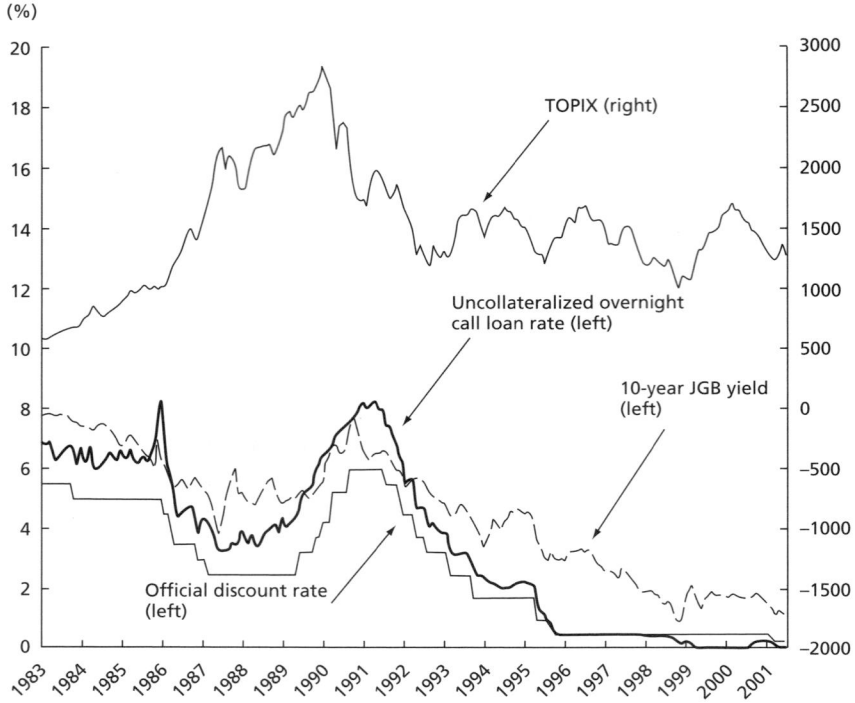

(%)

11.1. Short- and long-term interest rates versus the TOPIX.
Source: Nomura.

further pressure to use monetary policy as a means to alleviate the deflationary pressures stemming from the government's fiscal reforms and the related expected decrease in national expenditures. If the government's deficit leads to a rise in long-term interest rates, the BOJ could be pressed to step up its outright purchases of long-term JGBs or monetize the government's debt. Thanks to abundant savings in the private sector, deficit financing is currently not a major problem, and consequently, long-term interest rates have remained stable and are at relatively low levels (Fig. 11.1). But in the long run, given that private-sector savings probably will decline as Japan's population rapidly ages, long-term rates may rise because of the difficulty of financing the budget deficit through domestic savings alone (i.e., Japan would have a current account deficit). If those rates rise too high, the BOJ's policy decisions would attract considerable attention – and possibly harsh criticism. Figure 11.2 shows the monetary base and money supply.

(% chg. y–y)

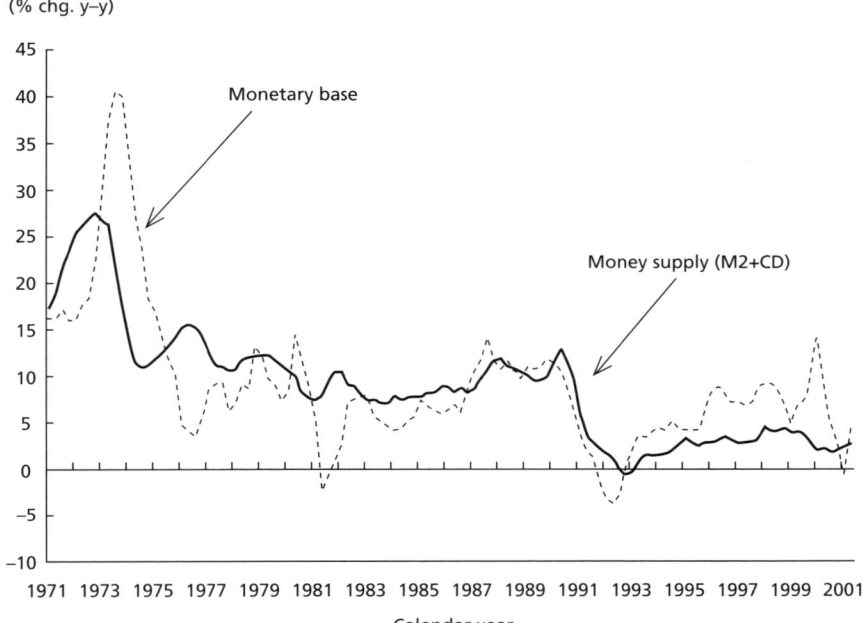

11.2 Monetary base and money supply.
Source: Bank of Japan.

In order to stand up to the likelihood of external pressure, the BOJ must further improve the transparency of its monetary policy decision-making process and strive to gain the support of the financial markets through dialogue with market participants. Until it succeeds in doing so, the BOJ will continue to face an uncertain future characterized by occasional confrontations with the government and market participants concerning its management of Japan's monetary policy.

CHAPTER 12 The Financial Services Agency

For a number of decades after World War II, the Ministry of Finance (MOF) held sole responsibility for all aspects of overseeing, regulating and supervising Japan's financial and securities markets. But this regulatory framework has changed drastically because of a series of problems that emerged during the 1990s, namely, two major securities industry scandals, the persistence of the problem of non-performing loans at financial institutions in the wake of the bursting of the bubble economy and the ensuing string of bankruptcies within the financial services industry, the need to inject public funds to shore up the financial sector, and revelations of malfeasance by MOF bureaucrats. The details of the repeated organizational changes that have been made are so complex that even financial market experts have difficulty grasping them in full.

That is not to say that the changes in the bureaucratic framework have been made merely in response to changes in the external environment. The reform drive undertaken during the Japanese Big Bang – the sweeping programme of financial deregulation that the government announced in November 1996 – has also had an enormous impact. One objective of this programme was to move away from the 'convoy system' of *ex ante* supervision and administrative guidance by bureaucrats of individual financial institutions (to protect them and keep them moving together at the same speed and in the same direction) and instead to apply *ex post* supervision based on transparent rules. Another aspect was the lowering of the barriers separating the various industries within the financial services sector; this change brought with it the need to reform the regulatory framework to make it less sectionalized.

This chapter presents an overview of the series of organizational changes in the regulatory framework as well as a discussion of their significance and some issues for future consideration.

From MOF to the Financial Services Agency

Before World War II, whereas Japan's banking and insurance industries were regulated and supervised by the MOF, the securities industry and stock markets were in the purview of the Ministry of Agriculture and Commerce and, later, the Ministry of Commerce and Industry. In July 1941, in order to strengthen the government's control over the flows of funds as part of the national mobilization for the war with China, responsibility for the securities industry and stock markets was shifted to the MOF, which thus achieved unified authority over the financial sector.

During the US Occupation after the war, a new Securities and Exchange Law was put into effect that was modelled on the US Securities Act of 1933 and the Securities Exchange Act of 1934. As in the US, regulatory authority over the securities industry was placed under the direction of a Securities and Exchange Commission (SEC). When the Japanese SEC was founded in July 1947, it was established as an independent administrative commission with power to set regulations; it consisted of three expert members and had its own permanent secretariat. The strong independence that the SEC enjoyed, however, hindered smooth communication between it and other administrative organs and delayed the processing of business matters. As a result, the commission was short-lived; it was abolished in August 1952 as part of the overall review of administrative organs that was conducted when the Occupation ended.

UNIFIED SUPERVISION BY THE MOF

With the abolition of the SEC, regulatory authority over the entire financial sector once again became concentrated in the hands of the MOF. Although the MOF's internal organization experienced some subsequent revisions, such as the establishment of the Securities Bureau in 1964, its basic framework remained unchanged from 1952 to 1992.

The approach that the MOF took in its supervision of banks and securities companies, which were licensed by the ministry, involved detailed supervision of their individual operations in order to ensure that not a single one of them would fail. This tactic, which eventually came to be commonly referred to as the 'convoy system', was based on the idea that all the institutions would be kept moving in the same direction at similar speeds under the MOF's careful protection. Indeed, for the most part, the rules governing financial and securities markets in Japan remained inflexibly uniform and exclusionary, at least until 1984, when the Japan–US Yen–Dollar Committee produced an agreement under which Japan liberalized and internationalized its financial sector. And the subsequent process of financial deregulation and internationalization was implemented largely under the leadership of the MOF and other regulators rather than at the initiative of the private sector financial institutions.

It is true that the MOF regulators wielded great discretionary power and that the regulatory process lacked transparency. The 'circular notices' (*tsûtatsu*) issued by the ministry were, properly speaking, no more than internal bureaucratic documents, yet they came to be seen as having the same force as formal legislation; regulators also frequently used administrative guidance to push individual institutions in the direction they desired. Moreover, the regulatory authorities often readily approved of business practices that restrained competition, which ultimately had the effect of sapping the vigour of private sector institutions.

Nonetheless, during the decades of the MOF's tight regulatory control, Japan's financial sector undeniably achieved dramatic growth without any serious confusion or failures, except for the market crisis of 1965. Banks and other financial institutions contributed greatly to the country's rapid economic recovery after World War II. Also, what should not be overlooked is that the protection and control provided by the convoy system enabled the financial sector to function effectively.

THE SECURITIES AND EXCHANGE SURVEILLANCE COMMISSION

A series of scandals in the securities industry in 1991 – including brokerage firms' compensation of losses for certain major clients, improper dealings with organized crime groups and high-pressure sales of speculative stocks – led to broad criticism of the MOF's supervision of the industry. Because the ministry was responsible for guiding and supervising securities companies on an everyday basis as well as enforcing regulations, it was essentially acting as both coach and referee at the same time. Hence, many called for the establishment of an independent agency that would function in the same way as the US Securities and Exchange Commission – an agency that could distance itself from the institutions under its watch.

As a first step toward reform, the Securities and Exchange Law was revised in September 1991 to forbid compensation for losses and securities companies' use of discretionary accounts, practices that were seen as having directly contributed to the string of scandals at the time. In May 1992 the law was revised again, this time to provide for the establishment of the Securities and Exchange Surveillance Commission (SESC) and the strengthening of the role of self-regulatory organizations. Other changes in the regulatory framework included abolition of frequent use of circular notices as a means of regulation.

The SESC was set up in July 1992. Unlike the Fair Trade Commission, which is an independent administrative entity, the new commission was established as a part of the MOF. It differed from the MOF's regular bureaus and departments, however, in that it was designated as a council with independent authority and was made up of a Chairman and two Commissioners appointed by the MOF with the approval of both houses of the Diet (Japan's parliament). Furthermore, care was taken to make the commission independent in practice; for example, the first Chairman was a former senior public prosecutor. Figure 12.1 shows the financial regulatory framework before and after the establishment of this commission.

The powers of the SESC include ensuring the fairness of securities transactions by brokerage firms and other financial institutions through inspections and reviews, investigating unfair practices, asking the Public Prosecutor's Office to prosecute violators, and recommending administrative remedies and policy measures to the Minister of Finance. Securities-related inspection responsibilities that were not placed in the hands of the new commission, such as the inspection of brokerage firms' financial soundness, are handled by a newly created Financial Inspection Department in the Minister's Secretariat.

The SEC in the US manages a broad range of duties covering the securities business as a whole, including registration of broker/dealers and securities to be issued or sold, the formulation of securities regulations, and market supervision and the exposure of violations. By comparison, Japan's SESC has limited powers and a relatively small staff of about 120 employees. Some have argued that its powers are insufficient, given that the SESC does not have the authority to prosecute violators directly or impose administrative sanctions by its own decision. Such views, however, ignore the

Until July 1992

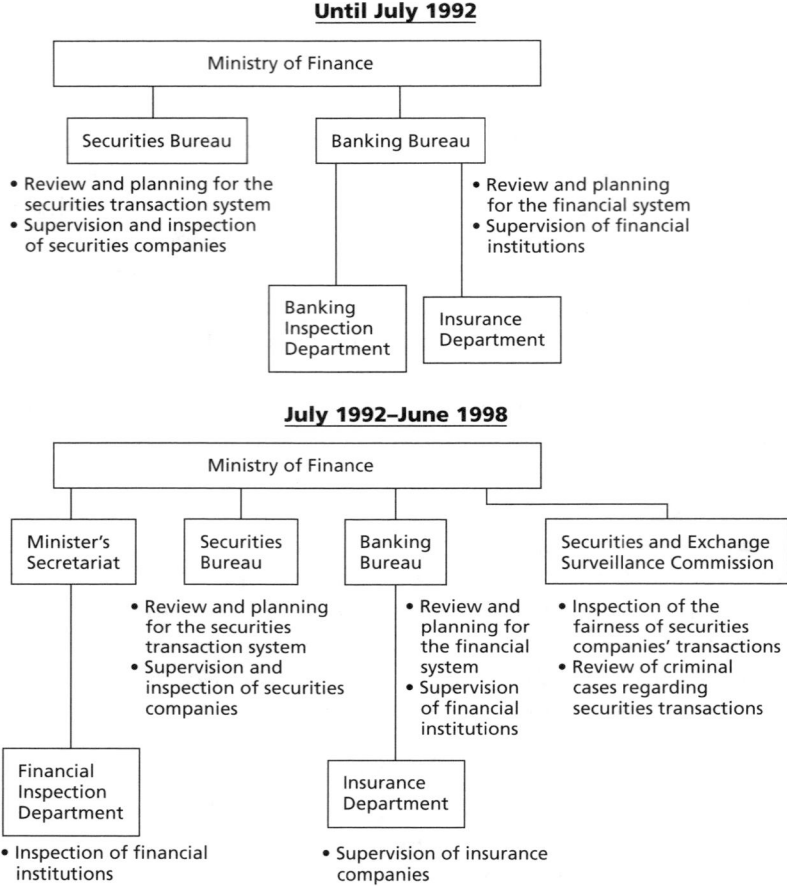

12.1 Japan's changing regulatory framework (1).

differences in the way administrative agencies operate in Japan and the US. The Japanese SESC possesses considerable power in terms of its core functions of supervising the securities markets and monitoring for violations, plus, unlike the US SEC, it has the authority to conduct mandatory investigations.

THE FINANCIAL SUPERVISORY AGENCY (FSA)

In 1995, criticism of the MOF's regulation of the financial sector once again came to the fore in the context of the debate over the dissolution of two failed credit associations and the disposal of the non-performing loan assets of the housing loan companies, known as *jûsen*. The reputation of the ministry was further stained by revelations that some senior MOF officials had colluded with executives of the failed credit associations. The MOF was also faulted for its handling of an incident that year involving the cover-up of huge bond-trading losses by the New York branch of Daiwa Bank. The criticism of the ministry induced many people to call for major reforms of the MOF that would have constituted a virtual dismantling of the institution.

Some proponents of reorganizing the ministry strongly argued that the MOF should not have the authority both to compile the budget and to regulate the financial sector. Others demanded that its authority to license financial institutions be separated from its authority to inspect and supervise them. In February 1996, the three parties of the ruling coalition (the Liberal Democratic Party, the Social Democratic Party and the New Party Sakigake, or Harbinger) established a working group to come up with concrete proposals for reorganizing the MOF and allotting greater independence to the Bank of Japan, thereby freeing it from the MOF's influence.

Based on the deliberations within the coalition, in December of that year, the three parties agreed on a proposal to establish a separate agency to take over the MOF's responsibilities for inspecting and supervising financial institutions. The MOF would retain its responsibility only for financial system planning. Just as when the SESC was created, some called for the new agency to be established as an independent entity similar to the Fair Trade Commission, but neither this suggestion nor the proposal that it be made a cabinet-level organ headed by a minister of state was adopted in the end.

At the same time, the ruling coalition decided that the SESC would be taken out of the MOF and included as an organ of the new agency. The SESC would continue to operate on a semi-independent basis as a council, inasmuch as it shared the new agency's nature as an entity responsible for implementation, not policy planning.

The ruling coalition's December 1996 agreement was implemented in June 1998, with the abolition of the MOF's Banking Bureau and Securities Bureau and the establishment of the Financial Supervisory Agency as an external agency of the Prime Minister's Office. As in the case of the SESC, care was taken to emphasize the independence of the new agency from the MOF and the departure from the previous administrative framework; the person chosen as the first Commissioner was a former President of a High Court.

CRISIS IN THE FINANCIAL SYSTEM

The period from December 1996, when the ruling coalition agreed on its plan for reorganization of the MOF, and June 1998, when the reorganization was implemented, was a time of dizzying change in the circumstances surrounding the financial regulatory system. The framework was also subsequently subjected to repeated further reorganizations at short intervals (see Fig. 12.2).

Among the first of the many changes, in the discussions between the ruling parties concerning the establishment of the Financial Services Agency (FSA), it was agreed that the financial system planning functions would be separated from the MOF as part of the planned future overhaul of the central government bureaucracy. Also, the Central Government Reform Law concerning this overhaul – which was enacted in June 1998, just before the Financial Supervisory Agency started its operations – provided for the establishment of a Financial Services Agency. This new agency would be part of the new framework in January 2001 and handle a full range of responsibilities from financial system planning to inspection and supervision.

Then, amid the restructuring, a string of failures of major financial institutions late in 1997, most notably the collapses of Sanyo Securities, Hokkaido Takushoku Bank and Yamaichi Securities (one of the big four brokerage firms) in November, prompted some serious concerns about the stability of the financial system as a whole. The government responded in February 1998 by enacting two laws aimed at stabilizing the financial system and including provisions for large-scale injections of public funds to shore up banks' equity capital.

One of the two laws, the Emergency Measures Law for Financial Stabilization, provided for the establishment of an Examination Board for Financial Crisis Management, which was created that same month. Consisting of the Minister of Finance, the Governor of the Bank of Japan and others, including examiners appointed by the cabinet and approved by the Diet, this board was given responsibility for reviewing and approving applications for injections of public funds into financial institutions on the basis of predetermined, objective standards; the injections were to take such forms as the purchase of preferred shares by the Deposit Insurance Corporation.

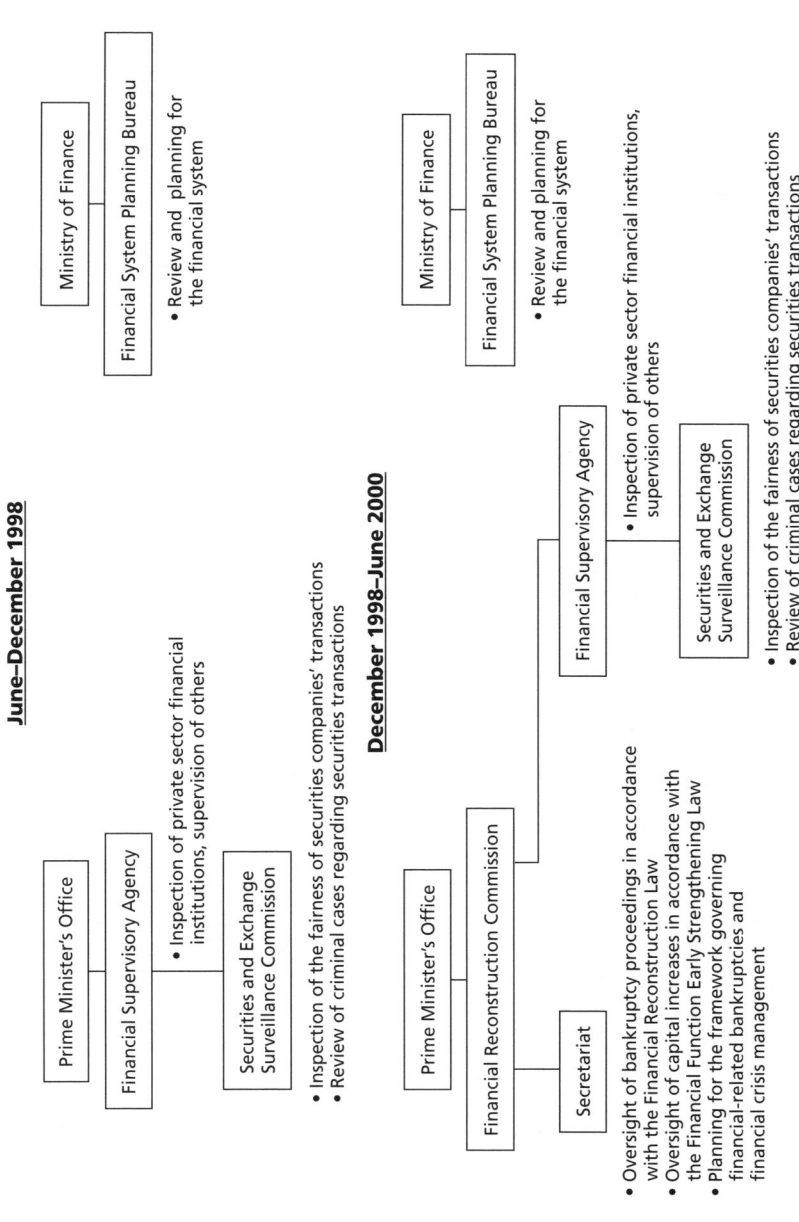

June–December 1998

Ministry of Finance

Financial System Planning Bureau

• Review and planning for the financial system

Prime Minister's Office

Financial Supervisory Agency

• Inspection of private sector financial institutions, supervision of others

Securities and Exchange Surveillance Commission

• Inspection of the fairness of securities companies' transactions
• Review of criminal cases regarding securities transactions

December 1998–June 2000

Ministry of Finance

Financial System Planning Bureau

• Review and planning for the financial system

Prime Minister's Office

Financial Reconstruction Commission

Secretariat

• Oversight of bankruptcy proceedings in accordance with the Financial Reconstruction Law
• Oversight of capital increases in accordance with the Financial Function Early Strengthening Law
• Planning for the framework governing financial-related bankruptcies and financial crisis management

Financial Supervisory Agency

• Inspection of private sector financial institutions, supervision of others

Securities and Exchange Surveillance Commission

• Inspection of the fairness of securities companies' transactions
• Review of criminal cases regarding securities transactions

12.2 Japan's changing regulatory framework (2).

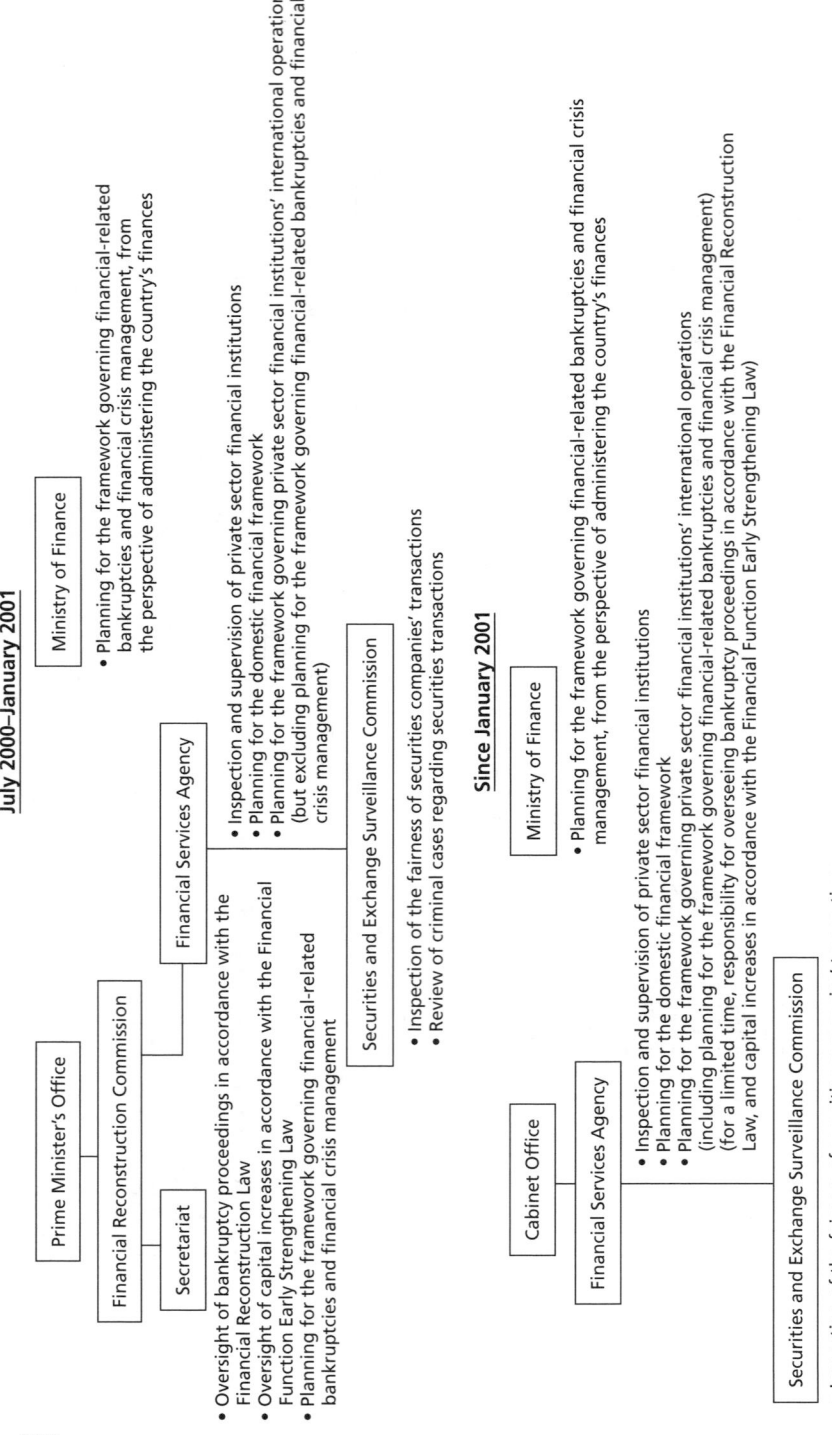

July 2000–January 2001

Prime Minister's Office

Financial Reconstruction Commission

Secretariat

- Oversight of bankruptcy proceedings in accordance with the Financial Reconstruction Law
- Oversight of capital increases in accordance with the Financial Function Early Strengthening Law
- Planning for the framework governing financial-related bankruptcies and financial crisis management

Financial Services Agency

- Inspection and supervision of private sector financial institutions
- Planning for the domestic financial framework
- Planning for the framework governing private sector financial institutions' international operations
- Planning for the framework governing financial-related bankruptcies and financial crisis management (but excluding planning for the framework governing financial-related bankruptcies and financial crisis management)

Securities and Exchange Surveillance Commission

- Inspection of the fairness of securities companies' transactions
- Review of criminal cases regarding securities transactions

Ministry of Finance

- Planning for the framework governing financial-related bankruptcies and financial crisis management, from the perspective of administering the country's finances

Since January 2001

Cabinet Office

Financial Services Agency

- Inspection and supervision of private sector financial institutions
- Planning for the domestic financial framework
- Planning for the framework governing private sector financial institutions' international operations
- Planning for the framework governing financial-related bankruptcies and financial crisis management (including planning for the framework governing financial-related bankruptcies and financial crisis management) (for a limited time, responsibility for overseeing bankruptcy proceedings in accordance with the Financial Reconstruction Law, and capital increases in accordance with the Financial Function Early Strengthening Law)

Securities and Exchange Surveillance Commission

- Inspection of the fairness of securities companies' transactions
- Review of criminal cases regarding securities transactions

Ministry of Finance

- Planning for the framework governing financial-related bankruptcies and financial crisis management, from the perspective of administering the country's finances

12.2 *Continued*

The scale of the capital injections approved by this board turned out to be small, however, and worries about the financial system persisted. In particular, concerns were heightening about the soundness of the Long-Term Credit Bank of Japan (LTCB), one of the institutions that received public funds. In October 1998, an additional package of legislation was passed that doubled the amount of public funds available for bank recapitalizations from ¥30 tr. to ¥60 tr. The package also established a new set of arrangements for dealing with failed institutions (including special public management of failed banks and the establishment of public bridge banks) and created a Financial Reconstruction Commission as an external agency of the Prime Minister's Office that would have responsibility over the FSA.

The Financial Reconstruction Commission was launched in December 1998 as a cabinet-level agency headed by a minister of state. It was structured as a council of four members who would be appointed by the cabinet and approved by the Diet. Among its responsibilities were handling the dissolution of failed financial institutions and helping to manage financial crises (previously the responsibilities of the FSA).

Finally, in November 1996, the government came out with its Big Bang programme of sweeping financial deregulation that was intended to make Tokyo an international financial centre on a par with New York and London. The bulk of the provisions of the Financial System Reform Law, a package of amendments to existing laws designed to help implement the Big Bang reforms, took effect in December 1998. The Big Bang did not itself directly lead to organizational changes in financial regulatory agencies, but the programme's objective of making Japan's markets 'free, fair, and global' became the operating principle for the FSA. Also, the reforms had a major impact on the actual nature of financial regulation; they included the change from a system of licensing to one of registration for securities companies and substantially relaxed the regulations that were previously applied on an industry-by-industry basis within the financial sector.

In addition, revelations in 1997 that major securities companies had been paying off racketeers served as the impetus for investigations by the Public Prosecutor's Office, which, in turn, led to the uncovering of lavish entertainment of regulators by financial institutions and to the arrests of a number of the MOF and BOJ officials as well. These scandals further sharpened popular criticism of the MOF and had various effects on the discussion of reform of the regulatory framework.

The present regulatory framework

The Financial Services Agency (FSA) was launched in July 2000 to oversee all aspects of financial and securities market regulation; structurally, it took over the organizations and functions of the former Financial Supervisory Agency as well as the MOF's Financial System Planning Bureau. Then, as part of the overhaul of the entire central government bureaucracy in January 2001, the FSA became an external agency of the newly created Cabinet Office. The overhaul aimed both to improve administrative efficiency and to strengthen the cabinet's policy coordination capabilities. It reduced the number of cabinet-level ministries/agencies from 23 to 13, and as originally planned, the Financial Reconstruction Commission was abolished at the same time. Though the FSA is not one of the 13 ministries/agencies whose heads are ex officio cabinet members, it is headed by a specially appointed minister of state.

As a result of this reorganization, the administrative functions of the government relating to the financial sector, after repeated rearrangements, have now been brought together again under the FSA. This change may be seen as representing, at last, the separation of the MOF's fiscal and financial regulatory powers that many had argued for earlier.

But as evident in one of the measures to stabilize the financial system – the provision of public funds to shore up banks' equity capital – it is not possible to completely separate the responsibility of safeguarding the stability of the financial system from the management of fiscal policy. Even after the overhaul, the MOF (whose name in Japanese was changed from Ôkurashô to Zaimushô but continues to be the 'Ministry of Finance' in English) is in charge of planning and policy making regarding failed financial institutions and financial crisis management. This responsibility is considered important for maintaining the health of the government's own finances.

ORGANIZATION OF THE FINANCIAL SERVICES AGENCY

At the top level of the FSA's organization are three political appointees: the Minister for Financial Services, the Senior Vice Minister and a Commissioner. These three are responsible for directing and overseeing the agency's activities as a whole. The FSA's major organizational units are a Planning and Coordination Bureau, an Inspection Bureau and a Supervisory Bureau, along with the

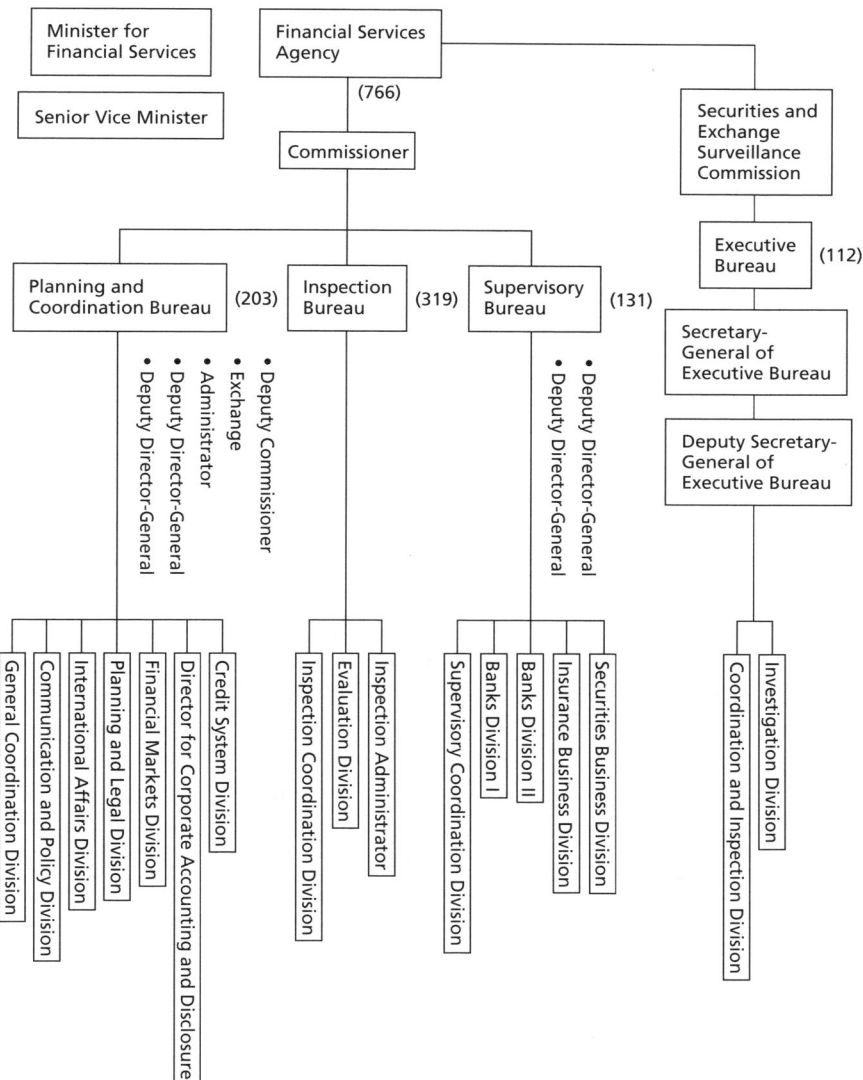

12.3 Organization of the Financial Services Agency, January 2001.
Note: Figures within parentheses represent number of authorized staff.

Securities and Exchange Surveillance Commission (Fig. 12.3). To take the place of the abolished Financial Reconstruction Commission, an advisory committee was set up with participants including the Minister for Financial Services and the Commissioner of the FSA; like the abolished commission, it functions as a council but is not an official administrative organ specified under the National Government Organization Law.

The FSA's authorized staff at January 2001 was set at 766, a substantial increase from the complement of 403 staffers assigned to the FSA at the time it was established. The biggest unit within the FSA is the Inspection Bureau, with a staff of 319. In addition, some 1300 employees are assigned to the financial inspection divisions of the MOF's regional financial bureaus, which are responsible for inspecting and supervising financial institutions in regions around the country. This personnel allocation clearly indicates that the focus of the new regulatory framework that has emerged from the financial and securities market reforms is not on *ex ante* intervention but, rather, on free competition between financial institutions and *ex post* inspection and supervision of financial institutions.

The structure of the present FSA is quite different from that of the MOF in the days when it was in charge of financial and securities market regulation as a whole. The former MOF organization included separate bureaus for banking and securities, each of which was basically responsible for the full range of administrative and regulatory affairs – from policy planning to inspection and supervision – relating to its respective industry (insurance industry affairs were handled by a separate department within the Banking Bureau). But these bureaus did have to coordinate their activities with the MOF's regional bureaus. The structure changed somewhat following the transfer of securities-related supervisory functions to the SESC and of financial institution inspection functions to the Financial Inspection Department in the Minister's Secretariat, but the basic organization continued to be divided along the lines of the separate industries within the financial sector rather than along functional lines.

By contrast, in the FSA, all the planning functions are grouped under one bureau, the inspection functions are in another, and the supervisory functions are in a third.

This kind of organizational reorientation is not unique to Japan. As the traditional distinctions between the banking and securities businesses become less meaningful and it becomes necessary for the authorities to deal with financial services conglomerates and products that span this division, other countries have also been moving to set up regulatory agencies responsible for the entire financial sector, such as Britain's Financial Services Authority.[1] Particularly

---

1 Britain's Financial Services Authority was established in 1997. Its main precursor was the Securities and Investments Board, which had been responsible for

pressing is the need to cope with the emergence of financial groups whose total risk exposures may not be evident through regulatory supervision of individual institutions; regulators need to look at such groups as a whole. Likewise, in Japan, it has now become possible for financial institutions to set up holding companies with subsidiaries in different financial industries. The organizational structure of the present FSA can be regarded as consistent with this global trend.

Another consideration behind the organizational shift was the problem under the previous framework that financial inspections, which require strict administrative capabilities backed by specialized knowledge, tended to be subsidiary to the functions of planning and supervision. When reform of the MOF was an issue, some suggested that this tendency contributed to the improper behaviour that came to light in relations between the MOF and the securities industry, for example. Of considerable significance in this regard is that the FSA has been organized with this issue in mind – the functions of planning, inspection and supervision have been assigned to separate bureaus of equal rank.

Progress to date and future issues

The FSA is aiming to achieve transparent and fair regulation of the financial sector largely by encouraging financial institutions to be responsible for their own affairs and by exposing them to market discipline. In place of the circular notices that were the mainstay of the old MOF framework, it has drawn up formal operating guidelines. The FSA uses its Web site to provide access to a wide variety of information, including the details of press conferences by senior officials and summaries of advisory council deliberations. In addi-

regulating and supervising the country's securities markets, but it also took over the powers of the Bank of England to supervise banks, the powers of the Department of Trade and Industry to supervise insurance companies, and the functions of inspecting and supervising investment service providers that had previously been entrusted to self-regulating organizations in each industry. It is thus a powerful regulatory agency that deals with the entire financial sector on a unified basis. Moves to create similar unified financial regulatory agencies are under way in places ranging from Scandinavia, Germany and Luxembourg to Ireland, Canada and Australia.

tion, it has made proposed revisions of existing ordinances and operating guidelines available for public review and comment. The agency's efforts to create openness represent a positive response to complaints about the former MOF framework, which was criticized for carrying out regulatory administration behind closed doors.

For a while, it seemed that regulators, in reaction to the earlier scandals involving the MOF bureaucrats, were trying to keep too much distance from the financial institutions for which they were responsible. More recently, however, FSA officials have been actively approaching financial institutions for exchanges of opinions. Also, the beefing up of the agency's inspection capabilities, which was the highest priority of the entire reorganization programme, will allow inspections of major banks to occur once a year; of regional banks, securities companies and insurance companies once every year and a half; and of other institutions once every three years. The agency has done much to incorporate the financial sector's views so as to be able to adapt to the rapidly changing realities of the market as well as to strengthen the inspection and supervision of financial institutions without compromising its independent authority.

In the future, the true mettle of the new agency will be tested. One question is whether it will be able to effectively coordinate its activities with those of the MOF in dealing with crises, such as the failure of a major financial institution. Another is whether it will be able to effectively inspect and supervise financial conglomerates. A third is whether it will be able to protect the interests of financial services consumers without blocking advances in financial technology and the introduction of new services. These are just some of the areas in which the FSA will need to prove itself.

Another point to note is that, for all the blurring of the lines separating the industries within the financial sector, these industries still exist, and regulators need to deal with them in accordance with the particular circumstances of each. Above all, one key issue under the new framework – in which the FSA is divided into bureaus along functional lines – will be the ability of those responsible for planning and coordination to communicate smoothly with those responsible for inspection and supervision of particular industries.

Another noteworthy development will be how the FSA follows through on its commitment to *ex post* supervision of the financial sector. In the final analysis, the financial and securities markets are based on trust in both the financial system and the individual institutions. Even if the FSA effectively establishes an *ex post* style of supervision, the financial markets are unlikely to be able to develop in a healthy direction if fraud, irregularities and financial institution failures are frequent occurrences. To a certain extent, *ex ante* co-ordination and intervention by regulators is necessary to head off problems before they occur. Such intervention is unlikely to turn into the sort of arbitrary regulation that drew criticism in the past. But maintaining a proper balance between *ex ante* and *ex post* supervision will be a major challenge for the FSA in its everyday operations.

CHAPTER 13 Securities exchanges

This chapter presents an overview of the development of securities exchanges in Japan and considers their role as participants in Japan's financial markets, and indeed as providing the essential infrastructure of those markets. (The structure and workings of the equity markets are considered in more detail in Chapter 16.) The myriad changes that have occurred in recent decades have led to many positive developments in Japan's financial markets, but an appropriate infrastructure must be established to keep pace with ever-increasing intermarket competition.

Securities exchanges can be viewed as the heart of the infrastructure that supports the financial and securities markets. A securities exchange lists the marketable securities, such as stocks and bonds, that meet its listing requirements and are traded by member firms meeting the standards of the exchange. The exchange places limits on the number of participants and trading hours, and transactions are conducted in accordance with established trading rules to ensure that securities are priced fairly and efficiently and are traded smoothly. The existence of such a secondary market makes it possible for companies to issue securities and raise funds in a stable environment over the long term.

Because prices on an exchange are determined by the decisions and assessments of a large number of market participants concerning the issuing company and security, these prices are widely used for valuation purposes in corporate accounting and taxation. Price trends on the major exchanges also serve as barometers of the health of national economies. Thus, securities exchanges are not only places for the trading of securities; they also play an important public role that has a great impact on economies.

Development of securities exchanges in Japan

The history of securities exchanges in Japan dates back to 1878, when the Tokyo Stock Exchange (TSE) Company was founded. Initially, trading on the exchange was predominantly in public debt that was issued along with the abolition of feudal privileges from the pre-modern era, but the proportion of stock transactions rose sharply as modern industries started to develop in Japan. Before World War II, however, the exchanges had a decidedly speculative flavour – they were dominated by speculative trading on a net-settlement basis rather than by cash trading based on the physical delivery of stock certificates. At that time, securities exchanges were profit-making corporations in that they listed their own shares on their exchanges, and in an attempt to increase their earnings they encouraged speculative trading of their own shares.

Even in the prewar period, the government realized that the very speculative nature of the exchanges made them unsuitable as a way either for companies to raise funds or for investors to manage assets responsibly. Numerous attempts were made to reform the system, especially by promoting the use of trading based on physical certificates, but changing the nature of the market proved to be no easy matter.

Finally, in June 1943, as part of the tightening of wartime economic control measures, the Japan Securities Exchange was established as a quasi-governmental company that combined the 11 extant individual stock exchanges. Trading on the Japan Securities Exchange was supported by major purchases by the Wartime Finance Corporation, so it cannot be characterized as a normal marketplace, but it continued to function until the Soviet Union went to war against Japan on 9 August 1945.

After World War II, under the orders of the Occupation authorities, exchanges in Japan underwent a complete overhaul. Immediately after the war, the Occupation authorities halted preparations by the securities industry and the Ministry of Finance to reopen the exchanges. The authorities permitted the establishment of exchanges but only under new securities transaction laws modelled after those in the US. To prevent traders from reverting to their prewar practices, the authorities centralized the trading of listed securities on the exchanges, established transaction records and banned futures transactions.

In May 1949, trading began on the Tokyo, Nagoya and Osaka securities exchanges. Later, six more exchanges were opened in

Kyoto, Hiroshima, Fukuoka, Niigata, Sapporo and Kobe. Of the 11 exchanges that were combined to form the Japan Securities Exchange during the war, three exchanges (Nagaoka, Nagasaki and Yokohama) were closed by the Japan Securities Exchange and the remaining eight exchanges were reinstated after the war. The Sapporo Securities Exchange was established after the war.

With the exception of the closing of the Kobe Stock Exchange in October 1967, Japan's system of securities exchanges remained more or less the same from the end of the war until the late 1990s. But during this period, the exchanges continued to develop and expand steadily: a margin trading system was introduced in June 1951; second sections for younger, growing companies were added to the Tokyo, Nagoya and Osaka exchanges in October 1961; foreign companies were listed on the TSE for the first time in December 1973; and a derivatives market was established in October 1985, starting with the trading of bond futures on the TSE. Meanwhile, stock trading activity steadily shifted from the regional exchanges to the TSE, forcing the other exchanges to scramble to find ways to survive. The Osaka Securities Exchange (OSE), for example, attempted to rejuvenate itself by promoting futures trading (Table 13.1, Fig. 13.1).

The Big Bang reforms of the financial system that started in 1996 led to some major changes in the existing framework for the exchanges. A revision of the Securities and Exchange Law included provisions for the merger of exchanges and other measures that encouraged regional exchanges, which had been struggling from a decline in the number of companies listing their shares on one exchange only, to close down. The Hiroshima and Niigata exchanges were merged into the TSE in March 2000, and the Kyoto exchange was merged into the OSE in March 2001. As a result of these moves, only five securities exchanges remain in Japan: Tokyo, Osaka, Nagoya, Fukuoka and Sapporo.

The structure of the securities exchanges

After the war, securities exchanges in Japan became membership organizations made up of securities companies. But a revision of the Securities and Exchange Law in December 2000 has opened the door for existing membership-based exchanges to become joint stock corporations. This move came after many securities exchanges outside Japan, in particular those in Europe and North America,

Table 13.1 Value of trading by exchange (¥ m, %)

Year	Total trading value	Tokyo	Osaka	Nagoya	Kyoto	Hiroshima	Fukuoka	Niigata	Sapporo	Kobe
1950	90 545	55.17	27.27	6.68	2.82	1.47	1.29	0.95	0.73	3.32
1955	442 197	64.21	22.44	5.47	2.18	1.48	1.95	0.32	0.37	1.59
1960	9 334 333	62.17	29.37	4.58	1.01	0.76	1.08	0.10	0.11	0.83
1965	5 782 977	69.25	24.64	3.02	0.84	0.81	0.35	0.35	0.09	0.64
1970	12 030 257	76.08	19.93	2.90	0.33	0.35	0.15	0.18	0.10	
1975	18 976 245	82.03	14.71	2.37	0.22	0.22	0.17	0.21	0.07	
1980	42 161 020	86.55	10.36	2.36	0.09	0.28	0.09	0.20	0.07	
1985	94 639 892	83.17	13.25	3.05	0.13	0.09	0.10	0.16	0.06	
1986	193 058 996	82.79	13.04	3.78	0.11	0.04	0.06	0.13	0.04	
1987	296 110 531	84.68	11.71	3.21	0.12	0.05	0.07	0.13	0.04	
1988	332 757 241	85.80	10.37	3.41	0.11	0.05	0.07	0.13	0.04	
1989	386 395 042	86.08	10.79	2.69	0.11	0.06	0.09	0.12	0.06	
1990	231 837 121	80.52	15.45	3.15	0.33	0.11	0.17	0.14	0.12	
1991	134 159 953	82.66	13.96	2.67	0.22	0.11	0.13	0.15	0.09	
1992	80 455 788	74.71	19.36	4.82	0.40	0.17	0.16	0.22	0.16	
1993	106 122 708	81.88	13.79	3.26	0.32	0.17	0.21	0.21	0.16	
1994	114 622 138	76.21	16.88	5.04	0.49	0.27	0.58	0.26	0.26	
1995	115 839 828	72.14	21.34	4.72	0.75	0.26	0.34	0.18	0.27	
1996	136 169 860	74.83	20.03	3.96	0.44	0.18	0.22	0.14	0.19	
1997	151 445 077	71.64	17.84	8.42	1.40	0.13	0.13	0.26	0.16	
1998	124 101 720	78.48	16.54	4.82	0.07	0.02	0.02	0.02	0.03	
1999	210 236 341	88.25	10.51	1.13	0.05	0.01	0.02	0.01	0.02	

Notes: The Sapporo Securities Exchange was established on 1 April 1950. The Kobe Stock Exchange was closed down on 31 October 1967.
Source: Nomura, based on the Tokyo Stock Exchange's *Shoken Tokei Nenpo* (*Yearbook of Securities Statistics*) and *Shoken Tokei Geppo* (*Monthly Securities Statistics*).

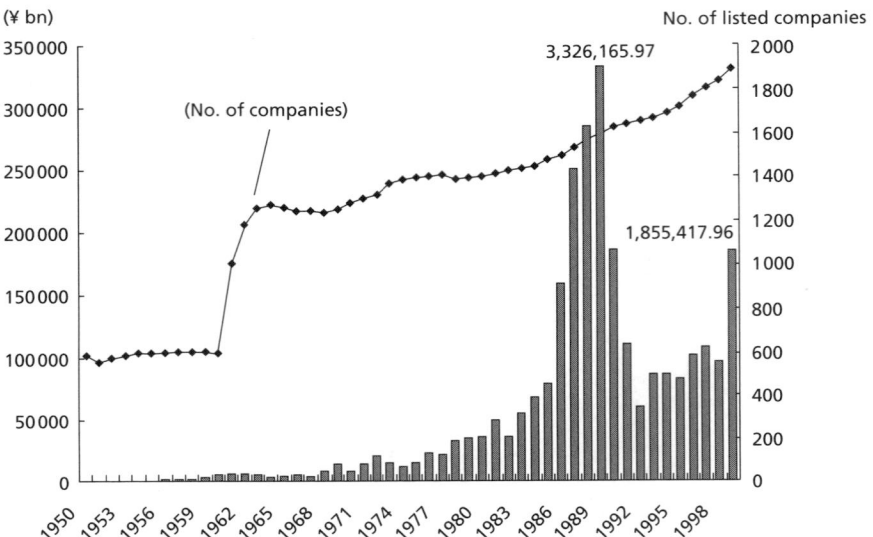

13.1 Tokyo Stock Exchange: value of trading and number of listed companies. Source: Nomura, based on TSE, *Shoken Tokei Nenpo* [*Yearbook of Securities Statistics*].

changed from membership organizations to corporations in recent years. After the Securities and Exchange Law was revised, the OSE became a joint stock corporation in April 2001. The TSE established a special committee to look into possible organizational changes, and then became a joint stock corporation in November 2001.

Many of the world's securities exchanges are membership organizations because they were originally created by the brokerage firms as club-like organizations. In Japan's case, the exchanges were reorganized after the war as membership organizations because the corporate structure of the prewar exchanges was considered to be conducive to speculative trading. But membership exchanges tend to become exclusive organizations concerned only with protecting the interests of their members. During the mid-1980s, the opening of TSE membership to foreign securities firms became a trade issue with the UK and the US. Thereafter, limits on the number of TSE members were eliminated, making membership open to any brokerage firm capable of executing transactions smoothly.

Exchange transactions are based on the auction method. The member firms take limit orders or market orders on behalf of customers and forward them to traders on the exchange; members also trade for their own accounts. The orders are then matched up on the basis of price and time. These transactions used to take place on the floor of the exchanges, and the flow of people around the floor, their body movements and their hand gestures were considered important indicators of market trends. Recently, however, developments in computer and communications technology have enabled transaction data to be disseminated in real time; transactions can now be conducted off the trading floor. The TSE started gradually automating the operations of its trading floor in 1982. All floor trading finally ceased at the end of April 1999, after the exchange had fully computerized its trading operations.

One important characteristic of an exchange is that it ensures the efficient and equitable pricing of securities through established trading rules and monitoring mechanisms. Exchanges regulate themselves by imposing rules on members and sanctions on those who break the rules. Also, to ensure the smooth execution of transactions, exchanges regularly check each member's financial condition and internal controls to ensure that they are in good financial shape and are capable of properly handling and settling orders.

Another important function of a securities exchange is to screen companies that seek to be listed. In Japan, going public and having shares listed on an exchange, particularly on the TSE, means more than just improved liquidity for a company's shares – the move also bestows a certain level of social standing on companies. Moreover, by listing its shares, a company ultimately benefits from better trade and financing terms and is better able to recruit employees. Until securities market reforms in 1983 led to the establishment of the JASDAQ market, only listed companies could raise funds through public stock offerings. Having become keenly aware of the importance of developing their markets, exchanges have recently been easing their listing requirements and screening processes. Nonetheless, the investing public still perceives listed stocks as relatively low-risk investments. By ensuring that listed companies meet certain standards, the exchanges' screening processes serve the interests of the general public.

Other types of exchanges

In accordance with the Securities and Exchange Law, the only products that can be listed and traded on securities exchanges are securities (as defined by the law) and futures and options derived from these securities. Futures and options on interest rates and currencies, as well as other financial derivatives not directly linked to securities, are traded on financial futures exchanges, whereas futures and options on non-financial products, such as agricultural produce and basic materials, are traded on commodities exchanges. In addition to the Tokyo International Financial Futures Exchange, which is Japan's only financial futures exchange, there are seven commodity exchanges nationwide, including the Tokyo Commodity Exchange, that trade products such as textiles, grains, rubber and sugar.

The over-the-counter market

Securities transactions need not take place on a securities exchange. Buyers and sellers can bypass securities exchanges if they can negotiate mutually agreeable prices. When a securities dealer is involved in such a transaction, it is called an over-the-counter (OTC) transaction. In OTC transactions, securities dealers display their bids and offers on securities to provide liquidity and ensure a smooth transaction flow.

OTC trades are common in the bond market, which is dominated by large trades between institutional investors and financial institutions. In the bond market, pricing can be based on a relatively limited amount of information, such as the coupon, the issuer's credit rating and the term to maturity. In Japan, many Japanese government bonds (JGBs) and other bonds are listed on the TSE, but almost all trading takes place over the counter.

In addition, stocks that are not listed on an exchange are traded primarily on the OTC market. Since the 1960s, OTC trading of stocks has been managed by self-regulatory securities dealers' associations.

THE DEVELOPMENT OF JAPAN'S OTC STOCK MARKET

Japan's OTC stock market began to take shape in the early 1960s, around the same time that the exchanges were adding second sections. Stocks that were unlisted at the time the exchanges were reopened after the war were traded over the counter among the exchange members, but most of this trading activity was taken over by the Tokyo, Osaka and Nagoya exchanges in October 1961, when they established second sections for smaller, growing stocks.

But OTC stock trading continued, chiefly in stocks that did not meet the listing requirements for the second sections. In February 1963, after the second sections of exchanges were created, regional securities dealers' associations established an OTC stock registration system. Members agreed to trade only those stocks registered with the system.[1]

The second sections of the exchanges expanded steadily by attracting fast-growing, mid-sized companies. But the oil crisis in 1974 put an end to the good times for start-ups. The bankruptcies of several second section companies prompted moves to make listing requirements tougher and to tighten other regulations of this segment of the market. In turn, it became difficult to maintain liquidity for stocks that had been delisted from second sections or that could not meet the newly tightened requirements of second sections. In July 1976, Japan OTC Securities (now JASDAQ Market Inc.) was established with capital from 187 securities companies (out of a total of 231 nationwide at the time). The company was set up to broker transactions between securities firms in order to promote the fair pricing and smooth trading of OTC stocks.

But the Ministry of Finance, which is the ministry that oversees the OTC market, has been somewhat cautious on the OTC market. Given that these stocks entail higher risk than listed stocks, it issued a circular notice (*tsûtatsu*) to brokerage firms prohibiting them from aggressively promoting OTC stocks to individual investors. As a result, Japan's OTC market has been positioned merely as a market that supplements the exchanges. Unlike the Nasdaq in the US, it has not developed into an entity equal in size and influence to the exchanges.

In the early 1980s, requests were set in motion to strengthen the role of the OTC market in the development of start-up companies. A number of major structural reform measures were implemented starting in 1983, including the easing of registration requirements for IPOs, liberalization of restrictions on brokerage firms' promotion of OTC stocks and a lifting of the ban on public offerings. To handle transactions more efficiently, JASDAQ also improved its infrastructure by adding a computerized quote system and a JASDAQ-market system for brokering transactions of OTC stocks. These improvements have paid off. By the late 1980s and early 1990s, both the

---

1 Stocks not registered with the OTC system were referred to as 'blue-sky stocks' in Japan.

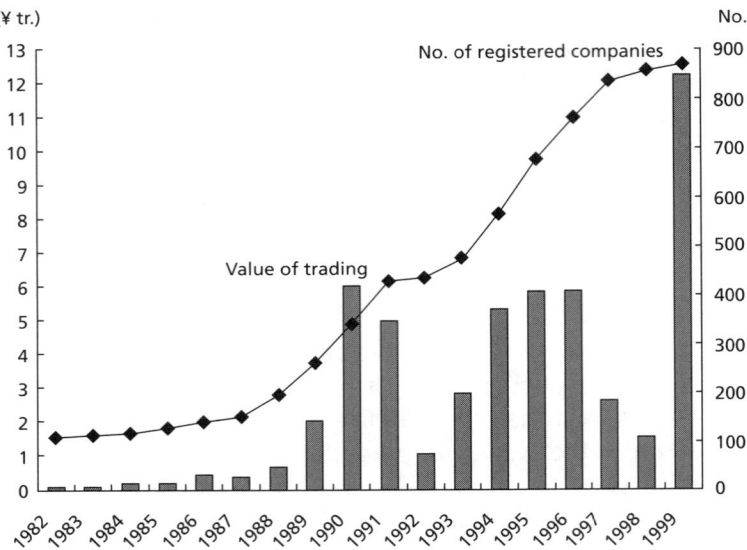

13.2 The over-the-counter market: value of trading and number of registered companies.
Source: as Fig. 13.1.

number of JASDAQ-registered stocks and trading volume had soared (Fig. 13.2).

OPERATION OF THE OTC STOCK MARKET

The legal status of JASDAQ changed significantly as a result of a December 1998 revision to the Securities and Exchange Law, which was a key part of the Big Bang financial reforms. Until that time, JASDAQ had played a secondary role to the exchanges, which were legally designated as the primary securities markets. But the 1998 revision put JASDAQ on a par with the exchanges as a marketplace for securities.

The JASDAQ market (it officially took its current name in July 2001) is operated by the Japan Securities Dealers Association (JSDA). JSDA is a self-regulatory organization of securities dealers, as defined by the Securities and Exchange Law, and regulates itself and its members through fair practice rules governing the operation of brokerage firms' businesses and trading on the OTC market. JSDA also serves as a securities industry group, representing the industry's interests and lobbying the government and political parties on such issues as tax reforms. The organization has recently made some structural changes, including the spin-off of JASDAQ Market Inc., which operates the JASDAQ trading system, into a subsidiary.

As previously mentioned, in a typical OTC market, dealers post bids and offers on securities in order to provide liquidity in the market; in the US, these dealers are called market makers. The US Nasdaq market, which is operated by the National Association of Securities Dealers (NASD) as an organized OTC market, can be regarded as nothing more than a large group of such market makers who display competitive bids and offers and help to establish an efficient pricing and trading mechanism.

In contrast, the JASDAQ market uses an auction system of trading similar to the one that has been used on the stock exchanges since immediately after the war, in part because for many years, tight restrictions were placed on proprietary trading by dealers. Despite the similarity of its name to that of the Nasdaq, the JASDAQ system introduced by Japan OTC Securities is actually a system for automating auction-style trading.

Some major problems have persisted on the JASDAQ market, where most of the stocks are those of smaller companies that do not meet the listing requirements of the exchanges: namely, insufficient volume to sustain continuous auction-type trading and poor liquidity. To remedy some of these problems, JASDAQ started to strengthen the market-making system in December 1998, at the start of the implementation of the financial Big Bang reform measures. Now, multiple market makers are displaying bids and offers for more than 300 stocks.

Settlement systems

In addition to the exchanges and OTC market, another key component of the infrastructure of Japan's financial markets is the delivery and settlement system, which comes into play after trades are made on the exchanges and the OTC market.

A security is a transferable, marketable certificate representing equity ownership of a company's assets and earnings (in the case of a stock) or a loan to a country or a corporation (in the case of a bond). Settlement of securities transactions traditionally entailed the transfer of funds and the physical delivery of the securities between two parties (or the securities firms representing the parties).

But with the broadening expanse of economic areas and the increase in non-face-to-face transactions, physical delivery and settlement in many cases impedes the execution of transactions. Physical delivery also increases the risk of counterfeiting, loss and theft. Meanwhile, developments in information technology have made it possible to accurately save and process large amounts of data. By replacing the physical certificates with electronic database systems, these advances have led to efforts to expedite transaction processing and reduce risks. Securities transactions are now settled through depository/settlement institutions, such as the Depository Trust Company (DTC) in the US. Another such settlement institution, Euroclear France,[2] has gone so far as to abolish stock certificates completely.

In Japan, the Japan Securities Depository Center (JASDEC) was established in December 1984 for the custody and transfer of securities and settlement of funds between participants. Still, the use of depository-based settlement has not become as widespread in Japan as in the US and Europe, mainly because of high custodial and other fees as well as investors' reluctance to have their securities held in the institution's name.

Meanwhile, for bond transactions, electronic settlement of registered JGBs at the Bank of Japan began in May 1990, resulting in the de facto abolition of JGB certificates. A corporate-bond electronic settlement network that links registered financial institutions, called JB Net, started up in December 1997 and has since then expedited the processing of bond transactions.

In recent years, an increasing awareness worldwide of the risks associated with financial transactions has led to efforts to shorten settlement periods and to a complete shift to the delivery-versus-payment (DVP) system, in which delivery and fund settlements take place concurrently. In Japan, the securities industry plans to shorten the settlement period on stock trades from four days (T + 3) to the next day (T + 1) by 2002; T + 1 settlement, which requires full-scale, completely paperless custody-based settlement and the abolition of physical delivery of certificates, could initiate a major change in the way transactions are processed in Japan.

---

2 Euroclear France was created out of a merger between Sicovam SA and Euroclear Bank SA/NV in January 2001.

Intermarket competition and the market infrastructure

Part of the impetus behind the late 2000 revision of the Securities and Exchange Law, which was a key part of the Big Bang, was the idea that the operation of securities markets is a commercial enterprise and that exchanges should compete with each other rather than be run as quasi-public agencies. As a result of the revision of the law, regional exchanges lost their local monopolies, regional companies are now permitted to list their shares directly on the TSE and OSE, and exchanges are allowed to establish new markets.

INCREASING COMPETITION

A significant step along these lines that heralded the beginning of intermarket competition in Japan was the announcement in June 1999 of a plan to set up a market called Nasdaq Japan. Nasdaq Japan is a joint venture between the NASD, which has developed the Nasdaq in the US into a market that rivals the New York Stock Exchange in influence, and Softbank, led by well-known technology entrepreneur Masayoshi Son. The establishment of a US-style stock market in Japan is a ground-breaking development – perhaps similar to the arrival of Commodore Matthew Perry's 'black ships' to Japan in the mid-1800s – that has generated considerable attention.

The TSE, which has always been viewed primarily as a market for stocks of mature, blue-chip companies, then launched in November 1999 a new market called Mothers (an abbreviation for 'market of the high-growth and emerging stocks'), targeted at start-up companies. The idea for the Mothers market had already been under consideration before the Big Bang started, but the creation of Nasdaq Japan undoubtedly hastened the establishment of the Mothers market. With the emergence of these new markets, JASDAQ – which had been the primary market for the stocks of relatively young, emerging-growth companies – has started feeling the heat and, subsequently, has begun restructuring its operations and promoting itself more actively.

This three-way market competition in Japan reflects a global trend toward greater competition among securities markets. In the US, the Nasdaq faces competition from electronic communication networks, or ECNs. Meanwhile, in Europe, competition is increasing as markets for newly emerging companies are opening up; in response, some existing exchanges have merged or partnered with each other. Amid this environment of global competition, the NASD helped to launch Nasdaq Japan in June 2000 as a part of its plan to create a global stock market and, in the process, touched off inter-market competition in Japan. Rather than setting up their own securities dealers' association, NASD and Softbank chose the more practical option of working with an existing market, the OSE.

By May 2001, 34 stocks were listed on the TSE Mothers and 63 were listed on Nasdaq Japan, a far cry from the more than 897 stocks registered on JASDAQ, but the two newer markets are steadily gaining ground as the markets of choice for initial public offerings.

As part of their efforts to attract candidates for IPOs, the three markets have greatly simplified and streamlined their procedures for screening companies (Table 13.2). Intermarket competition has made it easier for emerging-growth companies to launch IPOs, thereby broadening the financing choices available to them. The increased opportunities for IPOs – which serve as one exit strategy for entrepreneurs and their backers – have, in turn, contributed to an expansion of venture capital investments in Japan and greater opportunities for Japanese entrepreneurs. Over the long term, the development of the stock markets for start-up companies should contribute to the emergence of new industries and changes in Japan's industrial structure.

FUTURE CHALLENGES

The development of intermarket competition, however, is not entirely favourable; certain aspects of it need to be viewed with caution. For instance, in their bid to compete for business and bolster their own standing, markets that are subject to competition may be tempted to list or register companies too hastily by lowering their screening criteria. Among the possible consequences is the accept-ance of companies for stock listings that are otherwise not yet quali-fied to go public. In addition, in their race to list as many issues as possible, markets may solicit companies whose stocks are already listed on other markets, which would fragment the trading of stocks and lead to serious market inefficiencies.

Meanwhile, with IPOs within easier reach than ever before for many companies, some may decide to go public without fully under-standing the weighty social responsibility of being a public company owned by a large number of non-professional individuals and other ordinary investors. If companies can easily go public without con-sidering all the implications, investors may become dissatisfied with

Table 13.2 Comparison of major markets for emerging-growth companies (at May 2001)

	OTC	Mothers	Nasdaq Japan
Operated by	Japan Securities Dealers' Association	Tokyo Stock Exchange	Osaka Securities Exchange
Established	1963	1999	2000
No. of companies	897	34	63
Criteria for listing/registering stock	▪ Standard 1 is for ordinary companies, and Standard 2 is for emerging-growth companies. The latter are allowed to have losses at the time of registration. ▪ Stocks are no longer traded on the market if the average monthly turnover drops below 10 trading units (typically 10000 shares) over a six-month period or if the stock is traded on less than 20% of the days over a six-month period.	▪ Listings are allowed for money-losing companies or those with negative net worth, as long as the offering involves at least 1000 trading units and at least 300 new shareholders. Stocks are delisted if the average monthly trading volume over a one-year period drops below 10 trading units, or if the stock is not traded for a three-month period.	▪ The market has two sets of criteria, 'standard' and 'growth'. The 'standard' criteria are as stringent as those of the Nasdaq in the US. ▪ Under the 'growth' criteria, stocks are delisted if the free float drops below 500 trading units.
Trading method	▪ The main system is auction trading based on the JASDAQ system. Recently, a market-making system has been established for about 300 stocks.	▪ Trading is based on the same auction system as for the first and second sections of the Tokyo Stock Exchange.	▪ Trading is based on an auction system.
Other characteristics	▪ Part 2 of the securities registration application has been simplified, and the application review period has been shortened. ▪ JSDA also operates the 'Green Sheet' market for the trading of privately held stocks.	▪ Listed companies are required to produce quarterly earnings reports and hold regular meetings to brief investors. Reduced listing and examination fees have made it easier for companies to list on the market, and Part 2 of the securities listing application is no longer required.	▪ The eventual plan is to create a 24-hour trading environment by linking the market up with the Nasdaq systems in the US and Europe. Nasdaq Japan (a joint venture between Softbank and the NASD in the US) is in charge of seeking out companies interested in having their stocks traded on the Nasdaq Japan market.

Source: Nomura.

companies' management direction and information disclosures. A general loss of confidence in the markets themselves could result if the competition produces such side effects.

Of course, the three competing markets each have their own strengths: JASDAQ is aiming for a high level of liquidity through the use of the market-maker system; TSE Mothers emphasizes its fairness as a market operated by the long-established TSE; and Nasdaq Japan makes a selling point of its connection with the Nasdaq market in the US and, hence, its more international character. Nevertheless, it appears that the differences between the three markets are not all that evident to companies considering an IPO, which makes deciding which market to use rather difficult.

OFF-EXCHANGE TRANSACTIONS

In addition to the increase in competition between the small-cap stock markets, one often overlooked consequence of the Big Bang is the competition that exchanges face from the rising volume of listed stocks being traded off the exchanges.

As mentioned earlier, the trading of listed securities was centralized on the exchanges after the markets reopened after the war in accordance with the guidelines set down by the Occupation authorities. One motivation behind the move was to prevent OTC trading of listed stocks, which was widespread before the war, from compromising the fairness of Japan's securities markets. To be sure, market prices most accurately reflect supply and demand when all trading takes place on exchanges. But a strict enforcement of this rule makes it difficult for brokers to execute large orders from institutional investors and also limits the competition between exchange members and non-members. In the US, restrictions on off-exchange transactions were lifted in 1979. The ban on off-exchange trading in Japan was lifted in December 1998 as part of the Big Bang reforms. Exchange members can now trade listed stocks off the exchange, subject to the restriction that during normal trading hours, these transactions must be based on prices of trades on the exchange.

Because the most common off-exchange transactions are for special purposes, such as block trades by institutional investors and orders to be executed at volume-weighted average prices (VWAP), brokerage firms normally handle these customer orders by taking the other side of the trade. Off-exchange trades of this type involving TSE-listed stocks account for 10–15% of the trading volume on the TSE (Fig. 13.3).

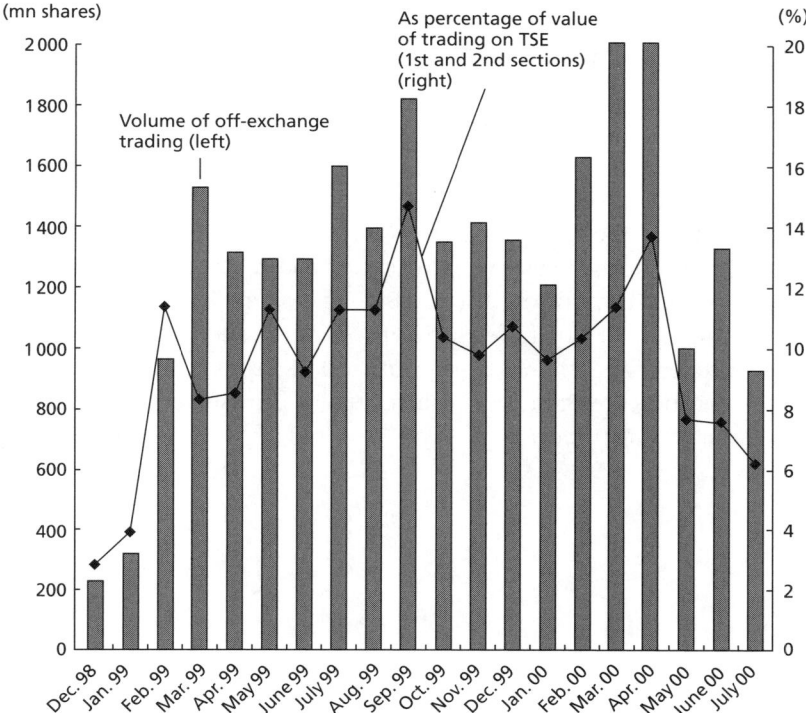

(mn shares)

2 000

1 800

1 600

1 400

1 200

1 000

800

600

400

200

0

As percentage of value
of trading on TSE
(1st and 2nd sections)
(right)

Volume of off-exchange
trading (left)

(%)

20

18

16

14

12

10

8

6

4

2

0

Dec. 98 Jan. 99 Feb. 99 Mar. 99 Apr. 99 May 99 June 99 July 99 Aug. 99 Sep. 99 Oct. 99 Nov. 99 Dec. 99 Jan. 00 Feb. 00 Mar. 00 Apr. 00 May 00 June 00 July 00

13.3 Trends in off-exchange transactions.
Source: Nomura, based on data from the Japan Securities Dealers Association and
the Tokyo Stock Exchange.

Another type of off-exchange transaction involves the use of proprietary trading systems (PTSs) operated by brokerage firms. A PTS
is a virtual securities exchange based on a computer network. These
systems were first developed in the 1970s in the US and are now
often called alternative trading systems, or ATSs. In Japan, such entities resembling exchanges were prohibited for many years under the
Securities and Exchange Law, but revisions to the law made as part
of the Big Bang have legalized PTS- (or ATS-) based trading.

At May 2002, only four PTSs used for stock trading in Japan were
in operation, including the 'BB Super Trade' system run by Japan
Bond Trading, which was licensed in June 2000 and began operation in September 2000. Unlike trading on the TSE, maintaining
liquidity in PTS-based trading is difficult, which decreases the likelihood that PTS trading will become widely accepted. But for
investors, such systems are beneficial in that they provide another
option for trade execution and thus help to reduce transaction costs
through competition. A total of five PTSs were in operation for bond

trading (six were established, but one was liquidated in April 2001), and are expected to be increasingly used by institutional investors.

FUTURE CHALLENGES

All in all, Japan does not yet have a market infrastructure on a par with that of the Nasdaq's National Market System, which consists of a variety of computer systems and order routing systems. The emergence of several channels for executing orders for the same stock leads to the risk of an increase in improper trades and a decline in market efficiency. A major task confronting Japan's securities industry, then, is the development of a requisite infrastructure for the age of intermarket competition.

The markets

14 The money market

This chapter consists of three sections: first, a summary of the way in which Japan's money market has developed and changed amid the liberalization and internationalization of Japan's financial markets; second, a description of the key financial markets, of trends within them and of the structure of various money market instruments; and third, a discussion of the outlook for Japan's money market.

The money market can be defined as the financial market for the buying and selling of short-term financial instruments with maturities of less than one year. Japan's money market comprises roughly two segments: the interbank money market, in which the participants are limited to financial institutions, and the open money market, in which a broad range of participants trade freely. In general, the main financial instruments transacted in the interbank market are call loans and bills, whereas the core instruments exchanged in the open market are certificates of deposit (CDs), commercial paper (CP), Treasury bills (TBs), financing bills (FBs), bond *gensakis* and cash-secured bond repos (repurchase agreements, or RPs).[1]

Changes in Japan's money market

The history of changes in Japan's money market, which did not become fully functioning until 1985, falls systematically into several five-year intervals.

1 As we note later in the chapter, *gensaki* are traded securities, whereas repos are transactions involving the borrowing and lending of bonds collateralized with cash.

THE 1985–90 PERIOD

From 1985 to 1990, Japan's money market became fully established and experienced rapid growth. As shown in Table 14.1, the outstanding balance of money-market instruments grew at an annual rate of 28.4% between 1985 and 1990, which was a significant increase over the annual growth rate of 13.3% between 1980 and 1985.

This strong growth can be attributed to two factors. The first factor was the release by the Ministry of Finance (MOF) of a report titled 'The Current State of and Outlook for Financial Liberalization and the Internationalization of the Yen' in May 1984. Following the release of the guidelines in the report, various measures to improve the functioning of the money market were set up for implementation in 1985.

The conclusions reached in the report had been coalescing for several years. With the cooperation of the US, Japan had begun to liberalize and internationalize its somewhat closed financial system in 1983, when the two countries established the US–Japan Yen–Dollar Committee. Thereafter, the environment surrounding the Japanese economy and its financial markets changed drastically and heightened the need for market reforms. The changes included the establishment of frameworks for international cooperation on financial and economic issues, such as the Plaza Accord in September 1985 and the Louvre Accord in February 1987.

These developments led to the start of unsecured call–loan trading in July 1985 and the liberalization of interest rates on large time deposits in October 1985. To support refinancing needs for the redemption of government bonds issued after 1975, the government began issuing discount TBs in February 1986; a secondary market for these instruments was established around the same time. In addition, regulations on the issuance of CDs were eased one after another, and CDs and FBs were added to the list of financial instruments that were used by the Bank of Japan (BOJ) to conduct its open-market operations.

Another significant change was the establishment of an offshore market as part of an effort to further internationalize Japan's money market. In response to strong demand, a domestic CP market was established in November 1987, which helped to broaden the short-term financing options available to corporations. In addition, between 1988 and 1989, the trading infrastructure for unsecured call loans improved, thanks to the introduction of a broader range of maturities and a competitive bidding system. A financial futures market was established as well. These improvements to the short-term money market greatly contributed to higher trading volume in Japan's money market.

The second factor that contributed to the strong expansion of Japan's money market was related to changes in the economic environment and a consequent increase in the transaction options available to market participants and the development of new financial technologies.

The expansion of the money market and the liberalization of interest rates provided market participants with various interest rate arbitrage opportunities. The growth of the money market afforded traders the chance to arbitrage spreads between short- and long-term interest rates and intermarket rates and between market interest rates and the interest rates that are targeted by the BOJ through its open-market operations. The development of a futures market also opened up opportunities for arbitrage between spot and futures prices. Moreover, interest rate arbitrage activity picked up after the BOJ began to permit financial institutions to borrow and lend funds simultaneously in March 1985.

The surge in arbitrage activity resulted in more-advanced trading techniques and the development of new financial technologies. The adoption of an accommodative monetary policy from 1985 to mid-1988 to stem the yen's appreciation led to a flattening of the yield curve (the spread between short- and long-term interest rates contracted), an outcome that reflected the market's expectations for a decline in interest rates. As interest rates started to increase in the second half of 1988, however, the slope of the yield curve steepened (the spread between short- and long-term interest rates widened) to match the market's expectations for a further rise in interest rates. This reversal in the market's outlook for interest rates, which was caused by changes in the economic climate, also stimulated activity in the money market.

THE 1990–95 PERIOD

From 1990 to 1995, the growth of Japan's money market levelled off. During this period, however, investors shifted funds between money-market instruments, which created a widening gap in the trading of the different money-market securities. As shown in Table 14.1, Japan's money market grew at an annualized rate of only 2.9% between 1990 and 1995. The outstanding balances of unsecured call

Table 14.1 Outstanding balances of money market securities, 1980–2000 (¥ bn)

	1980	1985	1986	1987	1988	1989	1990	1991	1992	1993	1994
Call loans (total)	4133.3	5110.4	10226.2	16037.9	15674.2	24485.8	23986.6	35316.9	44463.5	44720.3	42753.2
Unsecured call loans	0	821.5	1624.1	2941.9	6036.0	10065.2	12327.1	23448.0	31696.4	33963.8	33570.9
Secured call loans	4133.3	4288.9	8602.1	13096.0	9638.2	14420.6	11659.5	11868.9	12767.1	10756.5	9182.3
Bills	5738.1	14655.8	13544.4	13106.4	18036.4	20761.3	17060.3	16509.6	15606.1	9459.9	8260.7
CDs	2322.7	957.2	9926.3	10832.8	15972.9	21086.0	18859.8	17298.3	16782.2	19044.9	18483.9
CP	0	0	0	1698.2	9285.9	13065.9	15762.7	12400.4	12203.7	11050.6	9876.7
TB and FB	13965.5	13656.2	19227.2	23275.2	23251.9	26840.4	33110.1	30032.8	32777.0	34761.6	36143.4
TB	0	0	2076.2	2721.2	2039.9	4008.4	7605.1	9045.8	10369.0	10989.6	11298.4
FB	13965.5	13656.2	17151.0	20554.0	21212.0	22832.0	25505.0	20987.0	22408.0	23772.0	24845.0
Gensakis and repos	2496.1	4641.9	7116.9	6922.3	7350.2	6304.0	6811.4	6045.3	8848.4	8333.2	11673.2
Gensakis	2496.1	4641.9	7116.9	6922.3	7350.2	6304.0	6811.4	6045.3	8848.4	8333.2	11673.2
Repos	0	0	0	0	0	0	0	0	0	0	0
Total	28655.7	47721.5	60041.0	71872.8	89571.5	112543.4	115590.9	117603.3	130680.9	127370.5	127191.1

	1995	1996	1997	1998	1999	2000	1980–85	1985–90	1990–95	1995–00
Call loans (total)	38565.2	39852.7	39309.9	33609.6	21893.8	22893.8	4.73%	73.87%	12.16%	-8.13%
Unsecured call loans	29260.5	30503.7	30588.4	23811.5	12547.5	17574.0	n.a.	280.11%	27.47%	-7.99%
Secured call loans	9304.7	9349.0	8721.5	9798.1	9346.3	5319.8	0.75%	34.37%	-4.04%	-8.57%
Bills	9890.7	11060.0	10289.2	25724.3	3116.6	100.0	31.08%	3.28%	-8.41%	-19.80%
CDs	24309.1	32016.1	38553.7	39145.4	35471.5	38504.0	63.15%	19.06%	5.78%	11.68%
CP	10479.0	10844.8	12030.1	18205.8	21809.1	22651.1	n.a.	n.a.	-6.70%	23.23%
TB and FB	38088.9	39435.9	42716.2	48288.5	65870.2	73555.5	-0.44%	28.49%	3.01%	18.62%
TB	12798.9	12897.9	13098.2	15198.5	27519.2	33358.4	n.a.	n.a.	13.66%	32.13%
FB	25290.0	26538.0	29618.0	33090.0	38351.0	40197.1	-0.44%	17.35%	-0.17%	11.79%
Gensakis and repos	11079.8	38723.5	70414.5	76308.2	75611.9	71167.9	17.19%	9.35%	12.53%	108.46%
Gensakis	11079.8	11945.5	13647.0	11516.5	20798.6	22440.5	17.19%	9.35%	12.53%	20.51%
Repos	0	26778.0	56767.5	64791.7	54813.3	48727.4	n.a.	n.a.	n.a.	n.a.
Total	132412.7	171933.0	213313.6	241281.8	223773.1	228872.3	13.31%	28.44%	2.91%	14.57%

Notes: Figures are at the end of each year, as a rule. In line with recent practice, the FB figures represent the outstanding amount issued and not the outstanding amount sold in the market.

Source: Nomura, based on the Bank of Japan's *Financial and Economic Statistics Monthly*, *Principal Figures of Financial Institutions* and transaction statistics for call loans and bills.

321

loans, TBs and FBs (including bond repos) steadily increased, but the balances of secured call loans, bills and CP contracted slightly.

The previously mentioned steepening of the yield curve, which began in the second half of 1988, led to a shift in funds from short-term money-market instruments to long-term bonds. Moreover, the BOJ raised the official discount rate five times within a 15-month period starting in May 1989 in order to stem emerging inflationary pressures. The BOJ's actions prompted a sharp decline in stock and land prices, a downturn in economic activity and significantly slower growth in the money market.

Although the economic environment was not at all conducive to growth in the money market, measures intended to develop the short-term money market even further were steadily implemented. In 1988, the BOJ announced new guidelines on market operations that were designed to involve the full use of its influence over interest rates to ensure the effectiveness of monetary policy. Then, the Money Market Study Group released a report titled 'Japan's Short-Term Money Market and Key Issues' in 1990, which spurred a number of improvements to the money market; in particular, a broader range of maturities of unsecured call loans became available to money-market participants.

In 1991, the system of same-day settlement of trades was replaced by post-trade settlement (whereby funds are settled an unspecified number of days after the trade date). In March 1993, trading in 'tomorrow-next' contracts began. These trades involve an overnight contract that starts with the business day following the trade date. Then, in November 1993, the trading of 'spot-next' contracts began. These contracts involve an overnight agreement starting on the second business day following the trade date. The tomorrow-next and spot-next contracts continue to be key money-market instruments. Moreover, in addition to conventional 1/32-tick trades, 1/100-tick trading was introduced in February 1994. These changes helped the unsecured call loan market to almost triple in size between 1990 and 1995.

In the previously mentioned report 'Japan's Short-Term Money Market and Key Issues', the government anticipated that the core short-term money market instruments would be TBs and FBs. Various measures implemented in 1990 toward this end included the lowering of the minimum issuance unit for TBs and the approval of dealing by money-market brokers (*tanshi* companies). In 1992, tax exemptions were granted to foreign companies and transaction information was disclosed when Japan Bond Trading, a broker's broker, started handling TBs. These developments helped to improve the TB market infrastructure.

The motivation behind enhancing the functionality of the secondary market for TBs was the government's objective of increasing issuances of TBs; it needed to raise funds for the redemption of a large amount of deficit-financing government bonds that were issued starting in 1975 and were scheduled to mature starting in 1989. Consequently, the TB market expanded rapidly. Although the FB market did not grow as quickly as the TB market, it still expanded steadily because FBs are backed by the credit of the government and because non-resident companies were allowed to trade the securities.

In contrast, the outstanding balance of secured call loans, bills and CP decreased in line with a drop in the financing needs of companies as the economy weakened. As the open money market developed, companies avoided bills because of the high stamp tax imposed on the trading of bills as well as their lack of liquidity. In 1991, the BOJ was permitted to use government and corporate bonds for its discount bill open-market operations so that the central bank's adjustment of the money supply would not be hindered. In addition, the market for CP developed steadily. Issuing standards for CP were eased, which led to an increase in the number of companies that could issue CP starting in 1990. Furthermore, CP became recognized as a marketable security under the Securities and Exchange Law in 1993.

THE 1995–2000 PERIOD

As open-market transactions sharply increased, Japan's money market grew in size at an annual rate of 14.2% between 1995 and 2000. The outstanding balance of TBs and FBs continued to rise as a result of an increase in fiscal spending. Meanwhile repo transactions, which began in 1996, quickly became the core of the money market. But the interbank market, which had previously been the main money market, contracted slightly.

The main reason for these changes was the protracted slowdown in the domestic economy. In September 1995, the BOJ lowered the official discount rate to 0.5% in response to the prolonged economic recession and concerns about the stability of Japan's financial system. The cut in the official discount rate notwithstanding, the Japanese economy entered a deflationary spiral and a number of major financial institutions collapsed, both of which prompted additional fiscal and monetary stimulus. The central bank further lowered its target rate for the unsecured overnight call loan rate to 0.25% in September 1998 and then to 0.15% in February 1999. Also in February 1999, the BOJ moved toward quantitative easing by requiring excess reserves of ¥1 tr. and adopted a zero interest rate policy aimed at guiding the overnight call loan rate toward zero.

One result of the policy shift was an outflow of funds from the call market. The bankruptcy of Sanyo Securities in November 1997 led to the first-ever default in the unsecured call loan market and heightened concerns about credit risk. Also contributing to a marked contraction of trading volume in the unsecured call loan market were the bankruptcies of Hokkaido Takushoku Bank and Yamaichi Securities.

In September 1995, as part of measures to stimulate the domestic economy, regulations on the borrowing and lending of bonds were relaxed. After starting up in April 1996, the repo market grew rapidly – the outstanding balance of repos expanded to more than ¥40 tr. within a year – and quickly turned repos into the main instrument in the short-term money market. Factors behind the strong growth included the relative safety of repos and a large outstanding amount of Japanese government bonds (JGBs), the underlying securities that are the collateral for the repos.

The market for TBs and FBs expanded significantly thanks to various measures that developed the infrastructure. These measures included the start of same-day TB market operations in 1995; the issuance of one-year TBs, the introduction of public bidding for FBs and the elimination of withholding taxes for newly issued bills in April 1999; and the start of outright purchases and sale of TBs and FBs in October 1999. These changes helped to create a well-functioning Japanese money market.

The key money markets

THE CALL LOAN MARKET

Call loan transactions are legally defined as 'transactions pertaining to the borrowing and lending of money'. The call loan market in Japan was established just over a century ago. For an extended period of time following the Great Depression of 1927, most call loan transactions were based on collateral; however, amid an increase in the procurement of unsecured funds, such as Euroyen in overseas markets, overseas banks increasingly called for the elimination of collateral for domestic money-market transactions.

In July 1987, unsecured call loan transactions were allowed, resulting in both secured and unsecured call loan transactions in the market. Various measures were introduced to improve the functionality of the domestic unsecured call loan market. These measures included the introduction of a competitive bidding system, the quoting of call loan rates in percentage terms, the introduction of trades settled after the trade date and an increase in the number of available maturities. The call loan market also expanded steadily as a result of an increase in transactions that involved the simultaneous borrowing and lending of funds and a rise in demand for short-term investment options. In 1992, the outstanding balance of unsecured call loans stood at over ¥30 tr., making them the largest money-market instrument in Japan. For several years, the outstanding balance remained at a high level.

Starting in 1997, however, the size of the call market contracted significantly for several reasons. First, the number of unsecured transactions declined because of heightened concerns about credit quality stemming from defaults related to the bankruptcy of Sanyo Securities and several other financial institutions. Second, capital flowed out of the call market and into ordinary deposits and other financial instruments as interest rates dropped to almost zero. By August 1999, the outstanding balance of unsecured call loans dropped more than two-thirds from its peak to below ¥10 tr. During this period, the month-end outstanding balance of secured call loans was often higher than that for unsecured loans. Starting in August 2000, when the BOJ abandoned its zero interest rate policy, the outstanding balance of unsecured call loan transactions began to recover.

Money-market brokers are important participants in the call loan market. These brokers function as dealers for secured call loan transactions and as brokers for unsecured call market transactions. Their commissions on secured transactions are earned from the bid–ask spread. For unsecured transactions, for which the bid is the same as the ask, they charge a separate brokerage commission.

In the call loan market, trust banks, which are the largest providers of the funds, account for about 50% of the total. Specifically, the trust banks invest funds from their investment trust and investor-directed money trust (*tokkin*) accounts in call loans. Other major suppliers of funds in the call loan market include regional banks, financial institution federations and insurance companies.

City banks, which are by far the biggest borrowers in the call loan market, account for about 50% of available funds. During the mid-1990s, their share of borrowing in the call market was about 70%, but it has been declining gradually ever since. Other major call market borrowers include the long-term credit banks, overseas banks and trust banks, through their bank accounts. Recently, the number of direct call loan transactions – those conducted without brokering by money-market brokers – has been increasing as market participants try to reduce commissions.

The key instrument in the call loan market is the overnight unsecured call loan. As the name implies, the maturity of the instrument spans two days, from the trade date to the day following the trade date. The weighted-average rate for the loans is published daily. This product is significant because it is the main product used by financial institutions to adjust their daily funding requirements. In addition, the rate is an indicator of market participants' outlook on interest rates because it reflects the degree to which domestic financial institutions have built up reserves at the BOJ to meet minimum reserve requirements. The BOJ guides the overnight call loan rate to a target level by adjusting the demand and supply of funds based on the degree to which domestic financial institutions have built up reserves at the BOJ. From April 1999 to August 2000, the BOJ's policy was to guide the overnight call loan rate toward zero.

The collateral for secured call loan transactions typically has been JGBs, government-guaranteed bonds and bank debentures. Because only a portion of the face value of these bonds is counted as collateral for secured call loan transactions, the amount that can be raised in the secured call loan market is often significantly lower than the actual value of the securities. Until 1995, the collateral for secured call loan transactions was physically delivered by the money-market brokers. In 1995, however, when the Collateral Center for Short-Term Money Market Transactions was established, the need for physical delivery was eliminated. This development has greatly simplified the administrative work related to processing secured call loan transactions.

THE BILL MARKET

Along with the call market, the market for bills has played a significant role in the development of the interbank market. The bill market was established in May 1971, and the BOJ conducted its first open-market operations using bills in June 1972.

Two types of bills are traded on the market. Original bills are bills issued by non-financial companies and are held by financial institutions; examples include commercial bills, industrial bills and single-name bills. Consolidated bills are bills of exchange that are issued by financial institutions and are backed by financial instruments, such as original bills and government bonds, as collateral. Currently, most transactions in the market involve consolidated bills. In the bill market, a wide variety of maturities are available that range from overnight up to one year. Compared with the call market, the most frequently traded bill contracts are those with longer maturities of between one week and one year.

For many years, the BOJ used a so-called '*tanshi* method' for its bill purchasing/selling operations by going through the *tanshi* companies, or money-market brokers. Similar to the case of secured call loan transactions, *tanshi* companies act as dealers, with transactions conducted using a competitive bidding system. But in April 2000, the BOJ switched to a 'direct method'. The details of the change are outlined in the BOJ's statement of 'Principles Regarding Revision of Bill Purchasing/Selling Operations'. Under the direct method, the BOJ conducts buying and selling operations directly with counterparties, such as financial institutions, securities companies, securities finance companies and the money-market brokers, which maintain current accounts at the head office of the BOJ.

The reason for the introduction of the direct method was to facilitate market operations following the introduction of a real-time gross settlement system. RTGS, a system whereby settlements of fund transfers take place on a continuous, real-time basis for each transaction, is typically used for transactions such as bond trading. The BOJ used to employ two traditional types of bill purchase operation, namely, the 'limit-order system' and the 'auction system'. But for the direct method, these systems were combined into a 'conventional system' in which a discount rate-based auction is conducted. Under the old system, the maturities of instruments used for purchase operations ranged from one week to three months; the instruments were either immediately purchased or the offer to purchase was made during the morning of the business day before the scheduled operation. The new system offers increased flexibility in that specific terms, such as purchase dates and purchase amounts, are determined for each operation. Similar changes have been applied to both purchasing and selling operations.

The outstanding balance of bills began to rise sharply starting in 1985. The main reason for the increase was Norinchukin Bank's and other financial institutions' use of surplus funds that had been accumulating as a result of the BOJ's loose monetary policy to increase their investments in bills. Because of the high revenue stamp tax associated with bill issuance, however, companies gradually reduced the amount of bills they issued. Consequently, a shortage of collateral for the BOJ's bill-purchasing operations developed. To resolve this problem, JGBs and other public sector bonds became acceptable in 1991 as collateral for the central bank's purchasing operations. As a result, the balance of bills purchased by the BOJ ballooned and the central bank's share of total bills purchased rose to more than 90% in 1994, despite an overall decline in demand for bills. The city banks were the major sellers of bills, with their share reaching about 70%, an overwhelmingly high percentage that was on a par with their share in the call loan market.

Trading activity continued to stagnate despite measures to stimulate the bill market. In 1997, however, this trend changed drastically, when the deterioration in the creditworthiness of Japanese financial institutions in overseas markets resulted in the development of a so-called Japan premium. Foreign banks, which were able to procure yen-denominated funds inexpensively through currency swaps, aggressively invested in Japanese bills. Because the BOJ was now able to use repo operations as a new method to supply funds to the money market, the central bank significantly decreased its bill-purchasing operations. Foreign banks then became the largest buyers of bills, and the outstanding balance in the bill market rose sharply because of a surge in arbitrage activity.

Meanwhile, the BOJ aggressively conducted bill-selling operations, thus functioning as a borrower of funds, which were provided by foreign banks. During this period, the BOJ accounted for about 90% of total bills sold. By March 1999, the Japan premium had all but disappeared and purchases of bills by foreign banks had declined rapidly. The lack of buyers resulted in a sharp decrease in the outstanding balance of bills in the market.

THE CD MARKET

CDs, which are negotiable certificates of deposit, have for some time served as a key interest rate benchmark in the open money market. Three-month CD rates are published daily by the Tanshi Association.

The CD market was established in 1979 in response to companies' needs for products with higher interest rates than had previously been available and the strong need of foreign banks to raise funds through the issuance of CDs. At that time, companies viewed CDs as a substitute for time deposits. But the deregulation in 1985 of interest rates for large time deposits that led companies to shift funds from CDs to time deposits resulted in a temporary decline in the issuance of CDs. Nevertheless, in 1986, once the BOJ began using CDs for its market operations and investment trusts were allowed to buy CDs, the marketability of CDs improved.

The appeal of CDs as an investment product also improved because the minimum issuance unit was lowered, restrictions on maturities were relaxed and issuance limitations based on a company's net worth were eliminated. These changes led banks to issue CDs as needed, based on their interest rate outlook. At the same time, foreign banks and dealers aggressively set up arbitrage positions in unsecured call loans and Euroyen deposits.

The outstanding balance of CDs increased steadily, reaching ¥20 tr. in 1989 and ¥30 tr. in 1996. The maximum maturity for CDs was extended from two years to five years as part of deregulatory measures included in economic policies adopted in October 1995. This move increased opportunities for interest rate arbitrage and led to a rise in the amount of CDs issued.

Yet although the share of CDs issued by city banks remains high, trust banks, foreign banks, major regional banks, second-tier regional banks and credit banks have been reducing their amount of CD issuance in recent years. Because CDs are deposits, banks must maintain reserves against them, which means that CD issuance costs are relatively high.

Transactions in the secondary market for CDs are conducted through outright sales and purchases as well as *gensaki* (traded securities). Financial institutions, money-market brokers and securities firms trade CDs in an attempt to profit from interest rate arbitrage opportunities. Rates on CDs are determined based on the interest rates on other financial products, such as other domestic money-market instruments, foreign-currency-denominated deposits and Euroyen deposits.

The administrative procedure for the sale of CDs is complicated. Because the transaction constitutes a designated transfer of a claim under the Civil Code, sellers are required to notify the issuing financial institution with a notarized, date-stamped transfer notification document. Although trading was conducted through money-market brokers in the past, the number of direct transactions has increased in recent years, which mirrors trends in the call market. As a result, CD rates have no longer been published since September 2000 and have lost their significance as a benchmark money-market rate.

The BOJ began to use CDs for its open-market operations in 1986, but then it stopped in 1989 and did not resume using them until 1995. By then, the BOJ had changed the mechanism of its market operations. Under the previous limit-order system, the BOJ aimed for the announcement effect as a mechanism for targeting interest rates. In contrast, under the new auction system, which was in place once it resumed the purchasing and selling of CDs on the market, the BOJ aims to maintain flexibility in adjusting the money supply and providing liquidity. CD market operations are conducted through the money-market brokers, which, as the counterparty to auction participants, borrow funds from the BOJ to buy CDs.

THE COMMERCIAL PAPER MARKET

Commercial paper (CP) is legally defined as a promissory note issued by a corporation. To be eligible to issue CP, a company must be listed on a domestic securities exchange, or if a company is unlisted, it needs to have continuously disclosed the information that is required by the Securities and Exchange Law for three or more years. Non-resident companies that meet these conditions are also eligible to issue CP. In addition, eligible companies must meet the 'domestic CP standard rating' criterion. Specifically, a short-term rating must be provided by two or more designated rating agencies and at least one rating must be at least level 2, which is equivalent to A-2. In addition, except for some companies, a credit guarantee from a financial institution, or a backup line of credit, is required.

In November 1987, the CP market was officially established, thus broadening the financing options available to Japanese corporations. Following the establishment of the CP market, many companies took advantage of arbitrage opportunities between CP rates and rates on large time deposits and helped the CP market to increase in size to about ¥16 tr. by 1990.

With the collapse of the bubble economy, however, the size of the market contracted to about ¥10 tr. after reaching its peak in 1990.[2] Although the issuance of CP by financial institutions was not

---

2 See Chapter 10 for details.

permitted when the market was first established, securities companies were allowed to issue CP starting in 1990, followed by non-banks and leasing companies in 1993 and life and casualty insurance companies in 1994.

In 1993, when CP was legally recognized as a marketable security under the Securities and Exchange Law, the necessary legal infrastructure for the financial instrument was finally created. The government also permitted a broader range of CP maturities. CP with maturities shorter than two weeks were allowed in 1995, and CP with maturities of up to one year were permitted in 1996. Furthermore, the eligibility standards for CP issuance and issuance limits were relaxed, and in May 1997, restrictions on the use of proceeds from the issuance of CP by non-banks were lifted. Before these restrictions were lifted, non-banks could not use CP to finance their lending activities. In April 1998, issuers were permitted to sell CP directly to institutional investors, and during the same year, banks were granted permission to issue CP. These deregulatory moves contributed to a gradual expansion of CP trading volume starting in 1997; by 1999, it had reached around ¥20 tr.

CP is issued as promissory notes with a face value of ¥100 m or more and maturities of less than one year. The instruments are sold to intermediaries at a discount. Discount rates incorporate various costs, such as fees paid for backup credit lines and revenue stamp tax expenses. Intermediaries include financial institutions and securities companies, which have dealer contracts with the CP issuers. CP is sold to investment trusts and other institutional investors as well as to money-market brokers, but it cannot be sold to individual investors. CP is often used with other money-market instruments for interest rate arbitrage transactions, whereas investment trusts and corporations use the product for short-term *gensaki* investments.

Although the BOJ used CP for open-market operations starting in 1989 as a new means of implementing monetary policy, it rarely did so after August 1990. The central bank then resumed CP operations in 1995, but by then, the mechanics associated with these operations had been revised several times. Under the old system, only money-market brokers were eligible to participate in CP open-market operations, but under the current system, financial institutions, securities companies and other investors are also allowed to participate. The BOJ conducts an auction in which participants can place bids on a yield basis or put in limit orders based on yield. CP open-market operations are conducted using only CP issues that have been approved by the BOJ, and all CP sold must be repurchased on a specified date within three months.

As part of a review to improve the functioning of the CP settlement system, a study group under the auspices of the Ministry of Justice and the Ministry of Finance issued a report in 2000 on the creation of a paperless book-entry system for CP and the shortening of the settlement period for CP trades. A law on book-entry settlement for short-term corporate bonds was passed in 2001, and took effect in 2002. Under this law, CP is defined as 'short-term corporate bonds', thereby allowing CP to be settled in a paperless manner, using account transfers through clearing institutions.

THE FB and TB MARKET

FBs are issued to raise funds to finance temporary shortfalls in the national Treasury or special accounts. TBs are a type of refinancing bond issued based on the Debt Consolidation Fund Special Account Law. These securities are issued to ensure the smooth repayment of government bonds as well as a means to secure necessary funds to refinance government debt.

Initially, there were three types of FBs. Treasury FBs were issued in accordance with the Public Finance Law to cover temporary funding shortages resulting from time lags between the receipt of national-Treasury revenues, including tax revenues and revenues from bond issuance, and the payment of fiscal expenditures. Food FBs were issued based on the Foodstuff Control Special Accounting Law to secure funds for the purchase of agricultural products in accordance with the national food control system. Finally, foreign exchange fund FBs were issued based on the Foreign Exchange Fund Special Accounting Law to procure temporary funds for currency market intervention.

In March 1999, these securities were combined and issued as short-term government securities. FBs and TBs have become core short-term money-market instruments, because of such attractive characteristics as low credit risk, a large issuance amount and low price volatility. Another advantage was that FBs and TBs with less than one year remaining to maturity were exempt from securities transaction taxes.[3]

Starting in 1956, FBs were issued using a fixed-price subscription system under which the bills were issued at a discount. If bids

3 This tax, however, has since been eliminated.

were insufficient to cover the auctioned amount, the BOJ purchased any remaining FBs. Because the actual discount rates were set lower than money-market rates, the BOJ effectively purchased almost all the bills, even though the auctions were technically supposed to be public offerings.

In May 1981, the BOJ began FB *gensaki* market operations, whereby the central bank sold FB holdings with RP agreements as a means to absorb excess funds in the market. Demand was very strong for these FB *gensaki* because the operations were conducted on market interest rates, not the lower rates at which the initial offerings were conducted. The FBs purchased through the market operations were occasionally resold by successful bidders to their customers. Consequently, a secondary market for FBs was established. The market operations were conducted directly with money-market brokers, which, in turn, notified financial institutions and securities companies of the details of the operations. To participate in the market operations, financial institutions must be participants in the call loan market and be members of the BOJ's book-entry system for government bonds; they must also submit written consent to the BOJ, indicating that they agree to resale restrictions. Financial institutions that purchased FBs from money-market brokers either held the securities or resold them in *gensaki* transactions to customers, such as institutional investors. Despite robust trading activity, the outstanding balance of FBs remained in the range of ¥2–5 tr. and the growth of the secondary market was limited because the supply of FBs to the secondary market depended on sales by the BOJ.

The situation greatly improved, however, with the introduction of a public auction system for FB offerings in March 1999. As mentioned earlier, the three types of FBs were integrated into a single short-term government security. The issuance of these securities was, in principle, conducted according to a competitive-bid auction system. Eligible participants were those financial institutions that were members of the BOJ's book-entry system and money-market brokers. The BOJ bought FBs if bids were insufficient to cover the total amount auctioned and when unexpected demand for government financing arose. Furthermore, the bank purchased FBs for trading with foreign central banks when needed. The initial maturity was 13 weeks, but 2- and 3-month FBs have been added.

In 1986, TBs were issued under a public auction system, as part of a series of measures aimed at coping with a large amount of maturing government bonds. Eligible participants were government bond-underwriting syndicate members who were members of the BOJ's book-entry system and licensed bond dealers. Although only 6-month TBs were issued at first, 3-month TBs were added in 1989 and 1-year TBs were added in 1999. When TBs were first issued, 18% of the redemption profit was withheld as taxes at the time of purchase. Certain entities, however, were granted tax breaks. Specifically, withholding taxes were immediately refunded for foreign central banks. In addition, for other non-Japanese entities, the last holder of a TB issue was allowed either to deduct the taxed amount from full-year corporate taxes or to obtain a refund irrespective of the period the company held the securities. In April 1992, foreign companies were permitted to receive a full refund at maturity under certain conditions. Therefore, profits on TB transactions were effectively tax-free for foreign companies. Thanks in part to these tax benefits, foreign central banks and other overseas investors with access to low-cost yen funds have long been major buyers of TBs in the secondary market.

The TB and FB markets have grown rapidly in line with a rise in fiscal expenditures and an increase in government bond redemption, and the amount of issuance is expected to continue to expand in the future. Therefore, improvements in the infrastructure for these markets are necessary to absorb the projected excess supply of these securities. In March 1999, in conjunction with the introduction of 1-year TBs and the issuance of FBs through a public auction system, the withholding tax system was changed. TBs and FBs issued after April 1999 have not been subject to withholding taxes at the time of issuance. In addition, for non-residents and foreign corporations, the tax was eliminated on the redemption profit. Moreover, to improve the BOJ's ability to flexibly conduct open-market operations, regulations were revised to allow the central bank to use TBs and FBs. Specifically, regulations governing the central bank's FB *gensaki* selling operations, which are used to absorb funds, and TB *gensaki* purchasing operations, which are used to supply funds, were integrated into one set of regulations covering 'conditional purchases and sales of short-term government securities'. Furthermore, in October 1999, the BOJ started using outright sales and purchases of short-term government bonds in its market operations.

To participate in the public auction of TBs and FBs, financial institutions must submit a document to the Ministry of Finance that delineates their obligations pertaining to the resale of TBs and FBs. For example, auction participants must hold purchased TBs and FBs as book-entry securities for the entire holding period, even after the bonds are resold (book-entry securities are JGBs held in book-entry form within a system established by the BOJ; all trades are settled within this structure). In addition, auction participants must agree to resell securities only to other auction participants and institutional investors that are familiar with trends in the financial and capital markets, such as publicly traded corporations or the equivalent. They are not, however, allowed to resell to individuals or corporations that are, in essence, similar to individuals. Another condition is that resales or pledges of securities must be made to the BOJ or to financial institutions that are allowed to participate in auctions. As part of the debate concerning possible changes to TB and FB regulations, one of the key areas of focus has been the obligation to submit the aforementioned document to the Ministry of Finance, because this obligation prevents the trading of TBs and FBs between overseas investors. As such, investment in TBs and FBs by overseas investors has been rather limited, thus prompting demands for further deregulation of the constraints on the resale of TBs and FBs in the secondary market.

THE MARKETS FOR *GENSAKI* AND REPOS

Gensaki and RPs, or repos, are, in essence, both financial transactions that are collateralized with securities. In addition, both transactions have the same economic impact. *Gensaki*, however, are traded securities, whereas repos are transactions involving the borrowing and lending of bonds collateralized with cash. Repos are typically used either as a means for raising funds or as short-term investments. In addition, repos are sometimes used as securities to cover short positions in fixed-income securities, which is similar to the function of reverse repos in overseas markets.

A *gensaki* transaction is the purchase or sale of a bond with the attendant condition that the bond is either repurchased or resold at a predetermined price within a predetermined period no later than one year. The *gensaki* market was established in 1949, in the wake of World War II, when bond issuance recommenced. *Gensaki* trading emerged as a result of a lack of a well-developed secondary market and the funding needs of Japanese securities companies. In 1965, when the Japanese government began to issue bonds, the scope of the *gensaki* market expanded. In March 1976, the Ministry of Finance, through the issuance of a circular notice (*tsûtatsu*), clarified the rules associated with *gensaki* transactions, thus establishing the foundation for these transactions.

At that time, however, several issues relating to the transactions remained unresolved. A key concern was the existence of a securities transaction tax, which made the effective cost of raising funds with *gensaki* transactions relatively high. Indeed, because of the tax, most *gensaki* transactions involved CDs, CP, TBs and FBs, which were not taxed, and very few *gensaki* transactions were based on interest-bearing government bonds as a means to raise capital. In addition, the development of the *gensaki* market was hindered by a requirement that when securities companies enter into a *gensaki* purchase agreement with a client, they must enter into a *gensaki* sale agreement with another client under the same terms and conditions except for the rate. This regulation, which was intended to prevent securities companies from engaging in synthetic lending activities, was effectively eliminated in December 1995, however, when securities companies were allowed to enter into *gensaki* purchase agreements without a corresponding *gensaki* sale agreement.

Gensaki operations include bond *gensaki* operations by the BOJ to adjust the supply of funds in the market and Trust Fund *gensaki* transactions used by the MOF to raise funds for the Trust Fund Bureau. Terms for bond *gensaki* operations are applied within two months, and Trust Fund Bureau *gensaki* agreements generally have maturities of two to three months. Currently, *gensaki* transactions are a key tool used by the BOJ to adjust the money supply. Previously, the Trust Fund Bureau used *gensaki* agreements as a vehicle for investing excess funds. Recently, however, the Trust Fund Bureau has been using mainly reverse *gensaki* transactions (now called 'fiscal investment fund *gensakis*'), which are essentially agreements to sell securities as a means of raising funds.

In March 1999, the securities transaction tax was eliminated, thus removing the cost disadvantage associated with *gensaki* transactions. In addition, a new *gensaki* system was implemented in April 2001. Under the new system, which is similar to the one for RP agreements in overseas markets, haircuts, margin calls and the substitution of the securities underlying a *gensaki* agreement are allowed. The current *gensaki* system is due to be eliminated and a full transition to the new system is planned.

Japanese repos are quite different from their counterparts in overseas markets. Japanese repos entail the borrowing and lending of bonds, collateralized with cash. Therefore, two payments are made in these transactions, namely, the interest on cash used as collateral and a fee for lending the bonds. The net payment is referred to as the repo rate, which is the base rate used for most repo transactions.

Repurchase agreement transactions were first introduced in April 1996. Until then, all bond lending and borrowing transactions were unsecured; however, heightened concerns over the risks associated with unsecured transactions and increased demand for funding mechanisms for interest-bearing government bonds led to changes in RP agreements that enabled the even exchange of cash collateral and the market value of the bonds. Two restrictions were eliminated – one that capped the interest rate on collateral to 1 percentage point below the secured call loan rate and another that required collateral of at least 105% of the market value of the bonds. The repo market has a degree of safety unlike that of other money-market instruments because of various systems and conditions, including the use of delivery-versus-payment (DVP) settlement (involving the simultaneous exchange of securities and cash), hair-cuts, marking to market and close-out netting. Close-out netting provisions allow counterparties to offset assets and liabilities in the case of the default of one of the counterparties.

At the time repo agreements were first permitted in 1996, the outstanding balance of government bonds was ¥300 tr. Given the minimal credit risk and high liquidity of government bonds, the repo market expanded rapidly; by 1997, it exceeded the call loan market in size and became Japan's largest money market. In November 1997, the BOJ began conducting repo market operations to provide liquidity. The number of participants in the repo market has been limited, however, mainly because transactions require the use of DVP, collateral must be carefully monitored and the processing of payments based on two rates is complex.

The adoption of a new system of *gensaki* agreements, as ordinary transactions similar to repos in overseas markets in terms of structure and accounting treatment, is likely to broaden investor participation in the money market.

The outlook for Japan's money markets

Under the RTGS system to which the BOJ changed in early 2001, significantly larger amounts of daily liquidity are required compared with under the previous designated-time settlement. The related increases in required funds and frequency of fund transactions are likely to stimulate money-market activity. Also, for the foreseeable future, the government will probably continue to issue and redeem considerable amounts of government bonds, which makes an increase in the issuance of TBs and FBs and the related growth in *gensaki* and repo transactions almost certain.

Moreover, the BOJ has significantly increased the money supply and reinstated its zero interest rate policy in an effort to resuscitate the ailing economy and stave off deflation. This environment bodes well for the continued expansion of the domestic money market. One key issue will be the extent to which qualitative improvements can be made to foster this growth. Pressing tasks include opening the market wider to the many global participants and continuing to strengthen the market's infrastructure through structural changes and tax reforms. Other desirable developments would be the introduction of electronic trading – which would broaden the transaction choices available to market participants and improve the efficiency of trading – and improvements in settlement, such as a shift to electronic settlement and a shortening of settlement periods. Such changes could significantly transform Japan's money market over the next few years.

CHAPTER 15 · The bond market

This chapter takes a look at Japan's bond market, in particular, the characteristics of the market's structure and how bonds are priced in the market. The focus is primarily on straight coupon bonds, with some discussion of the futures, options and yen–yen swap markets because of their increasing interrelation with the bond market. (Convertibles, bonds with warrants and other equity-linked debt securities are addressed in Chapter 16. Some other classes of securities that are traded by somewhat different market participants than those that trade other types of fixed-income securities include Treasury and financing bills, zero-coupon bank debentures and other money-market securities, which are covered in Chapter 14, and asset-backed securities, which are discussed in Chapter 18.)

Changes in the bond market

Since the second half of the 1980s, Japan's bond market has undergone profound changes. In conjunction with the globalization of markets, Japan's bond-trading system has moved closer in line with international standards. In addition, two prolonged periods during which the nation's monetary policy was loosened have revealed distortions in the bond market – and have promoted changes necessary to fix them. The last 15 or so years of dramatic changes in Japan's bond market can be broken down into five phases.

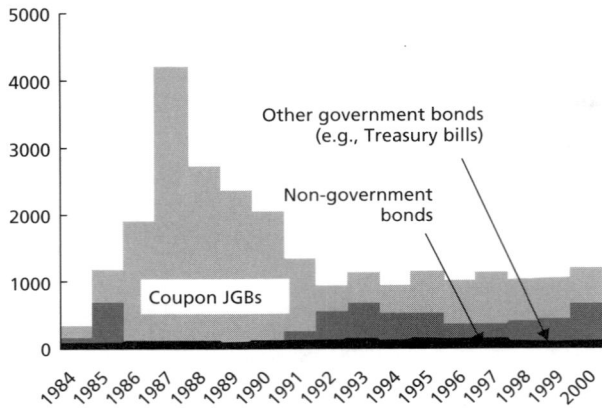

15.1 Over-the-counter trading in bonds (excluding *gensaki* transactions; ¥ tr.). Source: Nomura, based on data from the Japan Securities Dealers Association.

1985–87: EXPLOSIVE GROWTH DRIVEN BY BANK DEALERS

A major turning point that sparked the growth of Japan's bond market came in June 1984, when banking institutions were partially authorized to deal in public bonds for the first time ever. The market further expanded when trading in futures on long-term Japanese government bonds (JGBs) started up in October 1985, thereby bringing in a broader range of participants into the bond market. Throughout several major easing cycles, the Bank of Japan (BOJ) brought long-term rates down to unprecedented levels, and in what could be termed a speculative, dealer-driven market, buying in the market begat further buying (Fig. 15.1).

In April 1987, monthly turnover of coupon JGBs on the over-the-counter (OTC) market topped ¥950 tr., and the yield (simple yield) on the then-benchmark No. 89 JGB fell to 2.55%, which was nearly on a par with the discount rate of 2.5% at the time. But bond prices tumbled as expectations for further easing by the BOJ diminished after the weakening yen gave way to an improved outlook for the economy. Another factor that helped to prick the bubble in the bond market was related to supply and demand, namely, the variation in JGB settlement dates. The bond market contracted sharply. By September 1987, monthly turnover of the OTC bond market had shrunk more than 85% from the April peak to ¥120 tr. In early October 1987, the yield on the No. 89 JGB climbed as high as 6.40% (simple yield), an event that heralded the end of the unprecedented dealer-driven market.

Fuelled by funds with nowhere else to go, the bond market during these years attracted many traders who speculated by buying and selling the No. 89 benchmark JGB. Investor confidence in the bond market was badly shaken, and the market fell into a crisis when Tateho Chemical Industry's massive trading losses in JGB futures came to light on 2 September 1987 (in what is now referred to as the 'Tateho shock'). For better or worse, the bond market recovered, thanks to inflows of funds from the equity market in the wake of Black Monday, but the image of a dealer-driven bond market still lingered. Thereafter, pricing in the market gradually became more rational by reflecting supply and demand among bond investors rather than the dealers.

1988–89: A TOUGH MARKET CHARACTERIZED BY MASSIVE REDEMPTIONS

As a measure to improve the nation's fiscal deficit, the government decided to reduce issuances of deficit-financing bonds starting in fiscal 1980 and then eventually stopped issuing them in fiscal 1990. In the process, the government also reduced the amount of JGBs it issued. Of the amount of long-term (10-year) and ultra-long-term (20-year) JGBs issued in fiscal 1989, public subscriptions (excluding the amount bought by the Trust Fund Bureau, the postal savings system and the BOJ) totalled less than ¥9 tr. Moreover, the government started redeeming large amounts of high-coupon (7–8%) bonds in 1988, thus forcing bond investors to restructure their portfolios. Although long-term rates did manage to rise at one point from very low levels, they still hovered around 5%, making for a difficult environment for bond investors.

Given such circumstances, investors sought to replace their maturing bonds with higher-coupon bonds. The preference for a high current yield was also spurred by special accounting rules for banks at the time, one that excluded capital gains from net operating income and another that allowed life insurance companies to use only interest/dividend income to pay dividends to policy-holders. As a result of the prevailing preference for high-coupon bonds, low-coupon bonds (3.0–4.5%) issued in the dealer-driven market in 1987 were undervalued and, eventually, were used regularly for delivering on futures contracts. At the same time, because medium-term bonds with high coupon rates had relatively low yields, a distorted yield curve resulted.

By 1989, expectations of a tightening credit supply led to a gradual rise in short-term rates as well as an increase in yields on short- and medium-term bonds. When the BOJ raised the official discount rate (ODR) in its first round of tightening around 31 May, the yield curve was almost flat and short- and medium-term bonds did not appear overvalued. By the end of the year, the central bank raised the ODR another three times and generated further upward pressure on short- and medium-term yields. But yields on long-term bonds did not rise as much because of strong demand for the bonds. The resulting inverted yield curve – reflecting the distorted supply-and-demand balance in the bond market – stayed that way for an extended period.

1990–92: HIGH INTEREST RATES AND REDUCED DISTORTIONS

Long-term rates rose sharply in 1990 because of strong expectations of higher interest rates since the beginning of the year, a weakening yen and political uncertainty. To make matters worse, the BOJ raised the ODR by a combined 175 basis points (bps) in March and August to 6%. In part because of worsening tensions in the Middle East and banks' difficulties meeting capital adequacy requirements established by the Bank for International Settlements (BIS), the yield on the benchmark No. 119 JGB rose to a record high of 8.735% (about 8% on a compounded basis) on 26 September, shortly before the earnings season for companies' first-half results. Although short-term rates remained high thereafter, based on fears of a resurgence of inflation, long-term rates began to edge downward in anticipation of an economic slowdown. Short-term rates also began to fall when the BOJ started on its first round of rate cuts in mid-1991. Finally, a third rate cut by the end of the year more or less eliminated the inversion of the yield curve.

Because of rising interest rates, most long-term bonds were trading below par. And in part because banks adopted new accounting standards, investors no longer so strongly preferred current yield (high coupons) or disliked low-coupon bonds. Most bond investors began basing their investments on compound yield rather than simple yield, which had been the favoured criterion until then. Moreover, the futures market increasingly affected bond prices; for instance, deliverable bonds (with terms to maturity of seven to 11 years) were priced such that the net basis was zero. In these ways, the distortions in the bond market were gradually corrected. Also, during these years, investors began to distinguish between the creditworthiness of issuers of coupon bank debentures, which led to differences in the prices of the bonds.

1993–98: BACK TO ULTRA-LOW INTEREST RATES

The BOJ lowered the ODR to 1.75% in September 1993, a rate that was even lower than at any time from 1987 to 1989, a period when monetary policy was very loose. But the market did not overheat as it did during the dealer-driven market from 1985 to 1987. Long-term rates gradually drifted downward as the economic conditions and the supply and demand balance in the market were discounted. Although long-term rates rose in early 1994, in response to the Trust Fund Bureau's start of outright JGB selling operations, and again in the first half of 1996, on expectations of an improvement in the economy, the basic trend remained downward, mainly because of the so-called Heisei recession.

The BOJ then cut the ODR to an unprecedented 0.5% in September 1995, when the yen strengthened to a rate of less than ¥80 per dollar and contributed to a decline in the 10-year JGB yield to below 3%. Several years later, in the wake of Russia's debt crisis in 1998, the BOJ lowered its target unsecured overnight call rate to 0.25% (but left the ODR unchanged), and the 10-year JGB yield fell below 0.8%. Although different in character from the market in 1987, when trading was concentrated in a few issues, the 1993–98 bond market still constituted a bubble.

1999–2000: LARGE VOLUME OF JGB ISSUANCES

The bond market went through a major correction between late 1998 and early 1999, as the government stepped up its issuances of JGBs to help finance the budgets in the following years and as the Trust Fund Bureau ended its regular, outright purchases of JGBs. In a sharp bear steepening of the yield curve, the yield on the 10-year JGB rose to around 2.5%. The market was so weak at one point that it was commonly thought there would be no buyers of long-term bonds.

Fearing the negative impact that a rise in long-term rates would have on the economy, in February 1999, the BOJ adopted a zero interest rate policy, in which the central bank guided the unsecured overnight call rate as low as possible. Long-term rates began to settle down again around mid-1999, as the BOJ's new policy gradually started to have an impact. In 2000, the yield on the 10-year JGB moved within a tight range of less than 40 bps. In August 2000, the BOJ then abandoned its zero interest rate policy and raised its target unsecured overnight call rate to 0.25%. But the central bank faced

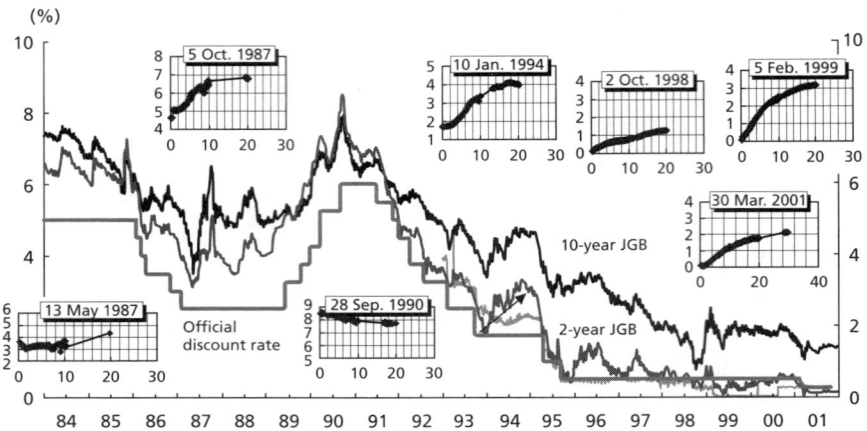

15.2 Official discount rate and government bond yields, 1984–2001.
Notes: The yields are the par yields (yield curves for coupon rates, assuming par bond values at different maturities) for each maturity.
Source: Nomura.

pressures in early 2001 to ease monetary policy again, because of the stock market's decline and concerns about an economic slow-down. On 19 March, the central bank switched its monetary policy to an entirely new direction by pursuing quantitative easing, whereby its focus became the level of banks' current account balances at the BOJ rather than interest rates (Fig. 15.2).

The government issued substantially more JGBs in this period to make up for dwindling tax revenues and to finance emergency economic packages and measures to shore up the financial system. The amount of public subscriptions of JGBs (based on initial budgets) rose from slightly more than ¥37 tr. in fiscal 1998 to nearly ¥90 tr. in fiscal 2001. The amount of JGBs outstanding increased to about ¥350 tr. by the end of 2000, putting Japan's JGB market on a par with the US Treasury market in terms of size. It is only a matter of time before Japan's market overtakes the US market. But Japan has lost its sterling credit rating – Moody's Investors Service (Moody's), for instance, downgraded its rating on Japan's sovereign debt in late 1998. The amount of newly issued and outstanding JGBs continues to grow; public subscriptions of new JGB issues could soon exceed ¥100 tr. a year.

The JGB market infrastructure was also expanded through a series of measures during this period. Non-resident investors were no longer subject to a withholding tax in September 1999, and a real-time gross settlement system was adopted in January 2001. JGBs with a broader range of maturities were also offered, including 5- and 30-year bonds (fixed coupon) and 15-year bonds (with a floating rate based on the 10-year JGB yield). In addition, benchmark JGBs – which were at the centre of the dealer-driven market from 1985 to 1987 – lost their significance, and the Trust Fund Bureau halted its JGB purchases in fiscal 2001 (these purchases had contributed to volatility in the market a number of times). Although some argue that Japan's bond market is still developing, by a number of measures, it is surely becoming a market on a par with global standards.

THE SECONDARY MARKET

With the goal of internationalizing the yen, the Japanese government initiated efforts in the mid-1980s to make the structure of Japan's bond market similar to that of Europe and the US. The major moves included the introduction of derivatives trading, diversification of maturities and types of JGBs and other bonds, and the development of the settlement system and other aspects of the market infrastructure (Table 15.1).

Overview of the bond market

TYPES OF BONDS AND THE SCALE OF THE MARKET

Straight coupon bonds (i.e., not asset-backed or equity-linked securities) publicly issued in Japan include government bonds, publicly offered municipal bonds, government-guaranteed bonds, coupon bank debentures, straight corporate bonds and yen-denominated foreign bonds (samurai bonds).[1] Although Euroyen bonds are technically not domestic bonds, they are traded in more or less the same manner as samurai bonds. Most bonds issued by public sector corporations and local municipalities are not publicly offered; still, they are traded on a secondary market. In fact, the secondary market for privately placed municipal bonds (munis) should not be ignored because it is larger than the one for publicly offered bonds. This chapter, however, focuses only on the market for publicly offered bonds because of the transparency of this particular market.

---

1 Issuances of FILP agency bonds got fully under way in fiscal 2001.

Table 15.1 Major changes in Japan's bond markets

Date	Key event
June 1984	Banks start dealing JGBs
Jan. 1985	Trading of futures on long-term JGBs begins
Feb. 1986	Market auctions on Treasury bills begin
July 1986	Increase in number of settlements per month from two (20th and end of the month) to three (10th, 20th and end of the month)
Oct. 1986	Syndicate underwriting of 20-year coupon JGBs begins
Aug. 1987	Increase in number of settlements per month to six (5th, 10th, 15th, 20th, 25th and end of the month)
Apr. 1988	Introduction of book-entry system for JGBs and uniform withholding tax on interest income for individuals
Apr. 1989	System of tax-exempt savings limited to seniors; trading of OTC bond options allowed
May 1989	Short-sale rules for bonds revised; margin trading for bonds begins
May 1990	BOJ-NET (the BOJ's online transaction processing service) expanded to include JGB transactions
Oct. 1990	T + 3 rolling settlement of Treasury bills begins
Apr. 1992	Foreign institutional investors exempted from the tax on original issue discount for Treasury bills
Feb. 1994	Market auctions on 6-year JGBs begin
Apr. 1994	BOJ-NET expanded to include DVP (delivery-versus-payment) settlement of JGB transactions
Apr. 1996	Cash-secured margin trading for bonds effectively begins
Sep. 1996	T + 7 rolling settlement of JGBs begins
Apr. 1997	T + 3 rolling settlement of JGBs begins
Dec. 1997	JB Net (online settlement system for corporate bonds) starts up
Jan. 1999	Abolition of JGB call provisions
Mar. 1999	Abolition of securities transaction tax
Apr. 1994	One-year Treasury bills introduced; market auctions on financing bills begin (for 13-week bills, as a rule); Treasury bills and financing bills exempted from withholding taxes at the time of issue
Sep. 1999	Market auctions on 30-year JGBs begin; interest income becomes tax-exempt for non-residents
Feb. 2000	Market auctions for 5-year coupon JGBs begin
June 2000	Market auctions for 15-year floating-rate JGBs begin
Nov. 2000	Market auctions for 3-year zero-coupon JGBs begin (5-year zero-coupon JGBs no longer exist)
Jan. 2001	Real-time gross settlement system for JGBs introduced
Mar. 2001	Introduction of so-called reopening method (for calculating accrued interest for JGBs)
Apr. 2001	Expanded tax exemptions for interest income for non-residents; US- and European-style repo transactions introduced as a result of changes to the system of *gensaki* transactions

Source: Nomura.

Table 15.2 shows the outstanding amounts of the various types of bonds available in Japan. The proportion of JGBs to the total has become very high, in part because of the government's pump-priming fiscal policy. The 10-year JGBs are a core issue in the bond market, particularly in the secondary market. The maturities for coupon JGBs include 2 years, 4 years, 5 years, 6 years, 10 years, 20 years and 30 years.[2] A 15-year floating-rate JGB was introduced in fiscal 2000 to broaden the available types of bonds; the interest payment on the bond is based on the yield of the most recently issued 10-year JGB.

A total of 28 local public entities were approved to publicly offer municipal bonds at the end of 2000. Most of these municipal bonds had maturities of 10 years, but 5-year issues were introduced in fiscal 2000. Government-guaranteed bonds are issued by public sector corporations and are backed by the national government. Most government-guaranteed bonds also have maturities of 10 years; recently, however, the Japan Finance Corporation for Small Business started offering 5- and 6-year bonds and the Deposit Insurance Corporation 4-year bonds. In fiscal 2001, Fiscal Investment and Loan Programme (FILP) agencies, or public sector corporations that participate in the government's credit programme, started publicly issuing bonds that are not backed by the government (see Chapter 9 for details).

Coupon bank debentures, which are particular to Japan, are issued by seven specific financial institutions – Industrial Bank of Japan, Shoko Chukin Bank, Norinchukin Bank, Shinsei Bank (the former Long-Term Credit Bank of Japan), Aozora Bank (the former Nippon Credit Bank), Shinkin Central Bank and Bank of Tokyo-Mitsubishi. Most of these bank debentures have maturities of five years; some of the banks issue 1-, 2-, and 3-year debentures.[3]

MARKET PARTICIPANTS

Major participants in the secondary market other than bond dealers include city banks (including long-term credit banks), regional banks, trust banks, agricultural financial institutions, insurance companies (life and property/casualty), investment trusts, foreign investors and the postal savings/postal life insurance system (Fig. 15.3). Some of the city banks and trust banks (through their bank

2 Four- and 6-year JGBs were no longer issued after fiscal 2001.
3 New bank debentures have not been issued since October 1999, when banks became allowed to issue straight and subordinated bonds.

Table 15.2 New issuances, outstanding amounts and trading value of bonds (¥tr.)

	Outstanding amount	New issuance	Trading value	Par value included in NOMURA-BPI	
Public bonds (publicly offered)	400	113	2407		
JGBs	359	106	2364		
Public subscriptions	257	99	2364		
15-, 20-, 30-year JGBs	27	5	52		
10-year JGBs	130	17	976		
6-year JGBs	21	4		194	65.8%
5-year JGBs	10	10	247		
2- and 4-year JGBs	37	18			
Medium-term zero coupon	1	0	1		
Treasury bills	29	44	1088		
Purchases by Trust Fund Bureau, BOJ, others	102	7			
Publicly offered munis	16	2	11	15	5.1%
Gov't-guaranteed bonds	25	5	32	22	7.6%
Corporate bonds	63	9			
Straight bonds	50	8		39	13.2%
Electric power bonds	16	2	13		
Other straight bonds	32	6	26		
NTT, JR, JT bonds	3	0			
Asset-backed securities	1	1	0		
Convertible bonds	12	0	3		
Bank debentures	50	21			
Discount	12	12	2		
Coupon	38	9	37	21	7.3%
Non-resident bonds (yen-denominated)	8	3			
Samurai bonds	8	2	5	3	1.1%
Asset-backed securities	0	0			
Privately placed munis (*1)	36	4	30		
Special bonds	46	3			
of which, public subscriptions	11	2	3		
Privately placed corporates	4	0			
Total	607	152	2527	294	100.0%
(Ref.) Financing bills	40	188	1556		

Source: Nomura, based on data from the Japan Securities Dealers Association.

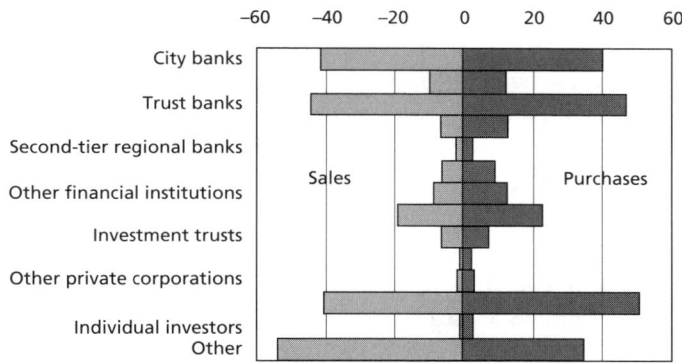

15.3 Trading value of public and corporate bonds by investor categories (excluding Treasury and financing bills; ¥ tr.).
Note: 'Other' includes the postal savings/postal life insurance system.
Source: as Fig. 15.1.

accounts) hold bonds in their investment portfolios as a substitute for lending, and the net amount of their bond purchases and sales changes in accordance with changes in interest rates and the growth in their lending. These financial institutions typically buy and sell bonds with short durations, whereas trust banks (through their trust accounts, which hold pension assets) and insurance companies – both of which have liabilities with long durations – usually buy and sell bonds with long and super-long maturities. The agricultural financial institutions, which are a cross between banks and insurance companies, and the postal savings/postal life insurance system have had a major impact on Japan's bond market. Given the huge amount of assets they manage, they tend to take on significant duration risk. They were major buyers in the market during the time the BOJ instituted a zero interest rate policy. In addition, foreign investors – who often use different bond valuation metrics than Japanese investors do – have been increasing their share of the bond market, and their influence, each year.

TRADING, SETTLEMENT AND TAXES

Bonds in Japan are typically traded on a simple-yield basis; dealers rarely provide the market prices of bonds. The relationship between the simple yield (the simple yield to maturity) and the market price is as follows:

$$\text{Simple yield} = \frac{[\text{coupon rate} + (100 - \text{price})/\text{term to maturity}]}{\text{price}}$$

Compared with the yields given by the compound interest method used for US Treasuries and the ISMA (International Securities Market Association) compound interest method used for Eurobonds, the simple yield is generally higher when the bond is trading below par and lower when the bond is trading above par. Japanese dealers have long been using simple yield because it is simpler to calculate and coincides with the rate of return shown on the books. Although it is debatable whether the simple yield is an appropriate basis for making bond investment decisions, trading based on this yield has had an important impact on Japan's bond market. Lately, most market participants have been using the compound interest method that is used in the US as a basis for their bond investment decisions, thereby contributing to more rational pricing of bonds and the elimination of market distortions. The significance of simple yield as a metric for investment decisions has also been waning because of the widespread trading of non-JGBs based on the yields of JGBs with different maturities and on the spreads versus swap rates.

Bonds are registered based on the Corporate Bond Registration Law and the Law Concerning Government Bonds, and changes in the registered owner are handled through the registration agents (the BOJ in the case of JGBs). But this administrative task has become much more complicated with the expansion of the secondary market. A book-entry system for JGBs was introduced in 1980, and since then a sharply increasing proportion of JGB trades has been settled using the book-entry system because of tax considerations. In December 1997, Japan Bond Settlement Network started up JB Net, an online system designed to streamline the settlement of corporate bond transactions while keeping the registration system intact.

TAXES ON BOND TRADING

Interest income from bonds is subject to a withholding tax of 20% (15% in income tax and 5% in local taxes), except in the case of designated financial institutions and other entities that are exempt from withholding taxes. Non-resident investors are exempt from local taxes, and those in countries that have a bilateral tax treaty with Japan benefit from lower or no withholding taxes.

Even so, the withholding tax on bond income hinders secondary market transactions. Most non-resident investors simplify the settlement of their bond trades by holding their bonds in street name (using the name of a designated Japanese financial institution and delivering request forms for a change in registered name after a trade). In an effort to tackle this problem, non-residents' book-entry holdings became exempt from interest-income taxes in September 1999, as part of a package of tax reforms for fiscal 1999.[4] These tax reforms also resulted in the abolition of a securities transaction tax that had applied to bond transactions.

LISTING OF BONDS ON THE STOCK EXCHANGE AND THE JAPAN SECURITIES DEALERS' ASSOCIATION'S (JSDA) BOND QUOTES

Two-, 5-, 10-, 20- and 30-year JGBs are listed on the Tokyo, Osaka and Nagoya stock exchanges (2-year bonds issued starting in April 2000 are listed). Many other bonds have been listed to provide indications of fair market price. Some trading in samurai bonds has been required to take place on exchanges, but this requirement was abolished in December 1998, resulting in effectively no new bond listings on the exchanges and a dwindling of JGB trading. Exchange trading thus ceased to provide indications of fair market prices for bonds.

In place of prices determined by exchange trading, bond prices are now most frequently based on OTC quotes, or reference prices, provided by the JSDA. These prices are averages of quotes as at 3.00 pm for trades involving denominations of ¥500m from association members. The JSDA's system covers a very broad range of bond issues. Nevertheless, for a number of bonds, these prices can be quite different from actual market prices.

BENCHMARK INDEXES

Nomura's bond index, the NOMURA-BPI, is a widely used bond index; it tracks the performance of publicly offered fixed-coupon bonds with a remaining issue size (total face value) of at least ¥1bn, a term to maturity of at least one year, and for corporate and samurai bonds, a rating of at least A (Fig. 15.4). The types of bonds in the index are as shown in Table 15.2: JGBs, publicly offered municipal bonds, government-guaranteed bonds, coupon bank

---

4 The exemption initially applied only to bond holdings kept at domestic depository institutions, but was expanded in April 2001 to include holdings kept at global custodians.

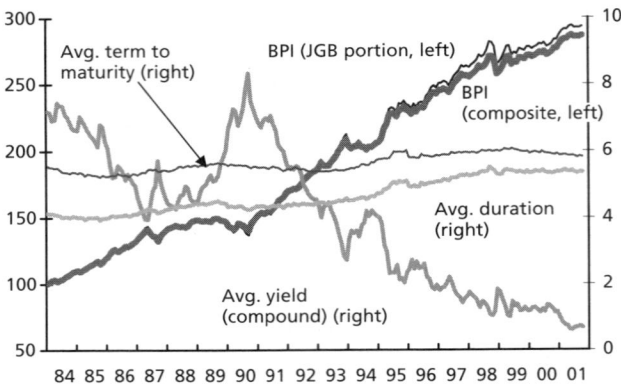

15.4 NOMURA-BPI index (at end-2001).
Source: Nomura.

debentures, straight corporate bonds and samurai bonds. JGBs, however, have been accounting for an increasing proportion of the index in recent times; their share now stands at more than 65%.

As can be seen in Fig. 15.4, the average term to maturity and duration of the index have been increasing as a result of the government's issuance of massive amounts of JGBs in recent years. At the same time, the average yield has fallen to around 1%, a decrease that reflects the impact of the BOJ's prolonged policy of keeping interest rates near zero.

Bond futures and options

THE DEVELOPMENT OF THE MARKET

Bond futures and options trading in Japan actually goes back further than most probably expect. Futures on 10-year JGBs first started trading on the TSE in October 1985, and they were followed by futures on ultra-long-term JGBs in July 1988, OTC bond options in April 1989, options on long-term JGB futures in May 1990 and then futures on medium-term (five-year) JGBs in February 1996 (Table 15.3). Also, the product characteristics defining medium-term JGB futures were changed in May 2000, and calendar spread trades were started in August of the same year; an evening session began in September and options on medium-term JGB futures started trading in November.

Table 15.3 Major characteristics of bond futures trading

	Medium-term JGB futures	**Long-term JGB futures**
Standard contract	3% 5-year JGBs	6% 10-year JGBs
Contract months	March, June, September, December (the nearest three contract months are available at any one time, i.e., the longest-term contract is nine months)	March, June, September, December (the nearest three contract months are available at any one time, i.e., the longest-term contract is nine months)
Trading unit	JGBs with a face value of ¥100m	JGBs with a face value of ¥100m
Delivery date	20th of every contract month (the next business day if the 20th is a weekend/holiday)	20th of every contract month (the next business day if the 20th is a weekend/holiday)
Deliverable issues	JGBs with a term to maturity of at least 4 years and no more than 5 years, 3 months	JGBs with a term to maturity of at least 7 years and no more than 11 years
Minimum price fluctuation	1/100th of a point (per ¥100 par value)	1/100th of a point (per ¥100 par value)
Daily price limits	+/– ¥2 from the previous trading day's settlement price (¥3 if extended)	+/– ¥2 from the previous trading day's settlement price (¥3 if extended)
Last trading day	7th business day prior to each delivery date	7th business day prior to each delivery date
Trading hours	9.00–11.00 am 12.30–3.00 pm 3.30–6.00 pm	9.00–11.00 am 12.30–3.00 pm 3.30–6.00 pm
Launch date	16 February 1996	19 October 1985

Source: Tokyo Stock Exchange materials.

But because there is effectively no longer any futures trading on ultra-long-term JGBs and trading of futures on medium-term JGBs remained thin (as of the end of 2000), bond futures trading nowadays essentially refers to trading of long-term JGB futures. Options on futures and calendar spread trades also apply, more or less, only to long-term JGB futures.

THE SIZE OF THE MARKET

Trends in Japan's bond market are essentially determined by long-term JGB futures. Given the underdeveloped state of the cash bond market, the futures market provided liquidity as well as a benchmark indication of long-term interest rates. The impact of the futures market on the cash bond market was so significant that it was

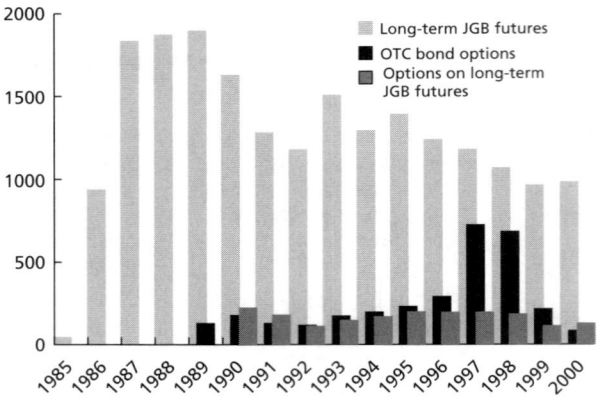

15.5 Trading volume for bond futures and options.
Note: Units are trillions of yen, in terms of par value.
Source: Nomura, based on data from the Tokyo Stock Exchange and the Japan
Securities Dealers Association.

commonly said that the cash market would not function without the futures market. The volume of futures trading has recently been declining, but even so, at more than ¥1000 tr. a year (or ¥4 tr. a day) in 2000, such volume makes Japan's bond futures market the largest in the world (Fig. 15.5). It is also on a par with the volume of cash trading (on a round-trip basis, excluding *gensaki* transactions), which means that the futures market is much larger than the cash market.

The bond options market, meanwhile, is not quite as large as the futures market, even though it is an important one. The volume of listed options trading has recently been declining because of a prolonged decline in volatility in the market, but it still amounts to more than ¥100 tr. per year (about ¥500 bn per day).

MARKET PARTICIPANTS

The bulk of bond futures trading consists of banks and other domestic institutional investors selling to hedge long cash positions, brokerage firms buying for their own accounts and non-resident investors buying mainly for arbitrage strategies. Ever since bond dealers started to shift most of their inventory-hedging trades with customers to the repo market, the impact of their futures trading is probably neutral on average. Brokerage firms and banks each account for about a 40% share of the market for futures trading; non-resident investors for slightly more than 10%; and other market participants the remainder.

Domestic investors typically trade OTC options on specific bond issues, and hence brokerage firms and non-resident investors have a higher share of the market for listed options than they do for the futures market. In other words, listed options are primarily used by dealers to adjust their positions in OTC options.

The yen–yen swap market

Along with bond futures and options, one of the leading interest rate derivative products is the yen–yen swap, or interest rate swaps based on yen interest rates. Yen–yen swaps were initially used by companies to increase their fund-raising flexibility and only recently have been used for trading. They are actively bought and sold by market participants in Japan and other countries and have become established as a crucial product in the interest rate-related trading markets.

By serving as a benchmark in the primary and secondary markets for JGBs as well as corporate bonds, in a determinant rather than derivative fashion, yen–yen swaps have contributed significantly to the development of Japan's bond markets. With the increasing liberalization of financial markets in Japan and the continuing progress in developing mark-to-market and other accounting standards, the interrelation between the swap and bond markets is likely to strengthen.

DEVELOPMENT OF THE JAPANESE SWAP MARKET

The simplest and most common type of swap transaction involves an agreement over a fixed period of time between two parties to exchange the payment or receipt of a fixed-rate cash flow for the payment or receipt of a floating-rate cash flow. A swap is an off-balance sheet transaction that has the same economic effect as a bond transaction; specifically, parties can borrow funds either to buy bonds or sell bonds and invest the proceeds for the short term. Swap transactions are often used in place of bond transactions or to complement them, and hence, the swap market, like the bond futures market, is closely related to the bond market. Beyond the exchange of different types of cash flows, swaps have come to include the exchange of credit risk and other types of complex option-type transactions; this section, however, deals mainly with yen interest rate swaps.

Swaps got their start in Japan in the first half of the 1980s, mainly as a currency hedge for major companies' bonds and loans. Later on, they became increasingly used as a tool for generating financial earnings, by taking advantage of spreads with bonds with warrants, which were issued in huge volume as the stock market picked up in the latter half of the 1980s, for example, and by creating structured bonds and structured loans. The main players in the swap market were foreign banks; Japanese financial institutions and companies primarily used swaps as end users.

The swap market got fully under way and included more active participation by Japanese companies in the early part of the 1990s, when trading in yen interest rate swaps expanded. This development was driven by a number of factors. First, the progressive deregulation of interest rates made both borrowing rates and investment yields more closely tied to market rates, thereby encouraging banks to manage their assets and liabilities more carefully. Second, with the implementation of capital-adequacy requirements by the BIS, banks increasingly used swaps as a way to use their capital more efficiently. And third, a cycle of monetary tightening by the BOJ that pushed interest rates up and contributed to a sharp correction in the stock market compelled financial institutions and companies to become increasingly aware of the need to hedge their risks. In addition, the establishment of a Euroyen interest rate futures market in June 1989 and the lifting of market entry restrictions on domestic brokerage firms in November 1990 helped to set up all the right conditions – in terms of demand, infrastructure and participants – for the growth of the swap market.

SWAP RATES AS THE BENCHMARK LONG-TERM RATES

Yen–yen swap rates for different maturities can be looked up as the Tokyo Swap Reference (TSR) rate (Telerate Screen 17143). The TSR, which is the official swap rate based on rates provided by 25 leading banks, brokerage firms and other market participants at 10.00 am and 3.00 pm every day, is widely used as the reference rate for valuation purposes. The TSR is also used as the reference rate in industry-standard ISDA (International Swaps and Derivatives Association) contracts.

The JGB yield curve is based on benchmark yields for all the different maturities. For a long time, however, only a few maturities and specific issues had benchmark characteristics because of significant differences between issues stemming from disproportionate issuances of certain maturities and different supply and demand for different issues. The participation of Japanese banks and other major financial institutions has added depth to the swap market, which has played a major role in serving as a reference for market levels of medium- and long-term yen interest rates. The L spread, defined as the yield on a bond minus the swap rate for the corresponding maturity, has become a commonly used measure of fair value in the primary and secondary markets. Hence, the swap market has played not a secondary but rather a leading role – ahead of the JGB market – in providing benchmarks of absolute levels of market interest rates for a broad range of maturities.

MARKET PARTICIPANTS

The market makers for swap transactions include major banks (city banks, debenture-issuing banks and trust banks), non-Japanese banks and brokerage firms. Market participants include regional and second-tier regional banks, the *shinkin* banks (small cooperative deposit-taking institutions), credit cooperatives and other local financial institutions, financial institution federations, insurance companies and non-financial companies seeking to establish hedges, manage financial assets and liabilities and lower their funding costs.

The main transactions in the yen–yen swap market, as noted before, consist of swaps in which city banks, which have short-term liabilities and long-term assets, pay a fixed medium- or long-term rate, and debenture-issuing banks and trust banks, which have long-term liabilities and short-term assets, receive a fixed rate. But with city banks now able to issue bonds and thereby better match the interest rate exposures of their assets and liabilities, an increasing number of swap transactions are no longer for asset–liability management purposes. And thanks to the standardization of transactions based on ISDA master contracts and the formation of an active interbank market by foreign and Japanese banks and securities companies, it is not rare for city banks to use swaps instead of bonds to receive a fixed medium- or long-term rate on a trading basis.

Trading opportunities for ultra-long-term swaps (over 10 years) are somewhat limited because of low demand. They also depend

Table 15.4 Highlights of the bond market, November–December 2000

Date	Key regular events
21 November (Tuesday)	Auction for ¥1.6 tr. of 10-year JGBs
22 (Wednesday)	Determination of terms for government-guaranteed bonds and publicly offered municipal bonds
24 (Friday)	BOJ outright-purchasing operation for JGBs (¥200bn)
28 (Tuesday)	Auction for ¥900bn of 5-year JGBs
30 (Thursday)	Last day of trading for December options on futures contracts
1 December (Friday)	Trust Fund Bureau purchase of JGBs (¥100bn); auction for ¥1.4 tr. of 2-year JGBs
5 (Tuesday)	BOJ outright-purchasing operation for JGBs (¥200bn)
7 (Thursday)	Auction for ¥500 bn of 6-year JGBs; IBJ and other leading banks decide to lower long-term prime rate by 15 basis points
11 (Monday)	Last day of trading for December futures contracts
12 (Tuesday)	Auction for ¥800 bn of 15-year floating-rate JGBs
15 (Friday)	Trust Fund Bureau purchase of JGBs (¥100bn)

Source: Nomura.

on the environment for arbitraging between currency rates and foreign interest rates. Nonetheless, through the use of asset swaps, trends in long-term investments by foreign pension funds have become an important driver of the swap market.

The secondary bond market

This section, by using events from late November to mid-December 2000 as illustrations, outlines the latest trends in the secondary bond market (Table 15.4). Although the events represent only a sample of the market activity at the time, the aim of this section is to highlight the key themes on which market participants were concentrating.

JGB AUCTIONS

As noted earlier, JGBs account for a rather large proportion of Japan's bond market (Table 15.5). The market cycle revolves around the JGB auctions, which reflect the supply-and-demand environment. The auction schedule has become increasingly crowded recently because of the broadening range of maturities being offered, but the

Table 15.5 JGB auction results, December 2000

	10-year JGB	5-year JGB	2-year JGB	6-year JGB	15-year JGB
Auction date	21 November	28 November	1 December	7 December	12 December
Issue number	No. 226	No. 9	No. 179	No. 36	No. 10
Nominal coupon (%)	1.8	1.1	0.6	1.2	–
Offering amount (¥bn)	1600.0	about 900.0	about 1400.0	about 500.0	about 800.0
Amount of bids accepted (¥bn)	945.9	887.2	1375.8	496.3	799.6
Amount of competitive bids (¥bn)	2720.7	2430.9	2631.4	1696.6	2422.3
Weighted average price (per ¥100)	101.17	100.07	100.09	100.59	–
Lowest accepted price (per ¥100)	101.05	100.06	100.08	100.56	0.89%

Source: Nomura, based on Ministry of Finance data.

offering for 10-year JGBs is the most important. The market cycle usually starts with the 10-year JGB auctions and lasts for one month.

Ten-year JGBs are issued on the 20th of every month (which is also the payment due date). Auctions are typically held after the 20th of the preceding month (with the exception of the JGBs issued in January, in which case the auction takes place at the beginning of the month). Next in the monthly issuance cycle are 5-year, 2-year and 20-year JGBs (issued quarterly up through fiscal 2000 and then every other month starting in fiscal 2001), 30-year JGBs (issued semi-annually) or 15-year floating-rate JGBs (issued quarterly); auctions every other month for 4-year and 6-year JGBs started in fiscal 2000, but these JGBs have not been issued since fiscal 2001.

To take December 2000 JGBs as an example, 10-year JGBs were auctioned on 21 November; 5-year JGBs on 28 November; 2-year JGBs on 1 December; 6-year JGBs on 7 December; and 15-year floating-rate JGBs on 12 December. Of these, only the 10-year JGBs were issued using a syndicate underwriting system, in which 60% of the issue is sold to syndicate members through a competitive auction and the remaining 40% is allocated to the syndicate based on preset shares. Participants factor in the underwriting commission of ¥0.63 per ¥100 of face value into their bids. For the other JGBs, the entire issuance amount is sold through competitive auctions with no under-writing commission. The majority of JGB auctions use the conventional pricing method, in which the issuance price is the bidding price (starting with the highest bidding price). The 30-year JGBs are currently auctioned using a Dutch auction system based on yields, and the 15-year floating-rate JGBs are auctioned using a Dutch auction system based on yield spreads (versus the 10-year JGB yield).[5]

One week before the scheduled auction, the Ministry of Finance (MOF) formally announces at 10.30 am on that day (at 8.30 am for 10-year JGB offerings) the planned offering amount and other offering terms. Participants have until noon to submit their bids through the BOJ-NET; MOF announces the results of the winning bids at 1.30 pm,[6] but the winning amounts of each participant are announced by various media organizations based on their own surveys.

TERMS FOR GOVERNMENT-GUARANTEED AND MUNICIPAL BONDS

When the 10-year JGB auction is over, the market's attention shifts to the determination of issuance terms for both government-guaranteed and municipal bonds. Based on the results of the 10-year JGB auction, the terms for the 10-year bonds are determined by the syndicate members in consultation with the MOF and the Ministry of Public Management, Home Affairs, Posts and Telecommunications on the day after the auction (excluding April-issued bonds). For example, the terms of the December 2000, 10-year government-guaranteed bonds and 10-year municipal bonds were set on 22 November as shown in the accompanying table. The recent differences in the issuance terms for government-guaranteed bonds and municipal bonds versus JGBs are shown in Fig. 15.6.

	Coupon	Issuance price	Offering amount
Government-guaranteed bonds (10-year)	1.8%	100.00	¥371.0 bn
Municipal bonds (10-year)	1.8%	99.00	¥230.0 bn

Government-guaranteed bonds are issued by special public sector corporations, and municipal bonds are issued by local governments, yet the terms of issuance for these bonds do not differ according to the issuer. Differences between these issues do develop

5 The amount of bids accepted is allocated starting with the highest bid price (lowest bid yield), and the same issuance price (the lowest price, or the highest yield, up to the offering amount) applies to all successful bidders (i.e., all those who bid at least the lowest accepted price).
6 Until May 2001, the announcement time was 2.00 pm.

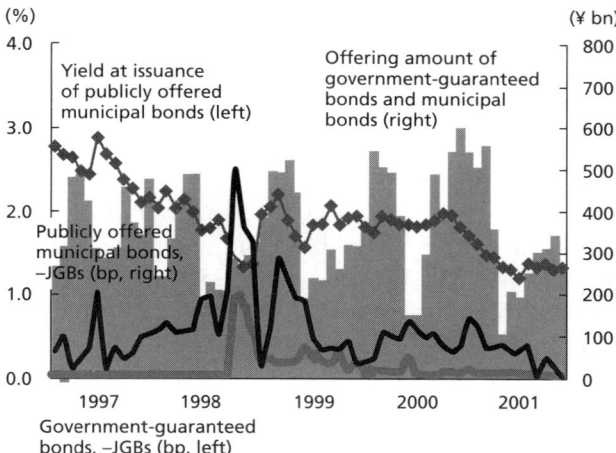

15.6 Differences in issuance terms between JGBs and other public bonds.
Notes: Differences in issuance terms are based on simple yield and do not include price fluctuations after JGB auctions; April-issued bonds are not included because of the difference in timing of the determination of issuance terms.
Source: Nomura.

in the secondary market, however, and bond dealers sell at a discount to the market price of the bonds, as a form of giving up some of the underwriting commission. Many believe that how well government-guaranteed bonds (which are less liquid than JGBs) are subscribed to has a significant effect on bond prices thereafter.

Of the newly available maturities for public bonds, the 5-year publicly offered municipal bonds have their issuance terms determined at about the same time as the 10-year bonds. In addition, the Japan Finance Corporation for Small Business, the Deposit Insurance Corporation and some other issuers have issued 4-, 5- and 6-year government-guaranteed bonds through competitive auctions.

ISSUANCE TERMS FOR COUPON BANK DEBENTURES

The issuance terms for the core 5-year coupon bank debentures are determined around the 10th of every month. One of the main issuers of bank debentures, the Industrial Bank of Japan, first determines its long-term prime rate and then sets the coupon rate on its debentures at 90bps or lower (the issuance price is typically ¥100). The yield in the secondary market on the portion issued in the previous month is an important factor in determining the coupon rate on the new ones to be issued; in this sense, it could be said that the prime rate is determined by adding 90 bps to the coupon rate for the IBJ debentures. The debentures issued by other banks used to be based on the coupon rate for IBJ's debentures, but since Japan's banking crisis hit in 1997, their issuance terms have typically been based on the creditworthiness of each bank.

The issuance terms for coupon bank debentures sometimes have an impact on the supply and demand for medium-term bonds. The issuance of 5-year coupon JGBs has diminished the presence of bank debentures, but how well the bank debentures are subscribed to every month still remains important for determining the supply-and-demand environment for JGBs with medium-term maturities.

BOJ bond operations

The BOJ's open-market operations have recently begun to affect the bond market, particularly the JGB market, more than in the past. The various ways in which the BOJ can adjust the money supply include purchases/sales of bills, and a variant in which the central bank supplies banks with funds by using bonds as collateral; purchases/sales of Treasury bills/financing bills with repurchase agreements; purchases of commercial paper with repurchase agreements; JGB repo operations (borrowing of JGBs); outright purchases of Treasury bills/financing bills; and outright purchases of medium- and long-term JGBs. The JGB repo operations and the outright purchases of medium- and long-term JGBs have had a direct impact on the JGB market. The latter type of operation is watched particularly carefully by bond market participants, because it has had a discernible impact on long-term interest rates.

Outright purchasing operations involving JGBs are targeted at 2-, 4-, 5-, 6-, 10- and 20-year coupon JGBs that have been outstanding for one year.[7] Although all such JGBs are eligible as a rule, the cheapest to deliver (CTD), and those that were absorbed in large quantities in previous operations, are typically excluded. Outright purchases of long-term JGBs in fiscal 2000 were conducted twice a month, and each time, the purchases amounted to ¥200 bn (for a total of ¥400 bn each month).[8] These purchases are not conducted

---

7 Before June 2001, the only JGBs targeted for the outright purchasing operations were the 10- and 20-year bonds.

8 The monthly purchases were increased to three times, or ¥600 bn, in August 2001.

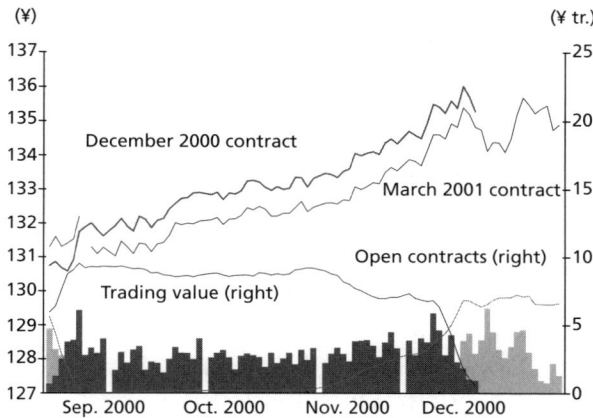

15.7 Futures prices and open contracts.
Source: Nomura.

according to a set schedule. The BOJ puts out a notice on the operation at 10.10 am;[9] dealers have until 11.10 am to put in bids; and the results are finally announced around noon. Bids are submitted in terms of a spread relative to the previous day's reference simple yield (announced by the JSDA) and are accepted starting with the lowest yield. In addition, in a fashion similar to the BOJ's outright purchases of medium- and long-term JGBs, the Trust Fund Bureau conducted regular purchases of JGBs twice a month in fiscal 2000; each purchase amounted to ¥100 bn (and thus a total of ¥200 bn each month).[10]

The BOJ started its outright purchases of medium- and long-term JGBs in 1967 for the purpose of supplying the funds necessary for economic growth, but in recent years, the operations have drawn attention for their impact on long-term interest rates by affecting the supply–demand balance in the bond market (Fig. 15.7). Among the changes are the enhancement of dealers' market-making capabilities and improved liquidity, because the BOJ can absorb the relatively illiquid 20-year JGBs from the market. In addition, the outright JGB purchasing operations generally tend to minimize the fluctuations in the yield curve; the spread-based bidding makes it easier for dealers' bids on issues with short terms to maturity to be accepted when the yield curve is flattening and for their bids on issues with long terms to maturity to be accepted when the yield curve is steepening.

9 The time has been 11.20 am since November 2001.
10 The Trust Fund Bureau's purchases ended in fiscal 2001.

FUTURES AND OPTIONS ON FUTURES

The last day of trading for long-term JGB futures is the seventh business day prior to each delivery date, which is the 20th day of every contract month (or the next business day if the 20th is a weekend or holiday). For December 2000 contracts, the last day of trading was 11 December (Monday). In the two weeks or so prior to the last day of trading for a certain contract month, when participants adjust their futures positions, the cash market is easily affected by the futures market. The technicals in the cash market are also easily affected by dealers' hedging their positions because the last day of trading for listed options on JGB futures is the end of the month before the contract month. Once the last day of trading for options on futures passes and traders roll over their positions to the next contract, the open interest for the nearest-term futures contract declines sharply.

Characteristics of the pricing of bonds

The pricing of bonds in Japan's secondary market is now based primarily on the yield to maturity. Still, some investors stay away from low-coupon bonds. In the past, accounting rules encouraged investors to favour current yield; this preference has not entirely faded away, as can be seen in the differences in yields between bonds with different coupons but the same term to maturity.

DISPARITIES IN YIELDS BETWEEN BONDS WITH DIFFERENT COUPON RATES

For instance, the No. 207 10-year JGB issued in the second half of 1998 had a nominal coupon rate of 0.9% and the No. 208 had a coupon rate of 1.1%, both of which were lower than other 10-year JGBs because of investors' dislike for low coupons (Fig. 15.8). At one point, the yield on the No. 207 was nearly 30bps higher than the yields on neighbouring issues (interpolated based on the yields of issues with similar terms to maturity). This spread compensated for the lengthened duration of the No. 207 as a result of the low coupon rate. But the bond gradually became less and less undervalued as non-resident investors bought it for arbitrage trades and as domestic investors started to buy it in response to the gradual decline in long-term rates. Such disparities in yields between bonds

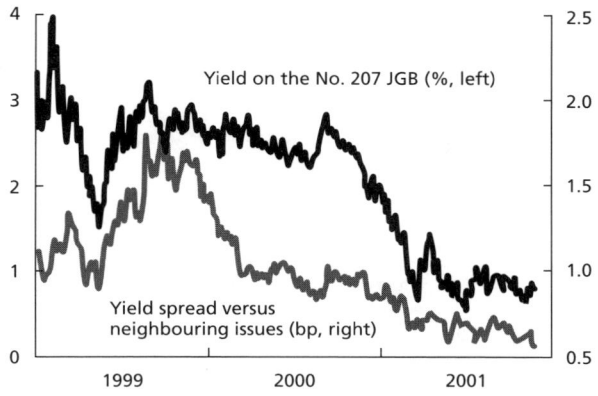

15.8 Yield spread on the No. 207 10-year JGB.
Source: Nomura.

with different coupon rates occasionally arise, but are difficult to explain rationally.

DIFFERENCES BETWEEN LISTED AND UNLISTED MEDIUM-TERM JGBs

Differences sometimes emerge between medium-term JGBs (2-, 4-, 5- and 6-year JGBs) and 10-year JGBs with similar terms to maturity. One reason is that nominal coupon rates can be substantially different depending on when the bonds were issued. From 1993 to 1998, banks' preference for current coupon pushed up prices of 4- and 6-year medium-term JGBs, but recently, these have fallen in price (Fig. 15.9).

In addition to the differences in the nominal coupon rates of medium-term JGBs and 10-year JGBs with similar terms to maturity, there are often differences between listed and unlisted JGBs (the listed JGBs are 2-, 5-, 10-, 20- and 30-year JGBs, and unlisted JGBs are 4- and 6-year JGBs). The effective differences went away when exchange-trading requirements for some JGB transactions were abolished in December 1998, but some of the differences in yields might be explained by whether a bond is subject to the BOJ's market operations. In other words, the 4-, 5- and 6-year medium-term JGBs – which were not subject to the BOJ's outright purchasing operations – may have had relatively high yields compared with 10-year JGBs with the same term to maturity, given that the latter are subject to the BOJ's outright purchases. This factor no longer explains the yield differences, however, given that the medium-term JGBs are now subject to the BOJ's outright purchases.

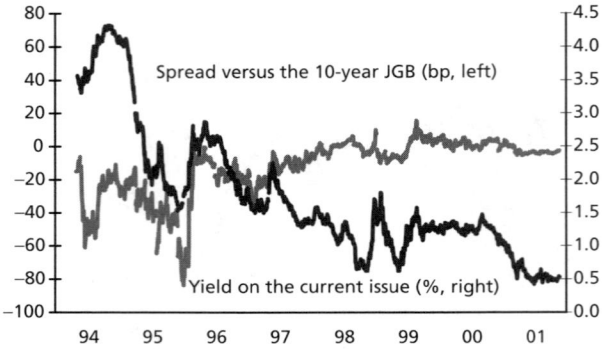

15.9 Spread on the 6-year JGB.
Source: Nomura.

SPREADS BETWEEN JGBs AND OTHER PUBLIC BONDS

Government-guaranteed bonds have the same creditworthiness as
JGBs do, but they tend to have higher yields than JGBs because they
are issued in smaller amounts and because their settlement systems
are not fully developed. The bonds of the Japan Finance Corporation for Municipal Enterprises, which are the most liquid and sizable
government-guaranteed bonds, usually have yields that are about
10bps higher than yields on JGBs with comparable maturities. The
spread, of course, varies depending on market conditions. For
other government-guaranteed bonds, the spread versus JGBs varies
slightly depending on the issuer (Fig. 15.10).

In the case of publicly offered municipal bonds, it is unclear
whether the credit that is being assessed is that of the issuer or the
national government (the Ministry of Public Management, Home
Affairs, Posts and Telecommunications). Recently, some munis have
been trading on the basis of slight differences between issuers, but
spreads have not developed in response to the fiscal situations of
the municipalities. Tokyo Metropolitan bonds, which have the
highest liquidity and creditworthiness of publicly offered municipal
bonds, usually have yields several basis points higher than comparable government-guaranteed bonds.

BANK DEBENTURES

Coupon bank debentures, which are leading bonds in the medium-
term zone, have traditionally had uniform yields between comparable issues, but their yields have recently come to reflect the credit

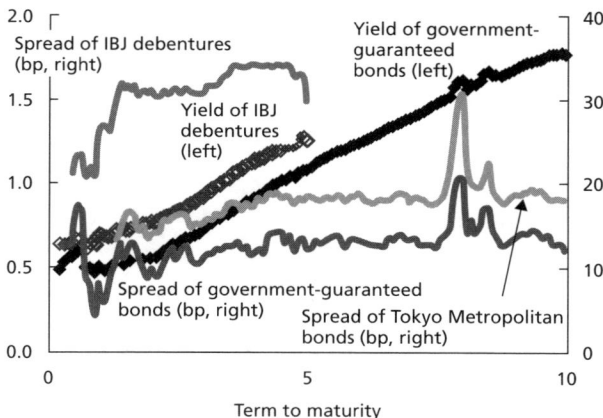

15.10 Spreads of public bonds and bank debentures versus listed JGBs (at end-2000).
Source: Nomura.

ratings of the issuers because of the troubles the financial system has been through. Bank debentures with relatively low yields include those issued by Shoko Chukin Bank, Norinchukin Bank and Shinkin Central Bank, all of which have relatively strong credit ratings.[11] Recently, with the stepped-up issuances of bonds by banks, bank debentures have been priced in comparison with bank bonds.

SPREADS BETWEEN CORPORATES AND JGBs

The 1997–98 Asian financial crisis and Japanese banking crisis had a significant impact on Japan's bond market. The spreads between corporates and JGBs widened significantly, making it more difficult for companies to issue new bonds. But since 1999, the government has used monetary and fiscal policy to help stabilize the financial system, and as a result, the spreads have narrowed sharply (Fig. 15.11). Also contributing to the narrowing of spreads has been the trend among some bond investors to look for high yields, given the difficulties they have had in an environment of ultra-low interest rates. Nevertheless, the prolonged economic downturn in Japan has

11 The yield spread on the Shoko Chukin Bank debentures, however, widened at times on concerns about the impact of the Koizumi administration's efforts to restructure public sector corporations.

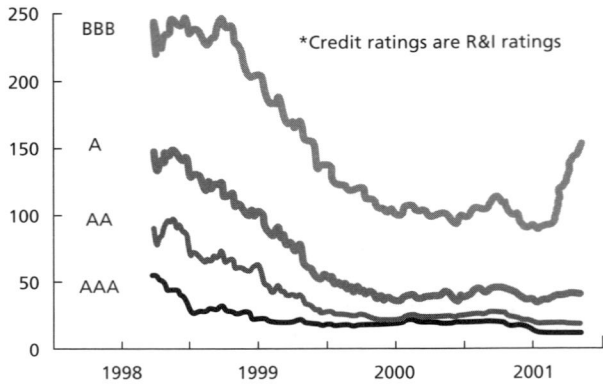

15.11 Spreads of corporates versus JGBs (bp).
Source: Nomura.

led to a rise in corporate bankruptcies and an unprecedented focus on the credit ratings and the financial condition of debt issuers. Hence, those companies that are rumoured to be struggling have seen the spreads on their bonds widen, resulting in a group of corporates with narrow spreads and another group with wide spreads.

THE SPREAD BETWEEN JGB YIELDS AND SWAP RATES

The spread between the yen–yen swap rate and the yield on the JGB with a comparable maturity (known as the LT or TL spread) currently shows a widening at longer maturities. But a look at the spread over time indicates that the term structure of the spread is not always stable (Fig. 15.12). Also, the level of the TL spread sometimes changes significantly. Arbitrage trades based on the TL spread are a major factor in the pricing of yen–yen swap rates, but for a variety of reasons, the arbitrage relationship does not always hold. In late 2000, for example, the TL spread narrowed sharply, and at the short end, the spread inverted.

Explaining this recent narrowing of the TL spread is not easy, but possible factors include the large amounts of JGBs that have been issued and downgrades of their credit ratings; increased issuance of yen-denominated and dual-currency medium-term notes by issuers with variable financing needs; an increase in the proportion of foreign banks that use the yen LIBOR rate; and the impact of mark-to-market accounting. The increased issuance of JGBs has contributed to a rise in JGB yields, and the increased issuance of medium-term notes and the greater proportion of foreign banks

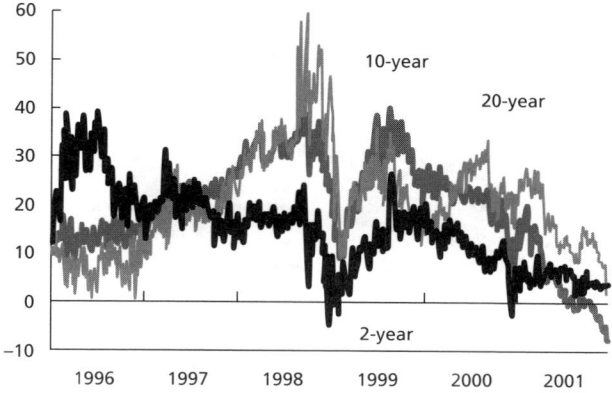

15.12 Spread between JGB yields and swap rates (bp).
Source: Nomura.

using the yen LIBOR rate have contributed to lower swap rates. The impact of mark-to-market accounting, meanwhile, needs to be made up for.

Until the end of fiscal 2001, only banks were allowed to use hedge accounting for those derivative instruments that are used as hedges on a macro or portfolio basis. Banks also did not need to account for the hedges on an individual basis, as long as certain conditions were met. One reason is that banks had been exempt from mark-to-market accounting rules for swaps, and their large swap, rather than bond, positions suffered from substantial declines in swap rates.

FUTURES-LED PRICING OF BONDS

Because the coupon rate for the standard long-term JGB futures contracts is set at 6%, well above the yields on the deliverable issues, the CTD has recently been set at those with a term to maturity of seven years. In other words, a strong arbitrage relationship holds between long-term JGB futures and cash JGBs with a term to maturity of seven years. In Japan's bond market, which is heavily affected by the bond futures market, the price of the CTD is relatively volatile, and the yields of other cash bonds tend to follow suit (Fig. 15.13). The volatility of the yield on JGBs with a term to maturity of seven years is significantly high. This trend was particularly evident in 1994 and 1999, when the bond market was volatile, and indicates the considerable extent to which yields in the bond market are affected by supply and demand for bond futures.

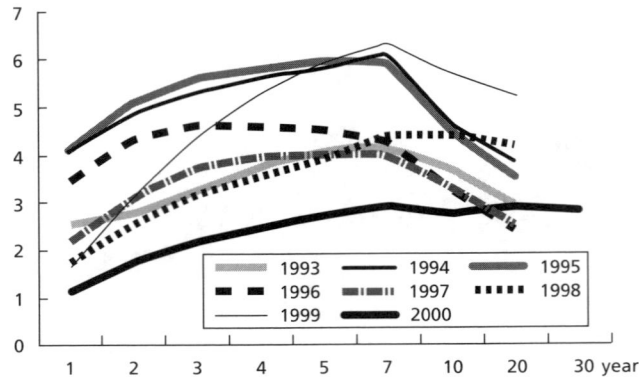

15.13 Standard deviation of daily change in JGB yields (bp).
Source: Nomura.

Conclusions and future challenges

Japan's bond market has developed to become the world's largest, and accordingly, its trading, tax and settlement systems are nearly on a par with those in other major markets. Nevertheless, some complexities peculiar to Japan's framework for bond trading continue to hinder liquidity. The increased amount of bonds issued in recent years has raised the weighting of Japan's bond market in global indexes and attracted the attention of foreign investors, but these non-resident investors still own only a small proportion of the amount of JGBs outstanding in Japan. In addition, they own so little of other types of bonds that they are not considered participants in those markets. More active participation by foreign bond investors in Japan's market will probably require further improvements in the characteristics of the fixed-income products and derivatives offered, as well as the underlying tax and settlement systems.

A lingering issue is the excessive impact of long-term JGB futures on the pricing of bonds in the cash market. Outside the deliverables zone, liquidity in the cash market remains low. The yen–yen swap market has drawn attention recently as a hedging vehicle, but the arbitrage relationship with the JGB market may not be sufficiently strong. Mark-to-market accounting rules for financial products are currently being phased in; once they are fully in place, distortions in the bond market should gradually disappear. The elimination of these systemic peculiarities should strengthen the arbitrage relationship between cash bonds and interest rate derivatives, such as futures and swaps, and help to make the yen interest rate market more transparent and convenient for market participants.

CHAPTER 16

The equity trading market

This chapter looks at the characteristics of recent trading trends in the equity-related cash and derivatives markets in Japan. The infrastructure of these markets was described in Chapter 13. The first section provides an overview of Japan's stock market, and the second section covers some of the major financial products that are available. The final section reviews the various measures that have been adopted in recent years to deregulate and reform the markets, the effects of these changes on trading and the outlook for the future.

Stock market indexes

The Nikkei Average is used far more often than any other index to represent the performance of the stock market. The index, which is calculated and published by the *Nihon Keizai Shimbun*, includes 225 of the leading stocks from the first section of the Tokyo Stock Exchange (TSE). (The Nikkei also publishes a number of other indexes, including the Nikkei 500 Stock Average, the Nikkei Stock Index 300 and the Nikkei Over-the-Counter (OTC) Stock Average, but the 'Nikkei Average' refers to the Nikkei 225.) Calculated continuously since the reopening of the TSE in May 1949, the Nikkei 225 is the best-known Japanese stock market index and regularly appears at the top of most economic news reports.

One index that has grown in importance in recent years is the Tokyo Stock Exchange Price Index, more commonly known as the TOPIX. (The TSE also publishes a number of sub-indexes based on market capitalization, but 'the TOPIX' refers to the index for the

Table 16.1 Comparison of Nikkei Average and TOPIX (at 31 December 2000)

	Nikkei Average	**TOPIX**
Type of index	Price-weighted (adjusted by par value)	Market cap-weighted
Calculation	Sum of par value-adjusted stock prices of index constituents/divisor	Sum of market capitalizations of index constituents/market value on base date
Criteria for inclusion	Leading stocks among those traded on TSE first section	All stocks traded on the TSE first section (except recent IPOs and those in the 'liquidation post', which are to be delisted)
No. of index constituents	225 (as a rule)	1445
Stock prices used	TSE prices (special quotes)	TSE prices (special quotes)
Adjustments for continuity	Divisor is adjusted for newly added stocks, stock splits and other corporate actions that affect the prices of index constituents	Base market value is adjusted for new listings, delistings or corporate actions that affect the market value of index constituents
Index changes	Regular index changes are conducted once a year (October), and unscheduled ones whenever a stock is delisted or moved to the 'liquidation post'	The index is changed whenever a new stock is listed on the first section (IPO or move from the second section), or whenever a stock is delisted or moved to the 'liquidation post'

Source: Nomura.

entire first section of the TSE.) The TOPIX is a market cap-weighted index of all of the stocks on the TSE first section (except for the so-called 'liquidation post' category of stocks to be delisted and new stocks that have been trading for less than one month), whereas the Nikkei Average is price-weighted. The TOPIX is used by the Pension Fund Association and nearly all of Japan's pension fund managers as a benchmark for their domestic stock investments. Among institutional investors, it has always been the most widely followed index. With the growing domination of the stock market by institutional investors and the growth of index funds, the TOPIX is becoming more commonly referenced. Table 16.1 compares the characteristics of these two leading indexes.

PROBLEMS WITH THE NIKKEI AVERAGE

As noted in Chapter 2, the Nikkei Average reached a record high of 38 915.87 on 29 December 1989, but fell sharply the following year and eventually hit a post-bubble low of 12 879.97 on 9 October 1998. It stood at 11 024.94 as of the end of March 2002, down more than 70% from its all-time high. The Nikkei Average, which is widely recognized and has historical continuity, is commonly referenced for long-term trends in the market, but a major change in April 2000 threatens to undermine this continuity.

To maintain the index's continuity, no changes whatsoever were ever made to the stocks in the index, except in the case of bank-ruptcies or mergers. But a problem eventually developed when the volatility of the index became exacerbated by arbitrage transactions involving component stocks that had become very illiquid. To remedy this problem, the *Nihon Keizai Shimbun* adopted new standards in October 1991 for the component stocks of the index. Although the new standards resulted in a number of sub-stitutions each year since 1991, they still did not help the index keep up to date with the rapid transformation of Japan's economic structure.

The *Nihon Keizai Shimbun* then announced on 15 April 2000 that it had revised its standards once again, thus initiating by far the largest-scale change ever in the index – the replacement of 30 of the 225 component stocks on 24 April (based on 21 April closing prices). Because most of the new additions were high-priced stocks, the 30 new ones alone accounted for about 40% of the new index at the time of the announcement and over 50% at the time the changes were actually made. As a result of the index changes, managers of Nikkei index funds (with assets of about ¥800 bn, as estimated by Nomura) and holders of index arbitrage positions (worth about ¥1.5 tr., as estimated by Nomura), had to adjust their holdings by making a massive amount of trades in only one week. Sales of stocks removed from the index and roughly half of the remaining stocks in the index amounted to more than ¥1 tr., and purchases of stocks newly added to the index surpassed ¥1 tr.

As a major price-weighted market index, the Nikkei Average has some peculiarities. For example, the Dow Jones Industrial Average, which is an even better-known market index, is a pure index – almost no funds are indexed to it. Some futures contracts are based on the Dow, but their liquidity is quite low compared with S&P 500 futures contracts, and arbitrage positions in Dow futures are not all that large. In contrast, a number of large funds are indexed to the Nikkei Average, and an active market exists for Nikkei futures. Thus, when the changes were made to the index in the spring of 2000, a massive amount of trading activity over a short time period overwhelmed the liquidity in the market for the affected stocks and futures contracts.

As a result of the Nikkei index changes, the prices of the new additions soared and those of the deleted stocks plummeted during the week between the announcement and the implementation of the index changes. After the changes were made, the newly added stocks gave back some of their gains while the deleted stocks recovered somewhat. But in the meantime, the value of the Nikkei Average before the actual reshuffle reflected only the declining prices of the stocks that were to be removed, and after the changes, the index reflected the significant pullbacks in the prices of the newly added stocks. Had the index changes been made at the same time they were announced, the Nikkei Average would have been more than 3000 points higher (by Nomura estimates). On top of this timing problem, the dramatic transformation of the composition of the Nikkei Average from the 'old economy' to the 'new economy' raises serious doubts about the historical continuity of the index.

PROBLEMS WITH THE TOPIX AND THE IMPACT ON PRICES OF TECHNOLOGY STOCKS

The TOPIX index, which has recently become more widely recognized, is not a perfect index either. Because stocks in the TOPIX are weighted by their market capitalizations, the index is not distorted by high-priced growth stocks the way the Nikkei Average is. But the weightings of the component stocks are based on the full market capitalizations of each stock, that is, the total number of outstanding shares (except in the cases of Nippon Telegraph and Telephone and Japan Tobacco, in which the government-owned shares are not counted). For some stocks, the discrepancy is huge between the number of outstanding shares and the free float, or the number of shares that are actually available in the market for investors to buy and sell. With more and more investment assets being indexed to the TOPIX, this discrepancy could lead to sharp volatility in the prices of some stocks.

The free float of a stock is often significantly lower than the total number of outstanding shares for several reasons. One is the common practice of cross-shareholding among Japanese banks and non-financial companies.[1] A large percentage of a bank's shares is often held by corporate customers for the purpose of maintaining a

---

1 See Chapter 17 for further details.

strategic relationship; at the same time, banks often hold shares of a large number of companies. Another reason is that the founders and affiliated persons still hold a significant portion of a company's shares after the company goes public.

A problem related to this difference between the free float and outstanding shares stems from the calculation of the TOPIX index on the total outstanding shares of a publicly traded subsidiary as well as those of its parent. For instance, about two-thirds of NTT DoCoMo's shares are owned by NTT, and one-half of Seven-Eleven Japan's shares are held by its parent Ito-Yokado. At one point, because of NTT DoCoMo's popularity as a leading technology growth stock, the company's stock accounted for 9.7% of the entire TOPIX index. When the stock's weighting reached a certain level, it became a must-have stock, not only for the TOPIX index funds but also for actively managed funds, which had to hold the stock or else risk deviating too much from the TOPIX in terms of performance. In other words, NTT DoCoMo's large market capitalization attracted new buyers, and these purchases further increased the stock's market capitalization, which then attracted more buyers and so on. Similar distortions affected the stocks of Softbank and Hikari Tsushin, both of which are substantially owned by the top executives. The sharp climb and then plunge in tech stocks between the second half of 1999 and 2000 were undoubtedly exacerbated by this problem with the nature of the TOPIX index.

THE PLAYERS IN JAPAN'S STOCK MARKET

This section provides an overview of the types of investors who are active in Japan's stock market, and their impact on the market.[2] Figure 16.1 illustrates the trends in trading by type of investor for the TSE, the Osaka Securities Exchange (OSE) and the Nagoya Stock Exchange between 1982 and 2000.

The first trend that stands out in Fig. 16.1 is the declining significance of domestic individual investors during the 1982–2000 period. These investors accounted for nearly half of all trading in the first half of the 1980s, but by the second half of the 1990s, they had become much less of a force and were no longer a major market participant. (Participation by individual investors recovered slightly in 1999 and 2000, when tech stocks drove the market and online trading became more prevalent.) Companies were major players in

---

2 For more detail on the major players, see Chapters 2 to 7.

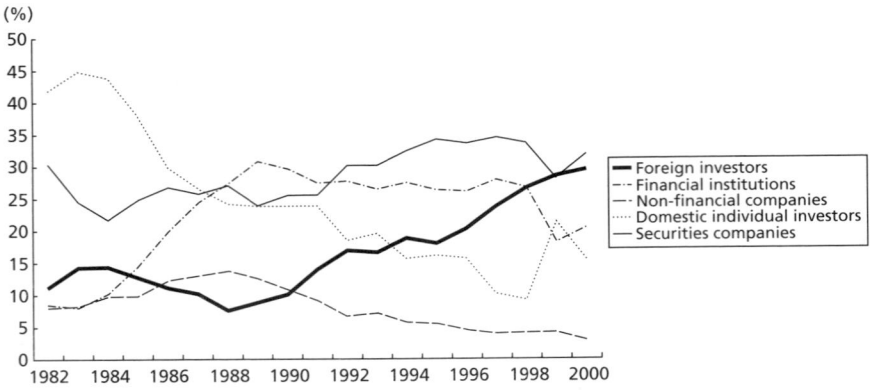

16.1 Three main exchanges, by share of total trading.
Source: Nomura, based on Tokyo Stock Exchange data.

the market during the economic bubble years in the second half of the 1980s, when they actively invested in various ways to generate non-operating profit, but now they are not much more than sellers of cross-held shares.

Currently, the three main participants in the stock market are securities firms, financial institutions and foreign investors. Securities firms have traded in the market in different forms over the years, and their activity has always had a major impact on prices. They were active in short-term dealing in the 1980s and in arbitrage transactions using futures in the 1990s; in recent years, brokerages have been active as counterparties in principal trading. The key roles played by the securities firms will be examined more closely later in this chapter.

After financial institutions increased their share of trading in the second half of the 1980s, they continued to be important players, despite losing some ground in 1999. Financial institutions' market investments primarily consist of trust assets managed on behalf of investment trusts and pension funds, the institutions' own funds and strategic shareholdings owned to maintain relationships with other companies. Of these, trust assets represent the largest share and are actively traded. In some cases, however, these trust assets are, in fact, public pension and postal assets that are invested in the market on behalf of the government for the purpose of supporting share prices (so-called 'price-keeping operations'); thus, they are more properly considered to be strategic rather than profit-oriented investments. The strategic shareholdings used to have little impact on the market because most of the transactions involving them were cross-transactions (simultaneous purchases and sales) to generate accounting gains. But they now have a much larger influence on market trends. After the accounting rules were changed in April 2000 so that profits realized from cross-transactions would no longer be recognized, the sellers were forced to wait a certain period before buying back shares or selling outright their cross-shareholdings.

In the 1990s, foreign investors accounted for a sharply increasing proportion of total trading. Among what are considered foreign investors are a certain number of so-called 'black-eyed foreigners', that is, investors that are nominally foreign but are managing funds originating from Japan that are being funnelled through overseas accounts to avoid investment regulations in Japan. A good example of such a 'black-eyed' foreign investor is the former Pension Welfare Service Public Corporation, which established limited partnerships overseas to invest its assets because it was not permitted to invest them with investment management firms.

'Black-eyed' foreign investors also include some hedge funds that are nominally non-Japanese. An increasing number of hedge funds have recently been using market-neutral strategies (i.e., hedging their long positions with short positions to generate steady returns). But the many restrictions on short-selling that apply to Japan-based funds prompted these funds to register overseas. Still, the majority of such hedge funds are owned and managed by foreign investors.

These and other foreign investors, including traditional long-term investors such as pension fund managers, have had a rapidly growing influence on Japan's market. Foreign investors used to follow a top-down strategy for their global investments; they determined their country weightings first and then selected individual sectors and stocks. In recent years, however, a rapidly growing number of foreign investors have paid less attention to country weightings and, instead, have focused primarily on specific sectors, such as technology or communications, in part because of the globalization of the industrial structure. These global bottom-up funds may be one reason Japan's stock market has become increasingly correlated with the US and European markets.

FOREIGN INVESTORS AND THE GLOBAL INDEXES

Japanese equities are a typical part of foreign investors' global equity investments. Many investors outside Japan use the Morgan Stanley

Capital International (MSCI) or FTSE indexes as a benchmark. Although MSCI generally avoids double-counting by including in its indexes only the parent company if it also has a publicly traded subsidiary, MSCI does not adjust for the free float of stocks, while FTSE does. After initiating a review of a free float adjustment in 2000, MSCI decided in December of that year to implement such a change.

The way in which MSCI made the changes to its indexes contrasts quite sharply with the approach taken by the *Nihon Keizai Shimbun*, which was outlined above. The *Nihon Keizai Shimbun* abruptly announced its changes, which affected about half of the value of the Nikkei Average, only a week before they took effect. In contrast, MSCI first publicly announced that it was considering changes more than one year before they were to take place. Furthermore, during the review stage, they publicized various proposals for adjusting for free float and sought opinions from the global investment community in an attempt to minimize the impact of the change on the markets and maintain the quality of the indexes as investment benchmarks. (A number of problems have nevertheless been found with the proposals.)

FUTURE TRENDS

As discussed above, the more commonly used indexes for Japan's stock market suffer from a number of problems, but the indexes are nevertheless unlikely to suddenly fall by the wayside. The Nikkei Average, for example, is not suited to be an investment benchmark because it is price-weighted and ignores the number of outstanding shares of the component stocks. Moreover, the drastic changes the *Nihon Keizai Shimbun* made to the composition of the index in April 2000 raise doubts about the historical continuity of the Nikkei Average. Some government-affiliated financial institutions have reportedly stopped using the Nikkei Average as a benchmark. Nevertheless, the Nikkei Average is likely to continue to be used by the mass media as an indicator of market trends, if only because it is well known among the general public and because it has been around for a long time.

An important factor in determining the quality of a stock market index as a benchmark for investment management performance is whether the index adjusts for free float, or the actual amount of investable shares of the stocks that make up the particular index. Nearly all Japanese pension fund managers currently use the TOPIX as a performance benchmark.

Like the Nikkei Average, however, the TOPIX is not a perfect index and has a number of problems that need to be considered. Stocks in the TOPIX index are weighted by their full market capitalizations, even though in many cases a substantial portion of shares are strategically held by investors. Moreover, the only qualification for inclusion in the TOPIX is that a stock be listed on the first section of the TSE. As mentioned, the MSCI and FTSE indexes, which are widely used as benchmarks by overseas investors, have been reshuffled to adjust for free float. In Japan, such a free float-adjusted index series already exists – the RUSSELL/NOMURA style index series. Some investment management companies already use these indexes as benchmarks. One likely trend in the future will be the increasing use of different indexes that are appropriate for different uses, based on an understanding of the different characteristics of the indexes. Any such move among fund managers to adopt different benchmark indexes could have a modest, but at times significant, impact on the relative value of Japan's stock market indexes.

Japan's equity and equity-linked markets

As explained in Chapter 13, Japanese companies can go public by either listing their shares on a stock exchange or registering them with the Japan Securities Dealers' Association (JSDA). In the latter case, the company is known as an OTC-registered company because its shares are traded over the counter by securities firms. But as part of revisions to the Securities and Exchange Law implemented in December 1998, the system for OTC stocks was defined as a 'market for securities traded over the counter', resulting in little difference with the stock exchanges other than the market-making function of the OTC market.

STOCK MARKETS

From the end of World War II until 2000, there were eight stock exchanges in Japan. The TSE absorbed the regional exchanges in Niigata and Hiroshima in March 2000, reducing the total number of exchanges in Japan to its current number of six as at December 2000 – Tokyo, Osaka, Nagoya, Sapporo, Kyoto and Fukuoka.[3] Some of

3 The OSE absorbed the Kyoto Stock Exchange in March 2001.

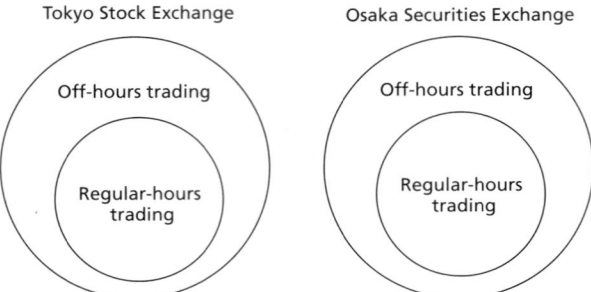

16.2 Conceptual view of trading of listed stocks.
Source: Nomura.

the exchanges are casually known by the districts in which they are located. For instance, the TSE is sometimes referred to as Kabuto-cho, and the OSE as Kitahama. The exchanges in Tokyo, Osaka and Nagoya all have a first and second section, with relatively large companies listed on the first section and smaller companies listed on the second section. Recently, the TSE's Mothers market and the OSE's Nasdaq Japan were established for start-up companies.[4]

As shown in Fig. 16.2, stock trades in Japan can be executed either through an auction system on the floor of an exchange during regular trading hours (for the TSE, as at December 2000, trading hours are from 9.00 am to 11.00 am for the morning session and from 12.30 pm to 3.00 pm for the afternoon session) or through an order-matching system outside regular trading hours (8.20 am to 9.00 am, 11.00 am to 12.30 pm, and 3.00 pm to 4.30 pm). In addition, the Securities and Exchange Law has been revised to allow the trading of exchange-listed stocks through an order-matching system without routing the trades through one of Japan's stock exchanges.

Compared with the listing standards for Japan's major stock exchanges, the requirements for registering on the Japanese OTC market have been relatively loose, which makes it easier for start-up companies with growth potential to go public. To further facilitate the registration of start-ups, in December 1998, the JSDA revised the OTC registration standards to create two groups of standards. The first set of standards is generally applied to all companies except start-ups, and the second group of standards is specifically designed for start-ups.

4 See Chapter 13 for details.

Table 16.2 Growth of Tokyo Stock Exchange and OTC market

	No. of stocks			Market capitalization (¥ tr.)			Avg. daily trading values (¥ bn)		
	TSE 1st section	TSE 2nd section	OTC	TSE 1st section	TSE 2nd section	OTC	TSE 1st section	TSE 2nd section	OTC
1986	1075	424	140	277.1	8.4	2.1	558.9	14.0	1.6
1987	1101	431	151	325.5	11.2	2.5	896.2	18.8	1.4
1988	1130	441	196	462.9	14.0	4.3	1024.6	21.1	2.6
1989	1161	436	263	590.9	20.2	12.5	1308.5	27.2	8.3
1990	1191	436	342	365.2	14.1	12.0	716.7	42.0	24.8
1991	1223	418	430	365.9	12.0	13.0	435.3	15.4	20.5
1992	1229	422	436	281.0	8.5	8.0	238.3	4.9	4.5
1993	1234	433	477	313.6	10.8	11.3	340.1	13.0	11.7
1994	1235	454	568	342.1	16.3	14.7	334.0	19.6	21.8
1995	1253	461	678	350.2	15.5	14.6	315.7	19.8	23.6
1996	1293	473	762	314.4	10.5	15.0	393.1	19.4	23.9
1997	1327	478	839	273.9	7.0	9.2	434.3	8.5	10.9
1998	1340	498	856	267.8	7.4	7.8	388.6	5.6	6.3
1999	1364	526	868	442.4	13.6	27.4	726.7	30.4	49.8
2000	1447	580	883	373.8	7.6	11.4	999.9	24.0	45.8

Source: Nomura, based on Tokyo Stock Exchange and Japan Securities Dealers Association materials.

As part of these reforms, the JSDA also implemented a new market-making system. To become a market maker for certain stocks, securities firms must simply submit a list of those stocks for which they want to make a market. As market makers, the dealers must continuously provide bid and ask quotes as well as the number of shares they are willing to buy or sell at those prices; dealers are obligated to take the other side of investors' trades and put through orders that meet these price and volume conditions. Stocks for which there are no market makers are typically traded through the same type of auction system used by exchanges in off-hours trading.

For both the TSE and the OTC markets, Table 16.2 shows the trend in the number of stocks traded on these markets, their market capitalizations and their average daily trading values during regular hours (including trading through OTC market makers for OTC stocks) from 1986 to 2000.[5] As shown in Table 16.2, the total market capitalization and trading value of stocks listed on the first section

5 In March 2001, the JSDA began referring to OTC stocks as 'listed' rather than 'registered' stocks.

of the TSE peaked in 1989 and then steadily declined into 1999. The stocks then recovered significantly later in 1999, primarily because of the strong performance of technology stocks. In 2000, average daily trading value for the entire TSE first section was about ¥1 tr., which was only about 20% of the level for the New York Stock Exchange and roughly on a par with that for the London Stock Exchange.

Nevertheless, in spite of the weak market, the number of publicly traded companies in Japan rose steadily by about 50% in the 10 years to 2000. The average daily trading value per stock listed on the first section of the TSE (based on the number of stocks at the end of 2000) was about ¥700 m in 2000. Average daily trading value, however, differs significantly among stocks, and trading has recently been highly concentrated in a small group of stocks. In 2000, only 217 stocks – or less than 15% of the total number of stocks listed on the first section of the TSE – had an average daily trading value in excess of ¥700 m, while more than 800 stocks had an average daily trading value of not even ¥100 m. Moreover, the 40 most actively traded stocks accounted for roughly 50% of total trading value. It is thus difficult for institutional investors that manage large sums – other than some of the aggressive funds that concentrate their investments in a small number of highly liquid stocks – to have their orders executed on the floor of Japan's exchanges efficiently, without having an inordinate impact on the market. Partly for this reason, principal trading in Japan has grown significantly. Principal trading is discussed in more detail later in this chapter.

The unique rules for trading individual stocks on the floors of Japan's exchanges include daily trading limits on both the upside and downside (based on the previous day's closing prices) and minimum quote increments. The prices of Japanese stocks vary widely, in part because the par values range from ¥50 to ¥50000.[6] In February 2000, when prices of technology stocks were nearing a peak, the shares of OTC-traded Yahoo Japan hit ¥100 m at one point. To reduce the daily volatility of stocks, daily trading limits are imposed based on the closing prices of each stock the previous trading day. When the price of Yahoo Japan soared in February 2000, the maximum daily fluctuation for all stocks trading at ¥10 m or more was ¥2 m, which was only 2% of Yahoo Japan's stock price of ¥100 m at the time. For a while, the price of the stock was volatile,

6 The rules concerning par value were eliminated in October 2001.

Table 16.3 Trading limits and quote inducements (at 31 March 2000) (¥)

Price	Trading limit	Price	Quote increment
100	30	2000	1
200	50	3000	5
500	80	30000	10
1000	100	50000	50
1500	200	100000	100
2000	300	1000000	1000
3000	400	2000000	10000
5000	500	3000000	50000
10000	1000	above 3000000	100000
20000	2000		
30000	3000		
50000	4000		
70000	5000		
100000	10000		
150000	20000		
200000	30000		
300000	40000		
500000	50000		
1000000	100000		
1500000	200000		
2000000	300000		
3000000	400000		
5000000	500000		
10000000	1000000		
15000000	2000000		
20000000	3000000		
30000000	4000000		
50000000	5000000		
50000000	10000000		

Source: Nomura, based on Tokyo Stock Exchange materials.

hitting its daily trading limits often, and almost no orders were filled. Shortly thereafter, the price of Hikari Tsushin's stock, which is listed on the first section of the TSE, dropped sharply, hitting the downside price limit for 20 consecutive trading days. No trades of the stock were completed at all for 13 of the 20 days, marking an all-time record.

Daily trading limits were relaxed in July 2000, as shown in Table 16.3, and special measures were instituted for stocks of bankrupt companies that are traded separately from other stocks in a special liquidation section on Japan's exchanges. Despite these improvements, daily trading limits are sometimes as low as 8% of the previous day's closing price, depending on the price range of the stock. Some continue to argue that the trading limits actually reduce liquidity in the market. Some also say that the minimum quote increments increase trading costs. The increments have been reduced in many cases, but they are still quite large for some stocks. For instance, the increment for stocks priced just barely above ¥1 m is ¥10 000, or about 1% of the price.

CONVERTIBLE AND WARRANT BOND MARKETS

Convertible bonds publicly offered by exchange-listed companies are traded on the exchanges, and convertibles issued by OTC-traded companies are registered as OTC securities. In addition, some convertibles are unlisted and privately placed outside of Japan.

From the second half of the 1980s to the early 1990s, a period when many Japanese companies heavily issued new equity, convertibles were very common. But recently, companies have not been issuing as many of them. Moreover, many of the recently issued convertibles come with downward conversion-price resets and other conditions that are designed to increase the probability of conversion. Nevertheless, because of the prolonged downturn in the market, more than half of the outstanding amount of convertibles today is accounted for by issues that have little more than straight bond value, because the embedded conversion options are practically worthless. Most of these issues were issued quite some time ago.

The daily trading value for most listed convertibles is relatively low, averaging about ¥10 bn, although a few exceptions exist. Most of the transactions are principal trades involving securities firms as the counterparty, during both regular trading hours and off-hours. Nearly all large convertible trades by institutional investors are principal trades.

Japanese companies issued a large amount of Eurodollar- and Swiss franc-denominated bonds with warrants during the latter half of the 1980s, but not much has been issued since 1990. Recently, companies have been privately placing a large amount of bonds with warrants to create synthetic stock options.

FUTURES AND OPTIONS MARKETS

The major equity derivatives traded on the exchanges include futures and options on stock indexes and individual stock options. The index futures are for various market indexes, such as the Nikkei Average, the TOPIX and the Nikkei Stock Index 300, and for specific sectors, such as the electronics and banking sectors. The Osaka Stock Futures 50 (OSF50) contract, which became the first stock index futures contract to be offered in Japan when it was introduced in June 1987, was for an index of 50 major stocks, but it is no longer traded. In September 1988, the OSE introduced a futures contract for the Nikkei Average, while the TSE introduced a contract for the TOPIX.

Then, in 1994, the OSE introduced a Nikkei Stock Index 300 futures contract, and in 1998, the OSE and the TSE each introduced futures contracts for three sector indexes. But because of the extremely low trading volume in its sector-index futures contracts, the OSE eliminated them in November 2000. Expirations for the index futures are quarterly – in March, June, September and December. Five contract months are available at any one time, with the longest expiration 15 months out. The last trading day for each contract is the business day preceding the second Friday of each expiration month. On the expiration date, open interest is settled based on special quotations (SQ), which are computed using the opening prices of the constituent stocks of the underlying market index on the business day following the last trading day.

Currently, Nikkei 225 futures are the most actively traded contracts, as shown in Table 16.4. These contracts are also traded on the Singapore International Monetary Exchange (SIMEX) and the Chicago Mercantile Exchange (CME). Because the index is well known, the contracts are traded by a broad range of market participants, including speculators. During periods of high market volatility, the futures market typically picks up in trading volume and drives the cash market as market participants put on arbitrage positions. Perhaps one of the main reasons for the popularity of the Nikkei index futures for arbitrage transactions is that the corresponding cash positions can be easily created with one minimum lot size of each constituent stock. Yet even though the TOPIX futures are not traded as much as the Nikkei index futures, they have been widely used by investors to hedge cash positions, partly because the TOPIX is a widely used benchmark among pension fund managers and other institutional investors. With the introduction of off-hours trading of Nikkei and TOPIX index futures and the formation of a

Table 16.4 Average daily trading value of index
futures (¥ bn)

Year	Nikkei 225	TOPIX	Nikkei Stock Index 300
1990	1 605.2	291.8	
1991	2 181.8	128.3	
1992	890.2	75.2	
1993	660.0	134.2	
1994	502.9	170.4	54.6
1995	503.5	153.0	24.0
1996	600.4	185.5	22.6
1997	559.1	172.1	16.8
1998	505.9	129.8	14.4
1999	624.8	179.8	16.5
2000	507.3	251.0	14.2

Source: Nomura, based on Tokyo Stock Exchange and Osaka Securities
Exchange materials.

market for trading spreads between futures contracts, traders now
have a broader selection of trading methods than before.

Index options are also available on the exchanges for the Nikkei
Average, the TOPIX and the Nikkei Stock Index 300 (they were introduced at slightly different times). The trading volume has been
relatively high for options on the Nikkei 225, which began trading
on the OSE in June 1989, but very low (effectively close to zero)
for options on the TOPIX and the Nikkei Stock Index 300. There
are eight expiration months for options on the Nikkei Average – the
same five as for the index futures contracts, plus the three near-term
months that do not overlap with the quarterly cycle. An index option
contract's final settlement price is based on the same SQ method as
for index futures. Each index option has eight exercise prices in ¥500
increments, based on the most recent closing price of the underlying index; four of the prices are above the index price and four
below.

Individual stock options started trading in July 1997 on both the
OSE and the TSE. Initially, options were available on only 20 major
stocks, but the number has since been increased by both exchanges.
Trading in the options got off to a strong start but has dwindled
ever since to nearly zero for most options.

Japan's derivatives markets are distinctive in two ways. First, as
mentioned earlier, the volume of stock trading is significantly higher
on the TSE than on the OSE. But the reverse is true for futures and

options trading volume. Admittedly, some of the relative strength of the OSE in derivatives trading is probably a result of the strong name recognition of the Nikkei Average. Another distinctive characteristic is that, in contrast with the US, individual stock options are rarely used in Japan.

OTC DERIVATIVES MARKET

Unlike listed derivatives products, which have for the most part not been widely used in Japan, a relatively wide range of OTC derivative products are available customized to meet the specific needs of traders and investors. Following the elimination of restrictions on OTC derivatives in Japan in December 1998, demand for the products has risen sharply. Major equity derivative products include long-term futures contracts, index-linked notes and exchangeable bonds. A comprehensive description of OTC derivatives is not possible because these products are unlisted and traded directly between counterparties.

The longest-term contract for listed futures in Japan is 15 months. These long-term futures contracts are often used by long-term investors (such as banks and companies involved in cross-shareholding relationships) that seek to hedge cash positions for periods longer than 15 months. Securities companies that take the other side of these investors' trades usually sell liquid, near-term listed futures to hedge their own positions and roll them over as the contracts expire, which is another way the cash market is affected by futures trading.

Index-linked notes are synthetic equity products. The redemption prices for these instruments are based on the price of a stock index, most often the Nikkei Average, when the note matures. These notes used to be traded mostly by institutional investors, but recently they have been made available to individual investors. Many of the recently issued index-linked notes are known as 'knock-in' and 'knock-out' products, meaning that the redemption prices for these bonds are fixed when the price of a stock index reaches a particular level some time before maturity. Just at the time these price levels are reached, the investment characteristics of the notes change considerably, unrelated to the changes in the linked index. Stock prices become volatile as both holders and the issuers of the notes trade to hedge their new risk exposure in the notes and also as other market participants trade in anticipation of these moves. The increase in market volatility in the second half of 2000 and the first part of 2001 can be attributed in part to the many Nikkei-linked notes with knock-out prices of ¥14000 or lower.

Exchangeable bonds resemble index-linked notes except that exchangeable bonds can be converted into equity instead of cash, based on the price of an underlying stock. These instruments typically offer comparatively high coupon rates and are sold primarily to yield-hungry individual investors. As with many other equity derivatives, the impact of exchangeable bonds on stock prices can no longer be ignored.

Strong demand for OTC derivatives is partly a function of trading activity among securities companies and other market participants, other than investors, seeking to hedge unnecessary exposure or generate profits by anticipating trading activity related to the derivatives. This trading in OTC derivatives affects the cash market in a variety of ways.

STOCK-LENDING MARKET

The stock-lending system in Japan serves an important function by providing investors with a broad range of investment opportunities and increased liquidity. Short selling of stocks used to be allowed only in conjunction with margin transactions, and the stock-lending market was thus used only by securities firms and securities finance companies. After the Securities and Exchange Law was revised in December 1998, however, the borrowing and lending of marketable securities became a part of Japanese securities firms' operations. As a result of the revision, securities firms are now allowed to borrow strategically held stocks from institutional investors and non-financial companies and lend them to investors or use them for arbitrage transactions and principal trades. For these negotiated margin transactions, the stock-lending period and fees are determined freely between securities firms and investors. Stock lending has become widely used as a means for investors to improve investment performance. Index fund managers, for example, can improve performance somewhat by lending out their shares.

Deregulation, market reforms and new trading tools

In March 1998, the Japanese government enacted the Financial System Reform Law, thereby paving the way for the implementation of Japan's financial Big Bang. The key changes in the new law relating to equity trading included the complete liberalization of brokerage commissions, the abolition of the securities transaction tax, an expanded range of allowable businesses for securities companies, the introduction of OTC derivatives, the deregulation of off-exchange trading and the introduction of proprietary trading systems (PTS). Among these changes, the liberalization of brokerage commissions had the most direct and significant impact on the securities industry.

BIG BANG REFORMS AND THE LIBERALIZATION OF BROKERAGE COMMISSIONS

In Japan, brokerage commissions were fixed for many years. In response to strong demand for a variable commission system among institutional investors, especially those that place large orders, commissions were liberalized for any transactions in excess of ¥1bn in April 1994. The impact of this partial liberalization of commissions was limited, however, because few transactions exceeded ¥1bn. In April 1998, commissions were further liberalized to include transactions in excess of ¥50m, and in October 1999, the fixed-commission system was completely liberalized.

When brokerage commissions were liberalized in the US and Europe, some securities companies raised the commission rates they charged individual investors because it was relatively expensive to handle smaller trades. But in Japan, online brokerage firms compete intensely on the basis of commissions, in part because commissions were completely deregulated just as online stock trading started to catch on.

The liberalization of brokerage commissions also resulted in intensified competition among Japanese securities companies to attract institutional clients. The strategies adopted by the brokerage firms vary widely. Some have taken the traditional approach of trying to provide research and other services to earn commission revenue, some have marketed themselves as discount brokers by offering comparatively low commissions, and others have focused on proprietary trading to improve profitability.

CREATION OF NEW MARKETS

The revision of regulations governing Japan's securities exchanges under the Financial System Reform Law played an important role in

Table 16.5 Listing criteria for TSE second section and Mothers market

	TSE 2nd section	**Mothers market**
Profits	At least ¥400 m in latest fiscal year and ¥100 m two fiscal years ago, or at least ¥400 m in latest fiscal year, ¥100 m three fiscal years ago and a total of ¥600 m over latest three years	No requirement (but the business that is the basis of the company's growth potential must be generating revenue)
Net assets	At least ¥1 bn on a consolidated basis and a positive figure on a parent basis	No requirement
No. of shareholders	At least 800, depending on number of shares listed	At least 300 new shareholders with an initial or secondary offering
No. of listed shares	At least 4000 trading units	At least 1000 trading units with an IPO
Proportion of stably owned shares	Less than 75% at the time of the listing	No requirement
Age of company	At least three years old	No requirement
Quarterly reporting requirement	No	Yes

Source: Nomura, based on Tokyo Stock Exchange materials.

promoting competition and reform among exchanges. One of the major improvements concerning the regulations for Japan's stock exchanges was the development of stock markets for start-ups. Many critics had argued that the relatively rigid listing requirements for the major exchanges made it difficult for start-ups to obtain capital just when they needed it most. One of the general listing requirements, for instance, is that companies must have been in business for quite a long period of time. In response to these criticisms, two new markets for start-ups were established between 1999 and 2000 – the TSE's Mothers market and the OSE's Nasdaq Japan, as discussed in Chapter 13. Furthermore, as mentioned earlier, the JSDA has established a special set of relatively loose standards for offering shares on the OTC market, which has traditionally been a market for companies with relatively short track records (Table 16.5).

The launches of the Mothers and Nasdaq Japan markets were greeted with much fanfare, partly because of fortuitous timing that coincided with a global bull market in Internet and technology stocks. Nevertheless, as investor sentiment on start-ups soured, the prices of many newly listed stocks fell below their initial offering prices and raised doubts about the role of these new markets for start-ups.

Meanwhile, Japan's stock exchanges have introduced new trading methods and revised regulations in an effort to make trading easier for investors. For example, off-hours trading, which is discussed in detail below, now plays a vital role. In December 2000, the OSE set up a new market that utilizes an electronic trading system called OptiMark, which was used mainly to execute large block trades by institutional investors. The market allowed investors to place orders in a variety of ways, enabling them to trade in a manner that best suited their needs while maintaining anonymity.

For instance, an investor wishing to buy a large block of a particular stock could indicate that he or she would offer ¥2000 per share if only 1000 shares are available but ¥2010 per share for 50 000 shares. But since almost no trades were matched up, the OptiMark market was halted after about six months. Nevertheless, the conceptual framework of the market and the OSE's effort to create the market are moves in the right direction. Moreover, concrete plans to implement proprietary trading systems are in place. In September 2000, Japan Bond Trading introduced a PTS, and a group of six securities firms led by Goldman Sachs announced that it planned to establish a market for after-hours evening trading for retail investors.

Nearly 90% of all stock trades (in terms of volume traded) in Japan are executed on the TSE. Yet the emergence of new markets and the development of an electronic trading infrastructure have led to increasing competition between the various markets as well as improvements in the markets. Therefore, whether or not the TSE will continue to be the leading exchange for stock trading in Japan remains to be seen.

PRINCIPAL TRADING

In a principal trade (or risk trade), a securities firm's dealing division takes the other side of a trade for a client that wants to quickly buy or sell a security when there is inadequate liquidity on the exchange floor. In contrast, in an agency trade, the securities firm passes client orders to the exchange.

Principal trading did not take off in Japan until the introduction of an off-hours trading system on the TSE in November 1997. Prior to the development of this system, securities companies conducted either partial or synthetic principal trades because all trading had to be conducted only during regular trading hours. In a partial principal trade, the securities company acts as the counterparty in a client trade involving a market order but absorbs only part of the order using limit orders. The synthetic principal trades are conducted through cross-trades on exchanges other than the TSE, such as the OSE and the Nagoya Stock Exchange, where the impact of other orders for the same stock is typically minimal. Many investors use off-hours trading now that it has become much more convenient than before; they can instantly execute trades at prices that are not too far away from the most recent regular-hours prices.

Eventually, all TSE off-hours trading moved to the TSE's ToSTNet system. The OSE set up a similar system in January 1999 known as the J-NET system. Principal trading in Japan further expanded when off-exchange trading was deregulated in December 1998, with the elimination of a requirement that trades go through Japan's stock exchanges.

EXPANDED TRADING METHODS AND HEIGHTENED COST CONSCIOUSNESS

Ever since full-fledged principal trades became possible, investors have had an even greater variety of available trading options. This development has had a large impact on market trends.

The use of principal trading, for instance, has improved the efficiency of basket trading, which involves the simultaneous trading of a number of stocks and is necessary for the implementation of computer-based investment strategies. Agency trades involving limit orders are problematic for basket trading because of the relatively long time required for orders to be executed. The non-simultaneous execution of the stock orders in an agency trade would lead to distortions in the client's portfolio because basket trades are often used to optimize a portfolio in terms of risk and return. In addition, executing basket trades using market orders during regular hours on the floor of the exchange often has an unacceptable market impact because of the insufficient liquidity in many cases. Principal trading enables instantaneous execution of basket trades for clients, with the fee incorporating the potential market impact when the securities firm unwinds its position and the firm's risk of holding the position until it is unwound. The larger the number of stocks in the basket trade, the more effective principal trading is; having many stocks reduces the overall risk of the basket, so the securities firm can offer an attractive price.

Exchange-for-physical (EFP) trades take full advantage of the benefits of principal trading. EFP trades entail the simultaneous purchase (sale) of a basket of stocks and the corresponding offsetting sale (purchase) of stock index futures. The risk taken by the securities company in these trades is limited to the tracking error between the cash basket and the index futures. The smaller the tracking error, the lower the risk absorbed by the broker and the lower the transaction costs, regardless of the market impact of trading the stocks that make up the cash basket.

Most principal basket trades are conducted outside normal exchange trading hours. The investor provides several securities firms with a list of stocks he wishes to trade and selects the firm willing to do the basket trade at the tightest spread relative to the last trade price on the exchange. The principal basket trade is then conducted before the next session of exchange trading starts up. Of the three off-hours trading sessions – before the regular morning session, during the lunch break, and after the close of the market in the afternoon – most trades take place during the lunch break. In addition, 'blind' principal trades are offered to institutional investors that prefer not to disclose beforehand the stocks they want to trade. But some say the intended impact of such trades is limited, because the stocks, the number of shares and the execution prices are fully disclosed by the exchange and the JSDA after the blind trades go through.

Commissions were still fixed in Japan (except for those on very large trades) between November 1997, when off-hours trading started and principal trading got fully under way, and October 1999, when the last remaining regulations on commissions were finally abolished. During this period, some investors used principal trades to lower their effective commission rates, even when market-impact costs were not a major issue. In these trades, investors asked securities companies to trade at low prices, which would still make the trade profitable for the brokerages considering the fixed commissions. But such techniques lost significance once commissions were fully liberalized, resulting in a modest decline in principal trading. Instead, one type of trade that has been catching on is the volume-weighted average price (VWAP) agency trade, which involves purchases and sales of a stock throughout the day (or the morning session or the afternoon session). Hence, in many cases, the opening price often determines the trend of a stock's price for the day.

The liberalization of stock-trading commissions in Japan has further heightened attention to trading costs by investment management companies and the pension plan sponsors they work for, as evidenced by the ongoing discussions about optimal trade executions. Even though commission costs have been declining, controlling other costs – such as market-impact costs, timing costs and opportunity costs – has become critical because the Japanese equity market is slightly less liquid than the US market, as mentioned earlier. Potential market-impact costs associated with large agency trades by institutional investors are relatively high, if the trades are executed as market orders.

Yet potential opportunity costs are high if these trades use limit orders because the trades may not be filled. Although VWAP agency trades can be thought of as trades with characteristics in between those of market and limit orders, actual market-impact costs and timing costs for VWAP trades are relatively high in many cases. Consequently, VWAP agency trades are not always an optimal solution.

Theoretically, an agency trade should be chosen if an investor's aversion (a risk coefficient expressed in terms of costs) toward the potential opportunity costs of having some trades go unfilled is lower than the securities firm's aversion toward the risk of holding positions as a counterparty. But if the investor's aversion is higher than the securities company's, then a principal trade is optimal. Unlike in the US, where institutional trading is dominated by agency trading, principal trading is likely to take on an increasingly important role in Japan, given the unique characteristics of Japan's stock market.

CHAPTER
17 Equity cross-shareholdings

In conjunction with the international harmonization of accounting standards, cross-shareholdings in Japan are now measured at fair value.[1] Financial accounting in Japan is in the midst of a transition, moving from a focus on parent financial statements and book value basis to an emphasis on consolidated figures and market value basis. One result of these changes is that companies will no longer be able to use unrealized gains on stock holdings as 'hidden reserves' for offsetting declines in operating profit, an accounting aspect that had been considered one of the advantages of cross-shareholdings. Moreover, companies will likely find it more difficult to justify holding, for an extended period, stocks that do not generate returns in excess of their cost of capital, unless the companies have clear business reasons for doing so. Consequently, even though the changes in Japanese accounting standards may not be the most significant factor behind the trend, they will probably stimulate the unwinding of cross-shareholdings.

The unwinding of cross-shareholdings is actually more closely related to some changes that have occurred in the traditional style of Japanese management, namely, the phasing out of lifetime employment and seniority-based compensation systems. During Japan's rapid economic growth period of 1952–73, cross-shareholding relationships were one of the most effective strategies for achieving long-term stability, a key issue for Japanese companies at the time. But faced with the enormous challenges of dealing with the

1 The rule took effect in fiscal 2001 (which ended in March 2002), although some companies adopted the rule early, in fiscal 2000.

prolonged downturn in the economy that has lasted for more than a decade and of surviving in the increasingly competitive global market, Japanese companies are being forced to alter their style of management. The urgency of these problems has brought about the introduction of new standards for valuing assets and liabilities at fair value, accounting for pension liabilities and valuing impaired assets. Whereas some companies unwound cross-shareholding relationships to bolster their accounting profits in the early 1990s, even more companies have been extensively doing so recently in order to manage their businesses better and more efficiently (see Chapter 7).

A history of cross-shareholding in Japan

The practice of cross-shareholding, which started in Japan after the domestic stock market reopened following the end of World War II, strengthened into the early 1990s. In 1949, when domestic stock exchanges reopened, individual investors owned a relatively high 69% of all shares, mainly because a large number of these shares owned by *zaibatsu* were sold to individuals as part of the dissolution of these prewar Japanese industrial conglomerates. The government at the time had also encouraged an increase in stockholdings among individual investors.

From the 1960s to the beginning of the 1970s, however, Japanese companies did increase their cross-shareholdings to build up bases of stable shareholders. During the market crisis of 1961–65, the first time after the war that the stock market tumbled sharply, the recently established Japan Security Holding Association (whose members were securities companies) and Kyodo Securities (whose members were banks)[2] tried to support the falling stock market by stepping in and buying stocks. As the stock market started recovering in 1965, these two organizations sold their shareholdings to investors they considered to be stable shareholders to soften any potential negative impact on the stock market and to prevent any particular investors or groups from gaining control of too many shares. The idea behind these moves resurfaced again in early 2001,

2 Kyodo Securities is now known as the Japan Kyodo Security Foundation, and Japan Security Holding Association is now known as the Capital Market Promotional Foundation.

when the Japanese government considered a proposal to establish the Banks' Shareholdings Purchase Corp., an entity to purchase stocks from financial institutions.

One key difference in this proposal is that the entity would buy stocks only from banks in order to speed up the final disposal of their non-performing loans and to help stabilize Japan's financial system. Moreover, the shares bought from the banks would ultimately be sold mainly to individual investors and such institutional investors as pension funds, rather than to the typical stable shareholders – banks and life insurance companies – as was the case in the early 1960s. In other words, the latest proposed method of transforming the ownership structure of stocks in Japan resembles the one used during the market crisis of the early 1960s, but it would shift ownership in the opposite direction, from banks and other stable shareholders to individual investors.

The liberalization of capital flows had also prompted Japanese companies to increase cross-shareholdings during the 1960s. Cross-shareholding relationships between non-financial companies and financial institutions as well as between non-financial companies were strengthened during this period to prevent acquisitions of Japanese companies by overseas companies. Then, another increase in cross-shareholdings occurred in the latter half of the 1980s, when companies issued a substantial amount of new equity; they increased their cross-shareholdings to keep stable shareholding ratios from falling.[3]

Although cross-shareholdings served their purpose during these two periods, they can be fraught with problems. Cross-shareholdings are mutual shareholdings in that one company agrees to own shares of another if the action is reciprocated, but in practice, the strategic and mutual ownership of shares between two or more companies is a narrow definition of the term 'cross-shareholding'. A broader definition of the term is the strategic but not necessarily mutual ownership of shares. The ownership of the shares of another company is termed strategic when the objective is to allow the executives of the other company to manage their business in a stable manner, not to seek an investment return on the stock. Because of this strategic aspect, cross-shareholdings have not only functioned as a buffer against poor operating results by offering unrealized gains during stock market upturns, but they have also contributed to the investment of surplus funds in unprofitable capital projects because

---

3 See Appendix 17.1 for a definition of the stable shareholding ratio.

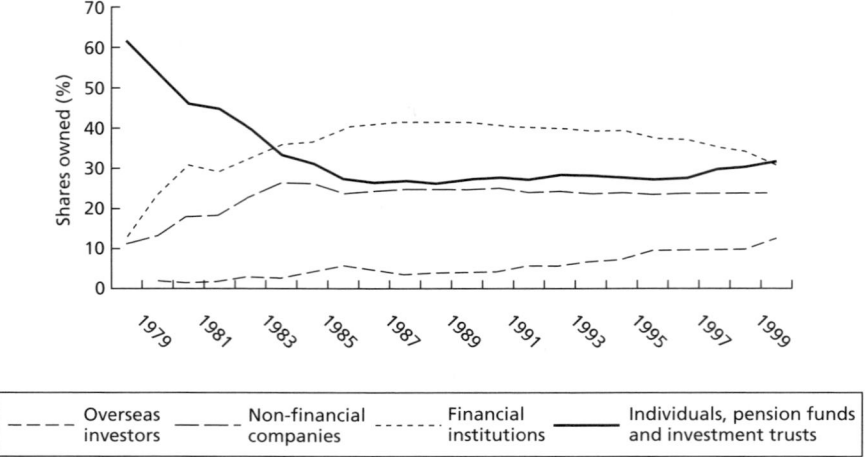

17.1 Stock ownership in Japan, by type of investor.
Source: National Conference of Stock Exchanges, *Shareownership Survey*, 1999.

higher shareholders' equity ratios have allowed companies to borrow money easily.

In fact, the expansion of cross-shareholdings through the 1990s and the related increase in bad investments, along with the prolonged downturn in Japan's stock and real estate markets in the 1990s, contributed to a rapid deterioration in the finances of many Japanese companies. Japanese banks have been hit particularly hard. It is estimated that about half of the total shares owned by Japanese non-financial companies are bank shares. In addition, banks own a massive amount of shares of non-financial companies. Indeed, on the evidence of their balance sheets, Japanese banks are essentially investing all their shareholders' equity in the stocks of non-financial companies. The Banks' Shareholdings Purchase Corp. is considered an emergency measure to help banks reduce their exposure to assets riskier than loans and to improve their finances.

As shown in Fig. 17.1, the structure of stock ownership in Japan has changed in two key ways during recent years. First, the proportion of shares owned by overseas investors has increased – 12.4% in terms of the number of shares and 18.6% in value terms, as at the end of March 2000. Overseas investors alone, however, will not be likely to fully absorb the cross-held shares that Japanese companies are seeking to sell, mainly because the stocks that overseas investors are interested in buying are not necessarily the same cross-held stocks that Japanese companies are trying to get rid of. This

Table 17.1 Stock ownership in Japan and the US, by type of investor

	Japan	**US**
Individuals, pension funds and investment trusts	25.2	83.8
Overseas investors	18.6	7.0
Financial institutions	29.3	8.2

Note: Units are percentages; figures based on market value of stocks at end-March 2000.
Source: Nomura, based on National Conference of Stock Exchanges' *Shareownership Survey* and Federal Reserve Bank's *Flow of Funds Accounts*.

mismatch has contributed to a divergence in the market, in the form of a group of strongly performing stocks and a group of poorly performing stocks. A possible interpretation of these developments is that overseas investors, who currently account for about 50% of total average daily trading volume on the Tokyo Stock Exchange and the two other major stock exchanges, are pressuring Japan to implement structural reforms.

The second major change in the structure of stock ownership is the marked decline in the proportion of shares owned by financial institutions. At the end of March 2000, the figure fell to 29.3% in value terms. The number of shares owned by financial institutions had declined for 11 consecutive years, falling from 41.5% at the end of March 1989 to 30.9% in March 2000.

A comparison of the structure of stock ownership in Japan and the US shows that in Japan, the combined proportion of shares owned by individuals, pension funds and investment trusts is significantly lower than in the US (see Table 17.1).[4] Also, the proportion of shares owned by overseas investors in Japan is higher than in the US. Another striking characteristic is that domestic financial institutions own roughly 30% of the total number of shares outstanding in Japan.

4 In Table 17.1, shares owned by Japanese individuals, pension funds and investment trusts do not include shares owned by public pension funds. Because the proportion of shares owned by public pension funds in Japan is very small, however, the inclusion of shares owned by them would not change the fact that the combined proportion of shares held by individuals, pension funds and investment trusts in Japan is significantly lower than in the US.

PROBLEMS RELATED TO CROSS-SHAREHOLDING

A variety of problems are associated with cross-shareholding relationships. First, Japanese companies, particularly banks, have tended to overlook the price risk of cross-shareholdings. But in response to the increased scrutiny of investors, companies have begun to realize that they had taken on more risk through their cross-shareholdings than they had originally anticipated. Investors have started to scrutinize companies more carefully as they come to realize they had overestimated the real value of these assets, now that the adoption of market-value accounting for assets and liabilities, in particular financial assets, has led to increased transparency on the value of businesses and assets of companies based on standardized criteria.

Second, cross-shareholdings tend to be an inefficient use of a company's capital. Comfortable cross-shareholding relationships often come at the expense of the efficient use of capital, but at the same time, as long as corporate executives seek to be able to manage their companies in a stable manner, incentives for cross-holding shares will exist. The reality is that the practice of cross-shareholding exists in countries other than Japan as well, albeit to different extents, which suggests that some business relationships cannot be justified in terms of immediate gains in efficiency alone. Such business relationships can be very effective when the parties involved have a clear and mutual sense of strategy for the intermediate term. Among the advocates of cross-shareholding ties is Harvard Business School Professor Michael Porter, who wrote on the topic in his 1990 book, *Capital Choice*.

Adding to the complications involved in these cross-holding relationships, however, is that distinguishing the leaders and laggards in the corporate world based solely on the stability of a company's management has become increasingly difficult. Even the stocks of some of the leading technology companies in the US, such as Cisco Systems, dropped by nearly half in the first quarter of 2001 alone, despite their popularity among investors. Likewise, in Japan, very few had imagined in the 1980s that Japanese banks and life insurance companies would ever go bankrupt. Yet some did collapse, and many banks are currently saddled with large amounts of bad loans, while many life insurance companies are stuck earning returns on their investments that are less than the yields they pay to their policyholders.

Clearly, as Japanese companies have come to put top priority on strengthening their own finances rather than worrying about other companies, the traditional structure of corporate governance in Japan – centred on cross-shareholding relationships – has started to unravel. It appears that Japan has finally entered a new era, one in which the efficient use of capital is considered important. The extent to which Japanese companies use their assets efficiently has significantly worsened in recent years, but many companies have been unwinding their cross-shareholdings and reallocating capital through merger and acquisition deals.

Third, the closed nature of cross-shareholding arrangements goes against the increasing tide of globalization. Cross-shareholdings are typically used to cement business ties between Japanese companies. Along with the system of *amakudari*, in which leading bureaucrats and other government officials are hired by private sector companies upon retirement, these relationships can lead to non-transparent, backroom agreements between companies. Amid the shift from competition between companies primarily in the domestic market to global competition, the extensive system of cross-shareholdings may be harming Japanese companies by preventing them from dynamically using their assets and resources more efficiently.

Despite these problems, Japanese companies continue to maintain cross-shareholding ties. One reason for this is the belief that their cross-shareholdings may help reduce agency costs – costs that result from a conflict of interest between managers and shareholders – because stable shareholders, who often have strong business relationships with managers as a result of the cross-shareholdings, are the ones monitoring managers. Simply strengthening ties with stable shareholders through cross-shareholdings, however, no longer appears to help reduce agency costs. Instead, cross-shareholdings may possibly result in higher agency costs.

THE AMOUNT OF CROSS-SHAREHOLDINGS AND THE UNWINDING OF CROSS-SHAREHOLDINGS

Table 17.2 shows the trend in estimated aggregate cross-shareholding ratios (based on three measures) for all Japanese companies traded on the exchanges and OTC market.[5] Because these ratios have been adjusted each fiscal year to maintain consistency over time, the results

---

5 Various organizations publish estimates of the amount of cross-shareholdings in Japan. Most estimates, however, are only for Tokyo Stock Price Index (TOPIX) companies and have not been adjusted to maintain consistency over time.

shown in the table are a relatively accurate indication of the extent to which cross-shareholdings have been unwound.[6] Typically, cross-shareholding ratios are calculated by dividing the cumulative number of shares held by all companies by total outstanding shares for each fiscal year. The figures in Table 17.2, however, are weighted by market capitalizations.

The use of market capitalization weightings has been considered inappropriate for calculating cross-shareholding ratios because of the relatively significant potential impact from stock price fluctuations. To avoid this problem and eliminate erroneous observations of changes in cross-shareholding ratios stemming from changes in stock prices and capital structure, the ratios have been adjusted using an index that results in the same market capitalization between two points in time.

The use of a ratio weighted by market capitalization also eliminates possible problems relating to newly listed companies, which may have an inappropriate impact on the simple average of the cross-shareholding ratio if the newly listed company's ratio is higher or lower than the average. With this method of retroactive adjustments, the trend in the ratios in Table 17.2 can serve as a measure of the extent to which cross-shareholdings have been unwound in Japan.

Most cross-shareholding data indicate that cross-shareholdings in Japan have been unwound more quickly than the data in Table 17.2 suggest. One reason for the discrepancy is that the stock prices of

6 The market capitalization-weighted cross-shareholding index is calculated as follows. Here, (″) denotes the use of market capitalization weightings for one period in the future, and (′) denotes the use of market capitalization weightings current at that point in time. Thus, the expression $h'(t_2)$ is based on the market capitalization weightings at time t_2, and the expression $h''(t_0)$ is based on the market capitalization weightings at time t_1. First, a cross-shareholding ratio weighted by the most recent market capitalization weightings for all listed stocks, $h'(t_2)$, is calculated. The cross-shareholding index for the most recent period $h(t_2)$ equals $h'(t_2)$. Next, the cross-shareholding ratio for the previous period, weighted by the most recent market capitalization weightings, is calculated and denoted as $h''(t_1)$. The degree to which cross-shareholdings have been unwound between the most recent period and the prior period, D_2, is equal to $h'(t_2)$ divided by $h''(t_1)$. Therefore, the cross-shareholding index for the previous period $h(t_1) = h(t_2)/D_2$. Similarly, the cross-shareholding ratio at time t_0 (two periods in the past) can be expressed as $h(t_0) = h(t_1)/D_1$. Note that $D_1 = h'(t_1)/h''(t_0)$. In this way, the cross-shareholding ratio for each period in the past can be calculated retroactively.

Table 17.2 Trends in unwinding of cross-shareholdings in Japan

	TOPIX companies			All listed stocks		
	Stable shareholder ratio	Unilateral shareholding ratio	Mutual shareholding ratio	Stable shareholder ratio	Unilateral shareholding ratio	Mutual shareholding ratio
1988	50.6	31.6	18.0	52.3	30.8	18.7
1989	50.1	31.8	18.4	51.8	31.0	18.9
1990	49.8	31.8	18.4	51.3	31.1	17.7
1991	50.1	31.9	18.8	51.6	31.2	18.2
1992	49.6	31.4	18.8	51.1	30.8	18.2
1993	49.6	31.4	18.9	51.0	30.8	18.0
1994	49.0	31.1	18.8	50.4	30.5	17.9
1995	48.9	31.3	18.8	50.2	30.7	18.0
1996	48.1	30.8	18.5	49.4	30.2	17.7
1997	47.8	30.8	18.4	49.0	30.3	17.6
1998	47.4	30.8	18.1	48.5	30.2	17.3
1999	44.1	28.2	16.3	45.4	27.8	15.7

Notes: Units are percentages, at end of each fiscal year in March. Figures, based on Toyo Keizai's major shareholder data and companies' securities filings, are adjusted for changes in equity capital.
Source: Nomura.

companies with relatively high cross-shareholding ratios have declined more than the stock prices of companies with comparatively low cross-shareholding ratios. In particular, the decline in the stock prices of Japanese banks, which have relatively high cross-shareholdings ratios, has made it appear as though overall cross-shareholdings in Japan are being unwound more quickly than the data in Table 17.2 would suggest. Similarly, the listing of NTT DoCoMo, which has a relatively high cross-shareholding ratio, and the subsequent sharp rise in the company's stock price have inflated other cross-shareholding data.

As shown in Table 17.2, cross-shareholdings in Japan were significantly unwound from March 1998 to March 1999. In addition, all three ratios – namely, the stable shareholder ratio, the unilateral shareholding ratio and the mutual shareholding ratio – indicate that cross-shareholdings were gradually unwound starting in the early 1990s.[7] Also, because of the inclusion of many companies heavily owned by the founders, all Japanese companies traded on the exchanges and the OTC market as a group have a higher stable shareholding ratio but lower unilateral shareholding ratio and mutual shareholding ratio than the Tokyo Stock Price Index (TOPIX) companies alone.

The relationship between cross-shareholdings and stock prices

Some argue that cross-shareholdings tend to push stock prices up whereas the unwinding of cross-shareholdings tends to put downward pressure on stock prices. Theoretically, as in the case of share buybacks, the impact of cross-shareholdings on stock prices should be neutral, assuming perfect capital markets with ample liquidity, the simultaneous receipt of information by investors and no transaction costs (see Appendix 17.2).

Share buybacks, however, can affect stock prices through the so-called announcement, or signalling effect, whereby investors have increased expectations of a rise in the value of the company because they regard the announcement of a share buyback programme as a sign that managers are serious about using assets more efficiently. Similarly, if cross-shareholding relationships are believed to

7 See Appendix 17.1 for further information on these ratios.

influence the fundamental value of a company, these relationships can impact stock prices, depending on the types of cross-
shareholding relationships already in place. In other words, the
impact of cross-shareholdings on stock prices is neutral only under
the assumption that they have no impact on the fundamentals of a
company.

Proving that cross-shareholdings actually have a neutral impact
on stock prices is difficult for two reasons. First, cross-shareholdings
can possibly have some influence on the fundamentals of a
company. Second, it is erroneous to compare two stocks and conclude that the stock with the higher price is overvalued. Therefore,
the conventional measure of the value of stocks is the price-to-
earnings (P/E) ratio, which is based on earnings per share (EPS)
under the assumption of a steady state. Because P/E ratios can be
influenced by cross-shareholdings, proving whether the impact of
cross-shareholdings on stock prices is neutral on the basis of P/E
ratios is difficult. This impact will be discussed in further detail in
the following section.

The relationship between cross-shareholdings and the P/E ratio

The P/E ratio for a company with cross-shareholding relationships
is said to be inflated[8] because whereas the stock is priced on the
basis of earnings from operations and capital gains from investments
in other companies, earnings in the denominator reflect only dividends received, not capital gains. Consequently, all other things
being equal, the P/E ratio for a company that owns another
company's stock tends to be higher than that for a company that
holds only cash. This problem, however, has more to do with the
P/E ratio itself rather than with cross-shareholdings; it can be
resolved by deducting from the numerator of the P/E ratio the
current market value of a company's capital invested in non-
physical assets (which is equal to the present value of the expected
future cash flows from these investments) and by deducting from

8 If a cross-shareholding relationship involves more than two companies, whether
P/E ratios are deflated or inflated is indeterminate and depends on the particulars
of each case.

the denominator the present value of the expected dividend income from the investments.

Cross-shareholding relationships in the form of mutual shareholdings can also result in inflated P/E ratios, which can be adjusted by deducting from the numerator the portion of the market capitalization that is effectively double-counted and by subtracting from the denominator dividends received from the counterparty in the mutual cross-shareholding relationship.

Note that the P/E ratio for a company in a mutual cross-shareholding relationship will equal the P/E ratio for a company not in a cross-shareholding arrangement if the dividend payout ratio for both companies in the mutual cross-shareholding relationship is 1. Mathematically, the coefficient for adjusting the P/E ratio when two companies have a mutual cross-shareholding relationship can be expressed as follows:

$$(1 - \text{cross-shareholding ratio})/(1 - \text{dividend payout ratio} \\ \times \text{cross-shareholding ratio})$$

Also, to compare average market P/E ratios between countries, the P/E ratios used are adjusted by multiplying the unadjusted market P/E ratios by the above expression.

If P/E ratios are boosted by cross-shareholdings, the implication is that investors recognize a relationship between cross-shareholdings and P/E ratios. But if investors do not take into account the aforementioned adjustments for the P/E ratios of companies in cross-shareholding relationships, then cross-shareholdings may not actually push up a company's P/E ratio. Because it is difficult to estimate the degree to which each P/E ratio needs to be adjusted for cross-shareholdings, most investors probably do not pay much attention to the possible upward bias cross-shareholdings may have on P/E ratios. Also, because investors do not base their investment decisions solely on P/E ratios, the possible impact of cross-shareholdings on P/E ratios is probably not very significant.

Cross-shareholdings introduce similar biases into other financial metrics. Because stock returns are closely linked to market capitalization and dividends, cross-shareholdings can influence returns on stock investments. Financial leverage can also be affected by cross-shareholdings because executives can increase shareholders' equity simply by increasing cross-shareholdings. Price-to-book (P/B) ratios, however, are not as significantly influenced by cross-shareholdings as other metrics are. P/B ratios are not directly linked to dividends, and market capitalization increases in line with shareholders' equity. Nonetheless, investors cannot solely rely on the P/B ratio to value stocks because book values reflect only the current liquidation value of a company, not expected future returns.

CROSS-SHAREHOLDINGS AND STOCK VALUATION

A determining factor of investors' expectations of future stock prices is the valuation metric used. When Japan's stock market rose during the economic bubble years of the latter half of the 1980s, investors shifted their focus from corporate profits to the value of a company's assets and increasingly based their investment decisions on P/B ratios rather than P/E ratios. As mentioned, however, it is problematic to base investment decisions only on P/B ratios because they do not incorporate expectations of future profits. As the domestic stock market declined substantially in the 1990s, traditional valuation measures came into question.

The fair market value of a stock based on the dividend discount model (DDM), one of the most commonly used valuation models, is the present value of future dividends expected on the basis of all currently available information. The DDM assumes that the cost of equity capital is constant, regardless of the time period. To use analysts' earnings estimates rather than dividends, the Edwards–Bell–Ohlson (EBO) model, which was developed upon the concept of economic value added (EVA), can be used.

The EBO model, which is derived from the DDM, can be rewritten as the reported book value plus an infinite sum of the discounted residual income. The EBO model makes understanding the relationship between economic profits and the value of a company in each period intuitively possible. In addition, the EBO model and discounted cash flow (DCF) models assume that in the long run, return on equity (ROE) reverts to the mean.

On the basis of the EBO model, there are two factors that may cause a company's P/B ratio to decline. First, an increase in a company's risk premium, because of a decline in market capitalization or a rise in credit risk, may put downward pressure on a company's P/B ratio. Second, a P/B ratio may decline as a result of lower expected returns. If the expected return on a stock is higher than investors' required rate of return and is not expected to revert to the required rate of return in the short term, a company's P/B ratio should be high. A relatively strong impact from a high-risk premium would suggest that a company's P/B ratio is closely linked to factors that affect the risk premium, such as the size of a company, whereas a relatively strong influence from expected returns would suggest that a company's P/B ratio is largely a function of expected ROE.

The remaining part of this section addresses the inputs for the EBO model. Because it is impossible to accurately forecast the future cash flows of a company, theoretical values for expected cash flows based on all currently available information are estimated. The projected ROE of a company, meanwhile, can be calculated on earnings estimates for the current fiscal year and the following fiscal year.[9]

In this analysis, based on the assumption that the cost of capital does not significantly vary among companies, the cost of capital is set at 5%[10] for all companies. Measuring investors' required rate of return is difficult. Although risk premia are assumed to be equal for all companies in this analysis, company size is considered separately as a factor that may cause risk premia to differ.[11] Financial leverage can vary even among companies with identical ROEs, resulting in differing volatility risk for ROE. Different financial leverage ratios among companies are typically reflected in their different costs of capital. It should be noted, however, that exceptionally high shareholders' equity ratios might affect the results of this analysis.

An examination of the relationship between the three types of cross-shareholding ratios mentioned earlier – the stable shareholder ratio, the unilateral shareholding ratio and the mutual shareholding ratio – and the estimated ROE for the next fiscal year based on earnings forecasts shows that the correlation between the stable shareholding ratio and ROE is positive, while the correlation between the mutual shareholding ratio and ROE is negative (Table 17.3). In other words, high ROE companies tend to have a high stable

---

9 Earnings estimates are Nomura estimates for parent after-tax earnings. When Nomura's estimates are not available, company estimates compiled by Toyo Keizai are used, and when company estimates are not available, analysts' estimates compiled by the *Nihon Keizai Shimbun* are used.

10 This figure is equivalent to a P/E ratio of 20x (the reciprocal of 5%).

11 It may seem inappropriate to assume the same risk premium for all companies, given the increasing differences in credit risk among companies recently. But some studies have confirmed that the cost of capital has very little impact on the results of cross-sectional analyses.

Table 17.3 Correlation between cross-shareholding ratios and estimated ROE based on next fiscal year's earnings forecasts

	Stable shareholding ratio			Unilateral shareholding ratio			Mutual shareholding ratio	
Date	Corr. coeff. (avg.)	Corr. coeff. (March)	Date	Corr. coeff. (avg.)	Corr. coeff. (March)	Date	Corr. coeff. (avg.)	Corr. coeff. (March)
1988	10.2	11.8	1988	10.3	11.7	1988	−1.5	−2.5
1989	12.4	10.4	1989	6.5	7.6	1989	−3.2	−0.2
1990	10.6	14.2	1990	2.5	4.1	1990	−5.3	−7.5
1991	10.1	8.1	1991	1.8	1.7	1991	−7.1	−3.9
1992	10.3	7.4	1992	−2.6	−1.8	1992	−10.6	−8.3
1993	11.3	10.7	1993	−4.3	−6.3	1993	−11.1	−12.7
1994	7.6	9.8	1994	−5.0	−5.9	1994	−7.3	−8.1
1995	8.6	12.8	1995	−3.6	−8.0	1995	−6.9	−12.7
1996	9.3	12.5	1996	−3.4	−6.1	1996	−9.7	−11.3
1997	8.0	10.2	1997	−1.3	−5.1	1997	−9.3	−10.9
1998	5.1	4.0	1998	−3.5	1.0	1998	−6.4	−5.5
1999	8.0	8.0	1999	−6.3	−6.2	1999	−8.8	−7.9
Total	9.3		Total	−0.6		Total	−7.2	

Note: 'Corr. coeff. (avg.)' is the average correlation between January and December, 'Corr. coeff. (March)' is the correlation at the end of March, and 'Total' is the average correlation from 1988 to 1999.
Source: Nomura.

shareholding ratio but a low mutual shareholding ratio. The primary reason for this outcome is that the same type of bias that exists in the calculation for the P/E can be found in this relationship. Mutual shareholdings reduce the observed ROE because the increase in shareholders' equity (the denominator of the ROE) is greater than the increase in profit (the numerator). Also, the correlation between the stable shareholding ratio and the mutual shareholding ratio is negative.

Empirical studies show that companies with a high stable shareholding ratio tend to have high valuations. This trend indicates the tendency of high ROE companies to have high stable shareholding ratios. At the same time, the empirical evidence does not indicate that a high mutual shareholding ratio lowers a company's value.

The impact of cross-shareholdings on Japan's capital markets

Cross-shareholdings, which include shares held by a company's own executives as well as shares held by major shareholders and institutional investors, serve to impose discipline upon executives. Nonetheless, cross-shareholdings can either strengthen or weaken the degree of control over managers. Cross-shareholdings can potentially strengthen shareholder control over corporations because institutional investors and other major shareholders generally have the incentive and ability to monitor executives. But when major shareholders have close business ties with their cross-shareholding counterparties, these large shareholders may become overly supportive of executives and thus function poorly as monitors of corporate managers.

In Japan, a non-linear relationship exists between the ratio of shares held by company executives and the value of a company. Studies have shown that an increase in the number of shares owned by company managers can increase the value of a company because it aligns the interests of managers with those of outside shareholders.[12] Yet a rise in the percentage of shares held by managers

12 See, for instance, A. Berle and G. Means, *The Modern Corporation and Private Property* (New York, Commerce Clearing House, 1932), and M. Jensen and W. Meckling, 'Theory of the Firm: Managerial Behavior, Agency Costs and Ownership Structure', *Journal of Financial Economics*, 3 (1976): 305–70.

and shareholders supportive of managers could serve to shield executives from outside shareholders. The resultant stable position of managers enhances the incentive for them to maximize their own interests rather than the value of the company.

The analysis in this chapter is based on three types of cross-shareholding ratios, as defined in Appendix 17.1. Among the three, only the stable shareholding ratio includes shares owned by managers. As mentioned, higher stable shareholding ratios tend to increase the value of a company because the interests of managers and those of outside shareholders are closely aligned. But the risk exists that corporate governance may be inadequate at companies with relatively high stable shareholding ratios. When the market regards a high stable shareholding ratio negatively, in terms of shielding corporate managers from unfriendly shareholders, a comparatively high ratio may reduce the value of a company. The earlier analysis of all Japanese companies showed that high stable shareholding ratios had a positive impact on the value of a company, which suggests that the value of a company would be hurt only if the stable shareholding ratio was very high.

The mutual shareholding ratio, on the other hand, measures the degree to which a pure cross-shareholding relationship exists because it excludes nearly all shares owned by executives. This ratio is highly correlated with the ratio of shares owned by financial institutions. It is therefore possible that corporate governance is inadequate at companies with relatively high mutual shareholding ratios.

ANALYSTS' EARNINGS FORECASTS AND CONSOLIDATED ACCOUNTING

Analysts tend to more fully incorporate management incentives into their earnings forecasts for the next fiscal year and beyond than for the current fiscal year. Analysts' earnings estimates for the current year are for profits generated from existing businesses and therefore do not need to take into consideration management incentives and corporate governance issues. Earnings forecasts for the next fiscal year and beyond, in contrast, should incorporate the ability of a company to generate added value through new projects because of the difficulty of increasing profits over the long run simply by maintaining a company's existing operations. In addition, because management incentives and supervision by outside shareholders are important factors in determining the ability of a company to generate value over the longer term, analysts cannot, for the most part, ignore the impact of cross-shareholdings in their earnings forecasts for the next fiscal year.

Since investors value stocks primarily on the basis of earnings estimates for the following fiscal year, a company's ownership structure is already discounted to some degree in the fair value of a stock. When valuing stocks, however, investors are likely to consider not only basic stock valuation metrics but also such factors as the impact of stable shareholders. With the ongoing harmonization of accounting standards worldwide, investors are increasingly focusing on consolidated earnings data. The correlation between theoretical P/B ratios, based on consolidated figures, and observed P/B ratios has been increasing each year, more so than the corresponding correlation for parent P/B ratios. Since 1996, however, the correlation between P/B ratios and the stable shareholding ratio has not been significant, in part because of a rise in corporate default risk. In seeking to avoid companies with significant default risk, investors have probably come to find more value in large corporations rather than in smaller companies with relatively high stable shareholding ratios but which are heavily owned by the founders.

Ultimately, the decision whether to consider the impact of cross-shareholdings on stock valuations depends on the valuation measures used by investors. Given that the share of Japanese stocks owned by foreign investors in value terms had risen to 18.6% by the end of March 2000, the measures by which stocks are being valued have been changing somewhat. Although it is difficult to directly incorporate cross-shareholdings into stock valuations, the analysis in this chapter suggests that cross-shareholdings could become an important factor in estimating the added value that is likely to be generated by companies in the future.

The outlook for cross-shareholdings in Japan

Amid the ongoing structural reforms in Japan, companies will need to adopt new types of management structures to survive the increasing competition. As a result, many companies are likely to continue to unwind their cross-shareholdings and increasingly participate in mergers and acquisitions. Any cross-shareholding relationships that manage to survive will probably change in nature.

In Japan, stable shareholders are typically executives, banks, life insurance companies, and parent and affiliated companies. Sales of cross-shareholdings by banks and life insurance companies are a particular problem for the stock market. Some argue that these sales, which were spurred by the adoption of mark-to-market accounting for cross-shareholdings in fiscal 2001, can put strong downward pressure on the stock market and thereby make it even more difficult for banks to dispose of their non-performing loans.[13] Meanwhile, life insurance companies are hurting because of the unprecedented low level of interest rates in Japan, which have depressed the returns on their investments to less than the yields they have to pay to their policyholders.[14] Struggling to strengthen their financial position, banks and life insurance companies are looking to reduce their cross-shareholdings to better manage their risk exposure. The Japanese government, however, is concerned that a large-scale sell-off of shares by the banks and life insurance companies could depress the domestic stock market even further.

A large equity stake controlled by the executives of a company is not considered a cross-shareholding. It does nevertheless constitute a stable shareholding because it serves to align the interests of management and shareholders, and therefore generally helps to increase the value of a company. But if the executives control too large an equity stake, then corporate governance may suffer because of the diminished ability of outside shareholders to monitor management.

Stable shareholding relationships involving parent and affiliated companies will most likely change significantly in the future. This transformation, however, will entail more than just the unwinding of cross-shareholdings. In this period of global competition, Japanese companies must strive to increase their value by restructuring, specifically by focusing on core businesses.

Extensive cross-shareholding relationships have also been rather common in Germany, which has started to reform its capital markets by adopting legislation that eliminates the capital gains tax, thus encouraging the unwinding of cross-shareholdings. Taking advantage of the new policy, Deutsche Bank transferred strategic shareholdings to an asset management company, which will manage the assets to maximize investment returns. The Japanese government,

---

13 Banks often realize gains on their stock holdings to help offset loan losses.

14 See Chapter 7 for a more detailed discussion of this topic.

meanwhile, is considering adopting an emergency measure to encourage companies to unwind cross-shareholdings. Although such policies are currently being debated, Japanese companies are likely to continue to gradually sell those cross-shareholdings they think are ineffective for increasing corporate value. Possible buyers of cross-shareholdings that are being sold include companies, which could buy back their shares from their cross-shareholding counterparty and either retire them or hold them as treasury stock; investment trusts, which can use the stocks for defined-contribution pension plans; and individual investors, whose participation in the stock market may increase thanks to deregulation and efforts to improve investor education.

Appendix 17.1 Types of cross-shareholding ratios

This appendix defines the terms 'unilateral shareholdings' and 'mutual shareholdings'. Throughout this chapter, the amount of cross-shareholdings has been assumed to be higher than the estimated amount of mutual shareholdings but lower than the estimated amount of unilateral shareholdings. A unilateral shareholding relationship is one in which Company A owns some of Company B's shares, regardless of whether Company B owns any shares of Company A. For instance, if Company A owns 1 million shares in Company B but Company B does not own any shares in Company A, the total number of unilateral shareholdings is 1 million shares (1 million shares plus 0 shares).

A mutual shareholding relationship is one in which Company A and Company B own each other's shares. For example, if Company A owns 1 million shares in Company B but Company B does not own any shares in Company A, then the total number of mutual shareholdings is zero (0 shares plus 0 shares). A mutual shareholding relationship exists only if Company A owns, for instance, 1 million shares of Company B and Company B owns half a million shares of Company A.

The total number of mutual shareholdings can be calculated in a variety of ways. In this example, the total number of mutually held shares could be considered to be 1.5 million shares (1 million plus 0.5 million), or it could be considered to be 0.5 million shares (0.5 million shares are held mutually, while the purpose of the remaining 0.5 million shares held by Company A is unclear). In this chapter, the half million shares of Company A's stock owned by Company B are considered to be a mutual shareholding; the 1 million shares of Company B owned by Company A are also considered to be a mutual shareholding; and the total number of mutual shareholdings for Company A and B is considered to be 1.5 million shares.

To analyse unilateral shareholdings and mutual shareholdings for each Japanese company, two sources were used: Toyo Keizai data on companies' major shareholders and company securities filings (*yuka shoken hokokusho*). Company securities filings contain various information on the stock holdings of publicly trading Japanese companies, such as the specific stocks, the number of shares owned and the purchase prices. These data are not perfect, however. For example, the category 'other holdings' does not include the names of these individual stock holdings. In addition, shares in affiliated companies are excluded because they are included in a separate section of the company securities filings. Furthermore, it is impossible to obtain data on shares owned by banks because they do not disclose their marketable securities holdings.

Toyo Keizai data on companies' major shareholders are therefore used to supplement the information available in company securities filings. The Toyo Keizai data include the top 20 shareholders of each Japanese company, including banks. For instance, if Bank A is one of the 20 largest shareholders of Bank B, with a holding of 10 million shares of Bank B, this information will appear in the Toyo Keizai data. Still, these data are not comprehensive because the coverage is limited to the 20 largest shareholders. The Toyo Keizai data include shares held by affiliated companies, as affiliates are often among the top 20 shareholders. If the data in the company securities filings and the Toyo Keizai data are identical, the latter source is used to avoid duplication.

For this chapter, we calculate the stable shareholding ratio, the unilateral shareholding ratio and the mutual shareholding ratio and use them as measures of cross-shareholdings.

The stable shareholding ratio is calculated by dividing the aggregate number of shares held by the largest 20 shareholders and all listed companies (including OTC companies) by total outstanding shares. This ratio encompasses a wide range of shareholding relationships, such as cross-shareholding ties between non-financial companies, those between non-financial companies and banks (primarily the main banks that they rely on most for loans and other banking services), as well as strategic investments by life insurance companies and investments by foreign companies and individuals.

The unilateral shareholding ratio is calculated by dividing the number of unilateral shareholdings, as defined above, by the total number of outstanding shares. The universe of companies used to calculate this ratio consists of all Japanese companies traded on the exchanges and OTC market. Mutual shareholdings constitute a subset of unilateral shareholdings. The unilateral shareholding ratio can be thought of as the stable shareholding ratio, excluding shares owned by major individual shareholders, privately held companies and life insurance companies.

The mutual shareholding ratio is calculated by dividing the number of mutual shareholdings, as defined above, by the total number of outstanding shares. The universe of companies used to calculate this ratio consists of all Japanese companies traded on the exchanges and OTC market. Companies with a relatively low mutual shareholding ratio include mainly the subsidiaries of large corporations. The mutual shareholding ratio does not take into account triangular cross-shareholding relationships. Therefore, based on the definition of mutual shareholdings noted earlier, companies that do not own each other's shares are not included in the ratio, even if one of them owns a significant amount of the other company's shares. In addition, because of the limitations on the available data, mutual shareholding ratios for *keiretsu* group companies may be underestimated.

Appendix 17.2 A theoretical discussion of the impact of cross-shareholdings on stock prices

An analysis of the impact of cross-shareholdings on stock prices follows. The example discussed assumes that a company purchases another company's shares in the secondary market.

The assumptions are as follows. Two companies, Company A and Company B, exist, and their current stock prices are denoted as P_A and P_B, respectively. The total number of outstanding shares, denoted as N, is the same for Company A and Company B. Company A buys α percent of Company B's total outstanding shares in the secondary market, while Company B purchases β percent of Company A's total outstanding shares in the market. Company A has surplus funds of C_A yen per share outstanding, and Company B has excess funds of C_B yen per share outstanding. Both companies will use some of their excess funds to establish a cross-shareholding relationship between themselves.

To purchase Company B's shares in the secondary market at the current market price, Company A will need $\alpha \times P_B \times N$ yen worth of funds. Therefore, after Company A purchases Company B's shares, Company A's excess funds will be $(C_A \times N - \alpha \times P_B \times N)$ yen. Similarly, Company B will need $\beta \times P_A \times N$ yen worth of funds to buy Company A's shares, and Company B's excess funds will be $(C_B \times N - \beta \times P_A \times N)$ yen after it purchases Company A's shares.

The share prices of Company A and Company B after the mutual shareholding relationship is established are denoted as $P_A{}'$ and $P_B{}'$, respectively, and the following two equations can be derived to represent each company's market value:

$$(P_A - C_A) \times N + (C_A \times N - \alpha \times P_B \times N) + P_B' \times \alpha N = P_A' \times N, \text{ and}$$
$$(P_B - C_B) \times N + (C_B \times N - \beta \times P_A \times N) + P_A' \times \beta N = P_B' \times N.$$

These equations can be used to prove that $P_A{}' = P_A$ and that $P_B{}' = P_B$, indicating that the stock prices of both Company A and Company B do not change after they purchase each other's stocks in the market, because neither company's market capitalization changes. The excess funds of Company A and Company B were simply transformed into stock investments, and the value of both companies was unaffected, assuming a perfect market.

In Japan, cross-shareholding relationships are often established through private placements. Below is an analysis of the impact on stock prices of cross-shareholding relationships formed through a private placement. Assumptions: Companies A and B buy each other's stock by issuing new shares and exchanging them through a private placement rather than using excess funds. Based on these assumptions, the following two equations can be derived to represent each company's market value:

$$(P_A - C_A) \times N + C_A \times N + P_B' \times \alpha \times N = P_A' \times (1 + \beta) \times N, \text{ and}$$
$$(P_B - C_B) \times N + C_B \times N + P_A' \times \beta \times N = P_B' \times (1 + \alpha) \times N.$$

These equations can be used to prove that $P_A{}' = P_A$ and that $P_B{}' = P_B$, indicating that the stock prices of Companies A and B do not change after they purchase each other's stocks through a private placement. Each company's market capitalization will increase in proportion to the increase in the number of shares outstanding, because their stock prices do not change.

CHAPTER

18

The securitization market

Japan's market for mortgage-backed securities (MBS) and asset-backed securities (ABS)[1] has developed rapidly in recent years. The market has expanded not only in size but also in terms of the types of assets securitized and the kinds of products available to investors. In 2001, the amount of MBS and ABS issued reportedly exceeded ¥3 tr. Japanese companies now have a better understanding of the benefits associated with using MBS and ABS to raise financing and improve their balance sheets, and more investors are now willing to invest in securitized assets. Many large Japanese institutional investors have established teams that specialize in investing in MBS and ABS.

The development of Japan's securitization market

Japan's MBS/ABS market dates back to 1973, when the first residential mortgage investment trust was established. The enactment of the Mortgage Certificate Law in 1931 had provided the legal framework for the issuance of mortgage certificates (mortgage notes), but these instruments were not really MBS. They were backed by the creditworthiness of the issuer of the certificates rather than by any specific assets. The next major catalyst leading to the development of Japan's MBS/ABS market did not occur until

---

1 A distinction is made in this chapter between MBS and ABS, although the distinction may not be a universal one.

the latter half of the 1980s to the early 1990s, when the Ministry of Finance implemented various measures to enable Japanese banks to securitize their assets, mainly loans, more easily. Also during this period, Citibank developed an asset-backed commercial paper program (ABCP) in the US for Japanese non-financial corporations to securitize their account receivables. This innovation helped to stimulate the development of the Japanese market for MBS and ABS.

One particularly major factor that contributed to the development of asset securitization in Japan was the establishment in 1993 of the Law Relating to the Regulation of Business Concerning Specified Claims. Often referred to as the MITI Law, this law was adopted primarily to broaden the fund-raising options available to non-banks. Before the law was implemented, non-banks were for the most part limited to funding their lending operations with bank loans. The rationale behind the new law was twofold. First, it lifted restrictions on the securitization of leases and other so-called specified claims through the establishment of trusts, partnerships or transfers. In addition, the law simplified procedures for perfecting an assignment against third parties.

The MITI Law specifies three methods for perfecting an assignment against third parties, but these were not specifically intended for the creation of the secondary markets for these securitized assets. Nevertheless, an increasing number of companies have issued ABS in the Euro capital markets by establishing offshore special purpose corporations (SPCs) with branches in Tokyo. In 1994, companies began to take advantage of the new law to issue ABS through a structure that entailed the transfer of assets to an overseas SPC.

Since the enactment of the MITI Law, the amount of securitized assets has increased steadily, reaching about ¥4 tr. by fiscal 1998. Assets that cannot be securitized within the scope of the MITI Law have been increasingly securitized through the use of overseas SPCs. Thus, although the amount of Japanese assets securitized has increased following the passage of the MITI Law, companies have been strongly calling for the establishment of a domestic SPC framework for securitizing assets.

Furthermore, a more comprehensive approach became necessary for the perfection of assignments against third parties when transferring assets. Accordingly, the government enacted two new laws in 1998: the Law Concerning Securitization of Specified Assets by a Special Purpose Corporation (the SPC Law), and the Law Concerning Exceptions to the Requirements for the Perfection of

Assignment of Receivables under the Civil Code (the Perfection Law). In addition, the government passed the Law Relating to the Issuance of Corporate Bonds for Lending Activities by Commercial Lenders (the Non-Bank Bond Act) to further expand the fund-raising options available to non-banks. The passage of these laws indicates that the government approved of the development of a legal and systemic framework for asset securitization in Japan. As a result, the amount of ABS issued in 1999 doubled from the level in 1998.

Major laws related to asset securitization

THE LAW RELATING TO THE REGULATION OF BUSINESS CONCERNING SPECIFIED CLAIMS (MITI LAW)

The MITI Law, which was passed in 1992 and took effect in the following year, has played an extremely critical role in the development of Japan's asset securitization market in terms of increasing the fund-raising options for Japanese leasing, consumer finance and other non-bank financial institutions. Before the enactment of the law, the Capital Subscription Law prohibited these non-banks from financing their lending operations by issuing corporate bonds. Non-banks thus had to rely totally on bank loans from other financial institutions to finance their business activities.

Another important facet of the MITI Law made transferring assets easier by allowing lenders to provide public notice to perfect an assignment against third parties. Prior to the enactment of the MITI Law, lenders were obligated to give notice to or receive consent from all obligors (debtors) to perfect an assignment against third parties. For assets involving many obligors, this requirement made securitization difficult because of the large number of administrative processes and high costs. Permitting public notification, however, eliminated these hassles.

The MITI Law covers lease claims, instalment loans (including credit card receivables) and leased equipment, all of which are classified as specified claims under the law. Two-thirds of securitized assets in Japan consist of lease claims, and the remainder are instalment loans. A very small amount of leased equipment has been securitized. At first, the law permitted the securitization of assets through trusts, partnerships or transfers. In 1996, however, the securitization of assets through the issuance of ABS or ABCP was permitted. As of the end of fiscal 1999, a trust framework was used for about 80% of asset securitization deals because of the comparative simplicity of the structure and the relatively low costs involved. Although the issuance of ABS or ABCP provides greater liquidity, the pricing of assets securitized through a trust structure is not that different from the pricing of ABS or ABCP deals.

THE LAW CONCERNING SECURITIZATION OF SPECIFIED ASSETS BY A SPECIAL PURPOSE CORPORATION (THE SPC LAW)

The SPC Law, enacted in 1998, was significant because it established the legal framework for SPCs. An SPC is treated differently from a general corporation under Japan's Commercial Code. Formally, the SPC Law brings together both the Law Concerning Securitization of Specified Assets by a Special Purpose Corporation and the Law Concerning the Establishment of Laws Related to the Implementation of the Law Concerning Securitization of Specified Assets by a Special Purpose Corporation.

The key aspects of the SPC Law are as follows:

1 An SPC can be established through a registration system if an asset securitization plan is submitted.

2 SPCs can acquire such assets as monetary claims to designated persons and real estate interests as well as trust beneficiary interests in these assets, but they cannot acquire marketable securities.

3 The requirements for establishing SPCs are looser than those for establishing a general corporation under the Commercial Code. Under the SPC Law, for example, the minimum required capital is ¥3m, compared with ¥10m for general corporations under the Commercial Code. In addition, an SPC requires the appointment of only one director, whereas regular corporations require the appointment of three directors.

4 SPCs are eligible for favourable tax treatment. For instance, if certain conditions are met, dividends are tax-deductible. In addition, SPCs are eligible for reduced taxes on the acquisition of real estate.

5 SPCs can issue preferred equity securities, debt securities and promissory notes. All of these securities are considered marketable securities according to the Japanese Securities and Exchange Law.

6 SPCs are considered recipients of assets, such as specified claims, under the MITI Law and special investors under the Real Estate Specified Joint Venture Enterprise Law.

The enactment of the SPC Law has had a profound impact on Japan's asset securitization market. By the end of 2000, more than 60 SPCs had been established. SPCs have become the standard structure for the securitization of real estate assets. SPCs are also widely used to securitize various monetary claims, such as lease claims, instalment-sale receivables, automobile loans and even life insurance companies' reserve funds.

The SPC Law has been revised and simplified in response to demands for various improvements to the law. Major problems included limits on the types of assets that could be securitized under the original law and problems pertaining to investors' exercise of voting rights. The new law, which will be discussed later, is called the Law on the Securitization of Assets, or the New SPC Law.

THE LAW CONCERNING EXCEPTIONS TO THE REQUIREMENTS FOR THE PERFECTION OF ASSIGNMENT OF RECEIVABLES UNDER THE CIVIL CODE (THE PERFECTION LAW)

The MITI Law created a structure for the securitization of assets and, within this framework, simplified the procedures for the perfection of an assignment against third parties when transferring assets, whereas the main purpose of the SPC Law was to create a framework for the securitization of assets and to deal with related tax issues. The Perfection Law, enacted in 1998, however, is an exception to Japan's Civil Code and is more comprehensive in its scope. It pertains broadly to the perfection of an assignment against third parties when transferring assets.

Under the Perfection Law, when a corporation transfers a claim (only claims with designated obligees, for which monetary payment is received) to a third party, the obligation to provide notification through a notarized date stamp, as stipulated in Art. 467 of the Civil Code, is deemed to be performed when a registration statement is filed at the time of the transfer. The Perfection Law thus permits the perfection of an assignment against third parties. The law does not, however, permit assignment against the obligor through the filing of a registration statement only. To effect perfection against an original obligor, separate notice to or consent from the obligor is required. In this case, notification must be provided in the form of a registration certificate.

The Perfection Law, which has been widely applied to asset securitization transactions, has had a significant impact on the administrative aspects of securitizing assets in Japan.

THE LAW ON THE SECURITIZATION OF ASSETS
(THE ASSET SECURITIZATION LAW OR THE NEW SPC LAW)

The revised version of the SPC Law, which will hereafter be referred to as the New SPC Law, took effect in November 2000. The new version of the law permits the establishment of special purpose trusts as another possible vehicle for securitizing assets. In addition, it expands the types of assets that can be securitized. The three main features of the new law are as follows.

Expanded range of assets eligible for securitization

Under the original version of the SPC Law, such assets as monetary claims to designated persons and real estate as well as trust beneficiary interests in these assets could be securitized. Under the New SPC Law, securitizing property rights in general has become possible. And because marketable securities can now be securitized, it is feasible to create such instruments as collateralized bond obligations (CBOs), a type of domestic bond, through the establishment of an SPC.

Simplification of the regulations regarding the establishment of an SPC

The following changes have been made to either simplify or improve the regulations:

- the registration system has been replaced with a notification system for the establishment of an SPC;

- the asset securitization plan no longer needs to be included in the articles of incorporation of an SPC;

- the minimum required capital has been reduced from ¥3 m to ¥100 000;

■ a trust structure has been established for capital contributions;

■ reductions in the outstanding amount of preferred equity securities are now allowed;

■ the issuance of convertible bonds and bonds with warrants (warrants would give the holder the right to purchase preferred equity securities) is now allowed;

■ funds can be borrowed for the acquisition of assets to be securitized; and

■ changing asset securitization plans is now easier.

Allowing the establishment of special purpose trusts

The establishment of a trust for securitizing assets has been common in Japan for some time, especially for the securitization of specified claims. Under the New SPC Law, the same rules and framework that apply to an SPC apply to a special purpose trust. In addition, the new version of the law treats beneficiary certificates issued by a special purpose trust as marketable securities as defined in the Securities and Exchange Law. Even so, the certificates are not as liquid as corporate bonds. The certificates are treated as monetary claims to designated persons as defined in the Civil Code and, accordingly, are subject to the requisite procedures before they can be transferred.

THE LAW ON INVESTMENT TRUSTS AND INVESTMENT COMPANIES (THE INVESTMENT TRUST LAW)

The Law on Investment Trusts and Investment Companies, which used to be known as the Securities Investment Trust Law, was revised and renamed at the same time as the New SPC Law because both laws pertain to the establishment of collective investment structure (see also Chapter 6). The main purpose of this new law is to broaden the range of assets for which an investment trust structure can be applied to include assets other than just marketable securities, such as real estate. Unlike the New SPC Law, the Investment Trust Law stipulates that only licensed investment managers can manage assets.

The Investment Trust Law paved the way for the creation of real estate investment trusts (REITs). Introduced only in 1998, corporate investment trusts have had a very short track record. Nonetheless, because the closed-end corporate investment trust structure is well suited for REITs, the number of investment companies will probably increase substantially.

The profile of Japan's securitization market

Figure 18.1 shows the trend in the issuance amount of MBS and ABS, broken down by major asset type. The issuance amount for trust beneficiary interests and ABCP are not included, however. Although trust beneficiary interests are not included, the ¥211 bn Magic product, issued in 2000, is included in the residential mortgage category. Not only domestic asset-backed debt securities (including those issued through SPCs), but also Euroyen bonds and samurai bonds are included.

The size of the Japanese MBS/ABS market expanded signifi-

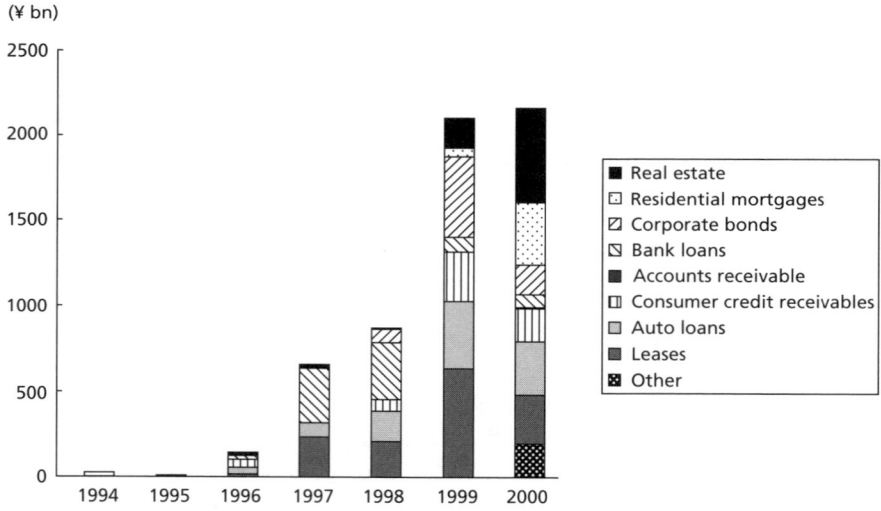

18.1 Trend in issuance amount of mortgage- and asset-backed securities, broken down by major asset type.
Source: Nomura.
Note: The amount of MBS/ABS issued through medium-term note programmes that is not clearly ascertainable is not included. The amount of MBS/ABS issued in 2000 in the category 'other' includes ¥180 bn in securitized reserve funds held by Nippon Life. Consumer-credit receivables include consumer loans.

cantly, from only about ¥140bn in 1996 to more than ¥2 tr. by 1999. During this period, lease and auto loan deals accounted for a relatively stable proportion of the total amount of MBS/ABS issued. In 2000, however, the main products in the MBS/ABS market were commercial and residential MBS.

KEY PRODUCT ATTRIBUTES

This section examines clearly emerging trends in the structures, credit ratings and maturities for MBS and ABS (Fig. 18.2).

Structures

In 1999, between 80% and 90% of MBS and ABS involved amortizing structures or a single 'bullet' principal payment on the maturity date; very few used pass-through structures. In 2000, however, around 40% of MBS/ABS deals were issued as pass-throughs. One factor behind the rise in the issuance of pass-through securities was a sharp contraction in the spreads for those securities structured as bullets. Demand for pass-through securities has increased particularly among investors seeking marginally higher yields. In addition, more pass-through securities have been issued because this structure is suitable for residential mortgages and other assets that have recently begun to be securitized. The proportion of pass-through securities will probably continue to increase.

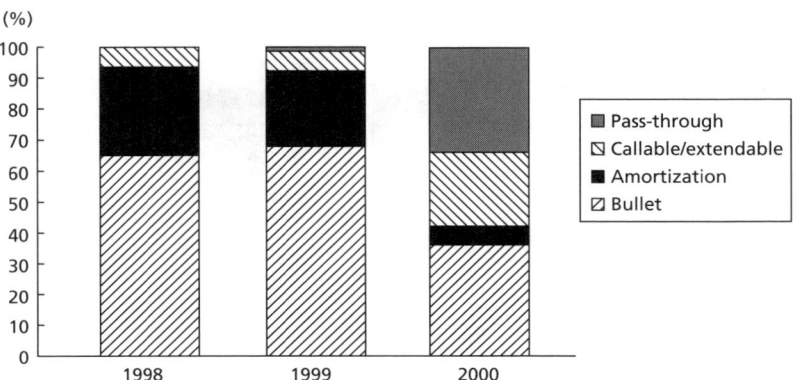

18.2 Trend in types of MBS/ABS structures as a proportion of total issuances. Source: Nomura.

Credit ratings

The amount of MBS/ABS deals rated below AAA or Aaa has steadily increased since 2000, although this trend is not evident in Fig. 18.3, which shows a breakdown of MBS/ABS deals by credit rating in percentage terms. Factors that have contributed to the rise in the ratio of ABS with credit ratings below AAA or Aaa include an increase in the issuance of real estate-backed securities and a contraction in corporate bond spreads and consequently stronger demand for higher-spread tranches with ratings below AAA or Aaa. In addition, in part because a large number of CBOs were issued in 1999 with the most subordinate tranches unrated, unrated securities have accounted for a sharply higher proportion of total MBS/ABS issuances.

Maturity

Because interest rates have remained so low for a long time, some institutional investors have been aggressively buying long-term fixed-income securities. This trend has contributed to the lengthening of maturities in the MBS/ABS market. As shown in Fig. 18.4, institutions are issuing an increasing proportion of longer-term MBS and ABS. In the past, more than half of all MBS and ABS, mainly those backed by leases and auto loans, had maturities of three years or less, but more recently an increasing proportion have had maturities of three to five years. In addition, a steadily increasing number of securities, primarily MBS, have maturities of 10 years or more.

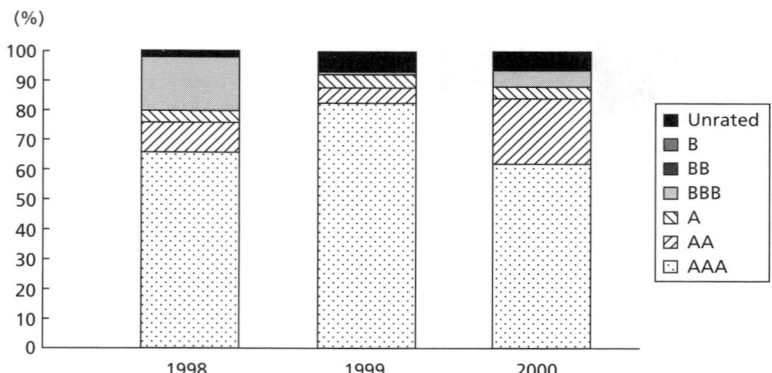

18.3 Breakdown of MBS/ABS deals credit rating in percentage terms.
Source: Nomura.

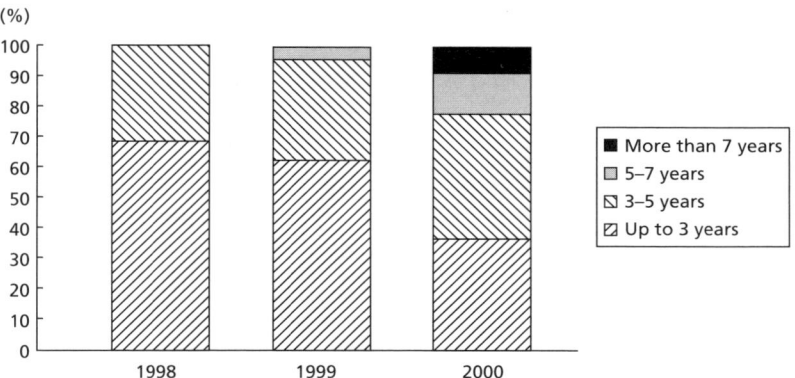

18.4 Breakdown of MBS/ABS deals by maturities.
Source: Nomura.

An analysis of the major types of MBS and ABS

As shown in Fig. 18.1, the major products in the MBS/ABS market in Japan have been securities backed by leases and auto loans. Restrictions on the ability of non-banks to issue corporate bonds and the enactment of the MITI Law contributed significantly to the sharp rise in the issuance of these securities. Banks issued a large number of collateralized loan obligations (CLOs) as a means to reduce their loan assets and meet capital-adequacy standards set by the Bank for International Settlements (BIS). CLO issuance fell sharply, however, in part because rules were tightened on the off-balance sheet treatment of these securities in cases where banks held the subordinated tranche of a CLO. As the issuance of CLOs slowed and banks cut back on lending, an increasing amount of CBOs were issued, with a structure unique to Japan. CBO issuance, however, fell sharply starting in 2000 when Japanese banks became more willing to lend after they were recapitalized with public funds. Since 1999, the amount of securities backed by residential mortgages and commercial real estate has risen significantly.

LEASE ASSETS

As mentioned, lease assets are one type of asset eligible to be securitized under the MITI Law. They now account for more than two-thirds of the specified claims that have been securitized on the basis of the law. About ¥3 tr. worth of lease assets was securitized on the basis of the MITI Law between April 1998 and March 1999, and about ¥2 tr. between April 1999 and March 2000. The value of lease assets that were packaged in the form of debt securities and sold to investors was about ¥630 bn in 1999 and about ¥290 bn in 2000. This decline may be related to an increasingly aggressive lending stance among banks. The amount of lease assets securitized each year is likely to be in the range of ¥2 to 3 tr.

AUTO LOANS

About ¥180 bn in auto loans were securitized in 1998; ¥390 bn in 1999; and ¥310 bn in 2000. Auto loans are also used as the underlying assets for trust beneficiary interests and asset-backed loans. Currently, the number of originators of auto loan-backed securities is limited. The issuance of auto loan-backed securities could rise sharply, however, if the financing subsidiaries of the major auto companies begin to aggressively securitize their auto loans.

CONSUMER CREDIT RECEIVABLES

Consumer credit receivables include those for consumer loans and consumer credit other than auto loans. The MITI Law covers the latter type of credit receivables. The amount of credit card and instalment-sale receivables securitized on the basis of the MITI Law rose from about ¥940 bn between April 1998 and March 1999 to about ¥1.3 tr. between April 1999 and March 2000. Consumer loan ABS are generally issued at higher spreads than are other types of ABS with the same credit rating.

Ever since the enactment of the Non-Bank Bond Act in particular, relatively small consumer finance companies have begun to securitize their consumer loans to raise funds. Medium-sized consumer finance companies have also been aggressively securitizing their consumer loans. Japan's major consumer finance companies, however, have not actively done so. The four major Japanese consumer finance companies had ¥5.5 tr. in outstanding loan receivables at the end of September 2000. Growth in Japan's consumer loan-based securities market will largely depend on whether the major consumer finance companies decide to securitize their loan portfolios.

ACCOUNTS RECEIVABLE

Commercial paper backed by accounts receivable was one of the first types of ABS in Japan. Most accounts receivable are securitized in the form of ABCP or trust beneficiary interests because of the relatively short maturity of most accounts receivable. Notes receivable are also typically securitized in the same way.

BANK LOANS

Bank-loan securitization deals first emerged in 1996 as a means to meet BIS capital-adequacy standards. Starting in 1999, however, the amount of bank-loan securitization declined sharply because of the treatment of subordinated tranches for BIS capital-adequacy requirements. The recapitalization of Japanese banks with public funds also significantly diminished the incentive for banks to securitize their loans. But the amount of bank-loan securitization is now on the rise again. The Japan Syndication and Loan-Trading Association, which was established in January 2001, has begun creating the necessary infrastructure for improving the secondary market for loans, which over the longer term should lead to a rise in the issuance of CLOs and CDOs (collateralized debt obligations).

In conjunction with banks' disposals of bad loans, a major trend that has developed since the second half of 2001 has been the securitization of banks' normal loans, often in the form of CLOs. This market segment, including synthetic CDOs, is likely to expand dramatically.

CORPORATE BONDS

Collateralized bond obligations came about in Japan for different reasons than in the US and Europe and are also structured differently. The first Japanese CBO was issued in December 1998 using only newly issued corporate bonds. Subsequently, a large number of CBOs were issued based on essentially the same structure (Table 18.1). The main factors driving demand for CBOs in Japan, as noted earlier, were tightened lending by Japanese banks and CBO yields that were relatively attractive compared with corporate bond yields. After Japanese banks were recapitalized with public funds and began to increase lending, the issuance of CBOs unique to Japan slowed. Among the CBOs listed in Table 18.1, only the J-Bond

Table 18.1 Japanese CBOs

	One-for-All Asset Funding			Ensemble			Twister Funding		
Issuer	One-for-All Asset Funding			Ensemble			Twister Funding		
Location	Japan			Cayman			Japan		
Place of issuance	Japan			Euro markets			Japan		
Type of offering	Public offering			Secondary offering			Public offering		
Value of collateral	¥70.0bn			¥91.5bn			¥88.0bn		
Number of bonds (number of debtors)	17			21			18		
Number of industries	15 industries			14 industries			11 industries		
Maturity	3 years			3 years			3 years		
Tranches and credit rating	AAA :	¥50.0bn	71%	AAA :	¥64.0bn	70%	AAA :	¥59.0bn	67%
	A :	¥8.5bn	12%	A :	¥7.0bn	8%	A :	¥7.0bn	8%
	Non :	¥11.5bn	16%	Non :	¥20.5bn	22%	Non :	¥22.0bn	25%
Coupon and spread	AAA :	1.100%	37BP	AAA :	1.500%	53BP	AAA :	1.320%	54BP
	A :	2.070%		A :	2.200%	123BP	A :	2.075%	130BP
	Non :	5.616%	134BP	Non :	6.000%	503BP	Non :	NA	
Issuance date	28 Dec. 1998			18 Feb. 1999			26 Feb. 1999		
Lead underwriter	Fuji Securities			NIP			Sumitomo Bank Capital Markets, Merrill Lynch, Daiwa Securities		
Rating agency	R&I			R&I			R&I		

	Symphonie	Concord Funding	All Aboard Funding
Issuer			
Location	Cayman	Cayman	Cayman
Place of issuance	Euro markets	Euro markets	Euro markets
Type of offering	Private offering	Private offering	Secondary offering
Value of collateral	¥48.5bn	¥25.0bn	¥35.0bn
Number of bonds (number of debtors)	18	10	10
Number of industries	14 industries	10 industries	10 industries
Maturity	4 years	3 years	3 years
Tranches and credit rating	Aaa : ¥28.0bn 58% AAA : ¥4.5bn 9% A : ¥5.0bn 10% Non : ¥11.0bn 23%	AAA : ¥16.0bn 64% A– : ¥3.0bn 12% Non : ¥6.0bn 24%	AAA : ¥22.0bn 63% A : ¥5.0bn 14% Non : ¥8.0bn 23%
Coupon and spread	Aaa : Zero 50BP AAA : 1.300% 60BP A : 1.950% 125BP Non : NA	AAA : 0.970% 54BP A– : 1.870% 144BP Non : NA	AAA : 0.940% 39BP A : 1.400% 85BP Non : NA
Issuance date	25 Mar. 1998	10 May 1999	23 Jun. 1999
Lead underwriter	Sanwa International	Tokyo-Mitsubishi International plc	Sakura Finance International
Rating agency	R&I, Moody's	R&I	R&I

433

Table 18.1 Continued

	Ensemble II			Collage Funding			J-Bond		
Issuer	Ensemble II			Collage Funding			J-Bond		
Location	Cayman			Cayman			Cayman		
Place of issuance	Euro markets			Euro markets			Euro markets		
Type of offering	Secondary offering			Private offering			Private offering		
Value of collateral	¥106.0bn			¥37.0bn			¥34.0bn		
Number of bonds (number of debtors)	27			7			61		
Number of industries	15 industries			6 industries			22 industries		
Maturity	3 years			3 years			4 years		
Tranches and credit rating	AAA :	¥78.0bn	74%	AAA :	¥14.0bn	38%	AAA :	¥8.5bn	28%
	A :	¥7.0bn	7%	AA– :	¥5.0bn	14%	AAA :	¥10.3bn	34%
	BBB :	¥3.0bn	3%	A– :	¥5.0bn	14%	AAA :	¥6.1bn	20%
	Non :	¥18.0bn	17%	Non :	¥13.0bn	35%	A :	¥1.6bn	5%
							BBB :	¥0.6bn	2%
							Non :	¥2.2bn	7%
							Non :	¥1.1bn	4%
Coupon and spread	AAA :	0.970%	37BP	AAA :	1.080%	37BP	AAA :	1.980%	17BP
	A :	1.300%	70BP	AA– :	1.280%	70BP	AAA :	1.090%	17BP
	BBB :	2.200%	160BP	A– :	1.630%	160BP	AAA :	1.240%	17BP
	Non :	5.250%	465BP	Non :	NA		A :	1.570%	50BP
							BBB :	2.370%	130BP
							Non :	NA	NA
							Non :	NA	NA
Issuance date	18 Feb. 1999			18 Feb. 1999			11 Aug. 1999		
Lead underwriter	NIP			NIP			NIP		
Rating agency	R&I			R&I			R&I		

	Symphonie II	Ensemble III	Scrum Funding
Issuer	Symphonie II	Ensemble III	Scrum Funding
Location	Cayman	Cayman	Cayman
Place of issuance	Euro markets	Euro markets	Euro markets
Type of offering	Private offering	Secondary offering	Secondary offering
Value of collateral	¥27.0bn	¥69.6bn	¥36.0bn
Number of bonds (number of debtors)	15	22	16
Number of industries	14 industries	15 industries	14 industries
Maturity	3.5 years	3 years	3 years
Tranches and credit rating	AAA : ¥14.4bn 53%	AAA : ¥48.6bn 70%	AAA : ¥22.0bn 61%
	A : ¥3.5bn 13%	A : ¥5.5bn 8%	A : ¥3.5bn 10%
	BBB : ¥1.5bn 6%	BBB : ¥2.5bn 4%	BBB : ¥1.5bn 4%
	Non : ¥7.6bn 28%	Non : ¥13.0bn 19%	Non : ¥9.0bn 25%
Coupon and spread	AAA 1.000% 18BP	AAA 0.840% 20BP	AAA 1.000% 2BP
	A 1.220% 40BP	A 1.040% 40BP	A 1.160% 40BP
	BBB 2.020% 120BP	BBB 1.540% 110BP	BBB 1.660% 90BP
	Non 5.000% 418BP	Non 5.000% 436BP	Non 5.000% 424BP
Issuance date	21 Oct. 1999	4 Nov. 1999	24 Feb. 2000
Lead underwriter	Sanwa International	NIP	IBJI
Rating agency	R&I	R&I	R&I

Table 18.1 *Continued*

Issuer	All Aboard Funding II			Ensemble IV		
Location	Cayman			Cayman		
Place of issuance	Euro markets			Euro markets		
Type of offering	Private offering			Secondary offering		
Value of collateral	¥15.0bn			¥95.5bn		
Number of bonds (number of debtors)	6			29		
Number of industries	6 industries			16 industries		
Maturity	3 years			3 years		
Tranches and credit rating	AAA :	¥5.0bn	33%	AAA :	¥67.5bn	71%
	BBB :	¥4.0bn	27%	A :	¥6.5bn	7%
	A :	¥1.0bn	7%	BBB :	¥3.5bn	4%
	Non :	¥5.0bn	33%	BBB– :	¥1.0bn	1%
				Non :	¥17.0bn	18%
Coupon and spread	AAA :	1.090%	24 BP	AAA :	0.940%	12 BP
	A :	1.250%	40 BP	A :	1.020%	20 BP
	BBB :	1.750%	90 BP	BBB :	1.520%	70 BP
	Non :	NA		BBB– :	2.000%	118 BP
				Non :	5.050%	423 BP
Issuance date	17 Mar. 2000			28 Apr. 2000		
Lead underwriter	Sakura Finance International			NIP		
Rating agency	R&I			R&I		

CBO was backed by bonds traded in the secondary market. This type of structure is called an arbitrage CBO. New CBOs consisting of only newly issued bonds are unlikely because this structure will be replaced with CDOs, which consist of loans, and synthetic CDOs.

RESIDENTIAL MORTGAGES

An increasing proportion of residential mortgages in Japan are being originated by the Housing Loan Corporation (HLC). Of the outstanding balance of about ¥180 tr. in residential mortgages at the end of March 2000, the HLC accounted for about ¥67 tr., about 37%, compared with not even 20% in 1975.

Private sector financial institutions

The first of the residential mortgage-backed securities (RMBS) in Japan, issued in 1999, was backed by residential mortgages originated by Sanwa Bank. This issue was in part a response to signs that HLC mortgages would be securitized. In the wake of the first issue, city banks decided to securitize their residential mortgages as well. In 2000, ¥372.5bn worth of RMBS were issued in Japan. Nevertheless, the pace of mortgage securitizations by city banks since then has slowed.

The Housing Loan Corporation

The main impetus for the HLC to start securitizing residential mortgages stemmed from the reforms of Japan's Fiscal Investment and Loan Program (FILP).[2] One of the government's key objectives for the reforms was to improve the transparency and efficiency of government-affiliated agencies by requiring these entities to raise funds on their own, that is, to issue FILP agency bonds, which do not come with any government guarantees. Two structures for these bonds have been considered. One structure is similar to that for straight bonds issued by corporations, whereby a bond's credit rating is dependent on the financial strength of the issuer. The second structure is an asset-backed security, which means that each bond's credit rating depends on the assets backing the bond. The HLC decided to issue MBS, and raised ¥50bn with the first issue in March

---

2 See Chapter 9 for details about FILP reforms.

2001. The agency issued a similar amount each quarter, for a total of ¥200 bn in fiscal 2001, and expects to issue ¥600 bn in fiscal 2002.

The RMBS issued by the HLC will be bonds issued by the HLC backed by mortgages held in a trust account for a third-party beneficiary. Accordingly, the securities are backed by the credit-worthiness of the HLC. Figure 18.5 shows how the HLC RMBS are structured. The major features are as follows:

■ when investors purchase the RMBS, it is indeterminate whether they have beneficiary interests;

■ if a loan held in trust becomes a non-accrual loan, the HLC replaces it with another loan;

■ the RMBS are redeemed in accordance with the repayment schedule (including prepayments) of the loans held in trust; and

■ in the case of certain events, such as the privatization of the HLC, investors acquire trust beneficiary interests and receive direct cash flows from the trust.

Any major change in the structure of the HLC, such as the privatization of the agency, would make it difficult to price the securities because this RMBS framework is based on the current legal status of the HLC. In addition, the analysis of prepayment risk is problematic, given the dearth of historical data on the HLC residential mortgages.

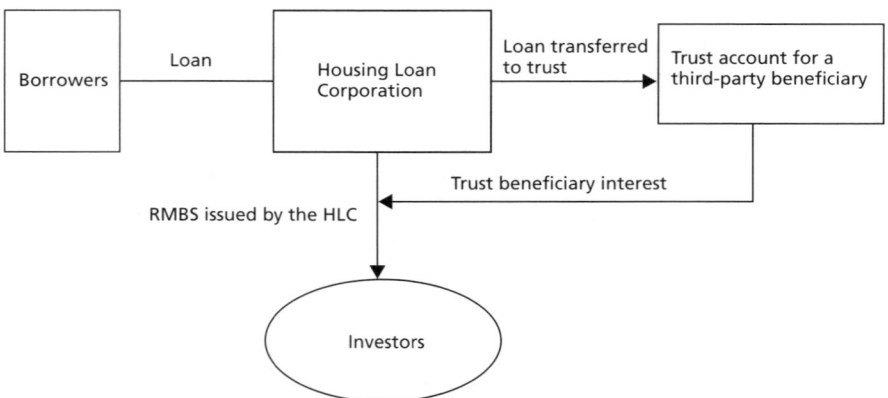

18.5 Securitization framework for Housing Loan Corporation mortgages.

¥75 tr. in mortgage loans, these amounts are relatively small. The HLC might issue a significantly larger amount of RMBS, depending largely on the outcome of the FILP reforms. The most important benefit associated with the securitization of HLC loans is that the resulting RMBS are standardized securities suitable for trading. Securitized lease assets and auto loan receivables are not attractive for trading because of their relatively short maturities. Although the potential investor universe for CMBS is limited because of the unique attributes of each issue, the HLC's RMBS can be valued by investors using a standardized set of parameters. Such a standardized security means the potential for the secondary market is huge.

OTHER GOVERNMENT-AFFILIATED AGENCIES

It is important to monitor the impact of FILP reforms not only on the HLC but also on other government agencies that are or can be originators, in particular those that mainly provide financing or those that have significant real estate holdings and facilities. The key issue to monitor is the extent to which these entities can balance the achievement of their policy objectives and the use of securitization to raise funds.

CHAPTER 19

The venture capital market

Venture capital is typically used to finance relatively new companies or businesses that are just starting to grow, but it is also increasingly used to provide capital to privately held companies that are in their mature or late stages of growth. Venture capital investing usually refers to equity investments in privately held companies, and the companies invested in are generally referred to as portfolio companies or venture capital-backed companies. In addition, private equity investing refers generally to investments in privately held companies.

Investments in privately held companies can be classified in several ways. The two most common methods are based on either the growth phase of the privately held company or the way in which funds are invested. Under the growth-phase classification, companies are categorized into one of three categories. Early-stage growth companies are ones that have been newly established; expansion-stage growth companies are characterized by expanding business; and later-stage growth companies are nearly ready to go public. Investments in privately held companies can also be broadly classified according to whether the companies issue new shares or whether outstanding shares are bought by a new group of investors. Whereas the former method results in new capital for a firm, the latter, typically referred to as a buyout, usually involves only a change in shareholders, not the provision of new funds, although in some cases new shares are in fact issued in exchange for fresh capital.

There are various types of corporate buyouts, the two common ones being leveraged buyouts (LBOs) and management buyouts (MBOs). In an LBO, borrowed funds are used to take over a company, with the assets and future cash flows of the target company used to back the loans made to finance the deal. In contrast, an MBO involves the buyout of a corporation by its existing management. This chapter focuses mainly on venture capital financing, which for the most part entails the use of venture capital.

Japanese venture capitalists

In general, the venture capital business involves investing in start-ups with the aim of ultimately generating returns on the investments. Venture capitalists (VCs) seek out promising companies or ideas and select those they will invest in by evaluating business plans. But VCs do not simply provide financing. One of their core functions is to increase the value of the companies in which they invest by providing managerial and personnel support to help them grow. Ultimately, VCs earn a return when the portfolio company is sold to another company or goes public.

In Japan, venture capital is provided through three main channels. The first involves direct investments from a VC. The second channel involves investments from a venture capital fund, a type of investment partnership established by various investors. The third conduit for venture capital financing is loans to start-ups.

Figure 19.1 shows the trend in the amount of venture capital financing by type. One of the distinguishing characteristics of venture capital financing in Japan is the relatively large amount of funds provided directly by VCs, although in recent years this amount has been declining, as shown in Fig. 19.1. Meanwhile, the amount invested through investment partnerships has been rising. Some venture capital deals are financed with both direct funding and with capital from investment partnerships. To avoid potential conflicts of interest, however, some large Japanese venture capital firms have stopped investing directly.

Another unique aspect of venture capital financing in Japan is the large amount of loans made to start-ups from the end of the 1980s to the early part of the 1990s, a period often referred to as the bubble economy era. During this period, venture capital groups functioned like non-banks in that they provided loans to start-ups. The assets, such as real estate, of the new ventures backed these loans. The problem, however, was that once asset prices began to fall sharply from their lofty bubble-era levels, many of the venture

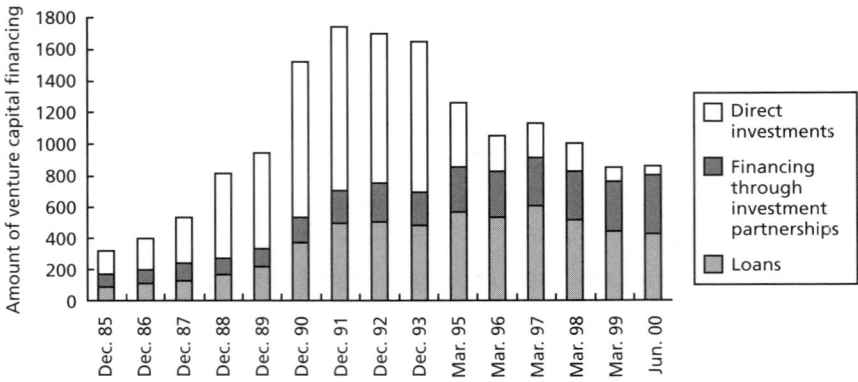

19.1 Venture capital financing in Japan.
Source: Nomura, based on Venture Enterprises Center data.

capital groups that provided loans during the bubble economy years were left with large amounts of non-performing loans. Since the latter half of the 1990s, the amount for venture capital financing provided in the form of loans has been declining.

Another defining attribute of Japanese venture capital entities is that few of them are independent. Many Japanese venture capital groups are affiliated with large companies, such as banks, insurance companies and securities companies. The venture capital firms affiliated with large companies often receive personnel and managerial support from their parent entities. Banks leverage relationships formed through their venture capital financing groups to become the main bank of their venture capital group's portfolio companies, while securities companies hope that similar relationships will result in future lead underwriting deals. These venture capital groups affiliated with banks and securities companies, therefore, do not necessarily expect to generate returns on the conventional venture capital business. Also, even if the venture capital arms of banks and securities companies are set up as investment partnerships, they essentially function as direct venture capital financing entities because the only providers of capital are the parent company and the venture capital entity.

US venture capital firms invest mainly in technology start-ups, in many cases, ones started up by people involved in cutting-edge technology research at universities and large companies. In contrast, Japanese venture capital firms back a disproportionately large number of ventures in the retail and service industries, most of which are established through the application of a technology developed within an already existing industry. The vast majority of Japanese venture capital firms thus focus on comparatively low-risk, low-return investments in that very few of the companies they finance are intended to contribute to the creation of a new industry, as in the US. Table 19.1 shows the distribution of recent start-ups by industry in percentage terms.

Another indication of Japanese venture capital firms' preference for low-risk, low-return investments is that most focus on investments with relatively clear exit options on the horizon. Figure 19.2 shows the distribution of the amount of venture capital financing for a company in percentage terms, broken down according to the age of a company when it first received venture capital. A relatively high proportion are later-stage start-ups, which are companies with considerably long track records that are approaching the initial public offering (IPO) phase. This tendency of Japanese venture capital firms to focus a relatively high proportion of their investments on seasoned start-ups also indicates that few of the VCs provide managerial

Table 19.1 Distribution of start-ups by industry, April–June 2000 (%)

Internet	21.9
Computers	12.4
Consumer services	10.8
Business services	9.8
Semiconductors and other electronic devices	8.7
Finance/insurance/real estate	7.6
Communications	7.2
Manufacturing	7.1
Medical/health care	2.5
Biotechnology	1.7
Construction	1.4
Industrial/energy	0.8
Transportation	0.5
Agricultural/forestry/fishing	0.0
Utilities	0.0
Other	7.5
Total	100.0
Total IT-related	50.3

Source: Nomura, based on Venture Enterprises Center data.

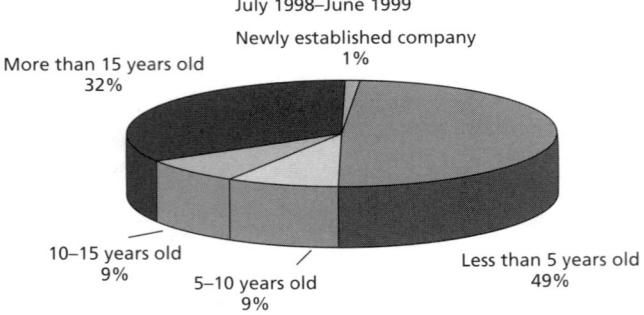

July 1998–June 1999

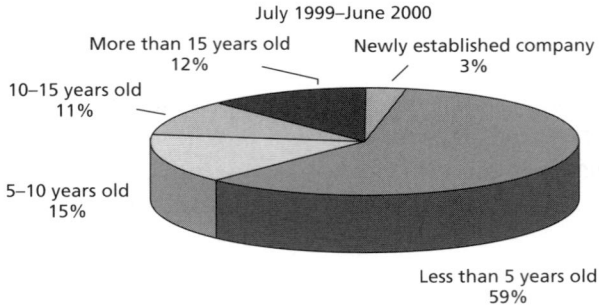

July 1999–June 2000

19.2 Breakdown of venture capital investments by age of company when funds were obtained.
Source: as Fig. 19.1.

support in an effort to develop a start-up, which is traditionally one of the key functions of a VC. Instead, most appear interested mainly in assisting start-ups to go public.

It is important to note that the tendency of Japanese venture capital firms to invest in later-stage start-ups is also related to the reluctance of the start-ups themselves to take in venture capital financing. Whereas US start-ups often expand by obtaining capital, financing and talent from VCs and other external parties, Japanese start-ups are often reluctant to obtain venture capital financing even if they need capital, because management is unwilling to relinquish control of the company or hesitant to divulge information to outsiders. Hence, even if Japanese venture capital firms are willing to provide early-stage funding, many companies are unwilling to accept it. Nevertheless, this reluctance appears to be abating. As shown in Fig. 19.2, the proportion of venture capital investments in recently established start-ups was higher for the one-year period to June 2000 than for the one-year period to June 1999. This trend will no doubt continue and result in an increasingly active role for Japanese VCs in developing new companies.

Japanese venture capital funds

Venture capital funds are one of the more popular investment vehicles that enable a multitude of investors to participate in venture capital investing. As shown in Fig. 19.1, an increasing amount of money has been invested through venture capital funds in recent years. These funds raise cash from designated investors and invest the funds for a relatively long period of time. A typical venture capital fund, for example, would require investors to commit capital for about 10 years. The general partners make the investment decisions for a venture capital fund.

The first venture capital fund in Japan was established in 1982. Figure 19.3 shows the trend in the number of new venture capital funds established in Japan each year from 1984 to 2000, and Fig. 19.4 shows the trend in the average size of Japanese venture capital funds over the same period. During the 1980s, the number of funds established each year as well as the average size of the

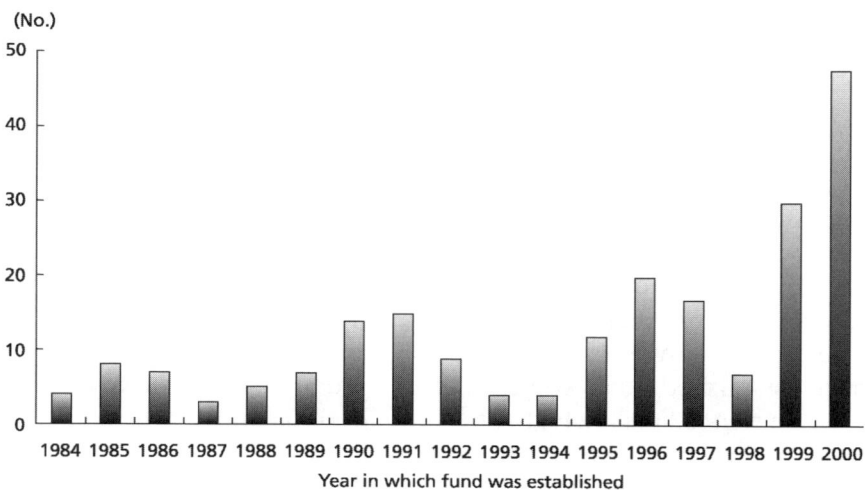

19.3 Trend in number of venture capital funds established each year.
Source: Nomura, based on Ministry of Economy, Trade and Industry data.

(¥ bn)

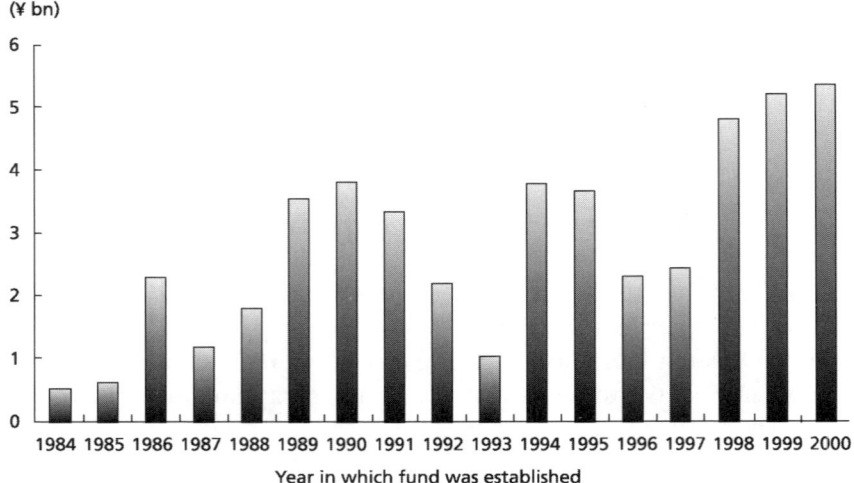

Year in which fund was established

19.4 Trend in average size of venture capital funds.
Source: as Fig. 19.3.

funds increased. In the first half of the 1990s, both the number of funds established and the average size of a fund declined, but both figures rose during the second half of the decade. In recent years, a large number of venture capital funds have been established that focus on companies in the technology and telecommunications sectors, given the projected strong growth in these businesses. The peak period for technology venture capital investing came in 1998–2000, when many large information technology (IT) venture capital funds were established.

Figure 19.5 shows a breakdown of the major types of investors in Japanese venture capital funds. As shown in Fig. 19.5, pension funds and individual investors are not major investors in venture capital funds. In the US and Europe, pension funds are major participants in venture capital funds, but in Japan the amount of pension assets allocated to venture capital funds is very small. Since 2000 or so, however, several pension funds have either started to allocate assets to venture capital funds or have indicated that they are considering such investments. Moreover, some venture capital groups have established funds specifically targeted at pension funds. In light of these trends, it is likely that the amount of Japanese pension assets invested in venture capital funds will increase.

When analysing the performance of venture capital funds, it is important to take into consideration several key factors. These include the use of internal rate of return (IRR) to measure the per-

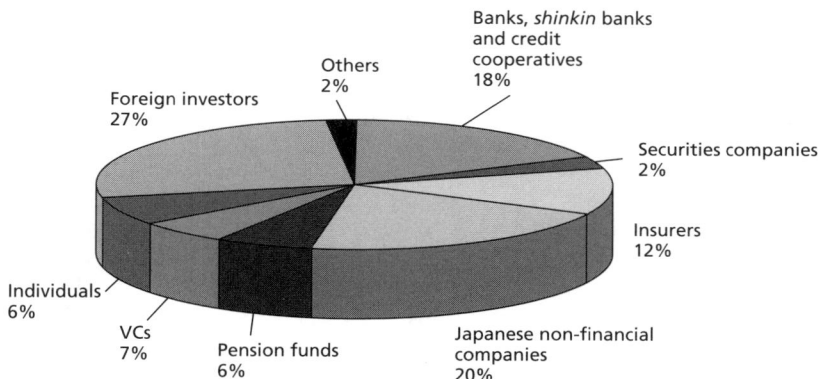

Foreign investors
27%

Others
2%

Banks, *shinkin* banks
and credit
cooperatives
18%

Securities companies
2%

Insurers
12%

Individuals
6%

VCs
7%

Pension funds
6%

Japanese non-financial
companies
20%

19.5 Breakdown of assets invested in limited investment partnerships, by type of investor, July 1999–June 2000.
Source: as Fig. 19.1.

formance of a fund, the difficulty of assessing the fair market value of the investments, different start dates among funds and the resulting differences in performance characteristics. Venture capital funds do not immediately begin to generate investment returns. In most cases, the funds start to gradually generate returns several years after they are established and then tend to produce significant returns during the latter half of a fund's life (Fig. 19.6).

Given that the performance of a venture capital fund depends to a large extent on the date the fund was established, it is important that the funds being compared were established at the same time. Figure 19.7 compares the performance of venture capital funds set up in the same year with the returns of other major asset classes. As shown in Fig. 19.7, the performance of Japanese venture capital funds has been higher than that of Japanese stocks, but not by a significant margin. The main reasons for the relatively low performance of Japanese venture capital funds are the inclusion of a substantial amount of fixed-income investments and relatively low exposure to high-risk investments.

Building up a strong venture capital system in Japan

To some extent, long-term investment capital is needed for a venture capital fund to succeed. One typical source of such capital is pension

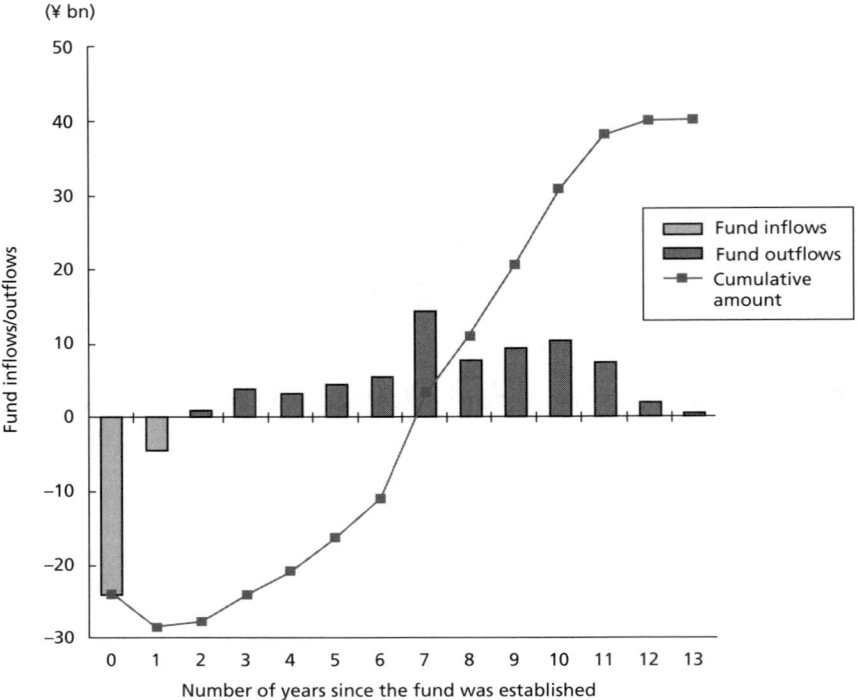

19.6 Typical growth pattern for a venture capital fund.
Source: Nomura, based on the Venture Capital Fund Performance Benchmark,
1998, published by the Ministry of International Trade and Industry.

funds; however, several problems prevented Japanese pension funds
from investing in venture capital funds. One is that venture capital
funds were recognized as voluntary partnerships under Japan's
Civil Code and thus were subject to unlimited liability. Another factor
that kept pension funds from investing in venture capital funds was
the lack of adequate disclosure, which made evaluating the performance of funds difficult.

Several changes have been implemented to address these
problems. The Law Concerning Small and Medium Enterprise Limited
Partnership Contracts (commonly referred to as the Limited
Partnership Law), which was passed in November 1998, limited the
liability of investors in venture capital funds to the amount of their
investments in a fund. In addition, new mandatory disclosure rules
have been implemented. These changes led to an increase in the
number of potential investors for venture capital funds. Moreover, in

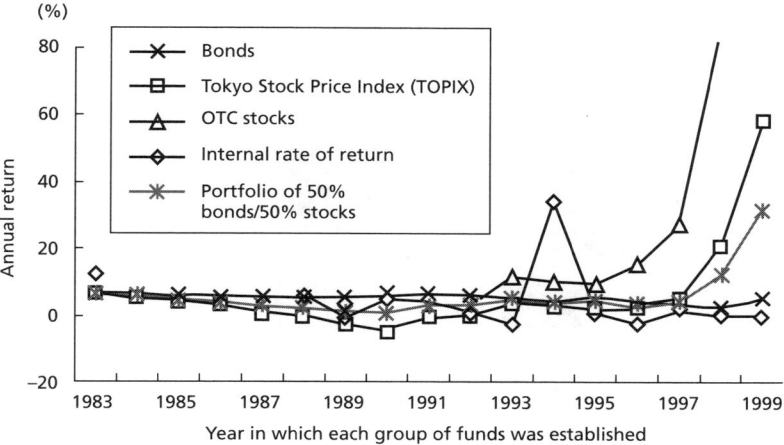

19.7 Investment returns for Japanese venture capital funds, to end-1999.
Notes: Annual return figures for each group of funds are from the year of
establishment to the end of 1999. The JASDAQ index is used to reflect the
performance of OTC stocks, and the NOMURA-BPI index is used to measure the
performance of the bond market. The performance of the portfolio of 50%
bonds/50% stocks is measured by the return on a portfolio with equal exposure to
the Tokyo Stock Price Index (TOPIX) and the NOMURA-BPI at the start of each
period. Returns do not reflect dividends or transaction costs. The internal rate of
return (IRR) of the venture capital funds is calculated on fiscal 2000 data published
by the Ministry of Economy, Trade and Industry.

an effort to improve the availability of information for evaluating venture capital funds, the Ministry of International Trade and
Industry (now called the Ministry of Economy, Trade and Industry)
published in December 1998 a report on venture capital fund performance benchmarks. Until then, performance data for venture
capital funds were for the most part not available, given that the funds
were private investments. The Venture Enterprises Center, an organization affiliated with the Ministry of Economy, Trade and Industry,
has been collecting and disseminating information on Japanese
venture capital funds for some time. The 1998 report on venture
capital fund performance benchmarks, however, was the first attempt
to gather comprehensive performance data. Since 1998, the ministry
has published the performance figures once a year. These data were
used to create Fig. 19.6.

The success of a venture capital fund in terms of investment
performance depends on the extent to which the fund can recoup
its original investments from portfolio companies. One of the most

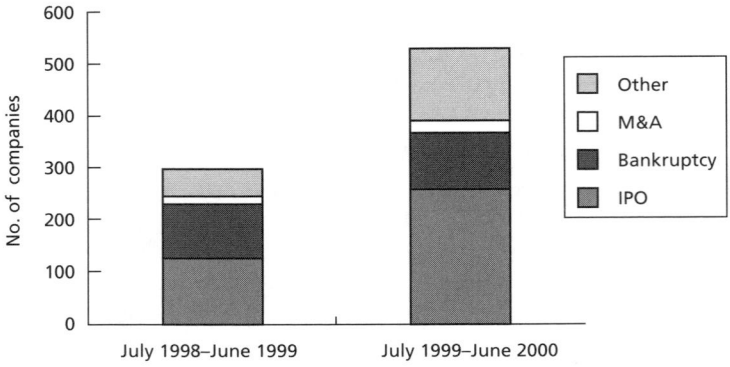

19.8 Exit strategies for venture capital companies.
Source: as Fig. 19.1.

common exit strategies for venture capital funds is selling shares of a portfolio company that is taken public. Therefore, a strong IPO market is one of the key elements needed to create an infrastructure conducive to venture capital financing.

Until recently, the most common choice for a privately held company to go public in Japan was to register on the over-the-counter (OTC) market. Since 1999, however, two markets with relatively relaxed listing standards – the Tokyo Stock Exchange's Mothers and Nasdaq Japan – have started up to make it easier for young growth companies to go public. A number of regional exchanges in Japan have also established markets targeted at new ventures. Among these are the Nagoya Stock Exchange's Growth Company Market Section (Centrex), the Fukuoka Stock Exchange's Q-Board and the Sapporo Securities Exchange's 'Ambitious' market. In addition, the OTC market established a set of relaxed listing standards (see Chapters 13 and 16 for detail). These new opportunities for emerging growth companies contributed to the sharp increase in the number of companies that went public between the one-year period ending June 1999 and the one-year period ending June 2000, as shown in Fig. 19.8. In addition, efforts are under way to create an online platform for trading privately held stocks. Increased merger and acquisition activity is another positive development for the venture capital industry, particularly in terms of providing yet another exit strategy for investors.

Key issues for Japan's venture capital industry

The infrastructure for Japan's venture capital industry has improved and partly contributed to an increase in the amount of funds invested in start-ups. Nonetheless, the industry is still underdeveloped compared with that in the US. One of the main issues that needs to be addressed to improve the venture capital business is the professional development of VCs, which takes time. A multitude of specialized skills is necessary to be an effective VC, including the abilities to assess new technologies, value companies, provide management and financial consulting, offer business support services and develop a broad network of connections to draw on. Because it is unlikely that any one individual will possess all these skills, venture capital firms and funds need to assemble teams of venture capital specialists.

The number of Japanese investors willing to invest in venture capital funds is likely to increase. In Japan, however, there is a dearth of professionals who are capable of both providing advice to investors on venture capital deals and acting as intermediaries between investors and venture capital funds. Developing such professional skills is therefore a key issue that must be addressed. Venture capital financing will probably play a significant role in helping to commercialize leading-edge technologies, such as those developed by universities, and creating new industries in Japan. VCs must also use their investment capital to help start-ups get what they need in order to expand.

The future

CHAPTER

20

Issues for the future[1]

As outlined in Chapter 2, the Japanese government has injected public funds into the banking system and taken other measures to help stabilize the financial system. Most of the measures in the government's Big Bang package of financial-system reforms have already been implemented. Indeed, as discussed in Chapters 3 to 19, Japan's financial markets have changed significantly in terms of the number, types and behaviour of market participants as well as the underlying trading rules and regulations. Despite major progress, however, the government has not yet fully achieved the goals it set out in its financial system stabilization policies and Big Bang package.

Even though several years have passed since the policies to stabilize Japan's financial system were initiated, the amount of non-performing loans at Japanese financial institutions has not markedly decreased. In fact, as part of his new administration's economic policies, Prime Minister Junichiro Koizumi said the government would require Japanese banks to completely remove non-performing loans from their balance sheets within two to three years. Furthermore, as discussed in Chapter 3, despite near-zero interest rates on deposits, most of Japan's household savings are currently kept in savings accounts. This situation indicates that Japan's capital markets are not functioning properly in terms of efficiently allocating capital.

1 This chapter is partly based on 'Establishing New Financial Markets in Japan', by Masatoshi Kuratani and Yukihiko Endo, *NRI Papers*, no. 6, June 2000. The author acknowledges the permission received from the co-author and the Nomura Research Institute.

Because the Japanese government is still struggling to resolve the bad-loan problem that continues to plague the financial sector, it has not been able to come up with ways to improve the international competitiveness of Japanese financial institutions. As a result, Japanese financial institutions are losing more and more market share, both in Japan and overseas, to foreign financial services companies. Because of a series of consolidations, Japanese financial institutions have grown larger and should therefore benefit from economies of scale, such as lower fixed costs for information systems. It is unclear, however, what new strategies Japanese financial institutions can come up with to compete against overseas rivals, many of which are significantly smaller.

Perhaps the main reason for the modest progress in Japan's financial reforms to date is that the transformation has only just begun. In other words, now that all the necessary components for a new framework seem to be in place, stability might eventually become a regular component of Japan's financial system. If so, Japanese financial institutions will be poised to regain their global competitiveness.

Unfortunately, because the government's blueprint seems to be missing some elements, it is not an easy task to visualize the final form of Japan's new financial system. In this context, this chapter discusses the importance of establishing rules to prevent the emergence of problems stemming from moral hazard. Creating a broader range of financial intermediary channels and improving the efficiency and expertise of the ones now in place are also necessary to promote stability and empower the reforms.

Preventing moral hazard

The term 'moral hazard' is originally an insurance term that refers to a situation in which the insured has an incentive to take greater risks than the person would if he or she were not insured. For example, a person covered by auto insurance may start driving more recklessly than if he or she were not covered by insurance. Similarly, a person with health insurance might use health care services to an excessive extent, assuming a highly elastic demand curve, because the insurance effectively reduces the cost of the services to near zero. In other words, the existence of insurance may distort the allocation of resources.

In the context of the financial system, moral hazard typically refers to the incentive for financial institutions and other market participants to take excessive risk because of the existence of a safety net, such as deposit insurance. But such incentives are not limited merely to financial intermediary institutions – others that are affected by moral hazard include depositors ignoring risk and lenders inadequately monitoring the behaviour of the borrowers and intermediaries.

Moral hazard could also be used to describe the tendency among Japanese households to leave too much cash in bank accounts, mainly as a result of excessive deposit insurance and a lack of understanding of the social costs involved in establishing such safety nets. Given the globalization of financial markets, the wide variety of financial products that are now available and the decline in trans-action and information costs, Japanese households should be able to construct optimal portfolios based on the risk–return characteris-tics of the different products available at home and abroad. In light of their liquidity and ease of use for settling transactions, bank deposits are understandably one of the main components of indi-vidual investors' portfolios. Nevertheless, as discussed in Chapter 3, for portfolios to be overly weighted toward cash is a problem because of the incentives provided by deposit insurance and the government-laid safety net of public funds for recapitalizing banks.

These distortions may have already been at work during the period of rapid economic growth, when the myth initially material-ized that Japanese banks would never go bankrupt and that deposits were safe. But given that this boom period was also characterized by a high marginal efficiency of investment capital and minimal eco-nomic volatility, banks at the time may have been an effective means of accumulating capital. With the changes in the economy, however, this myth surrounding the security of keeping money in the bank has ended up contributing to a bloated banking sector.

Strictly speaking, it may not be fully accurate to say that the banks have an information advantage merely because they can conduct credit checks on potential borrowers. In fact, the experi-ence of the boom years of the late 1980s suggests that most loans were extended simply on the basis of real estate collateral rather than reliable credit information about the borrowers. But when the falling price of land makes land an increasingly ineffective form of collateral and when economic volatility is rising, the ability of banks to screen and monitor borrowers becomes all the more important. Nonetheless, it remains to be seen whether the banking sector, which is in the midst of a swirl of changes, can maintain a competitive advantage over the long term in screening an increasingly diverse base of potential borrowers.

This summary assessment of the assets and liabilities of Japanese banks suggests that the role of banks as financial intermediaries has grown too influential in Japan. In the future, policymakers should make it their priority to establish an environment that would help individual investors to construct optimal, balanced portfolios, instead of overprotecting bank depositors through insurance.

Japan's banking system and the risk of moral hazard

Given the banking system's importance in terms of the stability of the overall financial system, this section outlines the impact of moral hazard on the behaviour of different types of market participants that stems from the existence of a safety net for the banking system.

Depositors:

▨ tendency to put too much of their assets in cash (see above);

▨ lack of incentives to learn more about personal finance, especially about the trade-off between risk and return, because of a heavy reliance on the government's protection of deposits; and

▨ selection of banks based solely on deposit yields, regardless of the financial health of the banking institution.

Banks:

▨ tendency to extend loans recklessly without adequately checking the creditworthiness of borrowers; and

▨ tendency to try to attract deposits by offering high interest rates without sufficient information disclosures.

Regulators:

▨ lack of incentive to deal promptly with banks that may fail because deposit insurance makes it relatively unlikely that a run on banks will occur; and

■ tendency to put off dealing with ailing banks out of fear that a bankruptcy would be seen as the responsibility of regulators.

As these examples indicate, the risk of moral hazard in the Japanese banking sector has been an issue for many years. The main reason the US established a new regulatory framework for banking following the Great Depression was to reduce the risk of the emergence of moral hazard created by the introduction of deposit insurance. As a preventive measure, US regulators established detailed restrictions on financial institutions to minimize the monitoring costs.

In response to such changing economic circumstances as the emergence of inflation, however, the US government began easing these rules in the 1970s. Not only were caps on deposit rates lifted, but also other federal- and state-imposed detailed restrictions were relaxed thanks to the initiatives of financial services companies. For example, bank holding companies went into the business of underwriting commercial paper and other securities. To guard against the potential risks that could emerge as a result of deregulation, the US government introduced capital-adequacy requirements.

Nevertheless, as evidenced by the savings and loan (S&L) crisis, the US government failed to prevent moral hazard following deregulation. The liberalization of interest rates on deposits enabled ailing banks and S&Ls to offer higher interest rates to attract deposits and, in turn, use the funds for such high-return but high-risk investments as real estate and junk bonds. In other words, deregulation made it possible for poorly performing banks and S&Ls to gamble. These high-yielding deposits were sold nationwide through brokers. Because deposits were fully guaranteed up to a specified limit, depositors had no incentive to assess the financial strength of financial institutions. Not surprisingly, the total costs of cleaning up the financial crisis caused by a series of S&L bankruptcies in the US ballooned when regulators and Congress put off dealing with the emergence of this moral hazard.

Eventually, the US government formulated a number of concrete policies for minimizing moral hazard. After the passage of the Federal Deposit Insurance Corporation Improvement Act (FDICIA) in 1991, the government encouraged competition by promoting the functioning of other market mechanisms. It also established procedures to 'quarantine' troubled banks quickly, in order to isolate and resolve problems before they spread to the entire financial system.

The government permitted struggling and uncompetitive banks to go bankrupt and took steps to make sure that the safety net for the financial system did not expand. For example, it adjusted deposit-insurance premiums paid by each bank to reflect each bank's risk profile and reintroduced ceilings on deposit rates paid by banks with low levels of capital. These moves were significant in that in its effort to contain moral hazard, the government moved away from the conventional regulatory approach of treating all regulated parties equally. To further strengthen supervision of the banking sector, some are currently suggesting forcing banks to issue subordinated debt, which counts as shareholders' equity, and thereby enhance the monitoring of banks by investors.

A recent major development in the US was the passage in 1999 of the Gramm–Leach–Bliley Act, which repealed the Glass–Steagall Act of 1933, the core of the post-Depression regulatory framework governing the US financial services industry. The new law permits banks, insurance companies and securities firms to enter into each other's businesses. This development confirms the US regulators' stance of continuing to deregulate, promote competition and improve efficiency in order to make the financial system more stable than it has been in the past.

The current state of Japan's financial system

Given the limits of relying on public funds, which are typically a safety net of last resort, it is becoming increasingly important for the Japanese government to consider measures to prevent the emergence of moral hazard. The government needs to establish a more efficient system for avoiding additional costs associated with resolving Japan's bad-loan problem. The government has already introduced some measures that are similar to those adopted in the US, such as a prompt, corrective action scheme for dealing with struggling financial institutions. Yet, that the term moral hazard has become a household phrase in Japan indicates a heightened awareness of the seriousness of the financial problems confronting the nation. Current measures, which are neither comprehensive nor consistent with the intended policy objectives of Japan's financial Big Bang, have yet to establish appropriate terms of competition for financial institutions and do not provide appropriate incentives to enhance operating efficiency.

To help stabilize the financial system while minimizing the possibility of moral hazard, the Japanese government does have two possible regulatory approaches at its disposal. One option would emphasize the stability of financial institutions through the implementation of detailed regulations. Alternatively, the government could treat the stability of individual institutions and the stability of the system as separate issues. It could implement measures to prevent the failure of individual financial institutions from destabilizing the overall financial system. At the same time, it could introduce incentive-compatible regulations that would discourage troubled banks and other market participants from taking unnecessary risks.

The US is clearly aiming for the latter approach, as is Japan, at least given the similarity of the latter approach to the Big Bang reform plan. And considering Japan's major role in the ever-changing international financial markets, it is highly unlikely that Japan will revert to the former approach.

One of the major financial sector problems confronting Japan today is that the establishment of an incentive-compatible system, which should accompany any financial stabilization policy, has been delayed. When taking over a failed bank, for instance, the acquirer is often required to assume all the outstanding financing extended by the failed bank and to keep them for, say, at least three years. This regulation may be necessary in the short run as an emergency measure to prevent a deterioration in the banking sector's ability to function as a financial intermediary. Nonetheless, promptly allowing the acquiring bank to conduct thorough credit evaluations and other normal operations should be seen as compatible with the original aim of stabilizing the financial system. As discussed later in this chapter, another way of dealing with the loans of failed financial institutions is the use of alternative financial channels, such as a secondary market for loan assets. Forcing an acquiring bank to assume the loans of a failed bank over a long period without such supplemental channels could result in the emergence of new types of moral hazard, in which borrowers would have little incentive to improve their balance sheets.

As a disciplinary measure to avoid incurring such risk, Japanese regulators require all banks that receive public fund capital injections to draw up restructuring plans. Yet the type of provisions contained in FDICIA aimed at preventing banks from taking on inordinate risk, such as restrictions on banks' pricing of financial products and the types of businesses they can engage in, appear inadequate. Because of economic stimulus measures, the Japanese government decided to postpone the imposition of a cap on the amount of deposit insurance available per bank deposit and the implementation of a prompt, corrective action system. But such postponements need to be discouraged. The point is not that such postponements are always unacceptable, but if the government decides to further delay the implementation of these measures, it should be prepared to justify its decision in terms of whether the move serves the original objective of stabilizing the financial system.

Financial intermediaries

Bank failures are a typical example of the type of event that can disrupt financial markets. The fallout from a bank failure can vary widely – from a breakdown of the clearing and settlement system and threats to the creditworthiness of other banks and financial institutions to losses for depositors and difficulties for borrowers in raising funds. The costs associated with dealing with these various potential problems can be extremely high.

One way to directly address the risks of moral hazard that stem from the introduction of a safety net for the financial system would be to strengthen the number of financial intermediary channels that are available other than the banking sector. Such a move would also simultaneously prevent a rapid deterioration in the intermediary function of banks. Simply increasing the number of financial intermediaries may not automatically eliminate moral hazard (for instance, it is still an issue for the securities markets), but enhancing alternative channels for the distribution of capital should help to at least minimize moral hazard: it would significantly reduce the likelihood of a sharp deterioration in the financial sector's intermediary function of allocating capital and would lessen the pressure to expand the financial system's safety net beyond the necessary extent.

In the US, the main services provided by financial intermediaries (other than banking services) include brokerage, M&A and corporate-restructuring advisory, asset management and private-equity placement. This diversification of financial intermediation services was prompted in part by financial deregulation during the 1970s and the resulting intensification of competition between investment banks and among institutional investors. The efficiency of the securities business improved thanks to a slew of financial product innovations, such as derivative instruments, junk bonds and the securitization of a multitude of financial assets. In turn, this development has reduced the relative importance of the traditional bank lending business. In addition, pension funds and other institutional investors with comparatively long-term investment horizons have become important sources of risk capital, mainly by investing in venture capital, mezzanine, and leveraged buyout funds. Through these developments, capital has become available at all different segments of the spectrum of investment options that represent varying levels of risk.

The US experience and the current situation in Japan suggest that the following measures are important in terms of developing multiple effective channels of financial intermediation. These measures are also relevant for resolving some of Japan's longer-term structural problems, such as its aging population, a bloated budget deficit and inadequate mechanisms for providing sufficient capital to help Japan move toward a knowledge-based economy.

CLARIFICATION OF THE ROLE OF FIDUCIARIES

Such alternative financial channels as the securities market – whether direct stock investments or investment trusts managed by institutional investors – differ from banking channels in that individual investors bear all the investment risk. To make these channels work effectively, it is essential to clarify the fiduciary duty of intermediaries, such as brokerage account representatives and fund managers, to act on behalf of investors with care and good faith.

In the US, the Employee Retirement Income Security Act (ERISA) of 1974 clarified the fiduciary duties of managers of corporate pension plans. After the Department of Labor cracked down on violations, the quality of investment management services provided by pension fund managers improved. These institutional investors also became suppliers of significant amounts of risk capital, through not only direct stock investments but also, thanks to their heavy use, a variety of innovative financial products.

Although the concept of fiduciary duty has become increasingly recognized to be important in Japan, the enforcement framework is still unclear and the impact of fiduciary duty on the professional capabilities of Japanese institutional investors has been limited.

ALTERNATIVE WAYS TO MONITOR START-UPS

Improving the infrastructure for the provision of capital to start-ups, which has been an oft-discussed topic, has led to the types of stock-exchange and OTC-market reforms discussed in detail in Chapters 13, 16 and 19. But because of the inherently high risks of investing in start-up companies, simply improving the infrastructure for channelling capital is not sufficient. The suppliers of financing also need to hone their ability to gather and analyse relevant information. Another issue is the potential for the emergence of moral hazard stemming from government subsidies to start-ups.

The information asymmetries between the lender and borrower of funds are greater in the case of venture capital than in the case of bank lending to established companies. Consequently, moral hazard is a chief concern. To create an environment in which equity capital is readily available to start-ups, professional venture capitalists (VCs) must be available to screen companies adequately beforehand and then monitor them after the financing is provided. Otherwise, individual investors may be exposed to inordinate levels of risk when such companies try to tap the capital markets for further financing.

A Canadian academic study has shown that the use of inside information is crucial in venture capital financing, because most start-ups have few assets that can be used as collateral and have very limited credit histories.[2] Hence, it is not common for VCs to recoup their investments by having their portfolio companies do an initial public offering. In far many more cases, however, start-up companies are acquired by executives and other third parties with key inside information or specific knowledge of the start-up's business. In the US, venture capital funds have been joined by a growing number of mezzanine funds, which specialize in financing small and medium-sized businesses by buying subordinated debt. This trend underlines the need for professional investors who can perform such screening and monitoring functions.

In Japan, the growing number of VCs has been accompanied by a corresponding growth in MBO funds and other funds that provide financing to help established companies restructure. Even so, further

---

2 Raphael Amit, James Brander and Christoph Zott, 'Venture Capital Financing of Entrepreneurship in Canada', in Paul J. N. Halpern, ed., *Financing Growth in Canada*, Calgary, University of Calgary Press, 1997.

improvements are necessary in terms of not only the amount of financing provided but also the quality of funding and management support.

DEVELOPMENT OF THE ASSET-BACKED SECURITIES MARKET

Medium-sized companies often lack name recognition and the financial strength to obtain credit ratings. As a result, they often have difficulty issuing enough securities to obtain adequate liquidity. Increased use of asset securitization is needed to provide these companies with ready access to capital. Although the asset-backed securities market in Japan is finally starting to take off, as discussed in Chapter 18, the number of participants in this market needs to be increased.

In the US, many mortgages are bought and securitized by government-affiliated agencies. Investor demand for these mortgage-backed securities is high because of the strong credit ratings of the agencies that guarantee the principal and interest payments on the securities. During the credit crunch of the early 1990s, there was a proposal for a federal agency (Velda Sue[3]) that would use a similar method to securitize banks' loans to small and medium-sized businesses. In the end, nothing came of the proposal; it was decided to let the private sector find a solution. In Japan, however, asset securitization is still in its early years, and an approach such as that of the Velda Sue proposal may be worth considering.

THE EQUITY MARKET AND CORPORATE GOVERNANCE

Equity rather than debt should become a much more important tool for exercising control over companies and the way they use funds. In other words, in addition to serving as a mechanism for allocating capital, the equity market should also play a more active role in corporate governance.

The US has a well-developed market for corporate control – in the form of hostile takeovers. The ability of investors to carry out LBOs by using junk bonds, as well as through shareholder activism by pension fund managers, means that even the largest companies

3 The name stands for Venture Enhancement and Loan Development Administration for Smaller Undercapitalized Enterprises.

can no longer escape pressure to improve their financial performance. Although Japan does not need to import such a market for corporate control immediately, a necessary first step to improving corporate governance in Japan would be to make it clear to pension funds that their fiduciary duties include the proper exercise of their voting rights.

If institutional investors were to exercise their voting rights more actively, they could use their expertise to put pressure on companies in a way that individual investors cannot. In turn, the risks of moral hazard – not just in the capital markets but throughout the economic system – would be reduced, and companies would be forced to enhance shareholder value. Ultimately, demand for equity capital would be stimulated.

HOUSEHOLD ASSET ALLOCATION

Despite the increasingly widespread use of the Internet for accessing information, households in general still have limited ability and expertise when it comes to choosing how to allocate their assets. The financial services industry exists precisely because of this situation. Households are also susceptible to the moral hazard that stems from deposit insurance, so the financial services industry plays a key hand-holding role in helping households to invest their assets wisely.

Given the government's plan to introduce a defined-contribution retirement plan system, it has become all the more important to expand the opportunities for households to learn more about personal finance and improve their ability to construct optimal portfolios based on reasonable assessments of risk and return.

There also needs to be more in-depth discussion of how individual investors should be protected. Discussions during the drafting stage of the Law on Sales of Financial Products included a proposal for a cooling-off period – similar to the kind that applies to purchases of physical goods – that would allow investors to change their minds about securities purchases. Yet although some sort of protections are needed for individual investors in the event they suffer losses because of unscrupulous behaviour on the part of financial services companies, the concept of a cooling-off period is not likely to be accepted because of the volatility of financial asset prices. Moreover, a cooling-off period could increase the risk of moral hazard.

Conclusion

Banks have played the key role in Japan's postwar financial system, particularly in terms of screening and monitoring companies and imposing some managerial discipline on them. The so-called main banks (Japanese companies typically designate one bank as their primary bank) have served as sources of both debt and equity financing; however, the slowdown in economic growth, a decline in the marginal efficiency of investment capital and the decreasing value of land as collateral have given rise to concerns that banks may be taking on inordinate risks if they continue to operate as they have in the past.

The fundamental question is whether banks – which raise funds mainly by accepting deposits that are highly liquid and important for fund settlement – should also be providing risk capital. Perhaps the desirable direction for Japan's financial markets is to move toward the development of multiple, alternative financial intermediary channels with different functions, which could be harmonized as necessary.

References[1]

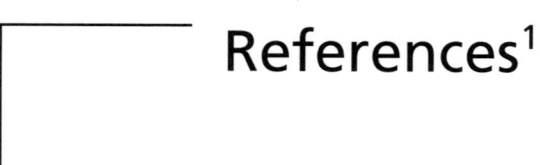

Chapter 1

Tokyo Stock Exchange Web site (http://www.tse.or.jp)

Chapter 2

Financial Services Agency Web site (http://www.fsa.go.jp)

Chapter 4

Ministry of Finance, Financial Bureau, 2001, *FILP Report 2001*.
Postal Service Agency, *Financial Results of Postal Services for Fiscal 2000* (July 2001).

Chapter 5

Hashimoto, Motomi, 2001, 'Japan's Recent Defined-Benefit Corporate Pension and Defined-Contribution Pension Laws', *Capital Research Journal* (Nomura Research Institute), vol. 4, no. 3 (Autumn).
'Nenkin Joho' (Pension Information), *Rating and Investment Information*, April 2001, no. 262.

---

1 References available in Japanese only have been omitted; for details, see the Japanese edition of this book, ed. Junichi Ujiie, *Nihon no Shihon Shijo* (Toyo Keizai Shinposha, 2002).

Chapter 8

Bank of Japan, *Balance of Payments Monthly*.

Chapter 9

Ministry of Finance Web site (http://www.mof.go.jp/zaito)

Wako, Juichi, 1996, 'The Government and the Public Bond New Issue Market', in Shigenobu Hayakawa, ed., *Japanese Finanical Markets*, first edn, Cambridge, UK: Woodhead Publishing.

Chapter 11

Bank of Japan, *Minutes of the Monetary Policy Meetings*.

Bank of Japan, 2000–2001, *Outlook and Risk Assessment of the Economy and Prices*.

Bank of Japan, Research and Statistics Department, 2000, *Price Developments in Japan: A Review Focusing on the 1990s*.

Miyano, Atsushi, 2000, 'A Guide to the Bank of Japan's Market Operations', Bank of Japan, Financial Markets Department, Working Paper no. 00-E-3.

Orphanides, A., R. Porter, D. Reifschneider, R. Tetlow and F. Finan (1999), *Errors in the Measurement of the Output Gap and the Design of Monetary Policy*, Federal Reserve Board.

Ueda, Kazuo [member of the Policy Board of the Bank of Japan], 2000, 'The Transmission Mechanism of Monetary Policy Near Zero Interest Rates: The Japanese Experience 1998–2000' (speech).

Chapter 15

Ikeda, Tetsuya, 1998, *Structure and Role of Derivative Transactions*, Monthly Report of the Ministry of Public Management, Home Affairs, Posts and Telecommunications' Institute for Posts and Telecommunications, March, no. 114.

Chapter 17

Fedenia, M., J.E. Hodder and A.J. Triantis, 1994, 'Cross-Holdings: Estimation Issues, Biases and Distortions', *Review of Financial Studies*, vol. 7, no. 1: 61–96.

Ikeda, Masayuki, 1992, 'Price/Earnings Ratios with Reciprocal Ownership', *Financial Analysts Journal*, vol. 48, no. 4 (July/August): 77–82.

Kobayashi, H., Y. Endo and S. Ogishima, 1993, 'New Directions in Japanese Banking Relationships', *NRI Quarterly*, Nomura Research Institute, vol. 2, no. 1 (Spring).

McDonald, J., 1989, 'The Mochiai Effect: Japanese Corporate Cross-Holdings', *Journal of Portfolio Management* (Fall): 90–94.

Ogishima, Seiji, 1994, 'Recent Trends in Japanese Stock Cross-Holding', *NRI Quarterly*, Nomura Research Institute, vol. 3, no. 3: 82–101.

Ogishima, Seiji, 1995, 'Empirical Tests for the "Mochiai" Effect in Japan', *International Society of Financial Analysts*, vol. 7, no. 2: 8–9.

Chapter 19

National Venture Capital Association, 1998, *1997 National Venture Capital Association Annual Report*.

Venture Economics, 1998, *1998 Investment Benchmarks Report – Venture Capital*.

Chapter 20

Kuratani, M. and Y. Endo, 2000, 'Establishing New Financial Markets in Japan', *NRI Papers*, no. 6, June.

Index